SECRETS

OF THE

SANDS

THE REVELATIONS OF
EGYPT'S EVERLASTING OASIS

HARRY THURSTON

ARCADE PUBLISHING • NEW YORK

Published by arrangement with Doubleday Canada, a division of Random House Canada Limited

Text image: a refyt bird from the temple at Deir el-Hagar

Photographs on pages 34, 55, 120, 300 and 340 are used with the permission of the Royal Ontario Museum. Copyright © ROM.

All other photographs are used with the permission of the photographer: Alan Hollett, page 6; Anthony J. Mills, page 72; Lech Kvzyzaniak, p. 93; Harry Thurston, pages 140, 279, 316 and 355; Catherine Thurston, pages 161, 183, 371 and 373; Stephen Homer, p. 210; Colin Hope, p. 233; and Peter Sheldrick, page 259.

Illustrations are used with the permission of the artist John O'Carroll, www.johnocarroll.co.uk

Text on page 42 is from *Mixed Memoirs* by Gertrude Caton-Thompson. Copyright © 1983 by Erskine Press.

Text on page 133 is from *Man in Nature, Historical Perspectives on Man in His Environment* by N.B. Millet. Copyright © ROM.

Text on page 359 is from *Pillar of Sand, Can the Irrigation Miracle Last?* by Sandra Postel. Copyright © 1999 by W.W. Norton & Company, Inc.

Every effort has been made to contact copyright holders. The publishers will be pleased to correct any errors or omissions in future editions.

Arcade Publishing books may be purchased in bulk at special discounts for sales promotion, corporate gifts, fund-raising, or educational purposes. Special editions can also be created to specifications. For details, contact the Special Sales Department, Arcade Publishing, 307 West 36th Street, 11th Floor, New York, NY 10018 or arcade@skyhorsepublishing.com

Arcade Publishing® is a registered trademark of Skyhorse Publishing, Inc.®, a Delaware corporation.

Visit our website at www.arcadepub.com.

10 9 8 7 6 5 4 3 2 1

Library of Congress Cataloging-in-Publication Data is available on file.

ISBN: 978-1-61145-734-6

Printed in the United States of America

I offer a special thanks to artist John O'Carroll for use of the wonderful drawings that grace the book

———————| |———————

for Catherine and Meaghan who shared this journey, with love

Neolithic petroglyphs *(John O'Carroll)*

CONTENTS

Acknowledgements IX
Prologue 1

PART I: ISLAND OF THE BLESSED
1. The Other Egypt 6

PART II: THE GARDEN
C.400,000 — 12,000 B.P.

2. Everlasting Oasis 34
3. The Garden 55

PART III: CROSSERS OF THE SAND
12,000 — 4000 B.P.

4. The Great Stone Ring 72
5. A Gift of the Desert 93
6. Crossers of the Sand 120

Part IV: Lords of the West
c.2700 – 332 B.C.

7. Lords of the West 140
8. New Light on the Old Kingdom 161
9. A Tale of Woe 183

Part V: A Curse of Sand and Salt
332 B.C. – 700

10. The Romans Are Coming 210
11. A Desert Pompeii 233
12. Skin of the Gods 259
13. Signs of the Cross 279
14. A Curse of Sand and Salt 300

Part VI: The Lost Oasis
700 –

15. The Lost Oasis 316
16. The New Valley 340
17. History's Lessons 355

Epilogue 371
Bibliography 373
Index 384

ACKNOWLEDGEMENTS

THIS BOOK COULD NOT HAVE BEEN WRITTEN WITHOUT THE co-operation of many members of the Dakhleh Oasis Project (DOP), who guided me through the desert and half a million years of human time on Earth. I must first acknowledge the support of the late Founder of the DOP, Geoffrey Freeman, and express my regret that he did not live to see this tribute to his vision. And I want wholeheartedly to thank Tony Mills, Director of the DOP, for making me welcome in Bashendi and cheerfully arranging and aiding my research at all stages; also, sincere thanks to Lesley Mills for creating a lovely environment in which to work. I am no less grateful to the following members of the DOP for the time and effort they freely expended in the field and afterward to help me better understand the significance of their research: C.S. "Rufus" Churcher, Maxine Kleindienst, Mary McDonald, Colin Hope, Gillian Bowen, El Molto, Peter Sheldrick, Ursula Thanheiser, Johannes Walter, Klaas Worp, Olaf Kaper, Marcia Wiseman, Alicia Hawkins, Tatyana Smekalova, Lech Krzyzaniak, Robert Giegengack, Jennifer Smith, Roger Bagnall, Jim Knudstad, Rosa Frey, Dan Tuck, Caroline McGregor, Manfred Woidich, Iain Gardner, Jennifer Thompson, Alan Hollett, Laurence Blondaux, Amanda Dunsmore, Richard Mortimer, Natasha Dodwell, Edwin "Ted" Brock, and Ines Tauber. Also, heartfelt thanks to Nick Millet and Roberta Shaw of the Royal Ontario Museum for their moral and practical support throughout the project. As well, I am grateful to Art Aufderheide of University of Minnesota, Duluth, School of Medicine; Ryan Parr, Paleo-DNA Laboratory, Lakehead University; Ian Brookes of York University; Henry Schwarcz of McMaster University; Georges Soukiassian of the French Institute of Oriental Archaeology; and Rudolph Kuper of the Heinrich-Barth Institute. Special thanks to Saad Muhammad for making accommodation and travel arrangements in Cairo, Mansour Beyumi Sayed for his fine cuisine and mazbut, and Ashraf Leltrabishi, Chief Inspector of Antiquities, Sohag Sector, for facilitating my research in the Dakhleh Oasis. I must also thank the National Geographic Society for permission to interview the DOP Prehistory Group whose research it funds.

Neither would this book have been possible without the patient and able guidance of my editors: John Pearce, Kendall Anderson, Suzanne Brandreth, and Rick Archbold. Thank you all. Also, I am grateful for the unwavering support of my publisher, Maya Mavjee, and my agent extraordinaire, Dean Cooke.

As always, deepest gratitude to my wife, Cathy, and daughter, Meg, who lived with this book and its writer for what must have seemed like ages.

Support for the Dakhleh Oasis Project may be paid as follows:

In the USA (specify the Dakhleh Oasis Project):
Society for the Study of Egyptian Antiquities
c/o Dr. E. Cruz-Uribe
University of Northern Arizona
Flagstaff, AZ 86011

In Canada (specify the Dakhleh Oasis Project):
The Society for the Study of Egyptian Antiquities
P.O. Box 578, Station P
Toronto, Ontario M5S 2T1

In the UK:
John Ruffle, Charman, The Dakhleh Trust
Rockcliffe House, Kirk Merrington, Co. Durham DH16 7HP

It is impossible to talk about the history of
human civilization without talking about water.

SANDRA POSTEL
Pillar of Sand, 1999

————┤ ├————

One may write a history of humanity principally guided by
two questions: What kind of man was the conqueror of man's
environment, and how did the conquered environment react,
and change man?

HANS ELEANDER WINKLER
Rock Drawings of Southern Upper Egypt, 1939

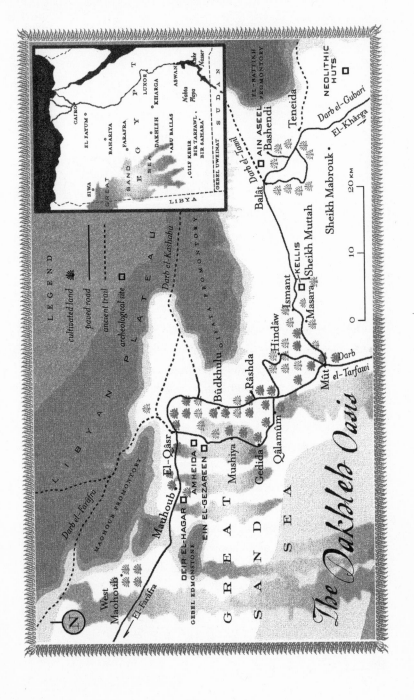

The Dakhleh Oasis

LEGEND
🌿 cultivated land
—— paved road
---- ancient trail
☐ archeological site

PROLOGUE

I HAD NO IDEA WHAT THEY COULD BE WHEN I FIRST LAID EYES on them. At a distance they looked like great red serpents, half buried, coiling through the sands.

These strange formations reared up at the far western edge of the Dakhleh Oasis in Egypt's Western Desert. Here, the oasis fields—so intensely green they almost hurt the eyes—end, giving way to mountains of yellow sand. Ranges of dunes receded into the Great Sand Sea: thousands of square miles of sand, more sand, and still more sand, and beyond, only Libya and the Sahara, desert stretching all the way to the Atlantic coast.

I was standing by a single upright column in the courtyard of a ruined Roman Age temple known locally as Deir el-Hagar, or "The Stone Convent." Scrawled on the column were various graffiti of nineteenth-century travellers who had ventured to this far western outpost. Most prominent were the members of the German expedition of Gerhard Rohlfs, their finely scripted names etched into the soft sandstone. At the bottom was the date: 1874.

Rohlfs had tried to cross the Great Sand Sea, an ill-fated mission which would surely have ended in disaster except for a freak two-day rainstorm that allowed him to reach safety in the northern oasis of Siwa. The only living thing he saw during his two-week desert trek was a great snake, basking on a rock. When he killed it and opened its stomach, he found only grains of sand.

Driven by curiosity to discover what the great red bands were, coiling snake-like from beneath the mountainous dunes on the horizon, I decided not to linger any longer at the temple.

Scrambling up a ridge of sand and over the ravaged and breached *temenos* wall that once surrounded and protected the sacred precinct of the temple, I walked out onto the Plain of Sio'h, which translates as "Throne of the Moon." It might as well have been the moon, such was its barrenness. The prevailing northwest wind was funnelling off the Libyan Plateau, driving sand into my face and eyes. I made my way toward the open plain, where the reddish ruins of Roman Age farmsteads stood out in sharp relief against the yellow dunes in the distance.

The plain had been stripped to the desert pavement, clay and bedrock, but there were plentiful signs of its past occupants. Potsherds large and small blanketed the ground like pieces of a puzzle. There were so many they could not be avoided, and they clattered underfoot, disturbing the profound desert silence. They were all colours of the earth, from black and grey to yellow and brown, but most were reddish. All were unglazed, the common, disposable ware of the common people. I reached down and picked up a large rim to which one handle was still attached. I recognized it as a Roman amphora. These were the trade containers of the Roman Empire. Perhaps it had once held olive oil or wine, or pickled fish products from the far-away Mediterranean. It could hold nothing now. The sides of the broken vessel were worn thin from centuries of sand blasting, and if left long enough, they would be abraded into oblivion, adding a few more grains of reddish sand to the Sahara's vast archive of sands. I returned it to its resting place, where the archaeologists would eventually map, collect, and draw it for posterity.

The potsherds were thickest on the ground near the old farmsteads. Some of these venerable structures were mere piles of rubble, others relatively intact; even some of the Roman-style arches had stood the test of time. Overall, however, they had the eroded look of sand castles after the tide has come in. They seemed to be dissolving into the landscape.

Leaving them behind, I continued walking west toward the dunes and the mysterious red bands snaking through the landscape. I could now see that there were several of these monumental structures linking the desert to the once-fertile plain.

I still had no idea what they could be.

It was only when I finally reached them that I realized how massive they really were and that they were human-made. I climbed up the side of one: about twelve feet. The top was concave, and at one time it must have been much deeper, with much higher sides. Like everything in this exposed location, it had been worn down by the wind. I walked across its width, measuring ten paces. It was then I noticed that the interior was carpeted with numberless tiny shells, their little turret shapes littering the surface just as they might any beach. I had seen these before at the sites of old, abandoned wells in the oasis. They were freshwater snail shells.

I realized then that water, lots of it, had flowed along these now ruined clay conduits from the high ground in the distance to irrigate the Plain of Sio'h below, where crops once grew as luxuriantly as they do in the still-fertile parts of the oasis.

My great red serpents of the dunes were aqueducts: Roman aqueducts.

PART ONE

ISLAND OF THE BLESSED

A map of Egypt *(John O'Carroll)*

CHAPTER ONE

THE OTHER EGYPT

Standing atop the 1,600-foot-high Libyan Plateau, a great limestone-capped prominence that shines white, pink or violet depending upon the angle of light and time of day, I peer over the edge at a dry ocean of sand, rippling with crests and troughs of golden, wave-shaped dunes. The seemingly boundless wastes of the Sahara are not all sand, of course. On the horizon, pyramidal hills rise up to meet the azure sky and long stretches of barren brown gravels separate the sands. In Arabic *Sahara* means "the brown void," or simply "desert." The planet's greatest desert stretches without respite 3,000 miles from the shores of the Atlantic Ocean to the Red Sea coast. Its driest core, its dead heart, is here in Egypt's Western Desert, 170 miles west of the verdant Nile Valley. Encountering it for the first time fills me with both fascination and dread. There is an insistent, ear-popping silence and, to the neophyte

---

A view of the Dakhleh Oasis from the Libyan Plateau

6

eye, a humbling vastness, seemingly unrelieved by any living thing. This is the desert that the early twentieth-century archaeologist Herbert Winlock characterized as "an infinite space of mystery and terror." Decades may pass between true rains: showers evaporate before reaching the ground. When the cold, dry winds blow, as they do almost daily, Saharan sand—the red rain—falls hundreds of miles out to sea, dusting the Atlantic.

To get here I have ridden in the back of a Land Rover, jarred and jolted by the rough terrain, along a road built by Nepalese soldiers during the First World War. It switchbacks up the pediments to the top of the Plateau, where it joins an old caravan route to the Nile Valley that is marked at intervals by the bleached bones of camels. Yellow sands that have travelled all the way from the Mediterranean flow over the lip of the Plateau in dry streams and fan out across the desert floor. Rains fell here hundreds of thousands of years ago and real waterfalls tumbled down, leaving gravels that remain today as pediments planed flat by the winds. These gravel ridges form giant steps, a great staircase used by desert foxes, people and donkeys to climb up to the Plateau. Between the pediments are dry *wadis,* rivers of white stone that were washed from the limestone crest mere thousands of years ago.

As I gaze down from my vantage point, a veil of dust hangs over the scene below. In the middle ground, several miles away, a green efflorescence glows faintly through the yellow haze. Training my binoculars on it, I can just make out the silhouettes of palm fronds and golf-course-sized patches of bright fields like rags sown onto a beggar's coat. The white dome of a sheikh's tomb, the needle of a minaret, the bulb of a water tower, and the flat roofs of mud-brick homes cluster at the edge of the greenery. A seeming mirage, it stands in defiance of the lifelessness that surrounds it. This is the Dakhleh Oasis, the place the ancients called the Island of the Blessed.

IT IS FEBRUARY 12, 1987, MY FIRST DAY IN THE OASIS.

In Arabic, *Dakhleh* means the *Inner* Oasis, that is, more interior to the desert than its neighbour, *Kharga,* the *Outer* Oasis. The Western Desert (so-called because it lies west of the Nile) occupies two-thirds of Egypt, and the only refuges in this waterless wasteland are five oases—Siwa, Bahariya, Farafra, Dakhleh and Kharga—that run in a north-south line roughly parallel to the Nile Valley. Dakhleh lies 400 miles southwest of Cairo as the crow flies, a twelve-hour trip by car.

In Cairo the Canadian Institute in Egypt had provided me with a young driver, Ibrahim, for the trip down the narrow corridor of the Valley, resplendent with its overarching date palms and fertile fields of winter wheat. At six in the morning, women swathed in black gowns emerged from the Nile with giant jars of water balanced on their heads; men rode into the impossibly green fields on squat donkeys, so that their sandalled feet nearly dragged on the ground. The scenes might have been lithographs etched in the family bible. To all appearances, Moses might still be hidden in the shallows, in his reed bassinet.

My enjoyment of these timeless tableaux was spoiled, however, by the maniacal habits of Egyptian drivers. Ibrahim passed every car, truck and bus on the road, more often than not on a corner or blind hill. I was glad to survive the vehicular roulette, the perpetual games of "chicken" indulged in by every Egyptian at the wheel, and relieved when at Asyut we set off across the nearly deserted roads of the desert. At a rest stop, we drank sweet tea served in glass tumblers to counteract the sweltering heat. Truckers carrying produce from the Valley stopped to pray at the squat mud-brick building which served as a way-station mosque, painted pastel blue with a two-by-four mounted at one corner in imitation of a minaret.

At Kharga, we stopped at the military check-post. A dispirited-looking group of soldiers, wielding Kalashnikovs and dressed in ragged wool uniforms, failed to ask for the military passes that we had spent half a day obtaining at the Ministry of Information in Cairo. Instead, one officer asked for my *stilo*. I explained that I was a writer and would need my pen; he seemed to accept my explanation, if grudgingly.

We descended from the barren plateau through a pass into the depression that links Kharga to Dakhleh, travelling on under a bright moon, the desert shining bone-white. Occasionally a pyramidal hill breached the horizon or the dark shape of a *yardang* (a sandstone butte) rose from the desert, like a sleeping lion. After fourteen hours on the road, we arrived at Dakhleh in time for supper and a raucous send-off party for the Australian contingent of the archaeological team, who were leaving the oasis the next day. That evening, two young villagers arrived at the archaeological compound to perform a stick dance in their honour. In a ritual bout performed since pharaonic times, the mock combatants jousted with long sticks that added their own loud clack to the energetic accompaniment of goatskin drums.

THE ARCHAEOLOGISTS WHO ARE MY HOSTS HAVE BROUGHT ME to the top of the Plateau on this first day to see, not the oasis, but what they facetiously call "The Grander Canyon," which spreads out at my back. It is an impressive dry gulch blanketed by variegated sands in colour gradations from straw yellow to rust red to graphite black. I clamber down the sandy embankment to the desert floor, which on this side is only a hundred yards or so below. It is ridged with outcrops of limestone that look like white-capped waves frozen in time—which, in a sense, is what they are, remnants of an ancient sea. As I scour the sands, assuming the posture of a working archaeologist, head down, eyes to the ground, scattered at my feet is a rich array of ancient marine flotsam: seashells whose scalloping has been so perfectly preserved they look as if they have just been washed ashore; also sharks' teeth, now as black as obsidian but retaining their deadly qualities of razor-sharp, serrated edges and points that might still draw blood. A little further on, I stoop to pick up a hand-sized brown fossil that proves to be a segment of a marine dinosaur skeleton. So rich is this ancient seabed that it has taken only minutes to recover an array of fossils representing the pyramid of past life, from lowly invertebrates to the most formidable carnivores. Here, in the depths of this wind-carved canyon, is where the story of life in Dakhleh begins. The archaeolgists are piecing together the entire history of this long-ignored region and the revolutions wrought here by earth movements, climatic changes, and, in due course, human beings. It is a story that encompasses the drying up of the Sahara, the birth of our own species, the invention of agriculture, and the rise and fall of ancient civilizations.

FOSSILS IN HAND, I CLIMB OUT OF "THE GRANDER CANYON" under the relentless glare of the sun, stopping again to rest on the high ground. Below my feet are layered eons of history, like pages of a great geological tome.

"There's a whole marine environment out there," says Rufus Churcher, a vertebrate paleontologist. A rangy man then in his sixties, he is the Dakheh Oasis Project's undisputed polymath whose formal training includes forestry, biology, paleontology and geology. I ask him to interpret the strata of rocks that, stacked one on top of another, make up the Plateau and the desert floor below.

"Seventy million years ago, there was no oasis and no desert," Churcher begins.

Instead there was a great sea that not only stretched across the vast barrenness that is now North Africa, but drowned what was to became Europe, the British Isles and southern Scandinavia. From the south a great river cleaved the land to the west of the present-day Nile. This ancient river system emptied into a shallow, wedge-shaped gulf of the sea that reached from present-day Libya to Jordan, and south to the Sudan. The river fanned out at its mouth to form a wide delta built up of rich continental soils, near where the oasis now sits. It was a lush, tropical place where giant ferns, horsetails and cycads flourished and sauropods, the giraffes of the dinosaur age, stretched their long necks to pluck the succulent leaves, cones and fruits. Armoured dinosaurs browsed the lush lower vegetation, and large carnivores stalked the herbivores along the coastal plain.

Nutrients from the centre of the continent flowed into the salty waters of the gulf, mixing with them and triggering a profusion of marine life. The warm waters seethed with single-celled green plants which fed a hungry array of molluscs that quilted the sea's sandy bed. Ten-foot fish cruised lazily, great skates flapped their wide wings in undersea flight, and turtles paddled through the murky inshore waters. Multi-chambered ammonites, encased in mother-of-pearl shells, propelled themselves with graceful rapidity by beating their trailing tentacles. Saw-toothed, giant sharks whipped their scimitar-like tails as they knifed through the water, releasing clouds of cardinal-coloured blood. But even they were no match for the marine reptiles that ruled the Cretaceous seas. Thirty-foot-long plesiosaurs, looking like giant turtles with snakes strung through them, contorted their elongated necks, seizing prey in needle-like teeth with deadly precision. Most dangerous of all, however, were the forty-foot-long mosasaurs, from whose yard-long jaws, armed with teeth the size of my thumbs, no marine creature was safe.

A great extinction at the end of the Cretaceous era spelled the demise of the dinosaurs and most of these magnificent marine creatures. In the deeper waters of the gulf, however, the shells of invertebrates and corals, billions upon billions of them, continued to pile up over tens of million of years; these are what now cap the great Libyan Plateau with a wintry whiteness like the cliffs of Dover.

With Churcher as guide, I could now read these great geological events in the face of the Plateau: the old red river muds at the base; later grey phosphate inshore beds in the middle; and more recent white, deepwater limestone at the top. No longer just a jumble of rocks, they formed a visual time line, milestones in the creation of the desert.

ABOUT 45 MILLION YEARS AGO, THE GREAT SEA BEGAN TO withdraw to the north, while the North African landmass also moved northward, sliding on its subterranean tectonic conveyor belt. The continents, then as now, were dancing across the earth's surface, a titanic bump and grind impelled by the seething mass of molten rock at the Earth's core. Monsoon rains fed river systems that cut across the continent, west to east. Now dry, from space they look like veins on a parched hand. Trees once grew along these ancient rivers, perch swam in their waters, and the ancestors of elephants and hippos wallowed along their banks.

Rains continued to fall on the newly exposed land of this still-tropical region. They filtered down through the porous sandstones laid down 100 million years ago, before the sea's encroachment. The sandstone lapped up the rains like a thirsty subterranean animal, and held the water in its belly. Whenever it rained through the succeeding ages, more waters seeped into this great reservoir.

Cataclysmic events accompanied the continent's slow crawl northward. Faults and fractures opened. Parts of the land were thrown up, while others sank. These massive movements created the depression that would become the Dakhleh Oasis. Over time it would be deepened by the relentless winds whipping down from the Plateau.

At about the rate fingernails grow, the African continent crawled northward until five million years ago, when its northwestern corner came up against Spain, closing the Straits of

Gibraltar, pushing down the Mediterranean basin and pushing up the European Alps. Now the Mediterranean—once part of the ocean—became a huge evaporation pan. As the waters dried up, a new river, the ancestral Nile, cut its way northward, picking up tributaries as it went, and carving a trench as deep as the Grand Canyon. Great waterfalls plunged into the Mediterranean and rainbows arced across the salt-white cliffs.

As the northern fringes of the African continent migrated further from the equator and its monsoonal rains, North Africa was also robbed of a reliable oceanic source of rainfall from the north. The waters of the Mediterranean basin were no longer renewed from the open sea. Slowly, the bordering lands were transformed into desert—into *Sahara*.

The Sahara, however, has not completely won its battle to claim North Africa. "The whole oasis basin has been scoured away, a hundred metres or more," Churcher points out. But when the winds penetrated the sandstone bedrock, water sequestered there suddenly burst through, nourishing a verdant island—an oasis. Below us, we can see the lines of acacia trees that shade the irrigation canals.

As the Sahara was beginning to assume its more inimical character, a new type of animal was evolving further south, in East Africa. Along rift valley lakes, a bipedal, large-brained primate, ancestral to modern humans, had learned to fashion crude tools from fist-sized cobbles. These early humans used stone balls to take down large game and smash the bones to get at the succulent marrow. They arranged lava blocks in circles, perhaps to anchor skin tents stretched over poles. More than one human-like species walked the African continent in the dawn of human prehistory. The one known as *Homo habilis,* or "handy man," seems to have been our first tool-maker. Although only four to five feet tall, they had the essential traits of humanity: a relatively large brain and two-footed locomotion.

Now another earth-shaping force kicked in, a major climate change that would further drive human evolution. Approximately 1.8 million years ago, cyclic astronomical forces tugged at the earth's axis so that less sunlight reached the northern hemisphere, causing the polar ice sheets to thicken and expand southward.

As the glaciers grew, they sucked moisture from the air to build their continents of ice, making the Saharan climate drier and colder. At about the same time, a larger human, *Homo erectus,* more like ourselves in stature and facial features, emerged in the rift valleys of East Africa. These new humans housed a bigger brain and had more expertise in working stone, producing almond-shaped hand-axes trimmed on both sides. These formidable weapons and practical implements were capable of slicing through the joints of the large game that roamed the new savannah lands. By now the savannah had spread northward; the Sahara then was akin to the present Serengeti Plain, with trees and grasses growing there, if sparsely.

Homo erectus had a questing nature. By one million years ago, they had occupied much of tropical and subtropical Asia as far east as Java. By 750,000 years ago, they had reached southern Europe, pressing northward in the shadow of the glacier. Perhaps they travelled out of Africa following the steamy banks of the ancestral Nile, or perhaps they walked north through the savannah lands.

These hunter-gatherers travelled in small bands of twenty to fifty people, tracking the migrating herds. Along the way they collected stones for fashioning their tool kit, dug tubers and harvested berries, and camped near ephemeral water supplies: *wadis* swelled by freshets, and watering holes filled to brimming during the rainy season. Water meant game and plants and a season of plenty—until the rains stopped and it was again time to move on.

Their wanderings continued generation after generation. But one day, one of these nomadic bands must have seen a great white Plateau rising above the rim of the plain, with more trees than

usual growing at the base. It is easy to imagine them walking a little more quickly, more eagerly, toward these promising signs of
life. They heard hoofbeats thundering across the plain and saw
herds of antelope, gazelle and hartebeest scattering before them.
On the ground were the tracks of larger animals. Within several
miles of the cliffs, they found a miraculous place, like nothing they
had ever encountered. Water gushed bubbling from the belly of the
earth and formed deep pools. There was a mineral pungency in the
air, which must at first have caused the people to pause. Was the
water sweet enough to drink? The leader's signalled approval would
have been a cause for communal celebration. Once the band discovered many more such springs, they decided that this place was
too good to leave. It was then that Dakhleh's human story began.
Since that time, people have always found refuge in this oasis.

Modern humans evolved here in Africa and spread to Europe
and Asia. Eventually they took to herding cattle and cultivating
crops. Later, the great civilization of ancient Egypt took root here.
Conquering armies from all points of the compass swept across the
desert and one at least was lost forever under gathering sands. The
empires of Greece and Rome profited from the oasis's waters, as
did the Islamic conquerors who followed. Today, rain falls so rarely
that many oasis dwellers have never experienced it. Nevertheless
people still survive on the desert's hidden waters.

IT IS LUNCHTIME AND I TAKE MY SEAT IN THE BACK OF THE
Land Rover for the uncomfortable, dusty trip down to the oasis.
On level ground again, we pass isolated fields of alfalfa and wheat,
more vibrantly green than any crops I have ever seen. A red fox,
here the colour of desert sand, darts across the road. We skirt a
high hill and follow a dirt track beside the date palm groves into
the village of Bashendi, threading through its narrow, walled
streets while warning pedestrians of our arrival with regular blasts

from the horn (a good horn seems more important in Egypt than good brakes).

Groves of date palms, silver desert light streaking along their spear-shaped fronds, surround the hilltop village that from a distance has the appearance of a single fantastic habitation that has grown, somehow, of its own volition. Once inside the village, the mud-brick houses are so interlaced and interconnected with walls and courtyards, it is difficult to know where one begins and the other ends. There are no harsh right angles; instead there is an organic flow of buildings threaded by narrow streets. Shy, dignified women, resplendent in purple, green, red and teal head-wraps and dresses, sit on low mud stoops, or *mastabas,* washing clothes in great metal basins, twisting strands of hemp rope and weaving mats; boys race by, kicking up dust in their spirited games of soccer; and old men smoking hookahs hunker down, backs against the walls, playing a complicated game of checkers, for which stones and dried donkey dung serve as pieces.

Beyond the villages, a patchwork of fertile fields flourishes wherever water freely flows or can be channelled. The oasis dwellers are engaged in a constant war with the desert sands that will eventually overwhelm their fields, roads, and even their villages. The borders of the oasis are not a permanent feature, but a battle line that is constantly being redrawn between human endeavour and natural forces, between will and fate.

When I remark on the fertility of the oasis over a lunch of local tomatoes, olives, fava bean soup, flatbread, bananas and dates, archaeologist Tony Mills observes: "It's a lovely life farmers have here. You throw the seeds on the ground and practically have to jump back. Then you sit on your hunkers for three months and go and cut it down. You feed yourself with very little effort."

Oasis dwellers farm the land year round. Water no longer bubbles from the ground. Deep wells now siphon waters from the desert reservoir. These waters nourish the bright patchwork of fields where the Dakhlans grow both their staple crops of rice and wheat, and fodder for their sheep, goats and cattle. The date palms yield the sweetest fruit in all of Egypt. Mud, water and straw provide essential building materials. Water and the soil laid down so long ago are all that these oasis dwellers need to make a life. Sand and wind are their only natural enemies.

The almost constant dry wind is the curse of the oasis: it propels the advancing sands that bury fields and roads, and sometimes whole villages. But it was the wind that excavated the desert floor down to the water table, releasing the waters sequestered there and allowing humans to live in the Sahara, in its archipelago of green islands. Of the five Egyptian oases, Dakhleh is the largest and has the richest history.

The blowing sand, while a curse to the farmer, has been a blessing for the archaeologists, preserving much of Dakhleh's past record. In the crowded courtyard of their rented compound are the treasures they unearth daily; white cotton bags of potsherds, metal strong-boxes packed with ancient bones, both human and animal, and trays of stone tools compete for space.

Before the 1970s, despite the venerable history of Egyptology, no archaeologists had concentrated their efforts on the oases, opting instead to study the magnificent ruins that border the Nile. Eventually, however, a team of archaeologists focused their attention on Dakhleh and began to chart an unbroken 400,000-year pageant of human endeavour.

THE DAKHLEH OASIS PROJECT (DOP) BEGAN VERY CASUALLY. IN 1966, Irish-born Geoffrey Freeman and his Canadian wife, Betty, decided to journey to Egypt on a second honeymoon. A successful insurance broker as well as history buff, Freeman had always found the culture of the pharaohs fascinating, but his knowledge of Egypt had been restricted to books until he set foot in Cairo.

At the time the Freemans visited, there were few other Western tourists. Chauffered from temple to temple along the Nile, Geoffrey and Betty found themselves not only fancy free but virtually alone. They had Egypt *carte blanche.*

In five weeks, they compassed a grand tour of Egypt's matchless trove of antiquities. There was only one disappointment for Freeman. Everywhere he went, guides gave him the same line, that this tomb or that temple was dedicated to the pharaoh, Ramses II. There is little doubt that Ramses II cast a large shadow over the history of ancient Egypt, living to the ripe old age of 92 and reigning over Egypt for 67 years, from 1279 to 1212 B.C. The largest monolithic statue ever undertaken in Egypt depicted a seated Ramses II and inspired Shelley's famous poem *Ozymandias.* Still, Freeman, a red-headed Celt with a fiery temperament to match, was skeptical: "I was mad that I couldn't read the hieroglyphics and the bloody guides were giving me the same translation for different hieroglyphs. I knew that they were giving me crap."

Even so, most mortals would have swallowed their umbrage, packed up their exotic souvenirs and returned home to carry on their life much as before. Not Freeman. Back in Canada, he immediately enrolled as a special graduate student in Egyptology at the University of Toronto and started plotting his return to the land of the pharaohs—this time as a private scholar.

Two years later, in 1968, he left the Great American Insurance Company and established his own general insurance agency. In midlife, at 47, he had recognized his true calling and, feeling driven by destiny, he now started to put in place a personal business plan that would free him from his career in insurance, which had long since lost its charm.

While continuing his part-time studies, in 1970, he established the Society for the Study of Egyptian Antiquities with a Ph.D. student Frank T. (Terry) Miosi and their University of Toronto Egyptology professor, Donald Redford. Freeman's motives were not entirely altruistic. He wanted to dig in Egypt and needed the aegis of a legitimate entity to apply to the Egyptian government for a permit and the Canadian government for funding. In 1970, the Society received a small Canada Council grant of $2500 to record the writings in the Temple of Osiris Heqa Djet, part of the great temple complex at Karnak in Luxor.

With further funding from the Smithsonian Institute and under the direction of Redford, Freeman spent three seasons deciphering the hieroglyphics of the temple. It was standard epigraphic work, a skill for which Freeman, always adept at languages, seemed to have a natural talent.

Although Freeman was now doing what he had dreamed of, he was restless. By 1972, he had taken a great dislike to the crowded confines of the Nile Valley, where there were too many Egyptians living one on top of the other, tourists everywhere you looked, and, for that matter, too many archaeologists digging one on top of the other. But if not in the Nile Valley, then where to dig next?

The solution presented itself during his third and final season at Karnak, when Freeman met the great Egyptian archaeologist Ahmed Fakhry, a figure renowned in Egyptological circles for his graciousness and vitality. Fakhry had gained a world-wide reputation as a lecturer with the travelling Tutankhamun exhibition, as well as a prodigious worker who published books and articles in four different languages. Being born in the Fayum, the district of lakes west of the Nile, had nurtured in him a lifelong interest in the oases. One of the first young Egyptians to study Egyptology at Cairo University, Fakhry helped to create a Desert Researches Section of the Egyptian Antiquities Service and served as its head from 1944 to 1960, conducting excavations in the oases of Siwa, Bahariya and Kharga. The University of Chicago Egyptologist John A. Wilson once wrote that Fakhry had "a genius for digging in the most productive places."

19

Indeed, in 1969, Fakhry made a remarkable and unexpected discovery: an ancient capital in the Dakhleh Oasis, replete with a Governor's Palace. Until then, no one had even suspected that the Old Kingdom Egyptians had been in the oasis. When Freeman met Fakhry, the Egyptian told him that Dakhleh was an archaeological gold mine and, best of all, that it was virtually untouched.

The nineteenth and early twentieth centuries were periods of unparalleled archaeological plunder in Egypt, as mummy, scarab and papyrus hunters clambered over each other to pilfer antiquities, a frenzy described by archaeologist and author Brian Fagan as the "rape of the Nile." In the process, these treasure hunters had destroyed all scientific context for these priceless artifacts and any hope of a later generation piecing it back together. But by virtue of its remoteness, Dakhleh had been spared. If Freeman dug there, Fakhry said, he would have the field to himself. Also, the notion of digging in the desert, pitching a tent under the star-filled Saharan sky, appealed to Freeman's romantic side.

Before returning home, he invited Fakhry to speak to the Society in Toronto. The audience that night in 1972 attracted a Who's Who of Canadian Egyptology, including Nick Millet, Curator of the Royal Ontario Museum's Egyptology Department, and the Assistant Curator, Tony Mills. In the tight-knit Egyptological community of Toronto, everyone knew each other. Fakhry's lecture proved to be the catalyst that brought them together for a common purpose— "He was a wonderful raconteur," Mills recalls—and by the end of his spellbinding lecture Freeman and Mills were fired up with enthusiasm over the possibility of digging at Dakhleh.

Another piece of Freeman's plan fell into place in 1972. He sold his business that year. Though reluctantly convinced to stay on part-time for two more years, increasingly Freeman dedicated himself to getting to the oasis. However, his first application to the Egyptian Antiquities Organization for a permit to dig was turned

down flat. The Western Desert had been declared an off-limits militarized zone because of hostilities with neighbouring Libya.
Undaunted, Freeman continued to apply year after year, and finally
a permit was granted in 1977.

Freeman, the able businessman and amateur, and Mills, the
experienced field archaeologist, set out in the winter of 1977 on a
reconnaissance mission. They eagerly anticipated examining
Fakhry's Old Kingdom desert capital. On arrival, however, it didn't
take them long to discover that the French Institute of Oriental
Archaeology, based in Cairo, was already excavating there. Fakhry
had also spoken of his Dakhleh discovery in France—where, in
fact, he had died suddenly of a heart attack in June 1973. The
Canadians were shocked and embarrassed to have travelled so far
only to discover that they had been beaten to the punch.

Although bitterly disappointed, Mills and Freeman decided to
spend their time reconnoitring the rest of the oasis. It proved to be
a very different place from the "Hollywood oasis" of a pond, a palm
tree, a camel, and an old temple that Freeman had imagined.
Instead, he and Mills found themselves exploring 800 square miles
of date palms, farms and villages—and regarded as curiosities by
40,000 people.

However, the scattered villages of Dakhleh still seemed
remote, in time and space, from the intense hubbub of the Nile
Valley. Freeman and Mills quickly decided this would be a good
place to work. Most of all, it was obvious that there was more than
enough to work on. Ample remains were scattered everywhere—
on the surface or poking through it—and ranged from Stone Age
tools to the medieval Islamic city of El-Qasr with its dark, winding
streets and soaring mud-brick architecture, a place of such mys-
tique it was enough, Freeman said, "to drive you crazy." They also
realized that there were other Old Kingdom sites, which lessened
the sting of the French scoop.

After each day of touring, sun-up to sun-down, Mills and Freeman returned exhausted but excited to a small guesthouse in the modern-day oasis capital of Mut, where they were only the sixteenth and seventeenth guests ever to register. Before supper, they repaired to one of the irrigation cisterns to wash off the desert grime and bask in the warm, spa-like waters. Over warm Stella beer and strong Turkish coffee, or *mazbut,* the two men, who shared an insatiable curiosity, talked long into the night about the potential of the oasis and the need to think outside the box of historical archaeology.

They decided not only to investigate the tombs, temples and hieroglyphs, the traditional concerns of Egyptology, but to determine how and why the oasis people came here. Similarly, they wanted to know how plants and animals had arrived here and if and why species had subsequently disappeared. They decided, then and there, to study the whole oasis in an effort to trace its entire cultural history. Most importantly, they agreed to enlist the help of natural scientists—geologists, paleontologists and botanists—to tie the evolution of the oasis cultures to the environmental changes that had taken place over time. Determining how the environment had shaped human activities and how humans had altered the environment would become the central mission of the project.

Freeman admits that it was perhaps naiveté that allowed him to conceive of such an ambitious undertaking. Not being an archaeologist, he saw no reason to limit the investigation to that discipline alone. On the other hand, Mills felt the same need precisely *because* of his prior experience in the field.

Like many archaeologists who came of age in the early 1960s, Mills had been part of the Nubian Salvage Campaign. The experience had a profound effect on his personal and professional life, and ultimately on the shape of the DOP.

The UNESCO-sponsored Nubian campaign was organized to rescue as much as possible of the archaeological heritage of the ancient land that once united Upper Egypt and northern Sudan along the Nile. The building of the Aswan High Dam meant that many undocumented sites were about to disappear under the dammed waters of Lake Nasser.

In Nubia, Mills discovered that field work appealed to his independent nature, but the salvage campaign also convinced him that this was no way to do archaeology. Despite gleaning valuable information, in the end, for Mills it was deeply unsatisfying. When the UNESCO money ran out, he and others had to abandon the field work before they could synthesize their data. Salvage is archaeological triage: you save what you can while you can and sacrifice the rest. Mills came away knowing very little about the geology of the area, or about the animals and plants, present or past: "A lot of the natural history escaped me." Also, he saw the drawbacks of compartmentalization: although the various international missions corresponded with each other to a certain extent, each was responsible for a particular time period or special area of interest. Mills resolved to do things differently the next time, and he sees Dakhleh as one of life's rarer gifts, a second chance.

First, Freeman and Mills had to secure the concession. On their return to Cairo, they were relieved to discover that the French were interested in excavating the Governor's palace and the tombs near Balat. They immediately applied to the Egyptian government for the concession to the whole oasis, except for the Old Kingdom sites discovered by Fakhry. To their surprise, it was granted.

In the fiercely competitive world of Egyptian archaeology, it was nothing less than a coup to be awarded the right to dig the entire oasis, which at 16 by 50 miles covers an area the size of Greater Toronto, Birmingham, or Cleveland. Archaeological sites were normally allotted piecemeal, sometimes yard by yard, in areas such as Luxor. This was an unheard-of dimension, and Freeman and Mills could hardly believe their good fortune. The truth was that no one else had wanted the long-ignored oasis—an oversight many have since come to regret.

The Project was to be a partnership between Freeman's Society and the Royal Ontario Museum (ROM), one of the world's great museums. The concession was granted in the name of the Museum, whose founder C.T. Currelly had a long and distinguished history of digging in Egypt. However, Freeman was the "mover and shaker" of the Project, which would never have come to fruition but for his terrier-like determination. All the pieces of his dream were now in place. As he says, "It was a perfect spot for archaeological work, untouched for 3,000 years, and I wanted that. I wanted Egyptology, I wanted Egypt untouched, and I got it."

Based on their reconnaissance report, Mills and Freeman sought funding for a full-scale survey of the oasis. In 1977, they received generous funding from the Social Sciences and Humanities Research Council for a five-year survey. On October 10, 1978, the DOP researchers became the first Westerners to explore the archaeological riches of Dakhleh since 1908, when Herbert Winlock of the Metropolitan Museum of Art had spent a short two weeks in the oasis.

When they began, their activities were of intense interest to the local population and, understandably, aroused suspicion in some. The night in 1987 when Mills shared with me the insights from his first decade of field work, he related what he called a *Raiders of the Lost Ark* story.

The technique for the initial survey was merely to walk along and catalogue whatever remains of human activity were visible on the surface. One morning during the second season, Mills dropped off his colleague Rosa Frey at a new site and proceeded north on foot toward the hills on one side of a village in the western half of the oasis. He walked through the hills in a wide loop around the village, and depressingly, failed to find a single site all morning. Coming out on the other side of the village, he was waiting for a truck to come along and take him back to base camp for lunch, when he saw another pickup barrelling down the road in a cloud of dust.

The truck stopped and the driver asked, "Are you the Canadian archaeologist?"

"Yes."

"What are you doing here?"

"Waiting for the truck to come and take me to camp," Mills said, pointing west in the direction of the village.

The man looked at him and said, "Don't go."

"What do you mean, 'Don't go?'"

"Well," he said, "I've just had trouble getting through the village. They finally let me through when I convinced them I had nothing to do with you. The whole village is up in arms. They're armed with rocks and sticks and hoes, lining the road through the village waiting for you to turn up—and they will stone and club you to death. Don't go there."

"What'll I do?"

The driver took Mills to the police, who said, "Don't be silly, these are superstitious local people, that's a problem for the mayor to solve, not for the police."

The driver then took Mills back to the edge of the village and found the local sheikh. Mills still didn't know what the uproar was all about, imagining that it was some sort of anti-European demonstration or that perhaps the Canadian government had done something to offend the Egyptian government.

The sheikh told Mills to accompany him, that the villagers wouldn't hurt him as long as he was with him. The crowds had dispersed somewhat by then, but there was still an air of malice, which was soon quelled by the sheikh. He interviewed the people and he and Mills drank innumerable cups of sweet, strong tea, in order to discover the reason for the hostility.

It seems that a little boy (let's call him Akhmed) had been playing with his mates that morning and, at one point, ran off. When his mother asked, "Where is Akhmed?" his playmates had replied, "He's gone off with the Canadian into the hills."

"By the time the woman had talked to her neighbours, the story had become, the Canadian had taken little Akhmed off to the hills to sacrifice and eat him at the entrance to the cave so he could gain access to the treasures and the gold—and the Ark itself perhaps," Mills laughed.

The fact that "little Akhmed" turned up not long afterward made no difference at all. By then the rumour had spread like wildfire and everyone in the village was upset enough to take up whatever weapons came to hand.

Mills recalled: "I think the thought that was uppermost in my mind was, 'My God, are we going to have to give up this project just because the local people don't want us here?'"

Today, it is difficult to countenance this story of ill will, or even suspicion, toward Mills, who is affectionately known as "Mr. Tony" throughout the oasis. Speaking his name is a passport to goodwill on the part of residents and Mills was honoured by the Governor of the Oasis, who presented him with the Order of the New Valley medal for his many good works in the oasis.

The superstitious uproar died down as quickly as it had arisen. Over the next four years, Freeman, Mills and a small survey team walked the oasis, west to east, also venturing into the surrounding desert and onto the Libyan Plateau in search of traces of previous human occupation. In all, they found 425 sites for future investigation (a number that has since topped 700 and is still growing).

"The results, even in the first two years, were quite stunning," Mills recalls. The team identified upwards of fifty Old Kingdom town sites and associated cemeteries dating from circa 2200 B.C., suggesting that the ancient pyramid builders had made a sizable investment in the oasis. Half of the sites in the western part of the oasis, however, dated to the Roman Period. At the far west end was the temple of Deir el-Hagar, dedicated by Emperors Titus and Nero. Nearby was the elaborately decorated tomb of Padi-Osiris, which blended classical Egyptian and Byzantine artistic traditions. At the abandoned Roman Age city of Amheida, a test hole in a large mud-brick building revealed a magnificent painted room, unique in Egypt.

On the outskirts of the present-day oasis, prehistorian Mary McDonald found a multitude of flints, grindstones, arrows, blades and scrapers, many in association with fossil spring mounds or shallow lake sediments, clear markers that the desert had once been a much wetter place and that the oasis had been much larger in prehistoric times. In fact, it was almost impossible to walk anywhere in the desert without stumbling over stone weapons and tools. Rufus Churcher uncovered scads of bone fragments—some displaying signs of butchering–that showed that when Stone Age humans lived in the oasis, the area was populated by savannah fauna similar to that found in East Africa today. Together, these discoveries helped to paint a picture of an environment with permanent standing water, seasonal rainfall, grassland and forest cover—precisely the kind of information Mills and Freeman had hoped to recover when they decided to include natural scientists in the dig.

In 1981, the survey crew moved into the eastern part of the oasis, where they continued to make newsworthy finds. There was the buried Roman Age city of Ismant el-Kharab, "a desert Pompeii" inundated with sand, and the temple of Ein Birbiyeh, built by Augustus near the present-day village of Bashendi. Rubble dismissed by previous Western travellers as foundation stones turned out to be the ceiling blocks of the first intact Egyptian temple discovered since the nineteenth century.

The exhilaration of discovery, however, was soon shadowed by personal tragedy. At the end of the 1982 field season, Freeman left the oasis, flying home as usual from Cairo via London. He was thrilled with the accomplishments of the five-year survey and anticipating the next season, when excavations would begin—if his fragile health did not scuttle his dream. Freeman had recovered from a heart attack, but had been slowly losing his eyesight for several years due to cataracts and macular degeneration, a condition which results in progressive loss of central vision until only peripheral vision remains. His loss of sight may have been related, in part, to multiple sclerosis, with which he was first diagnosed in 1932 as a boy of eleven. Mercifully, the progress of the disease had been slow until now. By the late 1970s, however, he could no longer ignore the symptoms of the disease, and on his desert surveys he was walking with a cane. Now, at the stopover in Rome, he realized that his sight was fast failing him and by the time he reached London, he was too blind to drive his rental car. Freeman would never return to the desert to see Dakhleh's treasures revealed. It was a sudden and tragic end to his career as a field archaeologist.

His legacy as founder of the project was secure, however. Tony Mills now made a dramatic commitment to carry on Freeman's work and vision. In 1983 Mills left his secure academic positions at the ROM and the University of Toronto to become full-time Director of the Project.

WHEN I ARRIVED IN DAKHLEH THE DIG HAD ALREADY BEEN running for five years under the congenial but efficient leadership of Mills. Jovial and quick-witted, he has been described by one longtime colleague as "a genius with people."

During the week I spent with his team in the oasis in 1987,

they showed me magnificent temples and tombs. They brought me face to face with mummies, whose withered visages returned my gaze over a divide of two millennia, and prehistoric petroglyphs depicting experiments in domestication with antelopes, cattle, ostriches and even giraffes. These wonders alone might have drawn me back to write about Dakhleh more than a decade later. But I had an even more compelling reason.

For most of my adult life I have been a writer specializing in the environment, especially contemporary environmental crises. Human-induced climate change, loss of habitat and bio-diversity, the squandering of finite resources, especially fresh water—these were topics I felt cried out for attention, more so than mummies, tombs and the temples of a dead religion, however intriguing.

The DOP caught me by surprise. It soon became apparent to me that its primary focus *was* the environment, particularly the interaction between environmental change and human activity, which it was tracking over nearly half a million years. Here, in a single, isolated place, was an opportunity to trace the entire history, not just of our genetic and cultural evolution, but of our relationship to the environment over hundreds of millennia, starting when as hunter-gatherers we left little impact on it except our footsteps and a scattering of stone implements, and continuing right up to the present, when industrial exploitation has reached even this remote spot.

The story of Dakhleh is a microcosm of the human drama being played out on our planet. It is a study of human survival in the past, but also potentially an object lesson for today's management of the environment. By understanding past mistakes here, we might derive vital lessons for a world that seems bent on using up its non-renewable resources in the shortest possible time.

In essence, Dakhleh's story is about water, its exploitation and conservation. By following the water, its rise and fall, we can trace the fate of humans not only in the Western Desert, but by implication anywhere on the planet.

It is an epic story in three parts: for much of human history—in fact, what we call prehistory—people adapted to the gradual drying up of the Sahara with their feet, migrating in response to the wet and dry cycles in the growing desert. In late prehistory, when the Sahara became what it is today, the largest of the world's hot deserts—a parched swath as large as the continental United States—people became tethered to the oasis, the only place where life was still possible. In the historic period, life in the oasis took a decisive turn. First the pyramid-building Egyptians and later their Roman overseers sought to transform the ecosystem and the desert itself by tapping the most precious resource they had, the waters secreted under the Sahara.

Without its gift of water, the oasis could not exist. I wanted to understand how human actions had affected the water supply and the welfare of oasis dwellers, particularly over the last 10,000 years. But I did not want to look only into the past. I wanted to examine contemporary water exploitation and what it might mean for the future of the oasis.

BACK IN 1987, I RETURNED HOME TO FILE MY ORIGINAL magazine piece, but it was obvious even then that it was impossible to cover Dakhleh in such an abbreviated format. A year later I had lunch with Nick Millet, whom I had met in Dakhleh.

"I'd like to do a book on Dakhleh," I proposed at one point.

Millet, a tall, kindly gentleman with an aristocratic bearing, paused over his meal. "Yes, a good idea," he said. Then added, "Wait ten years."

It was hardly what I wanted to hear, but I trusted Millet, whose vocation, after all, was the tracking of human time. He understood that there was much work yet to be done. It proved to be sound advice, for when I eventually returned in 2000, I found that not only has the DOP made a string of spectacular discoveries, but the story of the oasis has only become more compelling, its message more urgent.

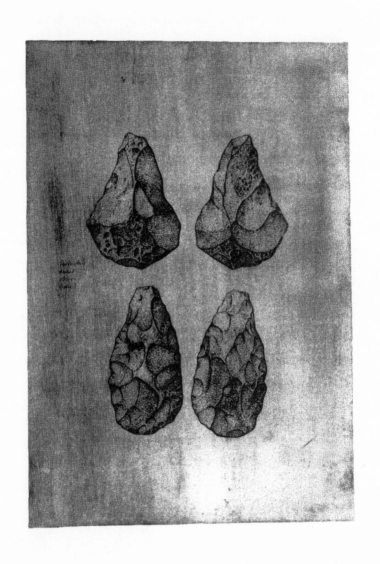

PART TWO

THE GARDEN

C.400,000–12,000 B.P.

Paleolithic tools *(John O'Carroll)*

CHAPTER TWO

EVERLASTING OASIS

In the beginning, the DOP's goal was to study the oasis only from the New Stone Age, 10,000 years ago, up to the present. But during the survey, it quickly became apparent that this was impractical: Mary McDonald was collecting many samples that were obviously much older—by hundreds of thousands of years. She and her mentor Maxine Kleindienst soon realized that Mills and his crew were unearthing in a single place the history of the evolution of humankind, stretching back to a time before the emergence of *Homo sapiens*. During the first decade of exploration, Kleindienst's academic commitments as Chair of the University of Toronto's Anthropology Department had kept her away from the field. Her long wait ended in 1986, when she was finally able to travel to the oasis to begin tracing first-hand the story of what she would later describe as the "Everlasting Oasis."

Acheulean hand-axes

When Kleindienst arrived in Bashendi, Mills handed her a cotton bag and said, "Here, these are for you." Opening it she found five "glorious Acheulean hand-axes." Having spent her early career in East Africa, in the cradle of humankind, she well knew what she was looking at: murderous-looking tools shaped to a keen cutting edge along their entire circumference by Early Stone Age people. It was during her heady student days that Kleindienst first made her acquaintance with the Acheuleans at Isimila and Kalambo Falls, and later Olduvai Gorge. Digging by day, she spent long nights describing, comparing and classifying tools by lantern light while listening to the footfalls and chilling mews of leopards outside her tent. The result was a field guide to the African Acheulean which is still in use. She showed that these early tool-makers were not limited to making large hand-axes, cleavers and knives. They also produced a variety of smaller tools in various shapes for specialized uses, including scrapers, chisels, push planes, and burins, or points, and other heavy-duty tools such as picks, choppers and hammerstones. The Acheuleans almost certainly used bone and wood for smaller, light-duty tools as well, but little of this perishable material has been preserved. "These people had a mastery of stone working. They're still my favourite people," says Kleindienst.

The five hand-axes—the Swiss army knives of the Early Stone Age—had been collected during the survey in the western part of the oasis near a spring mound, one of hundreds surrounding the modern oasis. However, they had been found during a sandstorm, so no one knew the exact location, nor could Kleindienst find it again later. It was an apt introduction to the challenges that she would face in her search for early humans.

In her first season in Dakhleh, the stocky prehistorian, then in her fifties, explored the desert on foot in a circle extending thirty miles, or two days, march for her Early Stone Age peoples, from the edge of the oasis. Her search took her into what she describes as the paleo-oasis, which, in the distant past, was a savannah-like habitat several times larger than the present-day island of fertility. Today it is an environment so alien in its barrenness that NASA has used the Western Desert as a surrogate for Mars exploration. Kleindienst knew her early humans needed two things: water and a source of stone for making tools. Where either was lacking, there were no people or, at least, people could not survive for long and were likely to leave few signs of their passing.

The most promising sites were south of the contemporary oasis, where hundreds of long-extinct "spring eyes" tower several yards above the otherwise featureless terrain, like diminutive Vesuviuses. "Springs" suggest subterranean water, but in the desert things are not always what they seem: time and wind have turned the landscape topsy-turvy. The relentless power of the wind has eroded the more vulnerable sandstone and claystone around the old spring eyes and whisked it south, on a long, inexorable journey to the Sudan, leaving the cement-hard spring sediments standing up as dry water silos, stained with yellow and red ochre deposits. Water once flowed here, and Kleindienst knew that ancient peoples would have clustered close by.

Most Acheulean sites are concentrated within easy reach of water or where water would be available with a slightly increased rainfall. Lakes, pans, swamps, permanent and seasonal watercourses, and springs are the favoured locales. The earliest Acheulean populations do not seem to have occupied country that was arid or waterless, or, for that matter, tropical forest. They preferred grass and park savannah.

Kleindienst found a few tell-tale tools embedded within the spring eyes themselves, but mostly the tools were scattered on the desert surface. She also hiked up the three great gravel-topped terraces that step up the escarpment. These barren terraces are alluvial sediments, six to thirty feet thick, left behind by rivers that once tumbled down the plateau. Planed flat on top by the wind, they are long and wide enough to be runways. These ancient river courses date from the Pleistocene, or last Great Ice Age (two million to 10,000 years ago), and were in turn criss-crossed several thousand years ago by Holocene rivers, now dry streams, or *wadis,* paved with chunks of white limestone torn from the escarpment.

The water-laid terraces above Dakhleh are proof that it rained hard and long during Pleistocene times. On the terraces, Kleindienst found cores and debris as well as isolated or unfinished tools. She concluded that the Early Stone Age hunter-gatherers probably used these elevated vantage points as workshops, fashioning tools and weapons as they kept watch for the big game—hartebeest, Cape buffalo, and zebra—ranging across the savannah below.

As springs broke through the escarpment, the tumbling streams formed aquamarine pools covered by thick mats of blue-green algae. Bulrushes rimmed the pools, and figs and other trees grew there, providing a change of diet for the meat-eating Acheuleans.

The view below would have been very different from what it is today. The plain would have been shaded by well-spaced acacia trees providing noon-day shade for both animals and roving bands of humans. At the centre of the oasis, thicker forest would have grown, a leafy haven alive with birdsong and the trumpeting of elephants.

Hunters would have congregated near the lowland springs, for that was where the animals gathered. Some of these springs, fed from artesian sources below ground, were powerful gushers, others mere trickles. They were mostly sources of warm, sweet water—though sometimes pungent with sulphur—surrounded by dense masses of green reeds whose blackened fossilized casts Kleindienst still finds embedded in the "spring eyes." The seepage from the largest springs would have formed fertile marshes, places for waterbirds to gather. Even today, a few marshes exist from the overflow of dug or deep artesian wells, and here spindly-legged black-and-white stilts bob for brine shrimp in the shallow waters. Such places would have been ideal for ambushing larger mammals, the reason so many tools are found in their vicinity, no doubt.

In isolated cases throughout North Africa, archaeologists have found evidence that these hunter-gatherers controlled fire and cooked their food. The Acheuleans may even have constructed crude shelters. At Olduvai, Mary Leakey identified a small ring of lava stone in the oldest bed with Oldowan tools. Perhaps it served as the foundation of a shelter constructed of tree branch ribs and animal hides. But the Acheulean people moved frequently, tracking the animals and the rains. Whatever else we can say about these early humans, we know they were successful and found no reason to change their lifestyle for a very long time. The Acheulean tool kit, with some minor variations, stayed in use for over a million years.

As a Pleistocene archaeologist, Kleindienst's method is always to climb uphill. She trudges to the top of every spring mound, ridge and hill, eyes on the ground, permanently set in search mode. Her object is to find the oldest material where it was originally dropped, eliminating the possibility that it has simply been washed down to a lower level. As a child, she found American Indian arrowheads in the Wyoming desert country. On the terraces, she draws on her childhood experience, as well as her field work in East Africa and in Nubia, to distinguish stones fashioned by early humans from the dense mantling of dark, wind-eroded gravels and cherts that can look deceptively like human-made objects.

Although Kleindienst was able to identify their tools, she was dogged by an inability to date them accurately. The wind that is the bane not only of the oasis dwellers but also of the desert archaeologist constantly scours the desert floor, lowering the level of the desert and with it the artifacts that once were buried under or lay upon it. The wind acts like a descending elevator, delivering all artifacts to the ground floor. Older and newer artifacts are thus mixed together, making it difficult to build up even a relative chronology, though exposure in the desert does make things easier to see and collect in the first place.

To establish a time line, the archaeologist needs to find artifacts where they were originally deposited (*in situ*), using the principle, borrowed from geology, of stratigraphy. The earth's surface is arranged in a layer-cake fashion, with the younger rocks lying on top of the older ones. In archaeology the assumption is also that older cultural layers lie under younger ones. As archaeologists dig deeper, presumably moving back through time, they discover that certain artifacts occur with greater or lesser frequency, as one tool kit is replaced by another. These seriation (ordering) techniques establish a relative chronology for the tools and the tool-makers.

After her first discouraging season, Kleindienst came to the gloomy conclusion that there were no datable artifacts to be found in Dakhleh. She found them either scattered on the surface of the pediments, or eroding out of spring mounds whose sediments had been hopelessly jumbled by the gushing waters. In neither case could she establish a reliable stratigraphy. But Kleindienst was determined to solve the dating conundrum, since knowing where you are in time is the *sine qua non* of archaeology. She desperately needed a relative chronology and some absolute dates before she could track the succession of cultures that had ebbed and flowed with the climatic vicissitudes of the Pleistocene. She believed that people had lived in Dakhleh since the Early Stone Age, using it as a refuge in the drying Sahara, but to prove it she had to find datable artifacts.

Faced with this seemingly intractable problem, Kleindienst decided to widen the field of inquiry to the Kharga Oasis, ninety miles to the west, in the hope of finding tools that could be compared to her Dakhleh finds—so-called cognates. She knew about a classic prehistoric study done in Kharga in the 1930s and the two oases were close enough and similar enough in their geology—both wind-scoured depressions at the base of the Libyan Plateau—to make comparisons valid. Most important, there were water-laid deposits called tufas, sedimentary rocks that look like huge black cinders clinging to the cliff-face. These tufas might be datable using a new absolute dating technique, uranium series dating, developed by Henry Schwarcz of McMaster University in Hamilton, Ontario. Schwarcz had been pestering Kleindienst for years to find some African tufa he could work on.

Uranium series dating is the latest in a battery of dating methods that grew out of the nuclear technologies developed during the Second World War. The best known is radio-carbon dating, but it has a limit of 40,000 years and so is of no use in dating Early Stone Age material. Schwarcz's method is based on the assumption that newly deposited freshwater carbonates, such as those found in the tufas, contain trace amounts of uranium (U) but negligible amounts of thorium (Th), the daughter compound that uranium decays into over time. It takes roughly 75,000 years for half of the uranium to decay to thorium, and that long again for half the remaining uranium to decay, and so on, which allows measurements of up to 350,000 or even 400,000 years.

If Kleindienst could combine the old study with the new technique, she might just be able to date her Dakhleh tools.

ON CHRISTMAS DAY, 1994, SHE AND HER PREHISTORIAN colleague, Marcia Wiseman, left their hotel in Kharga at 5 a.m. with two Egyptian drivers, Zemzemi Shahab Zemzemi and Hussein Abdel Halim. Their destination was Refuf Pass, a deep cut in the Libyan Escarpment. At the turn of the twentieth century, the pass had served as the access route for the Old Western Desert Railway and, for many centuries before, as a trail for camel caravans to and from the Nile Valley. In 1987, Kleindienst had tried to reach the Refuf tufas from the bottom of the pass, but her Land

Rover had become mired in sand. Not to be thwarted, Kleindienst hatched a plan to approach the pass from the top, and the DOP succeeded in finding a route in 1991. Kleindienst made the first geological survey of the youngest tufas in 1992 with Schwarcz, who pronounced them suitable for (uranium series) dating.

That Christmas morning, Kleindienst and Wiseman were driven up the escarpment on the paved road to the Valley, then along a dirt road to the head of the pass, where they picked up a camel trail. Then began a two-and-a-half-mile-long descent on foot. With sand and gravel shifting under them, it was a taxing trek. Kleindienst, by then retired, and Wiseman, who had finished her Ph.D. late in life, are testament to the need for field prehistorians to remain fit. They are a study in contrast: Kleindienst, a large-boned, sturdily built woman, and Wiseman, petite, hardly robust-looking, but, by her own admission, no less "bloody-minded" than her colleague.

When they entered Refuf Pass, they were following in the footsteps of two of their scientific heroes: prehistorian Gertrude Caton-Thompson and her geologist friend Elinor Gardner, who spent three field seasons from 1930 to 1932 studying the geology and associated archaeology of the Kharga Oasis. Kleindienst speaks almost reverently of both Caton-Thompson and Gardner, calling them "the grandmothers." Their work in Kharga was an exemplary regional study, and in many ways a forerunner of the DOP, bringing together as it did archaeology and the natural sciences, and placing human activity squarely in the context of the environment.

These two pioneers had found Acheulean hand-axes not only in spring mounds around Kharga, but also in deposits below tufas. Tufas are deposits of calcereous materials (largely calcium carbonate), created when water erupted long ago from springs in the escarpment. Rainbow hues must have reflected off the background of white limestone as the spring waters cascaded down, dissolving the limestone in the escarpment. Their erosive action also caused natural dams to form at the narrowest points of the *wadis* that carried the run-off, creating pools of the water. The pools evaporated, leaving deposits of dissolved limestone and building up terraces of tufa. These massive deposits had been noted by the Rohlfs expedition in 1874, but no one had taken a close look at them until the intrepid duo of Caton-Thompson and Gardner came along.

The two indomitable Englishwomen made the trip by camel, pointing out that "a camel is more easily replaced than a differential." First, however, they had reconnoitered the escarpment from the air, taking advantage of a visit from their friend Lady Bailey, who was piloting her own Puss-Moth, a then-popular single-engine monoplane.

In her autobiography, *Mixed Memoirs*, Caton-Thompson reminds us that landing a light aircraft in primitive desert conditions was anything but routine in those days. Before Lady Bailey's arrival, she directed the creation of a makeshift airfield in the desert near Kharga: for two days, a caravan of six camels carried tankfuls of water from a nearby well to water the sand in order to harden it. They were then marched around the periphery to make this "improvised aerodrome" visible from the air. Then, her heart in her mouth, Caton-Thompson waited for her friend's plane to appear in the clear blue sky: "From Luxor she came straight to us, and at about 9 a.m. on February 17th 1931 we saw her plane circling our heads at 4000 ft. She then made a wide detour out of sight and returned with the wind in the right quarter. As she dropped to landing level I was more petrified by fright than I have ever been. My heart was thumping. Then we lost sight of her in the dust-storm as she touched down. We all raced toward her . . . and found her calmly collecting herself. Her first words were, 'It was a very poor landing.'"

Undaunted by this close shave, Caton-Thompson explored "great lengths of this inhospitable region from the air" in the double-seater Puss-Moth, which, to her delight, featured a covered cockpit with side windows, "enabling photography and the unfolding of maps." The use of the plane saved Caton-Thompson and Gardner "weeks of foot-slogging" in the preliminary stages of their survey.

Nevertheless, Caton-Thompson and Gardner's expedition was carried out, as Caton-Thompson remarked in her usual understated fashion, "with not inconsiderable physical hardship." Six camels plodded the twelve miles to and from Kharga to re-supply their twelve-person camp. The two women lived in tents for weeks while they excavated several sites, from which they extracted Acheulean hand-axes, and intensively studied the adjacent tufas.

Early Stone Age tools were sealed under these tufas as if in a time capsule. Kleindienst believed that dating the tufas and the tools was key to figuring out both the sequence of climatic change and the succession of cultures that had prevailed in both Kharga and nearby Dakhleh. Like Caton-Thompson, she realized that the history of an oasis community, past and present, was tied inseparably to the question of water supply. Only by finding and following the water, its rise and fall, could she trace the comings and goings of ancient humans in the Western Desert.

As the Dakhleh prehistorians and their driver, Zemzemi, scrambled down the sand-filled pass they envied Caton-Thompson and Gardner their sure-footed camels. The tufas lined the walls of the Wadi el-Refuf, towering above Kleindienst and Wiseman like charred, petrified waterfalls. In sharp contrast, the limestone face of the escarpment formed a blazing white backdrop under the noon-day sun, and their voices and footsteps echoed around the natural amphitheatre.

They stopped occasionally to check their bearings and consult the 1930s map produced by their predecessors. The arduous descent was amply rewarded, however, as they rounded a turn and met a wondrous sight: the trench they had been searching for, Locus V, dug by Caton-Thompson and Gardner six decades before, still stood open much as they had left it.

Over the decades, not surprisingly, it had been partially filled with sand. Kleindienst and Wiseman began carefully removing the sand in the hope of finding some tools that had weathered out of the sides of the trench in the intervening years, but uncovered only a few flakes.

The trench had been dug at the base of a great greyish mass of tufas that dwarfed the two women. The artifacts were under the tufas, so dating the tufas would give a minimum age for the Acheulean tools discovered by Caton-Thompson in the trench.

Keeping an eye on the arc of the sun, Kleindienst reached for the geologist's hammer looped in the belt of her sturdy work pants and hacked off a fist-sized piece of tufa, which Wiseman labelled and deposited in a plastic bag, with the satisfaction of knowing she was carrying forward the unfinished work of their predecessors. They lingered a while to soak in the historic atmosphere before turning to make the arduous climb back up the valley, now in a foot-race against the fast-sinking sun. Along the way, they stopped briefly to sample successive terraces of tufa laid down at different humid prehistoric periods.

The three explorers toted their heavy packs of samples up the steep incline and were dog-tired by the time they reached the waiting Land Rover. Hussein, the DOP's chief mechanic and driver, thoughtfully greeted them with resuscitating cups of tea. Then it was another race against time through fields of *battikh,* watermelon-sized nodules of limestone. These car-wreckers were unnavigable in the dark, making it imperative to reach the gravel road before sunset to avoid spending a freezing-cold night on the Plateau.

The tufa samples were destined for Henry Schwarcz's laboratory for absolute dating. Caton-Thompson had not had access to such methods. She had been forced to compile a relative chronology of the succession of desert peoples based solely on their different tool types, the classic identification technique known as typology.

WHEN THE FIRST RESULTS FINALLY CAME BACK, MONTHS LATER, they more than rewarded Kleindienst's patience. She and Schwarcz had cracked the time barrier. With the data from the tufas and comparison of the Kharga and Dakhleh cognates, for the first time Kleindienst had a clear picture of the succession of Stone Age peoples through Dakhleh.

The oldest Acheulean material, from Caton-Thompson's trench, proved to be at the limit or just beyond the range of the dating method, or roughly 400,000 years old, confirming that people had been in the Western Desert for at least that long. The tests also pegged the first average dates for the older Middle Stone Age tools at approximately 220,000 years and for the younger Middle Stone Age tools at circa 125,000 years.

To Kleindienst's delight, the dating of individual tufas showed that Caton-Thompson's relative dates for the artifacts were now confirmed. Also, Gardner and Caton-Thompson's breakdown of climatic change has also been shown to be substantially correct: the later Middle Pleistocene (400,000–135,000 years ago) was generally wetter than the present with drier intervals, but the Late Pleistocene (135,000–10,000 years ago) was a generally dry period with wet intervals.

Each of the tufa terraces represents a time when there was an increase in rainfall, enough rain to cause springs to burst from the Plateau. Thanks to Kleindienst's perseverance, for the first time she was able to attach some dates to these periods of improved climate that created an ideal savannah habitat for the Acheulean tool-makers.

TWO YEARS LATER, KLEINDIENST'S PREHISTORY GROUP MADE another critical breakthrough in reconstructing the ancient environment of Dakhleh and the lives of the Middle Stone Age peoples, the archaic Homo sapiens who inherited the oasis from the

Acheulean hand-axe makers who are typically assigned to the species *Homo erectus*.

Kleindienst often carries out her quest to bridge the gaps in the chronology of the "everlasting oasis" in the company of her old University of Toronto colleague, paleontologist and archaeozoologist C.S. "Rufus" Churcher. For two decades, Churcher has been tracking the animals that lived in the oasis, from the Cretaceous period, seventy million years ago, right up to the present day—an evolutionary parade across an almost unthinkable span of time. Something of a savant, he says with self-deprecating humour that he possesses "a trivial mind—hit a professor on the head and you don't know what's going to fall out." Churcher nevertheless likes nothing better than to slide behind the wheel of a decrepit, bone-rattling Land Rover, strike out for the desert to the south, or the escarpment to the north, and once there to get down on his hands and knees and dig in the dirt.

His wife, Bee, complains: "You're always dragging me off to deserts." Indeed, Churcher has dug in deserts around the world: in Canada, East and South Africa, Australia and Egypt. These are his favourite hunting grounds, where, if "the bone goddess" is kind, he will find fossil bone. Each bone adds a chapter to Churcher's chronicle that traces the slow but steady extirpation of species in the oasis due to a combination of a deteriorating climate and, at times, human action.

To recreate the faunal community of past ages from mere spillikins of bone requires a lifetime of experience. Churcher, with his varied academic background and his intimate knowledge of Africa, is amply prepared. As well, he has certain native talents vital to the work of the archaeozoologist: he is good with his hands. While doing an Honours degree at the University of Natal he was given a crumbly fossil to reassemble. "Basically it was like a whole lot of cubes of sugar, and all the cubes were slightly disarrayed, but you could see they were part of a system," he recalls. He reassembled the bone puzzle, twisting the pieces this way and that until they fell into place, a trick akin to solving a Rubik's cube. Bee Churcher teases that she had to give up buying jigsaw puzzles as Christmas presents because Rufus would solve them before any other family member had a chance.

Kleindienst and Churcher have been trying to work out the links between the complex geology around Dakhleh and the evidence of the many human groups and animals that have lived or passed through there. It has proved a daunting challenge, but their enthusiasm has remained undimmed. These elders of the DOP, both now retired, stride off into the desert or scamper up the terraces of the plateau with the enthusiasm and pent-up energy of children let out of school.

For several weeks in 2000 I followed in their wake as they continued their two-decade-long geoarchaeological scavenger hunt for any scrap of bone or tool.

"Out there," Kleindienst said, pointing south toward a barren vista of outcrops and sand waves, "nothing is going to survive on the surface for more than a very short time—they're just gone."

"They weather into friable stuff," Churcher concurred.

Put simply, they turn into dust. The same is true of the ancient landscape itself.

"We always have to be mindful that most of the time we're walking on a surface metres below where ancient peoples might have walked," Kleindienst cautioned. Wind lowers the desert floor three or more feet every millennium. The extinct springs and flat-topped outcrops of sandstone called *yardangs* are pretty much all that remains of the ancient landscape. It has been Kleindienst's and Churcher's job to re-imagine from these fragments the landscape as it must have appeared to Stone Age peoples.

WHEN CHURCHER AND KLEINDIENST FIRST BEGAN POKING
around, they noted the greyish chalky soils—what they called
"CSS," or calcereous silty sediments—capping many *yardangs* in the
area of the Pleistocene springs. After years of pondering their origins, they concluded that these curious limey sediments, now sitting high and dry many feet above the desert floor, were marls, the
slurry that collects on lake bottoms.

If there were lakes here once, it would have had profound
implications for the prehistoric peoples and would also affect our
reading of the climatic changes in the Western Desert. However,
the geologist on the project at the time, Ian Brookes, strongly disagreed, saying the CSS could not have come from lakes. Churcher
demurred, but did not abandon his idea.

So matters rested until the winter of 1996, when Marcia
Wiseman suggested to Kleindienst and Churcher that they take a
closer look at the CSS icing one of the *yardangs* just southeast of
Teneida, the eastern access to modern Dakhleh.

Here the *yardangs* form a natural corridor across the desert to
the south. Each has been streamlined by the relentless northern
winds, so that the windward end is a blunt bow and the leeward end
tails away to the south to form a teardrop shape, the whole *yardang*
assuming the same aerodynamic configuration as sand dunes.
Furthermore, the wind and sand have cut the *yardangs* into vertical
terraces, broad at the base and narrow at the top, each terrace representing a previous drying phase when severe erosion took place. In
places, the sandstone has been scoured by the wind-driven sand into
paper-thin layers. From a distance the *yardangs* appear to be a dull
beige, but up close other more eye-pleasing colours leap out—
blushes of pink and rouge. This accounts for the Arabic name of
el-Gubari, "the painted road," which connects Dakhleh to Kharga.

Churcher steered the Land Rover off the paved el-Gubari road
and, shifting into four-wheel drive, climbed a steep incline beside

abandoned fields now given over to the spiny desert weed *alhagi,* or camelthorn. He parked beside the seventy-foot-high *yardang* and leaving Kleindienst and Wiseman to gather their packs, hurriedly began exploring. He noted a few Neolithic flakes at the base and, dug into the hillside, some open Roman Age graves which had been thoroughly plundered so that skulls, long bones, pelvic girdles and a host of smaller skeletal parts and winding cloth lay bleaching in the sun, intensely white and pathetic. Such spectacles of grave robbing are common in the oasis. As Churcher carefully scrambled up the steep-sided *yardang,* the crumbly soils gave way underfoot where grave robbers had been digging. His immediate reaction was that the site had been wrecked geologically and that there was little hope of finding anything intact and in its original position. On top of al-Hajir Hill, however, he spied a layer of the signature greyish-green CSS, the supposed lake marls, which had formed the roofs of the uppermost tier of graves. As he had done so often before to no avail, he knelt down and began chipping away with his spatula at the grey-green deposits. But this day, the bone goddess would smile upon him. As a white layer came to light, he smiled back, knowing that he had solved the mystery of the CSS. He shouted down to Kleindienst, "Snails! I've got snails! And bone!"

A few days later, primed for further surprises, Churcher and Kleindienst set about screening the loose material on the slope. They found some fish bones, later identified as Nile catfish, and also fragments of hippo bone. These were the clinchers, irrefutable evidence that they were dealing with standing water—a lake. They called it Paleolake Teneida.

Over the next two years, they built up an impressive list of fossil bones from the lake deposits, including various waterbirds, hyena, extinct Cape buffalo, hartebeest, extinct camel, warthog, antelope, gazelle, ostrich and monitor lizard. This was the first Pleistocene fauna discovered in the Eastern Sahara between southernmost Egypt and the Libyan coast and it provided critical clues to the prevailing environment. It was a momentous discovery.

Fossil casts of large reeds, possibly papyrus, suggested a permanent water body rather than a seasonal pan. Also, since the snails would have required fresh, moving water with low salinity, their presence confirmed that the lake was permanently fresh, not salty or even brackish as with seasonal pans. Catfish and hippos can tolerate seasonally low water levels and a degree of brackishness, but require some water at all times. The bones of waterbirds such as mallard, crane and turnstone further bolstered the water-as-lake hypothesis. Even the terrestrial species whose bones turned up in the marl argued for nearby water sources. Extinct African buffalo, like all cattle, probably required water at least once and preferably twice a day; warthogs and ostriches occupy savannah grassland or bush grassland but, like all animals, require frequent access to water; and Cape zebra generally require a permanent water source. The most common animal seems to have been the hartebeest, a large antelope whose lowing would have echoed across the lake.

When I returned to the site with Churcher, climbing up the hill past the human remains to the marl layer, he remarked: "The site is sadly contaminated with human bones."

With a spatula he flicked a moon-white shell from the marl. "This is *Limnae stagnatus*. It's found just around the Sahara as far as I can make out. It's almost like a desert snail."

After re-examining the marl for new species, he worked his way downhill, "into deeper water where fossils are less common." The bone goddess again smiled on him, however, as he turned up the tooth enamel (darkly coloured with manganese or iron) of a hippo, the atlas vertebra of an extinct buffalo which he surmised had been broken by humans, the scant remains of a small equid presumed to be a zebra, and parts of the carapace of a large turtle, again a faunal marker for water in the desert. "There is no past,"

Rufus declared with satisfaction at his day's finds. "There is only the present-past. Everything is still here!"

What had most surprised and delighted Churcher was that the animals from the Pleistocene lakes formed a perfectly good set of African fauna analogous to that found today in East and Central Africa, the community of animals that he grew up with in Kenya where his parents settled from Britain after the Second World War.

Most of the fossil bones were found near what would have been the shoreline of Paleolake Teneida. Apparently, the lake shrank or expanded in response to seasonal rains and longer-term climatic cycles. During low water, large animals—elephant, giraffe, buffalo and zebra—would have ventured onto the dry mud flats that would have formed. Dust devils would have wandered over them, and an occasional animal would have died out there. But, in Churcher's opinion, most of the smaller animals would not have ventured too far onto the exposed flats, as they would then have become obvious targets for pack animals, like hyenas, which probably survived in the oasis until at least Victorian times. The lake would have lapped around the higher hills, creating a landscape of coves, inlets and islands. This is, in fact, what Kleindienst sees when she scans this maze of *yardangs*: "You look around and you say, 'Lake, lake!' It was not an inconsequential body of water."

OTHER RESEARCHERS HAD SPECULATED ABOUT PLEISTOCENE AGE ponds in the Sahara, but this was more dramatic. Project geologist Robert Giegengack, Head of Environmental Studies at the University of Pennsylvania, now believes that there may have been three big paleolakes—Teneida, Balat and Kellis—and that at one time they might even have been joined to make one large lake, twenty by twenty miles. Clearly, the numerous spring mounds fed the lake, or lakes, from below, pumping artesian water like Jacuzzi jets. Rainfall and springs also fed streams from the Plateau which carried dissolved limestone—the source of the CSS—into the lake. This settled to the lake bottom, forming the greyish-green slurry. Such a large body of deep-blue water would have had profound implications. "If we had seventy feet of water all over here, this place would be as humid as hell," Churcher says. "You'd have everything from elephants downward along the lake edge—if man didn't kill them off."

DESPITE LAKES SURROUNDED BY SAVANNAH AND AN EAST AFRICAN fauna hanging around the water, humans were the missing element. There were no irrefutable signs of human presence in the form of datable tools, though there were signs that humans had been up to their killing ways, as Churcher found heavy fragments of hippo tibia in small clumps, piled like jackstraws.

For two years, Churcher and Kleindienst continued to scour the landscape, climbing up and down *yardangs* in search of tools, but time and again, they came up empty-handed. Then, in 1998, they began exploring near the northern border of Paleolake Teneida.

One day that winter, Kleindienst and Churcher parked the Land Rover at the northeastern corner of Paleolake Teneida and trudged up a ravine, a *wadi* that had once carried waters to the lakeshore. Near the top stood a twenty-foot-high spring mound. Large black hunks of iron-indurated sandstone, some the size of tennis balls, others the size of marbles, had rolled down its sides. They mischievously named it Iron Balls Spring.

While Churcher examined the area for fossil bone, Kleindienst wandered across the *wadi*, where opposite the spring mound she made a discovery as momentous as Churcher's freshwater snails. At her feet were beautifully preserved tools. Some had saw-tooth edges, others were points, and many were in mint condition. Most important, many were *in situ*, embedded in the CSS "gunk." After a decade of tramping the desert, she had finally found tools where they had been dropped by their makers.

It was the first time Kleindienst had found Middle Stone Age tools in Dakhleh in their original context. The only other place where Pleistocene artifacts had been found *in situ* in the central Western Desert was at Kharga, under the tufas. Now not only did Kleindienst have the tools, she had a way to date both them and the lakes. By comparing the tool types to those found in dated Kharga tufas, she was able to conclude that the lake was roughly 200,000 years old, or early Middle Stone Age—the time Caton-Thompson had speculated was perhaps the wettest in the desert.

"What we really get if we find what we call a site," says Kleindienst, "is a tiny snapshot from that period." It is perhaps more like a single frame edited randomly from an epic film. The illusion is that one day people did things one way and the next day they changed, although much of the plot, motivation and story line has been lost. Most of human history, in fact, is left on the cutting floor.

Change was taking place, however, though it is very difficult to pinpoint exactly when innovation occurred. These lake people at Teneida had shifted away from the production of large hand-axes and cleavers, instead making smaller bifaces that were trimmed at the point but not at the butt. For the most part, they are still what Kleindienst calls "big lunky tools." However, what Kleindienst found proved that the lake people were also beginning to turn out a few small, ovate bifaces that showed superior workmanship. Over time, the large bifaces gave way to this lighter-weight, smaller and more portable tool kit, consisting of a variety of points and scrapers. Indeed over the huge span of the Middle Stone Age, from 250,000 to 10,000 years ago, tools consistently got smaller, shrinking in size from large hand-axes to so-called microliths. This trend is analogous to current computer technology in which chips have become smaller over time and hardware has evolved from industrial-sized mainframes that filled rooms to computers that can be held in one's palm—all capable of doing the same amount of work. "As people make things smaller," Kleindienst says, "tools become more portable. It facilitates mobility. You can also use a wider range of raw materials. You're really tied to raw material sources if you need larger pieces. As your whole toolkit changes, how you do and see things, your whole information system, is presumably also changing."

It was by the shores of Paleolake Teneida that these Middle Stone Age people chose to camp, Kleindienst believes. Besides being close to water for themselves, they had convenient access to other important resources: fish in the lake, shoreline reeds for making baskets and temporary shelters; plant seeds, fruits, and roots; wood for fires; and not least, animals that lived near the lake. Women, children and older men would have foraged for the bulk of the food, while able-bodied men ventured into the green savannah for big game.

The savannah environment these lake dwellers inhabited, she observes, was very similar to that in which early *Homo* in Africa evolved with its varied resources: fresh water, seeds, fruits, roots, game, wood for fires, and stone and other materials for tools. By the time of the lakes at Dakhleh, about 200,000 years ago, *Homo erectus* had disappeared from the fossil record and had been replaced, world-wide, by the so-called archaic *Homo sapiens*. People, we know, were evolving; otherwise, as Kleindienst points out, we would still all be Acheuleans. Through the Middle Stone Age the process accelerated. By the time the Late Pleistocene dawned, around 120,000 years ago, anatomically modern humans are occupying the Saharan savannah and congregating in the Dakhleh Oasis.

CHAPTER THREE

THE GARDEN

WITH ITS LAKES AND FLOURISHING AFRICAN FAUNA, DAKHLEH must have been a very attractive place to be. At that time, it may even have seemed, in Kleindienst's words, "very Garden of Edenish."

"We do not know where or when humans left the metaphorical Garden of Eden and became 'ethicizing animals,'" Kleindienst has written. Like most Africanists, however, she believes that anatomically modern humans, *Homo sapiens sapiens,* originated in northern Africa between 200,000 and 100,000 years ago. The archaeological record of the Dakhleh-Kharga basin spans that critical period in human evolution when archaic humans such as the lake dwellers became biologically indistinguishable from us.

According to Kleindienst, wet periods, or pluvials, in the Sahara opened a doorway for migration out of Africa, whereas

---

A remnant wetland in the oasis

before there had been only a crack along the Nile corridor. She adds that during the Middle Stone Age the Nile Valley was not a very attractive place for human habitation and would have been difficult to traverse except by boat: "I wouldn't have lived down in the Valley. It's hot, there would have been insects, there are swamps and big fauna," she says. Most Middle Stone Age sites in the Valley are not living sites but workshops, found on the terraces and desert heights overlooking the river. Why not, she reasons, walk out of Africa through the savannah-land of the Western Desert? And if the first anatomically modern humans did take this route, they might well have passed through Dakhleh, long a gathering place and a cultural crossroads, whose central location makes it a natural jumping-off point—just as it has been for modern explorers—north to the Mediterranean, east to the Nile Valley, or south to the Sudan.

Water, of course, is the reason for the pivotal role the oasis has played. There always seems to have been water here. But while lakes surrounded by savannah provided an ideal habitat for Middle Stone Age people, unless a skeleton of "Iron Balls Man" turns up, we won't know, anatomically at least, where along the continuum of modernity Kleindienst's lake dwellers lie. It does, however, seem probable that at least some of them were amongst those who, 100,000 years ago, walked out of Africa and into Eurasia, bringing with them new ways of being. Behaviourally, they were truly "moderns," people capable of symbolic thought as expressed in language and art.

Originally, archaeologists believed that this revolution in human behaviour occurred approximately 40,000 years ago in Europe, with the development of language, creating the impression that the earliest modern Africans were behaviourally primitive. Africanists like Kleindienst argue that this theory demonstrates such profound Eurocentric bias as to be racist and stems from a failure to appreciate the depth and breadth of the African archaeological record, which demonstrates that modernity had its roots much further back in human history and emerged in Africa long before anatomically modern humans appeared in Europe. They claim that the components of modern human behaviour, such as the use of microlithic technology and blades, long-distance trade and art, have a much older pedigree in Africa. These behaviours were gradually assembled as a package and exported, which is why they appear to have arisen suddenly in Europe 40,000 years ago. Instead of the light coming on suddenly in full glare, as it might have appeared to in Europe, in Africa it is as if the lights of modernity were turned up gradually by a rheostat.

WHILE THERE WAS AN EXODUS OF PEOPLE FROM THE GARDEN of North Africa, other presumably modern groups stayed behind. From 90,000 to 70,000 years ago, not long after this "Out-of-Africa" migration began, North Africa saw the rise of one of its most enigmatic and specialized African cultures, the Aterians. More questions than answers surround them. They seem to have been supremely practical survivalists as well as aesthetes. Undoubtedly one of the most advanced of the Middle Stone Age cultures for which we have evidence, the Aterians appear, oddly, never to have made it out of their continent of birth.

The rise of the Aterians seems to have coincided with a temporary climatic improvement that opened up new hunting territory. That the Aterians were highly adaptable and ingenious is evident from the variety of environments that they were able to exploit, from marine beaches to mountains to semi-arid deserts, across the breadth of the Sahara from the Maghreb (Morocco, Algeria and Tunisia) in the west to the Kharga Oasis in the east.

Above all, the Aterian culture is distinguished from other Middle Stone Age cultures by the invention of the *tang* a projection, or stem, at the basal end of their tools which allowed for hafting: a wood, bone or horn handle could be attached to the stone tool or weapon. Other stone implements characteristic of the Aterian culture are the very finely worked points known as bifacial foliates. Attached to long handles, they could have been used as spears or lances; to short handles as knives or scrapers. Although earlier Middle Stone Age groups also produced foliates, the Aterian examples display unprecedented attention to detail and craftsmanship, which probably involved pressure flaking, or retouching, with bone or wood. These exquisitely fashioned points, often called laurel leaves for their shape, were not only practical for the Aterians but are aesthetically pleasing to the modern eye. Some have been worked beyond the point needed to be merely functional and may have held some symbolic or religious value. Kleindienst is not alone in considering the workmanship of the Aterian toolkit the high-water mark of Middle Stone Age tool-making throughout the Old World, including Europe.

Between 1995 and 2001, Kleindienst's field assistant, Alicia Hawkins, did her Ph.D. thesis, "Getting a Handle on Tangs," on the Aterians of Dakhleh and the Western Desert. Her mission involved long days of reconnoitering the desert, often alone. The daughter of 1960s back-to-the landers, this slight young woman was used to Spartan creature comforts and hard work.

In Dakhleh, all that she had to work with were surface remains. Hawkins, however, turned this apparent obstacle to her advantage. Desert erosion had exposed a large number of sites that in most places would otherwise lie buried. She set about mapping the Aterian patterns of land use. "Where you're looking at highly mobile hunter-gatherers, I think it's very important you look at the whole landscape," she says, "rather than one locality."

Hawkins has been able to establish what the Aterians were doing in different parts of the oasis by analyzing the proportion and types of tools found at various sites. She has broken these locations into three categories: workshops, occupation areas and specialized-use sites. She found the workshops on the pediments ascending the Plateau, where there was a ready source of chert. Here she collected cores and broken or unfinished tools. This ratio told her that this was where the Aterians did most of their knapping, carrying the finished tools with them to other sites rather than carting around the bulky raw material. Hawkins identified Aterian occupation areas south of the escarpment by the presence of dense clusters of finished tools. These were places to which the Aterians returned repeatedly. Finally, she identified specialized-use localities associated with springs or pans. Exactly what the Aterians were doing there is not yet clear. Waiting for prey seems most likely, but they may also have collected plants growing at the water's edge. The diversity of sites proves the Aterians were making logical decisions to exploit the resources at hand in a patterned way, strongly suggesting to Hawkins that the Aterians were indeed "true moderns."

Above all, art is the surest sign of symbolic thought processes and therefore modernity. Rock art is widespread in the Sahara, including at Dakhleh where, as we shall discover, there is a veritable gallery of New Stone Age petroglyphs. Although dating rock art is notoriously difficult, some Saharan engravings of extinct animals have recently been attributed to the Aterians, based on the presumed age of the drawings and some of the animals depicted in them. Slim as this evidence is, Hawkins points out that it should not exist at all if the Aterians did not have the capacity for modern thinking. Only *Homo sapiens sapiens* could be responsible for making art of any kind.

Perhaps the most convincing evidence that the Aterians were capable of symbolic thought comes from El Guettar in south Tunisia. The Aterians sometimes seem to have left finely finished tools at workshop sites, perhaps for religious reasons. At an Aterian spring in El Guettar, right in the centre of a cairn of carefully finished stone spheres arranged in a steep symmetrical pile, French archaeologists discovered a beautifully worked tanged tool.

In 1995, her first season in the field, Hawkins made a similar discovery at Dakhleh when she and Kleindienst decided to explore a knife-edge remnant of Pleistocene gravels capping a very steep hill, or *gebel*, at Gareet el-Afreets, west of Balat. Hawkins scampered up the steep talus slope, loose dirt and gravel filling the tops of her desert boots. There were cores and debris scattered all over the top, indicating that this was once a workshop site. Then, in a depression, her eye caught an artifact that seemed totally out of place— a beautifully worked Aterian point. Unlike most tools at workshop sites, it was neither unfinished nor broken. Hawkins stuck her head over the edge and shouted, "I think you better come up here!" Upon close examination, the archaeologists realized that the point was not only finished but had been retouched to sharpen it. The exquisite retouch strongly suggested that a consummate craftsperson had finished it by pressure flaking. But why had the toolmaker then left it among the workshop debris? Perhaps he had been forced to leave the area quickly and dropped it. But their best guess was that it had been placed there for religious reasons, as a kind of talisman.

Striking as it is, their technological prowess may not be the most remarkable quality exhibited by this distinctive African culture. Their pan-Saharan range indicates some leap in social organization. Their passage across its vast expanses has been compared to the Polynesians crossing the Pacific from island to island. Their ability to navigate the desert is in itself one of the more convincing arguments that they possessed modern behavioural traits. Perhaps, like the Polynesians, they did so by the stars, which in the ink-black, Saharan night sky are as luminescent as those over the ocean. Their colonization of widely separated habitable portions of the Sahara, from the Atlas mountains in the west to Dakhleh and Kharga in the east, is the mark of a daring and vigorous people. Kleindienst has suggested that their success might have been a result of having a common symbolic language with which they could share their knowledge of resources and tool technology across this vast region, although a technological system such as the Aterian could certainly impose some similarities upon vastly different peoples. All we have are the tools themselves, tantalizing but mute witnesses to the transmission of this mysterious culture.

At the very least, argues Kleindienst, "They had to have some form of communication, some social interaction that allowed that to happen—and again, that's modern behaviour." In the Central Sahara, J. D. Clark's research has shown that the Aterians were transporting raw materials from a source 170 miles away, and possibly even engaging in long-distance trade with other mobile groups. They were frequently on the move, following the rains in pursuit of game, and this fact alone would have encouraged cultural transmission of the idea of the tang and the haft. People would have been quick to recognize its innovative value and to emulate it, even without the aid of a common language.

Yet despite their evident mobility, the Aterians never crossed over into Europe, nor did they penetrate into the humid Nile Valley. Kleindienst asserts that such geographical boundaries exist only if there are cultural, linguistic or biological differences separating peoples. Whatever the reason, unlike their predecessors, they never got out of Africa. The question remains: Why not?

IF, AS SOME HAVE CLAIMED, THE RISE OF THE ATERIANS COINCIDED with a relatively humid period at the beginning of the last phase of the European glaciation, the Würm, it would have aided their epic spread across the Sahara. As the Würm glacier ground southward, however, the climate in the Sahara became increasingly arid and by 40,000 years ago had become very dry indeed. Kleindienst believes that the Aterians may have been a culture particularly well-adapted to semi-arid and arid environments, which might explain why they never settled in the Nile Valley.

Although definitive times have yet to be established, in Dakhleh the Aterians appear to have flourished between 70,000 and 40,000 years ago, a period during which Caton-Thompson believed that there was less than ten inches of rainfall annually and the rainy periods were only wet enough "to convert full desert into poor steppe," with some scrubby vegetation.

In the 1970s, Fred Wendorf of Southern Methodist University in Dallas, Texas, also tried to build up a climatic sequence for the Eastern Sahara. After spending a season in Dakhleh—during which a cobra once crawled into his work tent to escape a raging sandstorm, causing a mass exodus of workers—Wendorf moved on to Bir Tarfawi and Bir Sahara in southern Egypt, which he described as "one of the most desolate places on earth," and where today there are neither wells (*birs*) nor people.

Wendorf's excavations in southern Egypt demonstrated that there had been alternating dry and wet phases. Lakes—much smaller and younger than those discovered by Churcher in Dakhleh—rose and receded, were covered with invading dunes, then rose again as the rains returned. Humans, perforce, had to adapt to this unpredictable environment. Bir Tarfawi and Bir Sahara told a climatic story similar to Caton-Thompson and Gardner's at Kharga: there had been at least three wet events, all associated with lakes, and that the final two lake phases were more than 60,000 and maybe more than 80,000 years old. The fauna found there suggested a savannah landscape with large herbivores and their hunters—the enigmatic Aterians—concentrating around lakes, though they were more ephemeral than those exploited by the "Iron Balls" people.

Wendorf called the lakes "Aterian ponds," and noted that after 44,000 years ago, based on carbon dating, both people and fauna disappeared from the Western Desert. He believed that the climate became increasingly dry and cold throughout the Sahara in conjunction with the glacial maximum, and noted that during this time wind-blown sand shows up in seabed cores off the North African coast. His conclusion was that no one lived in the Western Desert for 30,000 years, until the glaciers started to recede and the rains returned at the beginning of the Holocene, 10,000 years ago.

This is what Kleindienst calls Wendorf's "empty desert theory." Caton-Thompson also painted a similar picture: "From the Aterian phase onwards the struggle for existence for man, beast, and plant must have become ever more severe with each succeeding century. The trees and ferns gradually died out, leaving the scarp in barren desolation, and with them went all the land and freshwater snails." Desertification made migration and the spread of culture across the Sahara impossible. The doorway that had opened wide with the onset of humid conditions, 400,000 years before, was now slammed shut, isolating groups of people such as the Aterians in areas where there was sufficient water. In effect, they became marooned on "desert islands." Migration out of Africa via the desert was no longer viable. Their larger garden turned to dust and the Aterians, it seems, were trapped on their continent of birth.

Today, there is a vigorous debate about whether desertification— the degradation of once productive lands to desert—is due more to human activity or to external factors such as cyclical climate change. (Even the term "desertification" is difficult to define but is distinguished from drought, which may have the same short-term effects, by long-term or permanent damage to an ecosystem.) The Saharan expert J. L. Cloudsley-Thompson has observed that in Africa the savannah evolved contemporaneously with humans and the destruction of forests began when the use of fire was first acquired, well over 50,000 years ago. Although fires occur naturally, deliberate burning by humans has a greater effect on vegetation because it occurs over the same ground more frequently. Deforestation leads to rapid soil deterioration and, ultimately, desert. We know that the Aterians had fire, so they might have contributed to the desertification of the Sahara. Even if the major cause was climatic change, as is likely, humans could make it drier through careless or deliberate use of fire. "Human beings can and do use fire to degrade the landscape. They accelerate the natural processes of erosion," says Kleindienst. In the present, women in Dakhleh carry home baskets of firewood every night. A more dramatic example is the current lucrative practice of cutting down acacia trees to produce charcoal for marketing to Valley restaurants. "It's appalling, just appalling," mourns Churcher.

Kleindienst, however, strongly disagrees with Wendorf's theory that after 44,000 years ago "there was nothing and no one in the desert except wind, sand and stars . . . until the Early Holocene." Kleindienst has never been one to shy away from scholarly confrontation. "I think I was the only person who ever told Mary Leakey she was wrong and lived," she says. Likewise, she has taken on Wendorf, the lionized author of *The Prehistory of the Eastern Sahara*, believing he has gone too far in declaring the entire Western Desert empty based solely on his work in southern Egypt.

Today, the desert is completely uninhabitable between Dakhleh and the Sudan, and Bir Tarfawi or Bir Sahara are no longer occupied. These areas are in the hyper-arid core of the Western Desert and would have been the first to be deserted at the height of any drying phase. "*His* desert might well have been empty," Kleindienst says. But she doubts whether Dakhleh was ever completely depopulated. Sitting as it does on one of the world's largest freshwater aquifers, she believes Dakhleh has always had water in one form or another and therefore has always had people. If, as Kleindienst believes, Dakhleh acted as a refuge for people even during the driest period of the glacial maximum, where might she find them? The drying out of the Sahara probably meant fewer people, making the challenge of detecting traces of them that much harder.

THE UNENVIABLE TASK OF FINDING THE PEOPLES WHO INHABITED the Western Desert after the Aterians, if any did, fell to prehistorian Marcia Wiseman, who studied under Kleindienst and now teaches anthropology at the University of Toronto. Wiseman made her first trip to Dakhleh in 1988 and was immediately faced with the perennial problems of wind erosion and an inadequate dating sequence for climatic change in the desert. "I don't mind the frustrations of the work, it goes with the territory," Wiseman says and, besides, she explains, the desert keeps calling her back—"the solitude, the quiet, the magic of it."

Current theory told Wiseman that the climate in North Africa became drier between 60,000 years ago and 10,000 years ago, with maximum aridity occurring around 20,000 years ago. However, evidence from the Nile Valley and elsewhere in North Africa showed ameliorating moist periods: from 35,000 to 26,000; from 23,000 to 21,000; and from 19,000 to 15,000 years ago. Furthermore, over three hundred hunter-gatherer sites have been identified in the Sinai, dating to around 15,000 years ago, when conditions there should have been about as arid as in the Western Desert. At the time, there were also sixteen distinct cultural groups living in the Valley and the adjacent Eastern Desert.

If the Western Desert was vacant, Wiseman asked herself, then where did the people go, and where did the people come from who later show up in the oasis during the early Holocene? Wiseman imagined people either adapting with their feet by migrating to a more congenial ecological setting, or staying put in Dakhleh and breaking into smaller, more mobile bands, moving from one temporary campsite to another, perhaps seasonally. If they migrated, they had only two options: the Valley or the

Mediterranean coast. However, between 40,000 and 20,000 years ago, there appear to have been relatively few people living in either region. Wiseman's hypothesis is that some people stayed in the desert and toughed it out. Toughing it out pretty much describes her own quest to find evidence of this missing post-Aterian culture, given that their campsites were likely temporary and subject to obliteration by the eternal wind. With poetic insight, she describes the desert as "a palimpsest," a manuscript erased over and over again by the wind. When Wiseman began looking in 1988, she wasn't even sure what she should be looking for, though Mary McDonald had noted small Levallois tools typical of Middle Stone Age technology in her travels, furnishing her colleague with a starting point, a search image.

On the last day of the field season in 1992, Wiseman's diligence was rewarded when she came across a concentration of small Levallois cores and flakes on the southern margin of the oasis. It was late in the afternoon and the light was low, just the right time for the sun to glint off the deposits of chert. The tools and debris were clustered in two adjacent hollows which, curiously, were surrounded on three sides by several standing sandstone slabs. Although apparently natural, the tallest slabs were conveniently situated to the north and west and offered welcome protection from the prevailing winds. Perhaps people had sought shelter there against the blinding wind-blown sand. At one time, it seemed, they had also sat there, backs against the slabs, chipping away at chert to make tools.

Wiseman was frustrated, for there was not enough time to map and collect this intriguing sample. She marked the site on the map, left Dakhleh, then had to wait a whole year before returning. When she did, the sun was higher in the sky, so that for a moment she could not make out the scatter of tools. Heart sinking, she wondered whether she had imagined them. Then the protean desert light changed and Wiseman breathed a sigh of relief: they were real, after all. Convincing other prehistorians of their significance was another matter.

The tools bore an uncanny resemblance to a technology Caton-Thompson dubbed the "Khargan Industry," which has been dogged by controversy ever since she first described it in the 1930s. By comparison to the finely shaped Aterian tools, these were ratty-looking things, which Caton-Thompson described in rather unflattering terms as "mutilated flakes." Wiseman herself says they look like "driveway gravel," and others have commented on their "singularly haphazard appearance" and suggested that they might not be tools at all but the result of accidental or natural agencies. Wisemen admits they have a "slap-dash" look to them, but with characteristic acerbic wit she notes they "seem to have been subjected to repetitive slap-dashery." Such a pattern, she feels, cannot be explained away as natural or accidental.

It is blatantly obvious that the people she called the Sheikh Mabruk (after a local village), with their slapdash flakes, are just not taking as much care as the Aterians, whom Kleindienst characterizes as "anal as anything." It may seem contrary to the notion of progress as an unbroken continuum that the Sheikh Mabruk should show a lesser degree of sophistication than their predecessors, but they were living in a drying, therefore more demanding, environment. Unlike the Aterians, they did not have the luxury of fashioning beautiful objects. (An analogy may be found in North American West Coast Indian cultures, which produced magnificent art in part because they lived in an environment rich in materials and food.) Times were hard for the Sheikh Mabruk and what mattered most was whether the tool or weapon did its job, not what it looked like. They expended their energies elsewhere, maybe because they had to, maybe because they wanted to. They may have built snares and traps, for instance, instead of fancy, if effective, spearheads.

Although water sources were obviously not now so widespread, Wiseman has environmental evidence in the form of phytoliths—microscopic, fossilized plant particles—that there were grasses growing around the Sheikh Mabruk sites. The savannah was shrinking, however, leaving isolated patches of vegetation in better watered areas; the oasis environment of the present day was taking shape. Much of the Sheikh Mabruk material follows the southern edge of the oasis, where spring vents occur and where there was enough moisture in the soil to support the growth of grasses, foraging animals, and human activity. Where water still seeped from the ground, there might still have been marshes.

Although still hunter-gatherers, the Sheikh Mabruk people seem to have been less mobile, or at least less widespread, than the Aterians. To date, their artifacts have been found only near Kharga and Dakhleh and in the much smaller oases of Kurkur and Dungul in southern Egypt. This suggests that the Sheikh Mabruk needed to stay close to a shrinking water supply. Wiseman is now convinced that the Sheikh Mabruk occupied Dakhleh at least between 40,000 and 20,000 years ago. Despite the inexorable forces that were creating the present-day Sahara, Dakhleh continued to be a garden, a place of shelter in an ecological storm for nearly a half-million years as the rains came and went and finally disappeared altogether.

IF HER THESIS OF THE "EVERLASTING OASIS" IS TO HOLD UP, Kleindienst must ultimately account for another troubling gap, of some ten millennia, after the Sheikh Mabruk people apparently disappear, until Neolithic cultures make their appearance in Dakhleh around 10,000 years ago. Critical to this task is getting "chronometric control," a set of absolute dates to establish the sequence of wet and dry periods. It is still not even clear whether more people would have been present in the Dakhleh-Kharga region during wetter cycles, or whether people were more likely to congregate there during drier cycles, using the oasis as a refuge, the interpretation Kleindienst presently favours.

She compares her search for evidence of prehistoric cultures in the desert to "a shell game with sand—every year, some things get covered, some things get exposed." The best strategy is persistence, returning year after year to the same terrain. "The typical pattern for North Americans," says Kleindienst, "is to come to Africa for a year or two, and then go away and write their book. I find that a very unsatisfying way to do archaeology. If you're going to do proper archaeology in an area, you should be sitting in that area for some considerable period of time."

From the beginning, Kleindienst has been in it for the long haul. Her personal commitment to Africa and to the people who occupied it in prehistory and ultimately gave rise to the human race as we know it, demands no less. Daily she dons her green Tilley hat, festooned with pins from archaeological conferences, slips on her photographer's vest, and, geologist's hammer in hand, heads happily into the desert. "You never know what's around the next corner," she says. "Dakhleh can still surprise us." It took her ten years to find the Iron Balls fauna, along with the evidence of the humans who hunted them. And it's a good bet that she, or one of the prehistorians she has inspired, will find the people who bridged the gap between the Old and New Stone Ages.

PART THREE

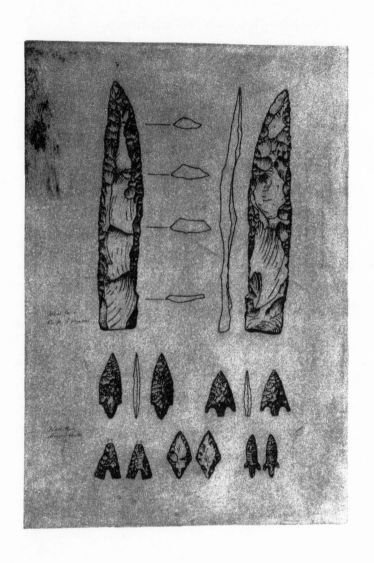

CROSSERS OF THE SAND

12,000–4000 B.P.

Neolithic knives and arrowheads *(John O'Carroll)*

CHAPTER FOUR

THE GREAT STONE RING

The dark age in Dakhleh came to an end around 12,000 years ago, when the glaciers started their rapid retreat northward. In concert, tropical monsoons also moved northward, wetting the thirsty soils of the Sahara, filling mud-cracked lakes and gorging dry wadis with water for the first time in 10,000 years. With the rains, plants that had been held at bay by the extremes of dryness also migrated northward. Large game animals followed the rains and the fodder. People were not far behind. The climate of the Western Desert was still arid or semi-arid, but even so, the seasonal rainfalls meant that as much as a third of the Sahara became habitable again.

The retreat of the glaciers ushered in the period that we know as the Holocene. Some places in the Sahara received more rainfall than others. Rivers ran five hundred miles from the Tibesti Mountains all the way to the Mediterranean, through the very core

---

Excavation of the oldest Neolithic dwellings in North Africa

of the Sahara. At the same time, catastrophic floods surged through the Nile Valley. The centre of the Sahara had been cold during the glacial maximum, but this new warming trend drew moisture-laden air in from the Atlantic. Now Dakhleh received not only these summer rains from the monsoonal belt of equatorial Africa, but also the renewed winter rains off the Mediterranean. Rivers rushed down from the Libyan Plateau, carrying blocks of white limestone and cutting into the old gravel terraces. The outflow pooled on the desert floor to form seasonal lakes, and with the seasonal rains the dry savannah leapt into life, becoming a shimmering, grassy plain.

This second greening of the Sahara allowed nomadic hunter-gatherers to again forage widely. Throughout the twentieth century, explorers of the Western Desert have found their hearths, now known as the "stone places of the Sahara." Widely distributed, these hearths seem to have been merely campsites, places where people stopped to sleep, or to eat and drink, and then moved on.

Prehistorian Mary McDonald has been tracking these nomadic groups, ever on the lookout for signs of when Africans took the first tentative steps toward becoming settled peoples and eventually farmers. The developments of prehistory have always held more attraction for her than historical ones, and none were more important to human culture than those that first took hold in the Middle East. The Neolithic Revolution was marked by the making of pottery, the building of permanent dwellings, and an epochal changeover from a hunting-gathering lifestyle to a more agrarian, settled way of life based on domesticated plants and animals.

As a student, McDonald carried on work that had been started in Iran in the 1950s by Robert Braidwood of the Oriental Institute of Chicago. There she excavated a village site, Seh Gabi, on the fabled Silk Road between Damascus and Tehran, where, 8000 years ago, people were raising goats and pigs, growing wheat and barley, making pottery and living in mud-brick houses.

McDonald had planned to return to work in Iran after completing her Ph.D., but was prevented by the Iranian revolution. Otherwise, she might still be working in the Zagros Mountains, one of "the hearths of agriculture," in quest of the origins of farming—an ambition she had nurtured since her girlhood on a dairy farm in Ontario, where, she admits, her fascination with ancient cultures was also fostered by watching such "sandal epics" as *Helen of Troy*. Concerning events in Iran, McDonald observes, "A lot of refugees from Iranian archaeology spread elsewhere in the Middle East, and a lot of them, like myself, fetched up in Egypt." She's glad she did.

McDonald found herself in Dakhleh in 1979, on the recommendation of Maxine Kleindienst. She quickly made herself at home in Bashendi and, twenty-four years later, is one of the respected "elders" of an ever more diverse company of scientists and scholars. She spent her first decade at Dakhleh mapping and excavating nearly three hundred Holocene sites in order to compile a chronology of the different groups that occupied the oasis during this period, and to figure out what kind of lives they led.

Almost every day, six days a week, she departs before dawn, long before most of her colleagues have kick-started their day. Her *modus operandi* is to walk directly into the rising sun, because this angle makes flints, her most common evidence, glint in the strong light. Invariably it is dusty work, far from water and shade, subject to the full force of the wind, which sometimes blows hot, other times cold, but *always* blows sand into her eyes, ears and nose. When the prevailing northwest wind is whipping off the Plateau, it can be cool enough to cause hypothermia. On other days, the temperature can rise to the low 90s under an unrelenting sun, causing dehydration. Regardless of the weather, McDonald caps her eight hours in the desert by taking a daily run. Her diligence and stamina are legendary among her colleagues, as well as the local villagers. "Strong woman," they say.

The many campsites McDonald found in the desert were marked by a thin scattering of flint, grinding stones used for milling grass seeds, sometimes the odd bit of bone, and by hearths that showed that these wanderers had stopped for a time to cook and perhaps warm themselves against the cold desert nights. Their tool kit was portable: small blades and bladelets. These were people on the move, wandering in search of game and the raw materials they needed to hunt, dress and cook it. McDonald decided to call these highly mobile folk the Masara, after a village that was near many of their campsites.

Almost all of McDonald's sites are far from the contemporary oasis margin. No one in the DOP has spent more hours in the field or covered more miles of the trackless desert. What she has to work with is minimal at best: stone chips, scant potsherds, scraps of splintered bone, hints of charred vegetable matter, and enigmatic stone structures. The day-to-day discipline of dealing with these parsimonious remains of cultures who left no texts to tell us how they lived or what they believed—how like or unlike us they were—spills over into McDonald's camp life. When not in the field, almost every waking hour in camp she is at her work station, sorting, counting and measuring. Her bench is littered not only with finished tools, but with the *debitage,* the debris left behind by the tool-makers. She dabs white nail polish on each artifact, then labels it with indelible ink. She analyzes collections from each site statistically to shed light on prehistoric mobility patterns, using the principle that the numbers and types of tools will be limited by the effort of transporting them. As mobility increases, tools become less diverse, more versatile, smaller, lighter, and more portable. As mobility decreases, the converse is true.

Over ten years of this daily grunt work, McDonald had come to distinguish three separate Masara cultures, based on slight differences in their tool kits. But despite heroic efforts, by 1990 she had still not found evidence that these peoples had ever abandoned their nomadic ways—no traces of an African-based Neolithic Revolution in the Western Desert. Frustrated but determined, she was about to discover that rewards in archaeology are not always won by systematic study or hard work alone. You also need a little luck.

In 1990, Greg Mumford, a student working with McDonald that winter, drew her attention to some enigmatic stone circles associated with the typical Masara tools. He had stumbled on them in the southeastern corner of the oasis, fifteen miles from Bashendi. When McDonald examined them closely, she quickly realized that what Mumford had found would fundamentally change our ideas about the people who inhabited the Sahara during the early Holocene period.

The structures differed from the typical stone places of the Sahara, which consisted of nothing more than a few stones and a heap of ancient ashes. To her delight, McDonald recognized that they were stone huts. She intensified her search along surrounding sandstone ridges, where she eventually discovered a total of seventeen such hut circles. Five of them were arranged in a semi-circle. Such a cozy configuration suggested a small family group. Here were the long-sought signs of Masara people settling down, taking the first step away from a nomadic lifestyle. McDonald knew it was a very early example of this lifestyle change for Africa, and carbon dating would prove her right. Dating to 8800 years old, these are the oldest architectural remains in Africa from the Holocene.

Unlike their more mobile cousins, this Masara group—identified by their distinctive blade tools—had at least settled down for an extended period during their nomadic rounds. McDonald quickly went to work to find out everything she could about these unique stone places, meticulously recording the placement and type of any artifacts.

The small stone circles were all about six or seven feet in diameter. The Masara had built the huts by first digging a subterranean floor, then erecting vertical slabs of sandstone for walls. They had apparently dug down a foot into the sandstone bedrock, using nothing more than stone tools and sticks. Even re-excavating them with a miner's pick was such hard work that McDonald had to let her blisters heal periodically before she could resume digging.

Attached to some of the huts she found storage bins. During her digging she uncovered abundant grinding equipment and ostrich eggshell beads that had been manufactured on site. She also found arrowheads, scrapers, awls and bones. The heavy grinding stones—which may have been used for milling wild cereals or mixing ochre for body paint—also pointed to a somewhat settled population, as they were too big to carry around. But there didn't seem to be enough artifacts to indicate year-round occupation, and the structures themselves seemed too rudimentary to function as permanent dwellings. McDonald believes that the huts may well have been roofed over with perishable material—perhaps brushwood, reeds or hides—like a North American wickiup or the temporary huts still constructed by nomadic sub-Saharan herdsmen. But the dug-out floors indicated the huts may have served as long-term base camps, becoming for part of each year a hub of activity, a place of preparation and processing, even though resources may have been gathered farther afield.

Simple as they were, the Masara huts stood in sharp contrast to the other, ephemeral hearths of the Sahara. To find a settled community of any kind in the early Holocene had come as a wonderful surprise and constituted a breakthrough in Saharan prehistory. Elsewhere in the Western Desert, peoples were continually on the move in search of water and resources, leaving their blackened hearths scattered across the desert like leopard spots. The huts at Dakhleh were the first solid evidence of adaptation to a more sedentary lifestyle. But, McDonald asked herself, what would impel these nomadic peoples to go to the trouble of building huts?

One clue was the particular place where the hut circles are situated: the Wadi el-Battikh is the terminus of a large *wadi* system and during rains would have delivered abundant water to the Southeast Basin. Significantly, the huts were not built on the lowest part of the plain but on slightly higher ground, presumably to prevent flooding during run-off. The question then became: just how wet was it in the early Holocene? As so often happens with questions of climate, the answers McDonald has been given are ambiguous.

Many researchers have considered the period from 12,000 to 8000 years ago to have been the wettest time of the era. However, throughout the Holocene, wet periods were interrupted by relatively dry intervals. There appears to have been a particularly dry phase between 8800 and 8600 years ago, precisely at the time the Masara were building huts. "It might be that they were settling in the oasis at a time when the desert itself was drier than usual," says McDonald. "They might have been 'dusted out' of the desert."

This was exactly the kind of question regarding the symbiotic relationship between humans and the environment that Mills had designed the DOP to answer. In the late Pleistocene period, if Kleindienst and Wiseman were right, the Sheikh Mabruk had also retreated to the oasis as the climate deteriorated. When climatic events resulted in a kind of "dust bowl" scenario, as it did in Masara times, it seemed probable that the relatively well-watered Southeast Basin again served as a haven for environmental refugees. Even today, when the desert is as dry as it has ever been, the occasional green bush can be found here.

So McDonald concluded that it was precisely the availability of water locally during a two-centuries-long drought that caused the Masara to become more sedentary, building crude shelters and living for months at a time in a place still wet enough to attract wild game. Churcher's analysis of their leftovers indicated that they hunted Dorcas gazelle, hartebeest, hare, ostrich and small wading birds, supplementing their diet with tortoises, lizards and toads.

Churcher and McDonald work at adjacent benches, McDonald analyzing the weapons and tools the ancient hunters employed and Churcher fitting together the fragments of bones of animals "Mary's people" saw as prey. Their complementary tasks mirror the predator-prey relationship that existed thousands of years ago. In the same symbiotic way, McDonald depends upon the work of the DOP's archaeobotanist to determine how "her people" might have utilized plants.

When McDonald scooped up charred remains from the hearths, she presented them to archaeobotanist Ursula Thanheiser. Thanheiser's task was to sort through this ashy material in the hope of isolating tell-tale remains of seeds, leaves, flowers and stems that would reveal what plants were flourishing then—information that would carry her a long way toward understanding what made this area desirable.

As a science, archaeobotany has come into its own only in the last three decades. Thanheiser is a research scientist at the Vienna Institute of Archaeological Science, and one of only three archaeobotanists in Austria. She is glad each year to escape to the desert, but while there wears white cotton gloves "because I have come from an Austrian winter and my skin is sensitive to the sun." She wraps her head in a white *shosh* like native women and, following their example, often dyes her hair with henna to produce reddish orange highlights. The camp pessimist, her mordant wit serves as a communal outlet for the frustrations of fieldwork and the complaints of living in an isolated oasis far from the comforts of home.

Originally trained as a biology teacher, after a year in the classroom she decided "this wasn't going to be the job of my life." With only a master's degree, she was unable to find research work, and to ease her growing discontent she decided to travel to Egypt. She had always had an interest in archaeology, often spending her holidays visiting archaeological sites in Europe. Now she heard about an Austrian excavation in the Delta that needed somebody to identify plant remains. She accepted their offer and learned her trade on site. Capitalizing on this field experience, she went on to work in Israel and to obtain a doctoral degree at Cambridge. Eventually she found herself in Dakhleh, at the invitation of Lech Krzyzaniak of the Poznan Archaeological Museum in Poland, who was studying the Neolithic rock art near Bashendi and wanted plant remains analyzed at that site.

The desert, she quickly learned, posed severe technical challenges. Just finding botanical remains is the first problem: the combined processes of wind-scour and extreme dessication sweep away or destroy whatever pollen or larger plant remains might have been preserved in the soils. The only Holocene plant remains preserved in the desert are those that have come into contact with fire, either by being burned in hearths or as the result of a grass fire. Then there is the problem of finding what is in this ashy material. The normal procedure for isolating plant remains is water flotation. The oasis soils, however, are very salty, and when Thanheiser added water to the sample, much to her distress, she discovered that the salt crystals caused the fossil plants to explode, transforming them into unidentifiable "black blobs."

She reluctantly concluded that her only recourse was to sort through the hearth samples by hand, peering at them under a microscope for hours on end, a method that was as maddening as it was inefficient. "It was just a crazy job," she says. "You sit there and brush dirt from one end of the Petri dish to the other and pick out things. And when I did that, at nine o'clock in the morning, I thought it must be lunch time. It just drags on and on and on—and you just go crazy." While McDonald continued to drag back bag after bag of dusty hearth remains to Bashendi for analysis, Thanheiser was able to process only one sample a week. A solution had to be found.

It came in 1993 at her laboratory in Vienna, where physicist Alfred Glaser, in what Thanheiser, tongue-in-cheek, calls the "The Department of Impossible Things and Inventions," developed a solar-powered, electrostatic device that separates the carbonized organic remains (ash) from the inorganic soils. Each carries a different electric charge and when passed through an electrostatic field, the plant remains are attracted and the soil less so. For all its seeming magic, mechanically it is a simple device and involves simply pouring the dusty sample into a hopper: the plant remains are collected in a paper bag for further analysis under a microscope, and the soil passes into a bucket for disposal.

Finally Thanheiser could keep up with the steady flow of new material. Her analysis has provided invaluable information on both the climate and human activities in the early Holocene. Previously, McDonald had only her rocks through which to peer dimly into the past.

Thanheiser has shown that the Masara sites were remarkably well-watered, considering how arid it was elsewhere in the Western Desert. As she expected, she found the ubiquitous acacia and tamarisk—trees that still commonly grow in the oasis—but much to her surprise there was a range of trees that today grow only in the Sahel. (*Sahel* derives from the Arabic, meaning shore, in this case the sub-Saharan shore of the world's largest sand sea.) At the northern edge of the summer rainfall belt, it seems Dakhleh became a refugium for many Sahelian plants, which apparently survived here long after they disappeared elsewhere in the Eastern Sahara. Even today, a few Sahelian trees remain. Behind Bashendi village stands a *Salvadora*, a tree that grows throughout the subtropical Sahelian zone as far east as India. Its young shoots are used as toothbrushes, its leaves are favoured by camels, and humans eat its fruit. An extremely old and ravaged tree whose roots have been exposed by wind, it looks like a giant spider crawling across the sands, or a Gorgon's head cresting a dune. Hideously deformed by time, it nevertheless survives as a living testament to a wetter climate in the past.

In addition to the trees, Thanheiser found a variety of grasses. Their presence might well explain the grinding equipment strewn about the hut circles; indeed, the people of the Sahel still mill grass seed today. The samples, however, were dominated by portulac, a moisture-loving edible herb found in open wet habitats, whose succulent leaves, much like spinach, are enjoyed today in salads.

All the plant remains, however, were strictly wild, with no sign of domestic crops such as sorghum or millet. Like their predecessors, the Masara were simply taking advantage of the natural flora. Neither was there evidence they had taken up herding. McDonald, nevertheless, had found people were capable of settling down in one place to make a living—even if they did so under duress and only seasonally. She had found the forerunners of the Neolithic Revolution in the Western Desert.

REVOLUTION IS NOT TOO RADICAL A TERM FOR, ARGUABLY, THE most important development in the history of humanity. Certainly it would be hard, to use Robert Braidwood's words, "to exaggerate the consequences of the first appearance of effective food production." It affected the whole range of human existence: diet, demography and diseases; social organization, politics, religion and aesthetics. It ushered in a completely new way of life that was largely sedentary. Previously, humans had followed the game animals or migrated between areas that provided plant food. Apart from their use of tools and weapons of stone, bone and wood, their existence was little different from that of the animals they hunted. They did not yet need pottery to store food, probably because there was such a limited and perishable supply at any one place.

It took perhaps a millennium, beginning 10,000 years ago, for the new food-producing way of life to fully take hold. Considering that the hunting and gathering mode had prevailed for more than a million years, this radical change occurred, in relative terms, overnight. Staying in one place was only the first, incipient step. When combined with cropping and herding, it opened the door to accumulation of material goods, which to the hunter-gatherer had been nothing but an encumbrance. Eventually the production and storage of surplus foods made it possible to support a larger population in villages and cities—which eventually led to monumental architecture, public works and writing.

The first stage of this revolution in Africa was pastoralism, but in Africa that did not imply always living in one place, as was the case with early Neolithic cultures in the Near East, in the Levant (Syria-Palestine) and in the Fertile Crescent of Mesopotamia (Iran and Iraq). As in the Sahel today, pastoralists followed a more nomadic lifestyle, moving their herds seasonally to greener pastures and migrating between water holes that might be hundreds of miles apart.

MacDonald first witnessed the living tradition of pastoralism at Seh Gabi in Iran. There she observed a present-day example of the cultural phenomenon she was excavating. Every spring, she saw long lines of local nomads, the Lurs, packing their black tents and herding their goats up the slopes to alpine pastures, and every fall she saw them descend again to the lowlands.

AFTER A TYPICAL LONG DAY IN DAKHLEH, MCDONALD ARRIVES for supper as punctually as a dinner bell; in effect, she *is* the dinner bell. She will not squander potential work time by arriving prematurely, and moments after McDonald's arrival, you can be sure Mansour Beyumi Sayed, the congenial camp cook, will usher the team into the dining room. McDonald quickly claims a place at the far end of the improvised long table, which seats up to twenty tired and hungry archaeologists and natural scientists. Her place might seem poorly chosen given that Mary insists on eating from one of the few flower-patterned plates and on being served one of the four corner pieces of any casserole. These quirks give rise to much good-humoured teasing as plates are shuffled down the table like cards at a poker game, and the dealer with sleight-of-hand palms a flowered plate from the bottom of the deck, to Mary's wide smile and everyone's collective relief. Mary watches the procession of the casserole with hawk-like intensity, knowing that in the end, however, a corner piece will be spared. This ritual is a nightly affirmation of the camp's prevailing atmosphere of tolerance and good-will. At suppertime the DOP team becomes one big family home from the fields, related by the passion for archeology in their blood. The impresario of this nightly good cheer is Tony Mills, affectionately referred to as the "*Mudir* of Everything," who insists on two things only: everyone does their work and everyone gets along, all in the service of a common goal—understanding how humans became what we are.

This common cause extends to the field, where investigators in different disciplines share their findings. In 1990, the same year Mumford chanced upon the Masara huts, geomorphologist Ian Brookes of Toronto's York University was examining aerial photos of the lowland depression known as the Southeast Basin, twelve miles southeast of the contemporary oasis, to identify water-laid sediments, always good markers for human habitation, when he detected an unexplained "disconformity"—a large ring. Word of this mysterious anomaly quickly circulated through camp. Lech Krzyzaniak, who was studying the remarkable Neolithic rock art in the area, urged McDonald to take a closer look. Was this anomalous feature simply a natural scattering of stones or, as seemed more likely, something constructed by human hands? Committed to digging elsewhere, McDonald delayed. Krzyzaniak and his wife, Karla

Kroeper, an archaeologist with the Berlin Museum of Archaeology, decided to have a look for themselves. They not only found the mysterious large ring but, about a half mile away, stumbled upon a cluster of smaller stone circles.

Their reconnaissance created a stir in the Bashendi compound, which every afternoon becomes a clearinghouse for the latest finds, as investigators gather for tea, *mazbut,* or a lukewarm Stella—a ritual McDonald usually eschews. But hearing the news at suppertime, and with the Masara finds fresh in her mind, the next day McDonald packed her maps and headed into the desert for a firsthand look.

Three hundred yards north of the el-Gubari road, she stood on an outcrop, gazing into a depression. The heat that day rose in shimmering waves, so that mirage lakes hovered on the horizon. She focused on the depression and slowly began to see distinct shapes—circles, ovals, crescents and rectangles—formed by the stones. She scurried down the slope for a closer inspection, walking rapidly from one structure to another. There could be little doubt now, but despite the breakthrough with the Masara huts, she was still not prepared for the scale of this site. She was astonished when she eventually counted two hundred huts, the largest collection of Neolithic hut circles ever found in North Africa. This was not a camp, but a village. "Oddly enough," McDonald admits, "I now realize that I had walked over these hut circles. You just don't see them until you start looking for them. Now I've got an eye for them. Due to the very eroded environment, you do get natural rows of rocks. Then you start seeing these things and realize they are not natural but are circles or crescents, and there's a bunch of them together. You start looking around and there's chipped stone and grinding stone and a bit of pottery. And it becomes pretty clear what's going on." By all appearances, many people were living here for at least part of the year. The inhabitants of this village belonged to a flourishing Neolithic culture that McDonald named Bashendi, after the DOP's home. Radiocarbon dating of artifacts indicates that the Bashendi occupied the Dakhleh Oasis for over two millennia, starting around 7500 years ago.

In 1992, McDonald got down to the exacting business of mapping the Bashendi village and excavating individual huts. "Once you start finding hut circles and patterns of hut circles, it puts you way ahead of the game," she says. The Bashendi huts, spanning nearly a thousand years from 7300 to 6500 years ago, were larger, more varied in shape and more elaborate in design than those of the Masara, which, on average, were 2000 years older. Rather than vertical slabs, the walls consisted of a few dark stones laid flat, one on top of another, as if to anchor some kind of superstructure. Perhaps the dwellings were roofed with a tent-like cover of stitched-together animal skins—Dorcas gazelle being the most likely candidate. However, nothing of these roofs survives, having either rotted or been eroded away.

Another common feature of the hut-circle construction is that the north walls are always higher, suggesting the builders needed protection against the winds funnelling through the *wadi*. This in turn suggests winter occupation. Like the smaller Masara huts, the Bashendi versions were either built into a natural hollow or, in some instances, these ancient architects had excavated the bedrock to make what might be considered a Neolithic split-level dwelling. Gaps in the walls marked the doorways, which were consistently positioned on the south side.

Some huts were thirty to forty feet long, comparable in length to a modern bungalow and probably similar in function to the Huron Indian longhouses of central Canada, which were designed to house extended family groups. In one such dwelling McDonald found two hearth sites, indicating more than one nuclear family group.

In looking for precedents, the closest examples McDonald could think of were in the Nile Valley at Merimda, on the western edge of the Delta. There, postholes and fragments of wooden posts indicate that the inhabitants lived in oval huts or wigwams. In some instances, a central wooden post supported the roof. But these Valley dwellings date to 6000 years ago, more than a millennium later than the oldest Bashendi prototypes.

In the middle of one cluster of huts McDonald uncovered a communal workplace. Here the Bashendi must have practised their crafts, whether bead-making, arrowhead knapping or stitching hides together for tents or clothing. At night, a ring of hearthfires would have lit up the desert night as the smell of roasted wild meat wafted through the cool air. On the floors of some huts McDonald detected the impressed patterns of reeds or mats. Some of the huts have "cubby-holes," separate small rooms where people could curl up against the cold.

Other Bashendi sites in the Southeast Basin flesh out the picture of the hut-builders' lifestyle. Rufus Churcher has found that most bones belonged to domesticated livestock, both cows and goats, rather than wild animals. Thanheiser, for her part, found traces of wild sorghum and millet, the ancestors of the first plants to be domesticated in Africa. Near the village, McDonald found a special processing area with reaping knives and abundant grinding equipment: platter-sized querns, or hand mills, their centres scalloped by the repeated grinding of seeds.

At last, McDonald had found all the tell-tale markers of the Neolithic Revolution she had spent so long tracking: a semi-permanent settlement, domesticated plants, and the bones of domesticated cattle, sure signs that the Bashendi were pastoralists. Such a finding in the Middle East would be passé, but in the Western Desert it was groundbreaking.

McDonald expects that the Bashendi pastured their cattle atop the Plateau during the rainy season, then retreated to their shelters in the lowlands during the dry winter season. The hut circles would have served as a seasonal meeting place. Such gatherings, she believes, fulfilled a purpose beyond mere subsistence, also satisfying the human need for companionship and celebration. McDonald's theory is bolstered by ethnographic evidence.

Often the archaeologist, faced with minimal material evidence, must turn to the ethnographer and anthropologist for models of human behaviour. "Anthropologists use the term 'aggregation' for the business of quite small bands coming together for social reasons," McDonald explains. "This is how you meet your mate, have your big rituals, your sundance or whatever it is, usually at a time when resources are fairly rich and you can support large numbers of people." For example, small bands of the San peoples of the Kalahari Desert still congregate today for gift exchange, gossiping and feasting. This could explain the proliferation of ostrich eggshell beads at the Bashendi hut circles, as well as the many finely-worked arrowheads. Among the San, these are common items of gift exchange.

The Bashendi may also have indulged in other rituals associated with modern herding cultures such as the Masai. Fred Wendorf found what he believes to be a ritual slaughter site at Nabta Playa in southwestern Egypt, and McDonald herself has discovered pits of fire-cracked stones with abundant bones of domestic cattle. Perhaps the Bashendi sacrificed cattle for festive purposes, as still occurs in some sub-Saharan herding cultures who ordinarily use cattle for dairy purposes, but at certain times of the year slaughter large numbers.

The most dramatic confirmation of the revolution that shaped the Bashendi lay over the ridge from their village. It was the stone ring that Krzyzaniak had first brought to McDonald's attention and that she first set out to inspect in 1990. A decade later she and I retraced her footsteps.

We crested a ridge and descended into a *wadi* of white stone. In full Holocene flood, 10,000 years ago, it would have flowed milky white, then jade green, as it slowly let fall its load of lime-stone. Of course, waters had not flowed here in several thousand years. It was now nothing more than a dry gulch, but I could still see where rivulets of water had once worked their way, vein-like, through the gravels. It was easy for me to imagine this as a swift-moving stream, having explored the "headwaters" of a *wadi* at the base of the Plateau where the white cobbles of limestone were the size of melons, as the Arabic place name, Wadi el-Batikh, suggested; here the torrential waters had slowed as they spread out over the desert plain, depositing the grape-sized, chalk pebbles that scrunched dryly underfoot.

Mary McDonald sprinted ahead. She was wearing her usual field garb: a plaid, long-sleeved shirt, green work pants, a white, floppy hat with a white handkerchief pinned at the back in French Foreign Legion style, and running shoes. Her long dark hair, now streaked with white strands, was pulled back in a pony-tail under her reverse-veil. She paused atop a sandstone butte, or *yardang*, her dark figure silhouetted against the polarizing noonday sky. As she scanned the horizon for her bearings, she unfolded her site maps, which flapped in the merciful breeze. But breeze or no, I found the shadeless heat, hovering in the low 80s, sapping my energy as I did my level best to keep up with the seemingly tireless McDonald. When I caught up with her, she muttered in a self-admonishing tone, "You'd think I'd know every wretched inch of this interfluve by now."

The use of a term connoting a ridge between river valleys seemed steeped in irony. From our vantage point, all I could see was the wan desert sands stippled with the domino-patterns of contrasting black iron-stained and white limestone pebbles, forming part of a lowland depression known as the Southeast Basin. The basin that once supported trees and grasses is now a scorched barrens, with neither a bush nor a blade of grass in sight.

But Mary McDonald saw a very different vista, the savannah landscape as it must have been seven thousand years ago. Giraffes reached up their long necks to strip leaves from the thorny acacia trees that lined the riverbanks meandering away from the plateau. Ostriches strutted through the fields of thin grasses rippling in the prevailing winds. Wild date and doum palms shaded the lowland watering holes with their fringes of rushes and reeds. Large savannah animals, such as extinct giant buffalo and elephant, and even hippo, drank and wallowed in the waters. Wading birds worked the shallows for fishes. Herds of zebra, hartebeest and gazelle took their turns at drinking, while keeping a cautious eye out for lions and hyena packs. And, of course, humans, armed with bows and arrows, stalked the birds and animals, and herded their own newly domesticated livestock to the watering hole.

Once McDonald found her bearings, we headed south along the ridge top. As we trudged through the ever-shifting sands, I could see our goal: a huge ring of iron-blackened stones. Plunked down in the middle of the desert, it had an otherworldly appearance.

"I know of no other such structure from that time period. Nothing even close to that size has been reported," McDonald noted with a hint of excitement creeping into her normally understated tone. Modest to a fault, she is not one to embellish the empirical evidence or to trumpet her successes. The stone ring, however, demanded a certain pride of ownership. "This is unique as far as I know. Certainly in northeast Africa."

"What do you think it is?"

"Fairy ring?" she offered with a sly smile.

As we descended the ridge into the cauldron, the desert floor rippled in the rising heat waves of midday, but McDonald seemed unfazed.

The desert is a *tabula rasa*, stripped of all vestiges of modern life and most signs of the prehistoric past. To suddenly come upon a structure of the scale of the stone ring is somehow exhilarating, life-affirming, in the face of so much barrenness. The stones that form the ring rise above the flat plain like the wake that forms when a stone is dropped into a still pond.

McDonald and I crossed over the tiers of dark, iron-stained Nubian sandstone that form the rim of the stone ring. The flagstone-sized fragments clattered underfoot like broken bone china. The thick walls were thirty feet wide in places. Now collapsed, they had once been stacked in three tiers to make a sturdy barrier, three to six feet high. Rather than circular, it is actually a huge oval, 115 feet in width by 154 feet in length. Without speaking, we gravitated toward its centre. The silence of the desert seemed to radiate out from the rim in concentric circles, and I sensed the power such a feat of architecture must have communicated. A desert wanderer chancing upon it seven thousand years ago would have immediately understood the ingenuity and strength of its builders.

What, then, was this mysterious structure? When she first laid eyes on it, different options raced through McDonald's mind. Her first thought was that it might be some kind of ceremonial centre. But she quickly discarded this theory in favour of a more practical interpretation: it was a corral. This conclusion was bolstered by the presence of two stone huts at what appeared to be the entrance, or gate. Perhaps cow- or goatherds kept watch over the herd from here, protecting it from nocturnal predators such as lions and hyenas.

When McDonald was unable to return to Iran, she had assumed she must abandon her quest for the early pastoralists and the roots of farming. Now, to her surprise, she had discovered one of "the hearths of agriculture" in Egypt's Western Desert. Clearly, the Bashendi were among the peoples, like those in Middle East, who had ushered in the Neolithic Revolution.

If McDonald was right, and the great stone ring was a corral, that corral also held profound implications for traditional views of the origins of the civilization of the pharaohs.

CHAPTER FIVE

A GIFT OF THE DESERT

McDonald had long known that there was already evidence for cattle-keeping in the Western Desert—even earlier than in the Near East. Fred Wendorf had found cattle bones in southern Egypt, dating back to 9500 years ago, along with Neolithic artifacts and a handful of huts dating to 8100 years ago. It appeared that other desert peoples, contemporaries of both the Masara and Bashendi, might have been keeping cattle by this time. Wild cattle were native to North Africa and had long been an important food source for hunter-gatherer groups. The question in southern Egypt was, were these wild or domesticated cattle? From just small fragments, it is a tricky business to distinguish between the bones of wild cattle and of domesticated ones, which on average are smaller than their wild ancestors'.

Until the work of McDonald and Wendorf, the best evidence

Rock drawing of humans tethering giraffes

93

that early Neolithic peoples had been keeping cattle was the rock art they left throughout the Sahara. These are petroglyphs, depicting humans and animals, that were incised, hammered and, on occasion, painted on the desert's vast canvas of stone: in caves of the Central Sahara, on the imposing faces of the Saharan massifs, and in the rock-tank basins of the Dakhleh Oasis. The urge to leave a visual record of one's presence in the daunting blankness of the desert is not restricted to prehistoric peoples but continues to this day; flowing Arabic script and other recent tourist graffiti is carved into stone along the el-Gubari Road and along other ancient camel trails, such as the Darb el-Tawil, that radiate from Dakhleh. Of greatest interest to archaeology, however, are the Neolithic petroglyphs which give us a unique insight into the behaviour and beliefs of these vanished artists—in particular, their relationship with animals at a critical stage in human cultural evolution.

The DOP first discovered rock art, including intriguing images of giraffes, during the third season of the survey. Most pictures were incised, but one image of a group of four-legged animals had been painted in a dark red pigment the colour of dried blood. The discovery did not come as a surprise, given the widespread occurrence of rock art throughout the Sahara and, more particularly, the work of German art historian, ethnographer and philologist Hans Winkler, who, in the late 1930s, documented a number of petroglyph locations at the eastern end of the oasis.

The first person to uncover this trove of ancient art in the Western Desert was Hassanein Bey, an adventurous traveller who might very well have served as the model for the classic Rudolph Valentino role in *The Sheik*. In photographs for his book, *The Lost Oases,* Bey looks the part of the nomadic Bedouin in his flowing white desert garb, the *jerd,* with a rifle slung over his back. It was a carefully cultivated image, for Bey was an Oxford-educated member of the Egyptian Diplomatic Service who represented his country in fencing in the Olympic Games.

In 1923, Bey made an epic journey of 2,100 miles by camel across the Western Desert to Darfur in the Sudan. It took him two and a half months. En route he discovered two "lost oases" at the southwest corner of Egypt. One was at Arkenu, where "the mountains rose before us like medieval castles half hidden in the morning mist." Here, Bey learned, local tribesmen pastured their camels in seasonally fertile valleys, where they left them unattended by walling up the entrances to the valley with rocks. Bey moved on, and four days later, the "dark masses of the Uweinat Mountains came into view."

In a valley of the Uweinat Mountains fed by a spring, Hassanein Bey discovered a remarkable collection of rock drawings:

"On a wall of rock there are pictures of animals, rudely drawn but not unskillfully carved. There are lions, giraffes, and ostriches, all kinds of gazelle, and perhaps cows, though many of these figures have been effaced by time . . . I could find no traditions about the origin of these rock markings, but I was struck by two things. There are no giraffes in this part of the country now, nor can they live in a similar desert country anywhere. Also there are no camels among the carvings, and one cannot penetrate to this oasis now except with camels."

The absence of camels suggested to Bey that the drawings dated to before 500 B.C.E., when the domesticated camel came to Africa from Asia, and the suite of African animals depicted showed him that the country had been much better watered in the remote past. For the first time, rock art revealed that a Saharan people had once prospered where it was now impossible to sustain life.

In 1933, the great Hungarian explorer Count Ladislaus de Almasy made a similar remarkable discovery in the Gilf Kebir, a precipitous sandstone plateau roughly the size of Switzerland, that was high enough to capture the moisture in tropical rain clouds from the south. The sheer cliffs of the Gilf rear up from the desert plain like some sea-girt island with flanks cut deeply by fjords. These steep valleys are haunted by a monotonous roaring of wind that sounds like breakers on a beach. Along with a native guide, Almasy scaled the nearly insurmountable cliffs to find more than a dozen large caves. In one of them were figures seemingly afloat in space, with arms and legs outstretched. Similar images from South Africa had been interpreted as depicting shamanistic states. Almasy, however, believed that the figures were "*nageurs*"—swimmers paddling in a prehistoric lake. He also located about a dozen smaller caves, "all covered with beautiful rock paintings in four colours, showing cattle and other animals, mostly tame ones, and human beings," including one curious pair, a slender man and an enormous woman, "Monsieur and Madame" of the cave.

Winkler was the first scholar to study this rock art systematically, publishing his now classic two-volume *Rock Drawings of Southern Egypt* in 1939. In Winkler's opinion, rock-drawings substituted for written records in prehistory and as such were a rich mine of information about dress, weapons, hunting, trade, and wild and domestic animals. They could even be a window into religious beliefs and social institutions.

Winkler's ambition was to survey the Western Desert, an area too vast to cover in its entirety. In 1937 and 1938, his search took him to Dakhleh. The sandstone outcrops on the el-Gubari road, he observed, "show yellow, red, and violet colours," and were covered with recent drawings, including names of English soldiers inscribed during the First World War, that, in some cases, were already half destroyed by wind and sand—only twenty years later. Such rapid erosion makes it all the more remarkable that ancient rock art has survived. North of the Kharga-Dakhleh road, however, Winkler found the artistic heritage of a previously unknown prehistoric people.

His prior investigations had led him to the conclusion that Saharan drawings fell into two main classes: "a period in which the artists knew and depicted cattle, and a pre-cattle period." What was unique about the Dakhleh drawings was their depiction of pregnant women with exaggerated bellies and buttocks. Despite the wealth of Neolithic rock art from the Nile Valley to the Atlantic, there was no parallel for these seemingly mystical figures, which Winkler believed were meant to depict goddesses.

Winkler identified two groups of Dakhleh artists at work. The people who did not know cattle, or at least never depicted them, he called the "Earliest Hunters." But living beside them was a group he called "the Early Oasis Dwellers," characterizing them as "clever stone workers, settled people, plant cultivators, probably adoring a pregnant goddess." Even though they knew cattle, Winkler did not believe that cattle breeding and nomadic herding was their main livelihood, nor was hunting. These people who drew the pregnant woman, he postulated, were settled plant cultivators. Despite little archaeological evidence to bolster his theories, Winkler's view held sway for the simple reason that after the Second World War—during which Winkler disappeared and was never heard from again—no further work was carried out either to prove or disprove his interpretation until the DOP retraced his steps.

IN DECEMBER 1985, MILLS MET LECH KRZYZANIAK IN CAIRO and invited him to join the DOP. At the time, Krzyzaniak was on his way to continue excavations of a Neolithic site in the Sudan. With more than two hundred papers to his credit over a forty-year career, he is one of the world's leading experts on the prehistory of North Africa, with a special interest in the origin and development of early food-producing cultures. Mills and Krzyzaniak were old friends who had worked together on the Nubian Salvage Campaign in the Sudan in 1971. Krzyzaniak was looking for a site where he could tie the rock art to evidence of living sites in the vicinity. In 1980 he had begun work in the Tassili-n-Ajer area in southern Algeria, famous for its prehistoric paintings and engravings, but had been forced to abandon the project. He was immediately attracted to the DOP's approach to the study of rock art as an important source of information on Neolithic cultural processes.

His first step was to find Winkler's original rock art sites. "Due to a lack of exact map locations, this was not as easy a task as it might at first appear," says Krzyzaniak. After finding the first few sites, however, he decided to take a drive to a remote, hilly location, well away from Winkler's route, far to the north of the el-Gubari road. Decades of experience in different parts of the Sahara and Sudan had nurtured "an ability to sense the association of certain environments with prehistoric human settlement." His archaeological sixth sense led him to what has become known as the Rock Art Basin, a half mile north of the Bashendi Neolithic village.

The area is marked by a series of flat-topped *yardangs*, the bases of which the ancient artists often chose as their canvases. He inspected row after row of these, numbering each petroglyph, describing it in words, making a schematic drawing, and photographing it. He also thoroughly inspected sediments, which suggested the area might once have been a seasonal lake or wetland.

During the first three field seasons Krzyzaniak located many other Winkler sites, although some have still not been found. Relying on McDonald's meticulous work, Kzryzaniak's aim was to relate the petroglyphs to artifacts in their vicinity, in the hope of identifying the artists. At the base of the petroglyph-bearing *yardangs*, McDonald identified the stone implements, potsherds and numerous fragments of ostrich eggshell left as signs of Bashendi occupancy. It appeared that her cattle herders were also the rock artists.

This astonishing collection of Bashendi rock art documents various stages in the development of human relationships with animals, in particular the transition from hunting to herding. Most wild animals are depicted without any association with humans. But others appear in dramatic hunting scenes. In one, a giraffe is being hunted by bowmen aided by dogs. One dog is attacking the snout of the giraffe while the bowman fires arrows at its jugular. Another hunter shoots from behind the animal. Krzyzaniak speculates that the animal may already have been weakened by the use of a poison dart. DOP botanist Johannes Walter has identified at least one source of poison in the contemporary oasis—the *Oshar* bush, whose waxy leaves exude a toxic latex-type substance—and ethnographic evidence also tells us that present-day hunter groups like the San employ poison darts to take down large game.

Of even greater interest to McDonald and Kzryzaniak were the drawings that depicted early experiments to domesticate animals. These are dramatic tableaux, showing the capture and taming of young animals, and their subsequent captivity in pens. In one scene, a human is pulling an antelope by a rope attached to its neck. Most surprising are pictures of giraffes tethered by the ankle, an image found elsewhere in the Sahara, including at Uweinat. There are also images of giraffes with lassos thrown around their elongated necks. It seems the Bashendi were experimenting with the control of wild animals of all kinds, although such connections, or "power lines," between animals and humans have also been interpreted in San rock art as showing symbolic control or simply identification with the animal.

One of the most telling images depicts the successful capture of a young giraffe. A human figure appears to lasso it while the adult giraffe, perhaps the parent, watches at a distance. There are also images of cows, which, despite the minimalist manner of their depiction, are demonstrably domestic, looking much like any cow fattening in Dakhleh today, where the oasis dwellers tether them in stubble fields.

There are other clearly domestic scenes, including a herd of long-horned cattle and a tethered bull. "There are cattle depicted where you can see the udders, the young near them, long horns and such," says McDonald. Such images strongly reinforce McDonald's belief, based on the corral, that the Bashendi had made the cultural leap to a pastoral lifestyle. But there seem to be some other aspects of Bashendi culture alluded to in the petroglyphs. On one, there are seven rows of geese, or perhaps ostriches, in a pen, watched over by a "little man" figure and near him an image of a much larger woman, her gender identifiable by an explicit venus or pubis.

IN HIS SEARCH FOR WINKLER'S ORIGINAL SITES, KRZYZANIAK also chanced upon several more of Winkler's seventy or so intriguing images of pregnant-looking women. While men were depicted naked (one with a feather on his head), the women were dressed in long skirts that covered their feet. The skirts displayed various patterns and were apparently woven. Often the upper part of the garment was plain but below the waist there was a "divided skirt" ornamented by short strips. Sometimes strings hung from the waist. In a few cases, the women wore "crowns" in several shapes, one resembling a high cap. Wavy lines indicated long hair or plaits. The artists had outlined a drawing by incising, and then smoothed the surface inside the outline. The result was a sunken relief, or engraving.

Many of the images of the pregnant-looking women were engraved on horizontal surfaces at the tops of hills, facing the sky. "It is obvious that we must look for a religious or magical explanation for these curious drawings," Winkler contended. His belief in the religious function of the goddesses was bolstered by the presence of large grindstones found all around the hills, and the fact that one of these contained an image of the pregnant goddess. "We may be on the right track in supposing that this pregnant figure was connected with the fertility of the earth. The position on top of hills facing the sky may connect these drawings with rain . . . did these pictures represent the fecundated soil thirsty for rain?" Winkler felt that the drawing of the richly ornamented woman on the grinding stone suggested a deity rather than a human woman, "possibly a goddess of virginal aspect." Her powers were to bring rain and/or to aid pregnancy—symbolically, to renew life.

His theory was given credence by one picture in particular, which had been deeply incised. The pregnant goddess figure was connected by a horizontal stroke to a bull or a cow, as if by a tether. The animal wore what might be an ornament on its head. A human being, "a little man" much smaller than the woman, pulled it by the tail. Winkler's reading was that the animal is about to be sacrificed to or blessed by the deity and that the ornament on the cow's head had a magical or religious function, signifying the oasis dwellers' dependence on rain and cattle, and ultimately on the favour of the pregnant goddess.

In 1988, Krzyzaniak found four of these female figures carved atop a solitary, conical hill, which he describes as a prehistoric "altar," overlooking a large *wadi* valley. In many respects, they closely resembled those described by Winkler, featuring large buttocks and slim upper bodies and small heads. However, the detailing, especially of the costuming, was unusually rich.

The women are wearing bracelets, anklets and neck rings. Particularly striking are the elaborate head-dresses, which, Krzyzaniak thinks, are woven of feathers or straw. They are worn over an elaborate hair-style with four free-hanging, braid-like projections. Decorative lines criss-crossing the upper body and partly reaching over the hip may be tattoos or other body decorations such as beads. The central figure also seems to be wearing a triangular mask, pierced in the middle by four centrally located holes, probably for the eyes and nostrils.

Winkler thought that these goddess images were depictions of statues. "I think they may have been of human-size or even a supra-natural size," says Krzyzaniak, based on the proportions of the goddesses, male figures, and animals depicted in the petroglyphs.

Young giraffes and antelopes, as well as domestic cattle, are being brought to the masked goddesses, probably for slaughter as offerings, according to Krzyzaniak. Although the Bashendi might have tamed the giraffes and antelopes, these animals were not amenable to domestication. However, such a practice with aurochs, a type of wild oxen, might explain the presence of domesticated cattle in the Western Desert from the onset of Holocene times, at which time Krzyzaniak believes the area may have been colonized by groups from the Nubian and Upper Egyptian Nile Valley, where aurochs were native.

Human figures with masks depicting animal heads are inti-mately associated with the magic rituals of pharaonic culture, where priests often wore masks during mummification and funeral cere-monies. For example, Anubis was a jackal-headed god who presided over the embalming procedure. Mask-wearing priests also assumed the roles of ibis-, falcon- and lion-headed gods. The image of the sun/ram with a disc on its head appears in Saharan rock art long before it becomes a stock image in pharaonic art. Also, the presence of rock art masks, not only at Dakhleh but at several prehistoric sites in the Sahara, suggests that the practice had much deeper roots in Egypt's past. Krzyzaniak says that the tradition of mask-wearing arose in prehistory when hunters donned masks of animals, "prob-ably to absorb the beast's power and speed," or simply as camouflage while hunting. In almost every case, mask-wearing seems to be asso-ciated with men as gods, sorcerers and hunters. Among the Bashendi, however, it is a woman who dons the magical mask.

Yet another group of five "Bashendi Ladies" shows two, face to face, in what seems to be a dancing posture. They each hold what appears to be a decorated drum in one hand and a stick in the other. The whole composition is alive with movement: one can sense the swirling skirts, almost hear the rhythm of the pounding drums, see the dust rising under their dancing feet. The picture is clearly a repository of important cultural information, but Krzyzaniak cannot tell whether the women represent a kind of totem, sorceresses, goddesses, or the elite of a social group.

Mary McDonald remains skeptical of Winkler's and Krzyzaniak's interpretation of the "Bashendi Ladies" as goddess figures: "It's a mug's game trying to relate cosmology or ideology to prehistoric peoples, because they have left no written texts. It's not very scientific. Perhaps the figures are related to goddess cults in Predynastic Egypt or in Europe, but who really knows?"

On the other hand, she trusts the hard evidence of artifacts. Rock art is notoriously difficult to date, but her study of the associated artifacts and the proximity of Bashendi living sites leaves her in no doubt that the rock artists were her Bashendi pastoralists.

LIKE A PICTORIAL ARK, THE PETROGLYPHS HAVE ALSO PRESERVED a record of the wild fauna during the time of the Bashendi. Rufus Churcher has found skeletal evidence for most of the animals depicted on the walls of the Rock Art Basin. However, there are some odd discrepancies. For instance, in the thousands of bones Churcher has examined, he has yet to turn up a single fragment of giraffe. "The art suggests that these things were around and now I gotta look for them," Churcher says ruefully. "It's annoying. The giraffes are all over the rock art and I haven't got a smell of giraffe, not even a hoof print, as you might say."

Churcher's field seasons are spent scouring the oasis margins and the escarpment, patiently trowelling the sands like a paleontological gardener. For shade, he wears a fifty-year-old black pork-pie fedora, once standard issue to Kenyan police officers. The fruits of his labour are scraps of bone abraded by the wind or smashed to smithereens by the powerful jaws of some predator, big cat or wild dog, or by the hammerstones of prehistoric peoples bent on extracting the last iota of the prey's protein, including the succulent and nourishing marrow secreted inside the bones. To add to Churcher's workload, his colleagues bring back bags of bones from their ongoing excavations—bones from Neolithic hearths, bones from Old Kingdom settlements, and scads of bones from the Romano-Byzantine city of Ismant el-Kharab.

These bags pile up in the DOP compound, begging for answers. What animal owned these bones? How did it die? Finding the answers is vital to the project's environmental mission. Every bone has a characteristic shape, some defining feature that says where it fits in the anatomy and what kind of creature it once belonged to, and knowing what animals were around tells us whether there was more or less rainfall and water. This tedious work finds Churcher at his table at the far end of the Bashendi laboratory, logging long hours in lock-step with Mary McDonald, who occupies the neighbouring workbench. Like her, he often has very little to work with, chips of bone that may tell him something about the size of the animal, or whether, for instance, it was a mammal, but little else. Churcher prefers some bones to others for the amount of information they can convey: teeth, skulls and jaws are at the top of his list, he says, while ribs are at the bottom.

The fauna group during the Bashendi time was not very different from what is found today south of the Sahara. "If you saw it tromping around East Africa, before people shot it out, you'd think nothing strange about it," says Churcher. Recalling the Kenya of his youth, he says, "I can make this place into a living savannah quite easily. Give it three or four inches of rain per year and it would be a savannah."

The fauna included elephant, giraffe (if the rock art is to be believed, and Churcher does believe the artists), hippopotamus, giant African buffalo, large and small antelope, gazelle, ostrich, and zebra—and predators such as hyena and, likely, lion. Churcher first catalogued this African fauna in the 200,000-year-old paleo-lakes. Surprisingly, they survived in and around the Sahara until the mid-Holocene. During arid episodes, the animals retreated south-ward to the Sahel, or persisted in watery pockets, like the oases, or in the highlands, such as the Gilf Kebir.

During the mid-Holocene, Dakhleh was still a relatively wet place. Showers fell frequently on the Plateau. Animals followed the rains across a vast open landscape, their trails eventually converg-ing at watering holes. The larger animals drank at will; the preda-tory lions and hyaena took their turn after the biggest animals— dangerous even to the large cats and dogs—had moved off; and finally came the wary antelopes, gazelles and other ungulates, like the hartebeest, twitching with nervousness at the lingering scents of the predators. During the wet periods of the Holocene, which usually lasted two to three times as long as the arid intervals, such watering holes would have been widespread. There were also abun-dant grasslands where species could find their own niches, dividing up the resources in the environment without putting undue pres-sure on each other.

Around 7000 years ago, Dakhleh seems to have been particu-larly blessed with rain. This was when the Bashendi first built their huts and stone circles, in McDonald's view, "tethering" themselves to the oasis. But the climate was growing progressively drier and by 6500 years ago the desert was beginning to assert its dominion. Thanheiser's archaeobotanical evidence indicates that grasses now dominated the flora, suggesting that the standing water of Masara times that had supported moisture-loving plants such as portulaca had disappeared. Grinding equipment found near the hut circles indicates that the Bashendi were now processing wild grasses, including wild sorghum and millet. As the desert expanded and the number and size of watering holes diminished, the movement of migrating herds became more restricted. And as the wild animals were forced to occupy a smaller and smaller area, so was the human population that depended on them.

It was during this period of environmental stress that pastoralism took hold. Researchers now agree that cattle-keeping was probably a response to the drying conditions. It first appeared in the Western Desert, including Dakhleh, and spread into the relatively well-watered Central Sahara only when it, too, became exceedingly dry. The strong likelihood is that as wild animals became not only more scarce but more scattered, people adopted pastoralism as a way of ensuring a steady supply of nutrition. Cattle-keeping was a banking system that replaced the unpredictability of wild resources. The Bashendi probably relied as much on by-products of the cattle—milk, blood and urine—as on meat from them. The African mode of pastoralism is less exclusively carnivorous than the Middle Eastern model, McDonald points out, and the practice of utilizing blood and milk persists even today among East African pastoralists such as the Masai.

The bones Churcher has found at the Bashendi sites strongly support McDonald's theory. Bones of Dorcas gazelle and hartebeest, along with those of larger game animals, are still found, and their presence, together with finely made arrowheads, indicate that hunting was still important. But the majority of bones, in later Bashendi times, beginning around 6500 years ago, belong to cattle and goats.

As we have seen, cattle were native to North Africa, but goats were not, their wild ancestors being indigenous to the Near East. This raised the troubling question: where did the domestic goats come from in the Western Desert? Until recently, it was assumed that goats arrived in Egypt by a route across the northern Sinai to the Nile Delta, then along the Mediterranean coast and southward up the Nile Valley. The problem with this theory is that goats appeared in the Western Desert around 7000 years ago, at Nabta Playa and Dakhleh, a thousand years before they do along the Nile. New research in the southern Sinai strongly supports a different migratory route: goats could easily have swam or been rafted across the narrowest strait of the Gulf of Suez, which was a relatively risk-free sea passage. They then diffused through southern Egypt and into the desert, where people like the Bashendi domesticated them and held them in pens that resembled giant stone rings.

This conversion of the Bashendi to pastoralism had disastrous consequences for the wild species that were able to hang on during the drying phase. Although the Bashendi continued to hunt, hunting pressure—which many scientists now believe accounts for the extinction of many large mammals in North America coincident with the arrival of humans on the continent—was not the primary factor in the extirpation of the Saharan wild animals. According to Churcher, the Bashendi eliminated them by the more passive but effective means of competitive exclusion.

The Bashendi would have herded their cattle and goats to a watering hole daily. While there, they would have guarded the precious water supply from wild animals, driving them away or in some cases killing them. Similarly, they jealously guarded the remaining pastureland. The wild species now had limited access to food and water, with negative consequences for the reproductive capabilities of their herds.

Ecologists now realize that the loss and fragmentation of habitat, due to agriculture, urban development and industrial activity, has had devastating impacts on biodiversity and wildlife populations. Island biogeography theory, pioneered in the 1960s by two Harvard biologists, the late Robert MacArthur and Edward O. Wilson, demonstrates convincingly the so-called "area effect"—stated simply, the larger the area, the more varied the species. Examining species diversity on islands worldwide, they and other researchers have consistently shown that the number of species approximately doubles with every tenfold increase in area. Of course, the converse is also true: a tenfold decrease in area, or habitat, means the loss of half the species. We are fast destroying and fragmenting remaining wildlife habitat to such a degree that scientists now estimate that human activity has increased the normal extinction rate by 1000 to 10,000 times, qualifying the present era as one of the great extinction events in geological history. Churcher believes that for tens of thousands of years Dakhleh acted as a refuge for African fauna until cattle-herding humans progressively destroyed them.

ONE DAY CHURCHER AND I HEADED SOUTH TO EXCAVATE A site he called Hyena Hill. We turned off the main road near Balat, and followed tire tracks over mounded terrain pocked with large potholes, the work of gravel diggers dating back to Roman times. We passed a few mounds of freshly dug earth, tailings from shallow wells recently dug, in the oasis dwellers' perpetual search for new water resources. "They are too close together," Churcher observed. "Local people don't seem to realize they will use all the water and there'll be none left for anyone. I'm afraid I'm not very sanguine about the future."

Leaving behind all vestiges of cultivation, we entered the wastes of the desert, and soon after stopped to inspect a sand dune. It crested up in a yellow wave beside the road and was sparsely vegetated with spare clumps of brown grasses. This desert grass, Churcher told me, was *halfa*. It appeared utterly lifeless, except for a single clump that sprouted green with a flowering head. Its neighbours must wait for rain to spring into life. However, there were other signs of life, however fleeting, in this harsh habitat. Churcher pointed out a trail of tiny gerbil tracks and, nearby, the pawprints of red fox.

We travelled further south into the desert, rattling along the rough track in the trusty Land Rover, one of the little-vehicles-that-can, and do, day after day, take this kind of beating in the service of science. It was the same terrain that desert scientists Ladislaus Almasy and Ralph Bagnold had travelled in their Steyr and Model T cars in the 1930s, a period of pioneer exploration of the Western Desert for which Churcher expresses unabashed envy.

Off to our right, at about two o'clock, was the flat-topped Hyena Hill. Churcher wheeled the Land Rover off the track and cut across the desert, parking up at the base of the *gebel*. Shovel and sieve in hand, we trudged up its flanks, which were wind-cut into three terraces. At the top was a cave, about three feet in diameter, dug into the soft greyish marls that in the distant past, 100,000 to 200,000 years ago, had been the lake bed. Two years before, when Churcher had climbed up here for a closer look, he had seen bones scattered around and had said to himself, "This isn't foxes." He found bones that he thought were hyena-cracked. "Hyenas keep clean dens," he noted, donning his zoologist's hat. "The bones tend to be on the edges of the den, on the outside, because the young hyenas play with the bones."

We began digging out the soft, wind-blown sediments that had sealed the mouth of the cave, spelling each other off in the increasingly hot sun. As we reached firmer, undisturbed sediments, Churcher commented that "the grave diggers gave up here."

In effect, we were tunnelling back through time. Churcher wanted to confirm, first, that this had indeed been a hyena den and he was looking specifically for traces of hartebeest bone. He had evidence of this large, greyish brown antelope from Neolithic remains, but suspected that it might have survived much later, into the Victorian era. The last reported sighting of a hartebeest in Egypt was in the Siwa Oasis in 1935.

Dorcas gazelle, donkey, camel, and fox bone and hair emerged as we shook the shovelfuls through a wire screen. The marl also was riddled with plant casts, the remains of reeds that had grown here underwater in the ancient lake.

As Churcher tunnels through time, he sees species dropping out of the fossil record, one by one, victims of environmental change and human exploitation, often in concert. "You ask yourself what's missing?" he says. "It's like intelligence work in the war. What they're *not* talking about is almost as important as what they *are* talking about. Absences raise the question, when did the water dry up?"

As we dug deeper, the soil became even harder, the consistency of tightly packed talcum powder, and cooler to the touch. Then the end of a long bone emerged from the greyish matrix. "Look there," Churcher said. He went to work with a trowel and brush to carefully extract the bone fragment. "That's a nice bit of bone. Maybe we've hit pay dirt here."

Digging out the six-inch fragment, he turned it over, musing all the while: "Larger than a goat, smaller than a cow." He looked at the end. "It's an adult.

"It's old," he said, pointing out its yellowish colour and smoothed surface. It was also chewed on one end. "Yes, hyena. I'm quite satisfied that I am into a hyena den now."

Holding up the bone, he said with satisfaction: "That may be our hartebeest."

Climatic change would have eliminated the larger animals first, such as elephant and hippo, as well as water-dependent species such as crocodiles. When trees such as acacia, which today are only found near irrigation ditches in the oasis, started to disappear, so did the giraffes that depended upon them for forage. Smaller animals such as gazelle and antelope became more vulnerable not only to natural predators but to humans as they were concentrated into smaller spaces by the ever-drier climate.

As grazing land is taken over by herds of cattle and goats, the large, wild grazing animals such as aurochs and buffaloes disappear.

Then the big gazelles drop out of the fossil record. Today, only the little Dorcas gazelle is left and it has become vanishingly rare.

The last straw for the wildlife populations in the Sahara that had survived the effects of a deteriorating climate throughout the Pleistocene may have been a shift in cultural values toward cattle being a status symbol: the more cattle you had, the more power you wielded. "As soon as the number of cattle people have becomes important for social reasons, then I think the wild animals are in real trouble," says Churcher.

The Bashendi, it seems, had already made this cultural leap. The large corral not only tells us that the Bashendi kept large numbers of cattle, possibly for status as well as subsistence, but reveals other insights into Bashendi society. Building and maintaining so massive a structure would have required an organized work force and, therefore, leadership. The same is true of the hut circles. Even if not all the huts were occupied at once, the population at any one time must have been several hundred people. "When you get that many people," says McDonald, "you almost have to have somebody playing a leadership role, to sort out disputes and to figure out such things as the best course of action to procure food."

The two hundred hut circles, the massive stone ring, and the rock art together demonstrate that the Dakhleh Oasis dwellers and probably other desert denizens were far more sophisticated than Egyptologists had previously guessed. The giant stone ring, however, is also important for another reason, as the earliest example in Egypt of what can be considered monumental architecture. It may seem a rather humble precursor to the great monuments that were to arise in the Nile Valley more than a thousand years later. But, filled with cattle, it would speak of the richness of these oasis dwellers, just as today size of a herd is a status symbol among Sahelian pastoralists. If it was a ceremonial centre—still a possibil- ity in McDonald's opinion—it may have been where the Bashendi celebrated a pregnant goddess with apparent magical powers over rainfall. Finding such a grand ancient work isolated in the desert makes one contemplate what other wonders this place may have held, and leads McDonald to ask what significance it held for the great Egyptian civilization that was to follow.

THROUGHOUT THE NINETEENTH AND TWENTIETH CENTURIES, two questions nagged Egyptologists: Where did the agricultural society of the Nile Valley originate? And why had it taken so long for this revolution to take hold? The earliest evidence of farming in the Nile Valley dates from around six thousand years ago, more than four thousand years later than in the other "hearths of agriculture." As we have seen, in areas such as the Levant and Mesopotamia, humans first cultivated winter cereals, especially wheat and barley, around 11,500 years ago, and first domesticated sheep and goats as early as 10,000 years ago. In the Nile Valley, meanwhile, people were still living as hunter-gatherers.

Since the 1890s, when British archaelologist Sir Flinders Petrie first began exploring the succession of Nile Valley cultures that led up to the 3000-year-long rule of the pharaohs, Egyptologists have claimed that agriculture spread into the Valley from somewhere to the east of Africa. Many of the domesticates—wheat, barley and flax, sheep, goats, and pigs—were not indigenous to Egypt but originated in the Near East. Also the Nile Valley Neolithic period shared some cultural traits, such as burial practices and storage pit types, with Southwest Asian cultures. The notion that the ancient Egyptians were not Africans, but came from somewhere else, had its ultimate expression in the theory of "a dynastic race." One of the prominent proponents of this theory of conquest of ancient Egypt was Walter Bryan Emery, Tony Mills' mentor in the Sudan. Emery was a renowned expert on Predynastic Egypt, who believed that the apparently rapid advance of civilization in the Nile prior to the unification of Upper and Lower Egypt in 3100 B.C. must have been due to the invasion of an advanced people from somewhere in the Middle East who brought with them not only agriculture but sophisticated concepts in architecture.

The theory was an attempt to account for the yawning gap—some four thousand years—between the rise of pastoralism in the Near East and its emergence in Egypt. There was, however, a dissenting but largely ignored minority of archaeologists who claimed that sources of Nile Valley Neolithic culture could be found much closer to home, in the Eastern and Western Deserts and in sub-Saharan Africa. When Mary McDonald joined the DOP in 1979, she was unwittingly thrust into the midst of this heated debate. Her subsequent discovery of the Neolithic village and the mysterious great stone ring were strong indicators that the Western Desert had played a hitherto unexpected role. The Bashendi were a pastoral society nearly two thousand years before farming replaced hunting and gathering in the Valley. Surely, she thought, it might be possible, even likely, that the Bashendi or other groups from the Western Desert had brought farming to the Nile Valley.

Even before she found the huts, McDonald had collected artifacts that supported early contact between the Western Desert and the Valley. Bifacial knives, similar to those common in the Valley, lay scattered on the surface. When she began to excavate the huts in 1992, more evidence emerged to show the Bashendi were part of a system of long-distance trade that extended west to the Central Sahara and east to the Valley.

McDonald discovered that the Bashendi adorned themselves with the fiery shell of the cowrie that came from the Red Sea and wore bracelets of conch shell. They also strung beads of amazonite, a green-coloured stone available only from distant sources in the massifs of the Central Sahara, like Tibesti, and possibly from the Gilf Kebir and Uweinat, as well as the Valley. It was obvious that the

Bashendi valued beautiful exotic objects. But they also carved pieces of locally available barite or calcite into the shape of nails and used them as lip plugs (labrets) or ear studs, the former probably stuck through the lower lip as is the custom in other parts of Africa and elsewhere today. They used "toggles," a type of oval-shaped button or clasp furnished with either one or two drilled holes—an artifact unique to the Bashendi—as a fastener on clothes, and made ostrich-egg beads, rounded or squared.

All these articles of personal adornment, with the exception of the toggles, have also been found in the Valley. Practical items such as pottery and stone tools found in Dakhleh also bear similarities to ones known from the Valley. McDonald has found pots with wavy designs impressed in the clay like those common in Khartoum, 750 miles to the south. She also collected many fragments of thin-walled, brown polished bowls with black tops exactly like those produced in the Valley. And the distinctive hollow-based arrowheads, or side-blow flakes, whose shape McDonald poetically compares to "a gull in flight," as well as polished axes, or celts, which were likely used as hoes, and distinctive bifacial knives which were used for reaping grains or grasses, occur both in Dakhleh and in the Valley.

Thanks to McDonald's doggedness, Dakhleh has produced a greater variety of artifacts for the Holocene than anywhere else in the Western Desert. The burning question was whether these artifacts first appeared in the oasis or the Valley. Before she began excavation McDonald collected ostrich eggshells (used for bead making or when whole as water carriers), which are commonly employed for carbon dating of associated artifacts. When the results came back, she was elated to find that nearly all of the shared artifacts occur in Dakhleh from 500 to 2,000 years before they show up in the Predynastic cultures of the Nile. This strongly suggested that the Bashendi, or desert people like them, introduced these items to the

Valley. It was now abundantly clear that the Western Desert had enjoyed a precocious Neolithic development.

AROUND SIX THOUSAND YEARS AGO, AN OVERWHELMING DROUGHT gripped the Eastern Sahara, as the summer monsoonal belt retreated south and the winter Mediterranean storm belt moved north. Its effects are dramatically obvious in the archaeological record: the number of Neolithic sites across the Western Desert suddenly drops off and human beings virtually disappear from less well-watered places. Even the number of sites at Dakhleh declines dramatically. The Western Desert did not become completely depopulated, but people were forced to move from more marginal areas or starve. Later, the prolonged drought triggered a "wave" of immigration, as desperate desert peoples sought better-watered places such as Dakhleh. After Dakhleh, the next closest such haven was the Nile. Small bands strung out across the desert, from previously occupied areas in the south and west, found themselves in a forced march against time to reach the refuges of Dakhleh or the Nile.

We are all too familiar with the tragic effects of drought in recent times in the Sahel, a region that in many ways must mimic the semi-arid Holocene environment of the Western Desert. Rainfall is always uncertain, varying from year to year and from decade to decade. Droughts in the late 1960s and early 1970s killed as many as 250,000 people and millions of cattle over six years. Another severe drought in 1984 put some thirty million people at risk of starvation.

The human cost of this ancient desperate migration must also have been great. Crossing the desert has always been a perilous undertaking, even for those accustomed to it. Stories are still told in Dakhleh today of the refugees from Kufra who made a forced trek of two hundred fifty miles during the Italian occupation of the Libyan oasis in 1931, skirting the southern edge of the Great Sand

Sea before striking north along old caravan routes to the oasis.
They straggled into Dakhleh in "a sorry plight," ragged and deliri-
ous with thirst and hunger. The worsening drought of six thousand
years ago would have presented the Neolithic desert peoples with
a terrible dilemma: wait for rain or leave. Their elders probably
held to their time-proven beliefs: rains had come before and they
would come again. When they did not, the braver among them may
have gambled on a march toward the Nile. Weakened by hunger, the
most vulnerable, children and the elderly, would have been the first
to succumb. The emaciated survivors, with their similarly gaunt cattle, would have straggled into the Valley.

They brought with them not only domestic tools and orna-
ments but also their technology and their knowledge of herding
and cropping. The arrival of these "environmental refugees" from
the Western Desert was a critical event in Egyptian history.

Until then the peoples of the Valley had been content to survive by gathering, hunting and fishing. The lush valley provided a
rich habitat for wild fauna and a diversity of plant resources
throughout the year; the river and marshes were teeming with fish.
Why tame the wild bull or till the soil when there was ample food
at one's doorstep?

The drought of six thousand years ago, however, also caused
dramatic and permanent changes in the flow of the Nile River. The
drought ushered in the extreme aridity we know today. The Nile
no longer flowed strongly all year round, but was marked by seasonal inundations followed by the slow draining away of the flood
waters. This jeopardized the comfortable lifestyle enjoyed by the
Nile Valley dwellers and coincided with the arrival of the Saharan
refugees and their cattle. Presumably, the combination of these two
factors compelled the people of the river to add herding and related
technologies to their traditional hunting and fishing strategies. It is
likely that at the same time peoples living in the Eastern Desert

and the Levant were also "dusted out" of their homelands and that some migrated into the Valley, bringing with them their sheep and goats, as well as their winter crops such as wheat and barley. The Nile Valley, in effect, became a melting pot of desert and riverine cultures. This convergence of cultures was the beginning of the Neolithic Revolution in the Valley, the event that eventually triggered the rise of the Egyptian civilization.

McDonald's discoveries have pegged Dakhleh as the centre for this cultural explosion. The reason artifacts from Dakhleh have more in common with the Nile Valley than those of any other site in the Western Desert now seems obvious. Dakhleh is both a natural crossroads in the Sahara Desert and the "everlasting oasis." The Bashendi continued to flourish there while other formerly occupied sites in the Western Desert were systematically abandoned. In times of stress, desert peoples sought refuge in Dakhleh, making it culturally richer than other sites.

Some of the desert refugees may have been the same people who congregated in Dakhleh for gift exchanges and celebrations. But Dakhleh's carrying capacity must have been exceeded during the worst of the drought. Some people would have stayed, but many probably used Dakhleh as a way station en route to the Nile. Some of the Bashendi themselves likely joined this great migration.

It is no longer necessary to invoke the century-old theory of a "dynastic race" being responsible for the growth of Egyptian civilization. The construction of a Neolithic village and monumental stone architecture; the domestication of cattle and the milling of grains; and, not least, the evolution of an artistic and probably religious tradition in Bashendi culture are all clear predecessors of later developments along the Nile.

No wonder Tony Mills characterizes the findings of Mary McDonald, his reticent and modest prehistorian, as "world-shaking." Even Mills' own views as a Pharaonic Egyptologist have been altered: "Work that Mary is doing will change people's ideas about the establishment of Egyptian Pharaonic civilization. Egyptologists have always felt that it came from the east, or it was autochthonous. There have been various theories, none of which included the Western Desert. It looks increasingly strongly that one of the major origins of Pharaonic civilization is out here in the Eastern Sahara. To us it has become a fact of life—it is up to us perhaps to broadcast this a little more strongly and widely."

McDonald, however, has found allies for her radical theory in other researchers working in the Western Desert. In the Farafra Oasis, north of Dakhleh, Barbara Barich of the University of Rome has found flint knives and other tools carved in a distinctive style that shows up later in the Nile Valley. Fred Wendorf and his colleagues uncovered what they dubbed "a Saharan Stonehenge" at Nabta Playa. Near this seasonal lake, 5000 to 6000 years ago, people erected a circle of six-by-nine-foot slabs, and dug two underground chambers, in one of which they ceremonially buried a long-horned bull. Wendorf suggests that the standing stones pointed north to "acknowledge the zenith Sun near the onset of the rainy season." Whatever its intent, such public architecture suggests a social hierarchy with someone at the top directing operations.

Farouk El-Baz, Director of the Center for Remote Sensing at Boston University and perhaps the world's foremost expert on the geology of the Western Desert, believes that the designs for both the pyramids and the Sphinx were imported from the Western Desert by nomads driven from the desert by the great drought. He suspects that ancient desert-dwellers studied them as models for monumental architecture. They would have seen that these shapes escaped destruction by leading the wind upslope, funnelling its erosive power toward the apex and dissipating it into the air. Thus conical hills, like the three between Kharga and Dakhleh (facetiously called the "Bashendi Ladies" by the prehistorians), inspired the pyramids, whose shape accounts for their longevity. El-Baz is also convinced that the Sphinx was carved from an existing *yardang*, which had been wind-eroded into a natural lion shape. Such "mud-lions" had been noted by early British geologists in the Western Desert, but, as El-Baz has observed, "the Egyptians of the past appear to have learned more about the desert than their modern counterparts."

EGYPTOLOGISTS' HEADS HAVE BEEN TURNED 180 DEGREES, from east to west, in their search for the origins of the great Nile Valley civilization. That the desert peoples, whom later pharaonic documents contemptuously refer to as "Crossers of the Sand," may have been, in the very act of crossing the desert, the catalyst for the rise of that extraordinary civilization seems increasingly certain. In light of these findings, perhaps we should revise Herodotus's oft-quoted observation, "Egypt is a gift of the Nile," to read, "Egypt is a gift of the Nile *and* of the desert."

CHAPTER SIX

CROSSERS OF THE SAND

AFTER THE ONSET OF FULL DESERT CONDITIONS IN THE SAHARA and the exodus of desert peoples to the Nile, some people clung to the oasis. The last traces of the Bashendi pastoralists disappeared around 5500 years ago. Their place in the archaeological record is taken by another culture of pastoralists whom McDonald has called the Sheikh Muftah, again naming them for a nearby village. Whether the last Bashendi chose to leave the oasis, or were replaced by or evolved into the new culture is impossible to know.

Over twenty-five years of wandering in the desert, McDonald has compiled a list of nearly a hundred Sheikh Muftah sites. The now salt-encrusted landscape the Sheikh Muftah inhabited imparts a feeling of desperation and doom, at least to the modern eye, an impression reinforced by the paucity of artifactual remains. "The Sheikh Muftah were very good housekeepers," quips McDonald,

---

Village headman, *omdah*, crosses the Gedida dunes

"so they haven't left a lot of stuff." Curiously, McDonald has found no built remains, perhaps because any structures were built in the oasis proper and have long since disappeared under cultivation. The most conspicuous sign of the Sheikh Muftah presence are ashy layers where they scooped out the earth to build a fire. Most sites seem like nothing more than temporary encampments.

McDonald is able to distinguish the Sheikh Muftah from their Bashendi predecessors based on unique tool types, including a winged arrowhead. Most telling is the type of raw material preferred by the Sheikh Muftah, a caramel-coloured tabular chert which was heat-treated, or tempered, to produce tools of a deep red wine colour. The material was exotic, and was almost certainly imported from the Kharga Oasis. McDonald also unearthed a number of copper rods, indicating that either the Sheikh Muftah knew how to work and smelt metal or had imported the finished items. She found fewer arrowheads than at Bashendi sites, indicating that hunting may have been less important to the Sheikh Muftah. Finally, pottery was more abundant and the Sheikh Muftah pots were generally bulkier than those fashioned by the Bashendi. To McDonald this meant that the Sheikh Muftah were more likely to stay in one place than the more nomadic Bashendi, for whom large pots were an impractical burden.

Wild animal remains also told McDonald a story. While she dug up the remains of large wild animals such as Cape buffalo, Grevy zebra and hartebeest, the most common species was Dorcas gazelle, an animal the size of a goat kid, particularly well-adapted to the drying climate. But, as Churcher discovered, domesticated animals outnumbered wild ones. Like the Bashendi, the Sheikh Muftah were keeping not only cattle but also goats.

Large fire pits found at a few sites indicate that the Sheikh Muftah occasionally enjoyed an open-air, Holocene barbecue. For the most part, however, the animal bones tell a story of hard times. It was Churcher who first noticed that the bones were broken into very small fragments. "You get this little pile of spillikins, and they tell you bugger all," Churcher complains, "except that someone was there breaking it up." After a community barbecue was over, and all that was left were clean bones, the Sheikh Muftah people apparently took a stone hammer and smashed the bones into pieces small enough to fit into a sturdy clay cooking pot. Setting it over the fire, they boiled the marrow soup to extract the last nutrients from the kill.

It seemed that, in the face of scarcity, the Sheikh Muftah were making every effort to maximize their resources. The cows that Churcher has identified are old animals, suggesting that they were used for milk, possibly blood, and as draft animals, and only killed when approaching the end of their lives. The goats were of all ages and probably kept by the Sheikh Muftah as ready sources of meat, milk and hides. Wild animals were becoming harder to find. They may have snared Dorcas gazelles and hares and hunted larger animals such as hartebeest. Churcher points out that still larger animals such as hippo and Cape zebra were available, but for some reason they do not seem to have been hunted.

The Sheikh Muftah undoubtedly supplemented their diet with plants. However, McDonald and Thanheiser have had little luck extracting and identifying the plant remains. So far, the few hearths found have not given them enough charcoal to determine what crops, wild or domesticated, the Sheikh Muftah were harvesting, and gypsum crystals in the soils have expanded and blown apart what few remains there were. But the presence of grinding stones and sickles indicates that the Sheikh Muftah were processing veg-etable foods of some kind. "They could be used on wild cereals, but I strongly suspect that they had agriculture," says McDonald. Massive stone scrapers and hoes, or celts, also suggest tilling of soil.

McDonald's most revealing insight came when she mapped the Sheikh Muftah sites and it became clear that they were clustered closer to the modern oasis, on the central lowland, whereas the Bashendi sites had been spread out, often on higher ground. While the Bashendi had been seasonal visitors, the Sheikh Muftah appeared to have clung to the oasis edges year round—"islanders" like the modern-day oasis dwellers, hemmed in by a hostile environment.

Presumably the Sheikh Muftah camped downslope of their predecessors to be nearer to diminishing water supplies and game. The desert was becoming ever more arid, so the people had to wait for the animals to come to them rather than risk forays into its waterless wastes. The monsoonal belt had withdrawn further south, but there was still enough rain to feed seasonal lakes. The rushes that rimmed them would have provided an excellent hiding place. Also, the Sheikh Muftah may have planted crops in the seasonally wet soils along the lake and led their cattle there to drink.

Today, these areas to the south of Dakhleh are marked by fields of salt that erupt from the desert floor in dirty waves like a fractured icefield. The brown-stained sheets of gypsum were formed as evaporates—salts—when the lake dried up. Snap off a piece and lick it, and there is little doubt of its briny nature. As the salts expanded, the crust cracked into plates that form "tepee" structures. Walk across this old lake bed, and the gypsum crust collapses underfoot like thin ice. Sheets of shallow water once lay here, and "the Sheikh Muftah folk," as McDonald calls them, appear to have liked to camp along the edge of these marshy areas.

Spring mounds emerge from these ancient lake beds like tiny volcanic islands, indicating that the shallow waters flowed from underground sources. By five thousand years ago, rainfall had decreased to nearly the level it is now (0.03 inches per year, though in many years it is zero) and such spring mounds dried up and the seasonal lakes with them, making the Sheikh Muftah's struggle for existence even more of a hand-to-mouth affair.

BACK IN 1987, I FOLLOWED MARY MCDONALD ON ONE OF her frequent scouting expeditions into the desert. As usual, she walked directly into the scorching sun and I did my best to keep pace. South of the village of Sheikh Muftah she directed me toward a scatter of flints flashing in the strong light. She pointed to fragments of ostrich eggshell, explaining that the vanished people probably sucked out the contents, then converted whole shells into water vessels and shell fragments into beads. Nearby were a few lumpy potsherds and a flat hand-sized piece of sandstone that McDonald identified as a grinding stone. And lying beside the simple artifacts in a mound of reddish clay was a human skeleton, curled in the fetal position.

"These guys are buried in permanent lake sediments," said McDonald. Yards away was a second skeleton. "It could have been an arm of a lake in the Neolithic—you tend to see water around everywhere."

Churcher had discovered this duo in 1982, in pink muds long since baked brick-hard under the desert sun. The two Neolithic individuals have proven indispensable in deciphering the elusive Sheikh Muftah, who were, and remain, the least understood of the three Neolithic cultures that occupied Dakhleh in succession. Neolithic human remains are extraordinarily rare in North Africa (most bones have long since weathered into dust) and this discovery has not only revealed what people looked like but how they were coping with the changing climate.

One individual, sex unknown, lay on his or her left side, the skull partially protruding from the earth as if the person were coming up for air. The second individual, a male, lay on his right side, the skull facing east. The vertebral column was clearly visible, and his legs were drawn up in the classic flexed burial position of the Neolithic period. There were no obvious grave goods, pots or tools, interred with them. However, someone had considered it important to give them what was, for the time, a proper burial. Though there were no provisions for the afterlife, as would become the custom in the Nile Valley, obviously someone had cared about these individuals.

The fossilized root casts of water plants surrounded the skeletons. There were spring mounds nearby, taller ones dating to Pleistocene times mixed in with smaller ones from the time of the Sheikh Muftah. The water that bubbled from them ran down a *wadi* in shallow sheets to form a seasonal lake. Burying them on its muddy shores must have been much easier than digging them out would prove, as the sediments, in drying, had assumed the consistency of cement. It would not be until 1998, sixteen years after their discovery, that these skeletal remains were finally freed from their five-thousand-year-old graves.

The rarity of these Neolithic skeletons demanded the specialized skills of a human paleontologist. In 1996 Jennifer Thompson, now at the University of Nevada, Las Vegas, joined the Dakhleh prehistory team at the behest of Maxine Kleindienst. Thompson was eminently qualified for the task, having worked on one of the most famous Neanderthal skeletons in the archaeological record. It had been excavated in 1908 at Le Moustier in France. Sold to the Germans in 1912, it was saved from the bombing of Berlin in the Second World War by being hidden with valuable art collections in underground bunkers. The skull was carted off by soldiers from occupying Russia, then returned to East Germany in the 1950s, where it remained packed until the 1960s. Finally, in 1989, when the Berlin Wall fell, the priceless specimen became available for study by Western scientists and Thompson took up the challenge. However, by 1996, after years cloistered in museums, she leapt at the opportunity to engage in fieldwork. The fact that Neolithic people were not well documented in North Africa was an added incentive to join the DOP.

Before Thompson could begin analyzing the skeletons, she had to somehow remove the two individuals from the recalcitrant soil of the lake deposits. "The earth didn't want to give up its dead," she wryly recalls. Instead of a trowel, she was forced to use a dental pick to extricate the fragile bones. Dropped at the remote location soon after sunrise, she had to wait until the sun warmed up the ground enough to allow her to begin excavating. Lying side by side with the ancient skeleton, it took her five frustrating days to dig out the brittle, salt-encrusted bones, some of which disintegrated at her lightest touch—"Only the birds and desert foxes heard my cursing." In the end she was able to salvage only the most important diagnostic portions: the skull, teeth and jaw. "Teeth always tell a story, so we're always anxious to get them," explains Thompson.

The male had very worn teeth, several caries, and a large abscess in the jaw. The wear and caries were typical of many prehistoric groups, caused by the coarseness of the diet and quite likely the liberal sprinkling of sand and grit in the food. The abscess, however, may have been the cause of his death, if the infection had leaked poisons into the bloodstream. Infected teeth were a frequent cause of death in prehistoric times. The other individual also exhibited anomalies in the teeth, with pits and lines scarring the tooth enamel, and overall opaqueness of the teeth. Both conditions occur when the teeth stop growing as a result of some stress. It was a common condition in prehistoric populations and may first develop when children are weaned and are exposed to poor drinking water or other infectious agents, or, denied mother's milk, simply suffer from poor nutrition. Both individuals' molars were also affected, indicating that they had undergone long-term stress, either from poor nutrition or disease, or both.

"I'm not quite sure what's happening," Thompson admits. "Whatever they're eating probably had sugar in it that promoted the bacteria." This high sugar level in the diet might have been a result of the domestication of date palms, which produce extremely sweet fruit, but a lack of botanical data leaves such a cause in the realm of speculation.

In 1996, while surveying with Thompson, Maxine Kleindienst spotted another bedraggled skeleton, several hundred yards from the first two burials. The wind had exposed it on the surface and erosion had reduced it to fragments. It, too, lay in a mound of pinkish lake sediments, but someone had protected it from erosion by capping the burial with sandstone boulders dragged from three hundred yards away. Kleindienst suspected that other skeletons might lie beneath the capstones and alerted Thompson, who began to dig carefully toward the centre of the mound, which sloped away on all sides over an area of twenty by thirty feet. The mound indeed hid two more skeletons. Had all five died at the same time, or was this a burial mound to which people returned to inter their dead? In any case, the Neolithic pallbearers had obviously expended considerable effort either to mark the burial site with the sandstone blocks, or at least to protect the dead from scavengers.

Like the first skeletons she examined, these three also showed signs of disease and, in Thompson's words, "a tough life." With one exception, they died between twenty and thirty years of age, itself an indication of stressors in the environment. One exhibited porotic hyperostosis, or "bubbly bone," in the eye orbits, a sign of anemia that can result from poor nutrition or disease. Thompson suspects malaria, which still occurred in the Kharga Oasis as recently as the 1940s. The swampy lakes around which the Sheikh Muftah camped could have been perfect breeding grounds for the malaria-carrying mosquito or other parasites.

If disease and poor nutrition did not kill you prematurely, then the lifestyle would eventually wear you down. The one long-lived person, a male who survived to be forty or thereabouts, was powerfully built, as indicated by the areas of muscle attachment on the skeleton. However, he had obviously suffered from the rigours of life in the oasis. He had compression fractures of his cervical vertebrae caused by repeated micro-trauma, possibly the cumulative effect of carrying heavy loads on his head. He also had arthritis in his shoulders and elbows, again likely due to his occupation. Lesions on his heel also suggested he had spent much of his time walking and running.

Two of the individuals, the forty-year-old male and a young female adult, who, Thompson determined, both had a broad face and a fairly broad nose, were buried side by side in an east-west orientation. "It's tempting to ask if they were related," she says. Perhaps they were father and daughter? Or, Thompson speculates, "The older male might have had the wherewithal to support a woman of child-bearing age." Eventually she hopes to submit the bones for DNA analysis, in an attempt to answer those questions but also to determine how closely the Sheikh Muftah are related to other populations in North Africa, or elsewhere. If the two individuals prove to be related, this may be a very early example of a family tomb.

By examining the flints and potsherds found near the skeletons, McDonald dated their death to between 5000 and 4000 years ago. It initially seemed that the Sheikh Muftah had not yet adopted the Egyptian practice of burying grave goods with their loved ones. However, as Thompson carefully excavated the forty-year-old male, picking away, bit by bit, at the stubborn matrix like a dental technician removing calculus, she saw a greenish stain in the soil underneath the man's pelvis. It was the oxidized remains of a copper pin. The fact that it was underneath convinced her that it had been buried with him. McDonald was elated by the find, since she knew that recently excavated burials in the Valley had shown that men from the Neolithic period often carried such copper pins in leather pouches strung at their waist. Finding a similar practice in the oasis (although the pouch had long since disappeared) suggested that people might have travelled from the oasis to the Valley and brought cultural ideas back with them.

Mills takes the view that because of Dakhleh's isolation, it is easy to spot when some cultural artifact is imported: "It sticks out a mile." Besides this copper pin, there are other concrete indications that such communication took place. Just as Bashendi pottery types showed up in the Valley, so Sheikh Muftah pottery has been found on the old roads leading to the Valley. As well, sherds of Predynastic pottery from the Nile Valley are sometimes mixed in with the local Sheikh Muftah pottery.

Sheikh Muftah pottery was handmade, either from a single lump of clay for small pots or coil-built for larger forms. DOP ceramicist Colin Hope has determined that they were fired in a "proto-kiln." The raw pots were placed on a smouldering bed of fuel, usually dung, and then more fuel was heaped over them, resulting in a slow-burning but intensely hot fire. This method produced firing colours varying from pale red to light brown to dark brown, frequently with grey inner surfaces. Most of the pottery took the form of bowls, but the Sheikh Muftah also produced a variety of small to mid-size jars, apparently for the storage of dry goods. Since the pottery was porous, it is likely that they stored liquids in animal skins.

Most of the Sheikh Muftah pottery is undecorated. Occasionally, however, the potter applied pressure with his or her fingers to make a "finger-track" or used fingernails to make a cross-hatch design on the rim top. A single large jar shows an impressed basketry design. Mostly, the pottery seems to be a local tradition, perhaps pointing to the isolation of the oasis, though it also appears that the Sheikh Muftah potters may have tried to copy the black-fired pottery being produced in the Valley by a Neolithic group called the Naqada I.

In the time of the Sheik Muftah, it was much drier than in Bashendi times, making the journey to the Valley by foot if not impossible, then fraught with danger. However, Churcher suspects that the Sheikh Muftah also had donkeys for the arduous undertaking. "The Sheikh Muftah," says McDonald, "were getting tabular flint from Kharga, which suggests that they had the ass to travel. And if they had that, it would make it at least possible to get back and forth to the Nile, though maybe not on a regular basis." The two Sheikh Muftah sites not clustered around the lake deposits are found on the Plateau along the Darb el-Tawil, an ancient route to the Nile Valley. These may have served as way stations.

THE CULTURE THAT THE SHEIKH MUFTAH WOULD HAVE encountered in the Valley bore little resemblance to their own. Since the arrival of the desert pastoralists, the Nile Valley had witnessed the development of a formidable and unrivalled culture, epitomized by the building of the great pyramids of Giza. How a simple Neolithic culture transformed itself in this way has long fascinated historians. In 1894, Sir Flinders Petrie, a self-educated, notoriously irascible Englishman, was the first archaeologist to discover the remains of the Predynastic Egyptian culture that spanned the thousand years of rapid development prior to the rise of the Egyptian nation-state. At Naqada, four hundred miles south of Cairo, he dug up 2100 graves which held a trove of goods: fired clay pots, palettes used for mixing pigments, and stone, bone and ivory amulets. Petrie used them to chronicle the succession of artistic styles and cultures. His system of sequence-dating earned him the sobriquet, "Father of Modern Archaeology," and has since been confirmed by radiocarbon methods.

Petrie's sequence demonstrates that the rise of the great riverine civilization did not occur overnight, as it were, but gradually, in a stepwise fashion. The Neolithic Revolution in the Valley began with a culture called the Badarians, probably a combination of Bashendi and other Western Desert peoples, perhaps mixed with Eastern influences. Six thousand years ago, between about 4000 B.C. and 3800 B.C., the Badarians practised industries—slate working, pottery manufacture, and the production of flint tools and weapons—that bear striking similarities to those found in Dakhleh. However, they still obtained most of their food by hunting and fishing in the marshes. But three hundred years later, the Amratians seem to have become true pastoralists, living in a string of small settled communities along the Nile, consisting of mud huts with grain storage bins and animal enclosures. By the Gerzean period, 3500 to 3200 B.C., rectangular mud-brick houses had replaced the humble Amratian huts. The Amratian and Gerzean peoples cultivated barley and wheat and raised sheep or goats, cattle and pigs; hunting had become by then only a marginal activity. They built sophisticated boats and had domesticated the ass by 3650 B.C.; both factors increased trade along the river highway.

During the late Holocene, the Nile floods varied in intensity, resulting in greater or lesser food production. To offset this, neighbouring communities began to pool their resources. Ultimately regional chiefs gained power by managing surpluses, their power being further enhanced by links to matriarchs who were thought to possess supernatural powers. Chiefs also consolidated their power base by the waging of war, against both outside invaders—Asiatics and Libyans—and neighbouring political regions. Fekri Hassan, of the Institute of Archaeology, University College, London, believes that the unification of Egypt was also stimulated by falling Nile levels at the end of the Predynastic period, which triggered competition and conflict between regions along the river, eventually resulting in unification.

There had always been a differentiation between Lower and Upper Egypt, but in 3100 B.C. the Scorpion King from Upper Egypt conquered the armies of the Delta in Lower Egypt. His successor, Narmer, completed the job and initiated the first Egyptian dynasty. Unification did not happen immediately, but more likely, proceeded over about 250 years. The first two dynasties lasted until 2700 B.C.

The golden age of Egyptian history was the Pyramid Age that began with the remarkable King Djoser and the Third Dynasty. It was during this time, known formally as the Old Kingdom, that the hallmarks of Egyptian civilization—writing, art and monumental architecture—were fully developed. Djoser and his famed architect, Imhotep, invented stone-built architecture by erecting the Step Pyramid at Saqqara, the prototype for the later smooth-sided pyramids of the Giza plateau—if Farouk El-Baz is correct, a design inspired by natural desert hills. The Pyramid Age was also marked by the production of magnificent statues and the exquisite reliefs in the Tombs of the Nobles at Saqqara, near the ancient capital of Memphis, all of which were executed not just for artistic but for religious reasons, much like the church paintings of medieval Europe. At the height of their power in the Fourth Dynasty, the pharaohs sent armies into Libya and Nubia, where they captured tens of thousands of prisoners. This was also a period of intensive activity at home. The pharaohs Cheops, Chephron and Mycernicus erected the Giza pyramids, monumental public works that were only possible under a centralized government system in which the king was the state.

While the Sheikh Muftah had contact with the Nile Valley, McDonald points out that there is little indication they participated in the growing prosperity and social complexity of Predynastic and early Pharaonic Egypt. History had not meted out its favours equally.

For all its accomplishments, no civilization was more tied to an ecological phenomenon—the annual innundation of the Nile—than that of the ancient Egyptians. By the end of the Predynastic period, they had already begun to build channels and dikes to control the floodwaters. These relatively simple measures, which enabled them to plant a second and sometimes a third crop, dramatically increased their ability to produce food. This stabilized the state, while at the same time fundamentally changing their relationship to the environment.

During the Old Kingdom, the Egyptians also established far-reaching trade links with Mesopotamian, Mediterranean and North African peoples. They were slow, however, to venture into the Western Desert. It seems odd that it was not until nearly two millennia after the desert pastoralists brought herding to the Nile Valley that the flow of people was reversed, but the reason is buried deep in the Egyptian psyche. Ancient Egyptians called the Nile Valley, with its fertile alluvial soils, Keme, the Black Land. The deserts that hemmed in their verdant corridor from either side, they called Doshre, the Red Land. "An important factor in the Egyptian character is a fear of the desert. This seems to have been true in ancient Egypt, and it seems to be, in some ways, still true," says Mills. "They don't like to go anywhere away from their river homeland. The Egyptians probably had a great reluctance to come to a place like Dakhleh."

To an ancient Egyptian, the valley and the desert were worlds brought into being separately by their gods and, therefore, meant to be kept that way. "The valley was home," writes Nick Millet in *Man in Nature*. "Only there could life be lived as it should be. His attitude to the desert . . . was essentially that it was foreign, and the word he used for it meant both 'hilly country' and 'foreign country.' Those who were doomed to live on it he referred to contemptuously as 'crossers of the sand.'"

The oasis dwellers seemed to have harboured no reciprocal prejudice. Since the time of the Bashendi, at least a few of them continued to make the perilous journey to the lush valley.

Individuals or small groups made the pilgrimage, off and on, over the next millennium, though, as the desert became progressively drier, the journey presented more formidable barriers to success.

Disaster no doubt marked some journeys. Though we have no record of the hardship these Neolithic travellers faced, even today, the old caravan routes are marked by the bleached bones and naturally mummified carcasses of unlucky animals—camels, cattle and donkeys—that did not survive the trek.

The standard mode of travel in ancient Egypt was walking. With nothing but a stick, loincloth and sandals, the traveller set out behind his donkeys, which were laden with his produce and vital water. To avoid dehydration, travel might be undertaken mostly at night. A trip from the oasis to the Valley might well have taken several days, stretching water supplies and fodder for the animals to the limit. Was the motivation trade, and if so, what produce did they pack on their donkeys and what goods did they return with? Perhaps they took their poor country produce of mats, plants, poultry and staves to the Valley. On the return haul, they might have brought pots and copper, or at least the knowledge of new and more sophisticated pottery traditions and of metallurgy.

The Sheikh Muftah travellers must have experienced profound joy at seeing their native oasis rise, green and shining, at the end of the long desert trek. Glad to be reunited with friends and family, they must also have seen the oasis with new eyes. Compared to the far greater oasis of the lush Valley, their own oasis may have seemed small and backward. When they told tales of people living in mud-brick houses and worshipping in grand temples, and of man-made mountains serving as burial places for the Valley's divine kings, their listeners may well have laughed or turned away in disbelief.

NEAR THE END OF THE OLD KINGDOM, AT LAST, THE FLOW OF people was reversed, and the two tributaries of ancient Egyptian culture—the desert and the Valley—were joined permanently.

The ancient Egyptians had already subjugated the Nubians to the south. They had also launched conquering forces to the east to subdue Syria and Palestine. A commanding officer named Weni has left us a vivid picture of an occupying force of "tens of thousands in the Levant," couched in the highly formal but bellicose language of the pharaohs: "His majesty sent me at the head of this army, there being counts, royal seal-bearers, sole companions of the palace, chieftains and mayors of the towns of Upper and Lower Egypt, from the villages and towns that they governed and from the Nubians of these foreign lands. I was the one who commanded them . . . This army has returned in safety; it has flattened the Sand-dwellers' land of the Syro-Palestinian region."

Given this expansionist policy, it was only a matter of time before the Egyptians extended their imperial ambitions westward. Around 2200 B.C. they finally made a move to occupy Dakhleh. There is no record of what form the occupying force took, but it seems unlikely that they would have required a force the size of Weni's army. Desert expeditions of the day, however, were sometimes a spectacle in themselves, consisting of three hundred or more pack donkeys, accompanied by kilted soldiers carrying shields and wielding knives, perhaps with a royal seal-bearer at the head. Certainly it would have been a sufficient show of force to cow the oasis dwellers and at the same time impress them with a show of royal pomp and ceremony.

Inevitably the two cultures clashed, though how that clash played out in Dakhleh is not fully understood. They also intermingled. Old Kingdom and Sheikh Muftah pottery has been found together, and the Old Kingdom people used the same tabular chert for their tool-making as the Sheikh Muftah. Either the Sheikh

Muftah were trading tools with the Egyptians or they were teaching them how best to use this local material. Rufus Churcher has suggested an interesting analogy to illustrate the relationship between the imperial newcomers and the indigenous peoples: the Hudson's Bay Company's relationships with native peoples in Canada, which was the basis of the great fur-trading empire and the key to opening up the North American continent to Europeans. While there was an exchange of goods, services and even technologies between the two groups, this in no way implies equity.

"The Sheikh Muftah would have had a simpler society. I hesitate to use the word 'primitive,' but they were obviously at a different socio-economic level," observes McDonald. Certainly, the Old Kingdom Egyptians would have seen themselves as superior to the local population and exercised their power, either by force or by more peaceful persuasion.

THE ARRIVAL OF THE OLD KINGDOMITES WITH THEIR SIMPLE yet more sophisticated irrigation technology, their ability to erect monumental architecture, and, not least, to produce more food than was needed for mere subsistence, fundamentally upset the precarious balance that had existed throughout the Holocene between human activity and the oasis ecology. The ancient Egyptians introduced new crops and weeds, as well as domestic animals. And they began to build large-scale buildings and settlements where before there had been nothing but trees and free-flowing springs, perhaps surrounded by modest huts. Essentially, they used their overwhelming technological superiority to introduce a well-organized, urbanized society into a subsistence economy.

With the arrival of the Old Kingdom, the prehistoric period in Dakhleh comes to an abrupt end. The story that we have been tracing, of the often heroic adaptations of humans to the changing environment of the Sahara over 400,000 years, is about to take a decisive turn. No longer will the people of the oasis passively take advantage of the gift of naturally occurring springs. For the next four thousand years, they will alter the environment for short-term goals, believing that they can control and exploit the life-giving waters of the oasis with no thought for the future. Their practices will permanently alter Dakhleh, transforming it from a naturally functioning ecosystem into a human-made desert island.

PART FOUR

LORDS OF THE WEST

C.2700–332 B.C.

Pharaonic sarcophagous mask *(John O'Carroll)*

CHAPTER SEVEN

LORDS OF THE WEST

In January 1947, a severe sandstorm swept off the Libyan Plateau. It raged for days, darkening the skies with heavy brown clouds. After the dust had settled, local residents noticed that the tops of massive ruins had emerged from their desert grave at a place they called Ain Aseel (Aseel Spring), near Balat at the eastern end of the oasis. The ruins had lain undetected for centuries. This desert dance, of veils of sand lifting and falling, covering and uncovering ruins, caused little excitement among the local residents, who considered this layering of time commonplace. After all, they lived among ruins and had names for such lost cities: Ismant el-Kharab (Ismant-the-Ruined) and Mut el-Kharab. Roman Age temples were everyday landmarks, their wind-eroded, red mud-brick facades visible for miles. The wind-resurrected ruins at Ain Aseel would, however, create a storm of their own in archaeological circles.

A view of the Southeast Basin from a Pharaonic watch post

It is not surprising that it was Ahmed Fakhry, the founder of the Desert Researches Section of the Egyptian Antiquities Service, who, hearing rumours of an ancient city's sudden appearance in Dakhleh, was the first archaeologist to take a look at the newly exposed ruins. Alone among Egyptologists, he had long taken a special interest in the oases, having made a first trip to Kharga and Dakhleh by camel in 1937 and developed what he described as "a mutual love . . . between me and the antiquities of the desert and its people." Fakhry took a cursory look at the city ruins in 1947, but it was not until 1969 that he was able to explore further. When he did, he discovered not only the ruins exposed by the wind storm, but four imposing *mastaba* tombs arranged in a north-south line along a low ridge at an adjacent site called Kila' el-Debba, one mile west of Ain Aseel. In 1970, he began to clear the sand from mud-brick facades of the tombs. Large stone slabs framed the doorways and lined and paved the corridors. Some bore inscriptions, from which Fakhry was able to identify three of the four people buried there. All three had served as Governors of the Oasis, which explained their ostentatious burials.

Fakhry returned again in 1971 and this time explored the conspicuous mound of ruins at Ain Aseel, an exploration that would enhance his reputation for digging in the right places. There was abundant pottery scattered about, as well as some inscribed stone blocks he thought might be associated with an ancient temple. Both were promising signs that something of significance lay not far underground. Fakhry dug a *sondage*, or deep test trench, into the heart of the site and soon realized he was probing an urban complex of impressive size and richness, probably associated with the massive mastabas. In 1972 he wrote a paper that was to set the Egyptological world on its ear. He boldly declared that Ain Aseel was the Old Kingdom capital of Dakhleh—an observation that has since been borne out by the extensive excavations of the French Institute of Oriental Archaeology.

Fakhry's discovery required a complete reassessment of the extent of Old Kingdom activities in the desert. The presence of a large urban complex in the Western Desert overturned the long-held belief that administrative centres in the Old Kingdom were confined to the Valley and Delta. It fundamentally changed Egyptologists' view of the ability of the Egyptian state to expand and adapt its Valley civilization at such an early stage in its history.

Fakhry was fired with enthusiasm. He believed that the mastaba cemetery and nearby city site would reveal a whole new facet of Old Kingdom Egypt. Then 66, he knew, however, that he would have to find someone to share his enthusiasm, since excavation would take several years (a wildly conservative estimate as it turned out). As we have seen, Fakhry's fervent lecture to the Society for the Study of Egyptian Antiquities eventually led to the Dakhleh Oasis Project. Fakhry also carried his message to Paris, where, several months later, he died on June 7, 1973. There, too, he made converts, and in 1977 the French Institute of Oriental Archaeology began digging at Kila' el-Debba and Ain Aseel. That same year Mills and Freeman arrived on the scene, only to discover that they had been beaten to the punch. The French have been there ever since, exposing and restoring the mastabas and excavating the city complex.

AIN ASEEL IS A FIFTEEN-MINUTE HIKE ACROSS THE DUNES FROM Bashendi. The desert floor, where the winds have whisked the sand away, is richly peppered with flints and potsherds, signs of the Old Kingdom settlement—home to the farmers and artisans—yet to be excavated by the French despite the quarter century of digging that has already taken place.

By comparison to Mills' Old Kingdom site, the French dig is on a massive scale, involving scores of local workers. A small trolley line running parallel to the site has carried away tons of earth over the last twenty-five years.

In 2000, I was met by George Soukiassian, a man of Old World civility who has been digging at Ain Aseel for two decades. "Here we can see only a small part of the settlement," he explained. "Most of the people living here were related to the administration, others were living like now. So we get a picture of the centralized administration at Ain Aseel and a lot of the small villages under its control." The French approach is historical, concentrating efforts on the architecture and documentary evidence, including many official letters, while, he argues, the "English" approach is "more anthropological-minded," focusing on the social life and environment. "They are complementary," he added, a view that Mills shares.

Ain Aseel's walls are preserved to a height of four feet or more and are constructed of the local red mud brick, in stark contrast to the golden desert sands that engulfed it. From the desert floor I looked *down* into the city ruins: at first glance a perplexing complex of rooms and structures, including, Soukiassian told me, four chapels and two ancient palaces (only one has been excavated) used by a succession of Governors of the Oasis. It is the best-preserved Old Kingdom settlement in Egypt and one of only two to be excavated, the other being at Elephantine, near Aswan.

What the French archaeologists have revealed is a three-stage development of the capital city. The original settlement was a fortified garrison, surrounded by a twenty-three-foot-high wall, with imposing circular watchtowers at the corners, as well as at the city gates to the north and south. Whatever danger they had anticipated apparently did not materialize, for the Egyptians soon expanded the city outside this fortified precinct. The Governor's Palace was built to the south of the original garrison and was left unfortified. In a third stage, the city spread south of the palace.

The Governor's Palace, befitting the station of its occupant as master of this isolated desert world, was an ostentatious structure. The complex covers some seventeen acres and includes not only the Governor's residence but also funerary chapels associated with his cult and the residences and work rooms of the battery of servants who would have attended to this desert ruler's every need. "The general picture is not people just surviving in the desert," Soukiassian said of the Old Kingdomites. "They lived well and enjoyed a high standard of living."

Two decades of excavation have exposed much of this once-grand residential complex, presenting a unique opportunity to see how the privileged lived at this early stage of Egyptian civilization. There is no comparable structure in the Nile Valley, where most Old Kingdom domestic architecture has been lost.

Though the roof line of the buildings has been stripped away by the wind, I could still sense the formal grandeur intended by the architects. On the way to the palace, Soukiassian led me along a small street flanked on either side by a series of magazines that once had vaulted roofs and were used as storerooms for grain and other necessities of the priesthood. The entrance to the palace proper was a corridor, lined with twelve-foot-high columns that once supported a flat-topped roof, that opened into a large court-yard containing a small chapel. Off the courtyard was a reception area that would have bustled with officials of the administration. It was here that the business of the oasis was conducted, visitors and their tribute to the Governor were received, and orders dis-patched. Soukiassian and his colleagues found many small memos and dispatches here. Strangely, they were written on clay tablets, as was the custom in the Middle East rather than on papyrus or potsherds (ostraca) as in the Nile Valley. Perhaps, however, clay tablet letters have not been preserved, or simply not yet found, in the Valley, where so few Old Kingdom settlements have survived the ravages of the river and modern development, and even fewer have been excavated. Many clay stamps were also found strewn about. It was common practice to place a stamp on parcels or boxes, or on a door once it was closed, so that if it was broken guards would be alerted to the breach of security.

I followed Soukiassian beyond the reception area, where inner corridors led into the living area, which once was surrounded by wooden columns set on a stone base. Overall, the architecture was intended to reflect spaciousness. Another courtyard served as an anteroom to the bedroom, which was sixteen feet wide, the widest span possible for a flat-roofed room. It was supplied with fireplaces to ward off the desert chill, which was not a problem that day as the unobstructed sun beat down. Remains of the columns that supported the canopy over the bed were still visible. A small side room served as an Old Kingdom version of the ensuite.

We circled back toward the south side of the dig, where local workers were excavating an arch at the entrance to a funerary chapel. The sandstone arch was scored with a long list of inscriptions. Running his fingers over the incised hieroglyphics, Soukiassian translated the ancient honorifics: "Governor of the Oasis . . . The Director of the Priests . . . The One Favoured by the King . . ." No fewer than four small funerary chapels, constructed during the lifetime of the governors, were associated with the palace complex. Although such chapels are mentioned in Old Kingdom texts, the only place intact examples have been found in Egypt is in the oasis. Again, this is largely because Dakhleh's isolation made it less vulnerable to destruction. The statues found in the palace and tombs, including one of a governor, were of very high quality, indicating that the oasis was prosperous enough to hire top-notch artists from the Valley. Grave goods such as alabaster vases also tell us that these were not deprived people exiled to the desert, but more like desert kings who enjoyed a high standard of living.

The governors were duly honoured in death. The massive mud-brick mastabas Fakhry discovered are excellent examples of early Egyptian monumental architecture. The earliest mastaba-style royal tombs date to the First Dynasty, and examples are found both at Saqqara, near the Old Kingdom capital of Memphis, and at Abydos, which was the traditional sacred burial place of the early kings of a unified Egypt. *Mastaba* is the Arabic word for "bench," which is what these ancient tombs looked like to modern Egyptians. Such small mud-brick benches project from the foundations of traditional dwellings throughout Egypt. They form a convenient and comfortable place to sit and watch the world go by or to perform domestic tasks out of doors. Daily in Bashendi, women sit on their mastabas preparing vegetables or winnowing rice, and men sit with their backs to the walls, smoking cigarettes or water pipes as they carry on heated discussions.

In fact, mastaba tombs bear only a faint resemblance to benches: the superstructure is rectangular and flat-topped with slightly sloping sides. Around 2700 B.C., the mastaba-style tomb was elaborated by Pharaoh Djoser and his esteemed architect Imhotep to produce the prototypical Step Pyramid at Saqqara, essentially a series of six mastabas, each smaller, stacked on top of one another. This concept would be further modified to produce the smooth-sided pyramids of Giza, which symbolically imitated the rays of the sun, and the sun god Ra, and served as a stairway to heaven for the king.

The sides of the mastaba were finished with mud brick and often decorated with pilasters and niches to give the impression of a palace facade. But the actual house for the dead was below ground and in many details imitated the earthly domain of the deceased. The body—which early in the Old Kingdom was merely wrapped in linen, not mummified—was placed in the bedroom. Pots containing food offerings were placed around the body as a funerary feast. This "House of Eternity" had surrounding rooms that were filled with other goods the dead person would need in the afterlife: garments, jewellery, weapons, furniture, drink, grain for grinding if his bread supply should run out, and nodules of flint for fashioning new tools should the old ones become blunt. Stone tablets called *stelae* were placed in niches; they contained the name and titles of the deceased. Often the burial chamber was more than a full storey underground; it was reached by a long central shaft that was filled with rubble and sealed with a large slab immediately after burial, in an attempt to frustrate grave robbers—a ploy that with few exceptions proved in vain.

After recording the dimensions and features of one of the superstructures at Kila' el-Debba, the French had to remove it to avoid the collapse of the badly cracked, brittle clay. A series of stairs and ramps then led them four storeys underground. At the bottom, they found the crushed burial of one of the Governors. It seems the underground structure had collapsed in antiquity, frustrating any attempts at grave robbing.

The French excavations demonstrated that Dakhleh in the Old Kingdom was much more than a provincial outpost. The presence there of high-ranking officials of the central Egyptian government suggests a degree of planning and purpose on the part of the Pharaoh. The Valley obviously felt it had a major stake in the oasis, for economic, political or cultural reasons.

All this investment led Mills and his colleagues to ask why the Old Kingdom Egyptians had come to Dakhleh in the first place. Was it for some resource found in the oasis itself, or was Dakhleh merely an entrepot?

Part of the answer surfaced in recent years when members of the DOP began finding crude, horseshoe-shaped stone structures on hilltops to the east and south of the oasis. The huts were oriented with an entrance to the southeast; to the northwest, their builders had stood large slabs on end to make a higher wall, presumably as protection against the prevailing winds. Maxine Kleindienst, who found the first one, might have mistaken them for Neolithic huts except for the abundant graffiti. The images were clearly of a different type than those found in the Rock Art Basin. In the 1930s, Hans Winkler had first described one of these enigmatic stone structures in Dakhleh and, based on the drawings its occupants had left behind, identified it as Old Kingdom in origin. In particular, he noted the "foot graffiti," a tracing of a foot or sandal that Old Kingdom people sometimes used as a personal signature. Besides these tracings, there were many depictions of human vulvae incised into the stone, some with holes graphically drilled into the apex of these pubic triangles. This made Winkler suspect that the rock artists were men "far from women." Not only were they removed from women's company, obviously they had been for long enough to begin fantasizing about their wives and girlfriends back home. Winkler concluded that they were stationed at a "watch post" of some kind.

Dutch-born Olaf Kaper, the DOP's epigrapher, has taken on the task of studying these curious inscriptions. An energetic man fluent in the three European languages—English, French and German—most commonly used in the Bashendi camp, Kaper originally joined the DOP in 1988 to translate the hieroglyphics of Roman Age temples. He has gladly added the watch post inscriptions to his duties and, when he took me to see them, he spoke about them with the same passion that he has for the more formal language of the temples.

The watch posts are located east of the present-day military check-post at Teneida, guarding the eastern entrance point to the oasis. Egypt declared the Western Desert a militarized zone in the 1970s, in the wake of the Seven Days' War with Israel and the sabre-rattling of Libya's Colonel Gadhafi. Young soldiers, dressed in frayed wool fatigues and wielding machine guns, still keep watch over oasis security, presumably against incursions from Libya. They dutifully checked Kaper's military pass and familiar face before waving us through the oil-barrel barriers. I could not help but think how little things have changed in four thousand years: Egyptian soldiers are still keeping watch over the oasis.

Hundreds of wind-carved *yardangs*, many eroded at the base so that they resemble vases poised on pedestals, preside over the Southeast Basin. This region has the look and feel of the badlands of the American southwest, with sandy corridors weaving in and out through groups of *yardangs*, and would make an ideal setting for a Hollywood western.

We stopped in a narrow valley and Kaper led me to a crude structure consisting of nothing more than some flat stones stood on end to form a windbreak. Further up the hill we found a second watch post capping this natural lookout, which afforded an unobstructed view of the eastern end of the oasis. The DOP agrees with Winkler's interpretation that they are Old Kingdom watch posts. "You can oversee this entire basin," Kaper said with a sweep of his arm. The green of the oasis, several miles distant, and the vague outlines of Bashendi and Balat, were indeed visible on the horizon. In Kaper's opinion, soldiers stationed at Ain Aseel could easily have lit fires in the fort towers to stay in communication with their comrades at the watch posts.

Climbing down, we drove on until we came to a large *yardang* about three storeys high that Kaper has dubbed "Nephthy Hill," for a graffito that bears a resemblance to the hieroglyphic symbol for that goddess. She acted, along with her sister-goddess Isis, as a protectress of the dead; she was associated with death and corruption, while her sister symbolized birth and growth. Difficult to define, she has been described as "the goddess of death which is not eternal." The symbol that Nepthys wore on her head [𓉠] looks like a bowl balanced on a stand and was found on a stone lying beside the watch post. This is one of the richest sites in the oasis for Old Kingdom graffiti. There are at least twenty-five petroglyphs carved into the hillside, including stock images of horned animals, birds, sandals and pubic triangles. One of the last is accompanied by the hieroglyph for love—a hoe—indicating the soldier may have been literate as well as lonely. On the side of the hill just above a narrow traverse is the most artfully executed of these images: a lion with a sun disc on its head. The proportions are so accurately rendered that there is no doubt the artist had seen his subject, either in the Valley or the oasis.

The most telling image is what appears to be a self-portrait of a soldier: a full-length depiction of a standing male wearing a triangular kilt, the common male garb of Old Kingdom Egypt. With a few deft strokes, the artist has sketched in hair and a mouth, and what appears to be a small beard. The chest is crossed by two bands and the figure wears a feather on his head, which is typical of soldiers' regalia. In his left hand, the man holds a lotus flower by its long stem. The lotus was a symbol for tranquility in Valley art, so may suggest a certain nostalgia on the soldier's part. Behind him is his equipment: a leather wrist-guard and a bow with five arrows, one of which is placed in the bow. Also, there is a hieroglyph identical to one found at Ain Aseel connoting "soldier."

Nephthys Hill has three watch posts on top. In all, the team has discovered fifteen such watch posts, including three in the south, which Kaper believes were all part of "an enormous defensive network going through the desert." Mills offers this analogy: the watch posts formed a kind of Distant Early Warning system, or DEW line, such as stretched across northern Canada during the Cold War. These ones were located, it seems, to guard the eastern entrance to the oasis, where the Darb el-Gubari and the Wadi el-Battikh meet. There may well be others farther east along the road to Kharga that remain undiscovered.

Kaper led me inside the hut on the highest peak to show me a further clue to the operation of these watch posts: a series of short, perpendicular lines scratched into the rock face. Such lines are common to most of the watch posts and seem to be some sort of tally system, as every tenth line is longer. What were they counting? The most likely answer is days, as the Egyptian week was ten days long. It would appear that some of the soldiers were on a two-week (twenty-day) tour of duty in these lonely and spartan outposts and were counting down the days until they could return to civilization in the oasis, to their womenfolk and their families. A hieroglyph for ten found on the watch post rocks also appears on clay tablets in Ain Aseel, where there are official records of provisioning water to soldiers. It seems that the soldiers were also provisioned with food because, with the exception of breadmaking moulds, there is no evidence of cooking and very little in the way of food remains. Gazelle hides found at one site seem to have been tanned and sewn into clothing while the soldiers endured their isolation.

Watch post duty can hardly have been pleasant; it may have felt more like imprisonment than duty. The circle of upright stones would have provided only minimal protection. In spring when the *khamsin,* or Fifty Days' Wind, blew, the sand must have been torture to the eyes and skin. At night in winter the temperatures dropped to freezing, and in summer, the relentless heat, soaring to nearly 120°F, beat down on them, unprotected by roof or cloud. To the north stretched the implacable whiteness of the Plateau and all around was lifeless desert. No wonder these men resorted to scratching graffiti on the stones, to ease the boredom—perhaps to preserve their sanity.

The question remains: what were they watching for? The concentration of sites in the Southeast Basin coincides with the largest number of living sites belonging to the Sheikh Muftah. Perhaps they were keeping a suspicious eye on these native oasis dwellers.

However, Sheikh Muftah pottery also occurs at the watch posts, suggesting some peaceable exchange between the two groups. If they were not guarding against a hostile indigenous population, then what was their purpose?

Kaper believes the watch posts may have been set up prior to the earliest days of permanent Old Kingdom settlement in Dakhleh. If so, they probably date to the late Fifth Dynasty, a period of Egyptian expansion, northwards and southwards, outside the Valley. There were maritime trading expeditions to Byblos, now Lebanon, probably for cedar wood, as well as to the Land of Punt (either southern Sudan or the Eritrean region of Ethiopia) on the Red Sea. Moreover, there is strong evidence the Egyptians had established a permanent presence in Nubia at least during the Fourth Dynasty. Given these precedents, Mills and Kaper felt it reasonable to believe that the pharaohs had sponsored exploratory expeditions to the Western Desert at the same time. The discovery by the French that there were eight separate Governors of the Oasis during the life of Ain Aseel also supports Kaper's time frame that encompasses the late Fifth Dynasty.

We know from written records that the Egyptians were active in the Western Desert by the time of the Sixth Dynasty, the last period of the Old Kingdom, which was dominated by two long-lived kings, Pepy I and Pepy II. Pepy I ruled for fifty years, surviving a conspiracy by his wife to overthrow him. During his long reign he maintained strong control of Upper Egypt, as well as Nubia, where he operated stone quarries. Pepy I was succeeded by two of his sons, first by Merenre, who continued his father's policy of expansion into the Nubian heartland, which was, among other things, a source of copper as well as exotic foodstuffs and luxury items for the royal court. Merenre died after a reign of only nine years and was succeeded by his half-brother Pepy II.

The oases served as stepping stones through the desert sea of sand and desolation. The famous *Darb el-Arbain* ("Forty Days'

Road") struck south from Kharga to Selima Oasis, then continued on to central Africa. Several desert routes radiated like spokes of a wheel from Dakhleh: from here a caravan or invading army could march north to Farafra and thence to Siwa; southwest to the Gilf Kebir and the Kufra Oasis in Libya; or south via Bir Tarfawi to the Land of Yam, that is, ancient Nubia.

One of the heroes of the extra-territorial forays undertaken during the reign of Merenre was Harkhuf, the governor of Aswan, whose tomb records his excursions into the Land of Yam. Once he travelled by the "Elephantine route," a trail that closely parallels the Nile. Such expeditions were undertaken on foot, accompanied by pack donkeys, and took months—Harkhuf's first expedition took seven months. His third journey was by way of "the Oasis road." Egyptologists have debated whether he passed through Kharga or Dakhleh. Kaper favours the latter for two reasons: Harkhuf left from Abydos, from where the modern route leads to Ain Aseel; and there is very little evidence of Old Kingdom material in Kharga. It was more arduous than the Elephantine route, but presumably was chosen as an end run to avoid conflict with Nubians along the river. When he reached Yam, however, Harkhuf found its chiefs already at war with the Libyan Tjemeh. The clever Harkhuf fell in behind the forces from Yam, followed them westward, and eventually overwhelmed them—depriving the Nubian army of its hard-won booty. On his return, the tribal chiefs of the Nubian border were so impressed with his retinue that they offered him guides and cattle, rather than attempting to plunder the convoy. "I came down with three hundred donkeys laden with incense, ebony, *hknw*-oil, *sat*-grain, panther skins, elephant tusks, throw sticks and all sorts of good products," he tells us proudly.

Harkhuf's expeditions continued into the reign of Merenre's successor, Pepy II. On one of the great explorer's forays into Yam, Harkhuf sent word to the young pharaoh—Pepy II was then a mere boy of ten years—that he was bringing with him a dancing dwarf, or "pygmy," anticipating the boy's pleasure at such a prospect. Pepy II's reply reveals the heart of youth and is a refreshing insight into the individual sentiment of a pharaoh, which is so often clouded with rote royal rhetoric:

> Come north to court at once, and bring with you the pygmy
> which you have brought living, in good condition and healthy,
> from the land of the horizon dwellers, for the amusement of
> the king, to rejoice and gladden his heart. When the pygmy is
> in the vessel, appoint trustworthy people to be on either side
> of him. Take care that he does not fall in the water. When he
> is sleeping at night, appoint trustworthy people to sleep
> beside him in his cabin, and make an inspection ten times a
> night. My Majesty desires to see this pygmy more than the
> gifts of Sinai and Punt.

Harkhuf's record should have alerted Egyptologists to the importance of the oases long before Fakhry's discovery of the capital at Ain Aseel. As Nicolas Grimal, a former director of the French dig at Ain Aseel, has since pointed out, the conquest of Nubia could only have been achieved through the control of the caravan trails, which implies domination of the oases.

There are only two ways into the Dakhleh oasis from the direction of the Valley. The old caravan road, the *Darb el-Tawil,* formed a direct route from the Valley to Ain Aseel. It is little used today, except by the archaeologists and local travellers. Those who follow this ancient caravan road see the skulls of camels baking in the sun as well as pottery shards spanning four thousand years. They also see graffiti scratched into the sandstone depicting Pharaonic boats. Strange as it may seem to find imagery of boats in the desert, the image probably relates to one of the titles of the Governors of the

Oasis, "Captain of the Ship's/Marines' Brigade." One such may have led the expeditionary force along this "cauldron road." A grassy basin known as *Halfat el-Bir* probably served as a convenient stopping place before starting the steep climb up to the Plateau. There are Old Kingdom potsherds scattered near some stone circular structures that are similar to structures in the Southeast Basin. The ridge provides a commanding look-out over both the pass through the Plateau and Ain Aseel, and so may have functioned like the watch posts in the Southeast Basin that presumably guarded this second access point to the Nile Valley along the *Darb el-Gubari*, now paved for day-to-day traffic.

Among the inscriptions Soukiassian had shown me on the stone lintel and jamb of the funerary chapel was one that hailed the Governor as "The Chief for Caravans and Expeditions," further supporting the theory that Dakhleh served as a hub for desert travel in the Old Kingdom. Recently, however, this anecdotal theory has been bolstered by hard evidence.

Today, archaeological exploration of the Western Desert is being spearheaded by the Heinrich Barth Institute, under the direction of Rudolph Kuper. Heinrich Barth was one of the great explorers of the African continent. In 1850 he set out from Tripoli with the explorer James Richardson on a British-sponsored expedition to central West Africa. Richardson died a year later, in northern Nigeria. A year after that, Barth's other colleague, the geologist and astronomer Adolf Overweg, also perished. Despite his own ill health and the loss of his expedition partners, Barth continued on to the famed city of Timbuktu in Mali. On his return to Europe, he produced a four-volume, 3000-page record of his findings, *Travels and Discoveries in North and Central Africa in the Years 1849–1855*. This classic tome, rich in anthropological, linguistic and geographical information, laid the foundations for interdisciplinary research in Africa, in particular, the study of the effect of the environment on human history.

It is this legacy that Kuper and his colleagues are carrying forward, under the umbrella of a fifteen-year study generously financed by the German Research Council. Kuper's dig house is located in Dakhleh, which in the tradition of desert explorers before him he uses as a convenient base for trips into the desert. It looks like a small palace with its domed, vernacular architecture, set among acacias and palms on the outskirts of Balat, a tiny oasis within an oasis.

Kuper is following in the footsteps not only of Barth but of a long line of nineteenth- and early twentieth-century European desert explorers, including his countryman Gerhard Rohlfs, who in early 1874 made the first attempt to cross the Great Sand Sea west of Dakhleh. Kuper seems to share the wanderlust and yen for adventure of this earlier generation of travellers. A vigorous, gregarious man with a grizzled close-cropped beard, he explained to me that he spends as little time as possible at Dakhleh, preferring the freedom of the desert. His long forays are also part of his mandate, as his group holds the concession to the entire Western Desert of Egypt, excepting the oases.

Like the DOP, Kuper's group is tracking climatic changes in the Sahara and human adaptations to the changing ecology, for good and ill. Life outside the oases necessarily depends upon finding water sources, which have been in short supply in the last 5000 years. Since the arrival of the Old Kingdom Egyptians coincided with the final drying up of the Sahara, where did they get their water if they were exploring beyond Dakhleh?

All of the early desert explorers recognized that there had to be some sort of water supply across this vast tract of desert, a well perhaps, or even a "lost oasis." Dr. John Ball, Director of the Desert Surveys, provided a partial answer when, on motor patrol during the First World War, he made a remarkable discovery about one hundred twenty miles south of Dakhleh. At the base of one of the thousands of hills that rise up from the barren plain, he found a huge cache of ancient pots, many the same shape as jars still used in the oasis, suggesting they had come from Dakhleh. This site was explored more thoroughly in 1923 by Prince Kemal el Din, who named the place *Abu Ballas*: "Father of Jars." In all, the prince unearthed about three hundred jars buried at the base of the hill.

Old residents of Dakhleh told Bell that a similar cache had been discovered in the middle of the nineteenth century when a party of Dakhleh people had repelled an attack of raiders and then followed them into the desert. There they found a deposit of water jars and smashed them to thwart future invasions from the south.

"Let me show you something," said Kuper, leading me to a room off the courtyard of his dig house. The lock made a hollow click as he opened the door into a darkened room, empty but for a huge collection of large, bulbous earthen pots. Each would have held several gallons of water, though many now have been eroded to paper-thinness by the wind, or in some cases have had holes sandblasted through them. These were not from Abu Ballas—most of those pots have long since been destroyed or carried off—but from a site further south recently discovered by Kuper. "All sites are endangered by tourists," Kuper worried. "All the off-road people who come here destroy sites. If a tourist finds this, he will easily take it." He was particularly concerned about the Paris-to-Darfur bike race that had recently roared through Dakhleh and along the now-paved desert road leading south to Uwenait. When we returned to the courtyard, he unrolled a large map of the Western Desert on the coffee table. "Here is Dakhleh," he said, pointing and running his finger south across the desert. This was the sector that the British Geographical Society characterized a century ago as "a humiliating blank" on the map of Africa. "There is Abu Ballas, and there are the valleys in the Gilf Kebir discovered by Almasy, and there is Kufra—130, 130, and 120 miles.

So these could well be way stations along the way." What Kuper had discovered was an ancient route across the desert. Caches were spread out between three natural sources of water—Dakhleh, Gilf Kebir and Kufra—each separated by approximately one hundred twenty miles, an insurmountable distance for donkeys, the only draft animals available to the ancient Egyptians.

With the help of a modern-day nomad by the name of Carlo Bergmann, Kuper has shown how the ancient Egyptians could have overcome these daunting barriers. A former manager of a car factory with a Ph.D. in economics, Bergmann now travels the desert by camel. Recently he has uncovered a series of these water depots south of Dakhleh, spaced approximately twelve miles apart, about a day's march for a donkey. Many are marked with cairns and some have petroglyphs, including depictions of donkeys. At some sites—clearly way stations but maybe also watch posts—there are stone circles, with fireplaces, pottery and grinding stones.

At one site, Kuper found this inscription: "In year 23 of . . . the steward *Mrj* goes up to meet the oasis dwellers." Without the pharaoh's name it is impossible to precisely date this rendezvous. Fortunately, archaeologists can use the pots themselves to provide accurate dates, based on their styles and the types of raw materials used. Many of the pots found so far date to the Old Kingdom and furthermore, the French say, they match the pots found at Ain Aseel. These depots of "bottled water" must have been periodically renewed in stages from Ain Aseel to maintain regular traffic. "Pottery is indicative of an organized route, not a casual one," Kuper points out. He has also found pots dating from the New Kingdom and even the Late Period, attesting to the long-standing use of the western route to the Libyan oasis of Kufra.

Kuper believes these desert roads had their origins in the Neolithic period. As the Sahara dried up, these routes remained "like strings," lifelines really, connecting the surviving watered areas. If Kuper is right, the first Neolithic pastoralists probably passed along these now fabled trails, herding their cattle from watering hole to watering hole as the climate became more arid. Even today, smugglers drive cattle up the Nepalese road behind Bashendi, then across the Libyan Plateau to the Valley, thereby avoiding tariffs. Kuper has found water and fodder caches on the Plateau, as well as cows that failed to survive the trip and became naturally mummified.

THE COMBINED EFFORTS OF THE THREE ARCHAEOLOGICAL missions headquartered in the oasis—Canadian, French and German—have now established that the Old Kingdom Egyptians' primary motive in coming to Dakhleh was trade, and substantially sketched in the desert routes by which they travelled into central Africa. It is not yet clear, however, what trade goods or resources they were transporting. Was it ivory, ebony, copper, cattle, or some other exotic product not yet identified?

Recently uncovered evidence has revealed that the New Kingdom Egyptians may have travelled to the western edge of the Great Sand Sea to procure a most unusual product: Libyan glass. Fragments of this yellowish-green glass are scattered across 2500 square miles of Egypt's Western Desert. NASA scientists first investigated these geological anomalies in 1979, when geochemical analysis showed traces of iridium, an extraterrestrial element, indicating formation consistent with a meteorite impact, twenty-five to thirty million years ago. When the meteorite slammed into the desert, it fused the silica-rich grains into glass which was scattered in tens of thousands of fiery fragments across the sands near the Libyan-Egyptian border. Recently, an Italian mineralogist has shown that one of the gems decorating King Tutankhamun's pectorals is made of Libyan glass. What other precious, or staple, products the desert furnished, only further research will reveal.

What is clear is that it was in the Egyptians' economic interest to maintain this western route.

From the sheer size of the administrative centre at Ain Aseel, Mills has concluded that the oasis was more than an outpost. It had economic importance and its strategic location made it a hub of commerce, all of which accounts for the presence of nobles, soldiers and expedition leaders. As today, however, most people in Old Kingdom Dakhleh worked the land. Surrounding the palace and forts were peasant villages that provided the necessities of life for the populace and the nobles alike. Daily, farmers tilled the soil with their wooden hoes and ploughs, harvested their crops with flint sickles and attended to their herds and flocks. Women ground the grain into bread flour on limestone slabs and plied their household trade as weavers, working the flax fibres into fine linens; flint-knappers fashioned exquisite knives and practical tools; potters turned out the earthen ware that decked the tables of the humble mud-brick homes standing in the shadow of the walled Governor's Palace and towers of the fort. It was the daily life of these common Egyptians that Mills decided should be the focus of the DOP's investigations of the Old Kingdom.

CHAPTER EIGHT

NEW LIGHT ON
THE OLD KINGDOM

AT FIVE IN THE MORNING, WITH THE TEMPERATURE STALLED at thirty-six degrees Fahrenheit, I joined Mills and his team as they shuffled through the cold and darkness of a desert morning in late January. After a quick breakfast of porridge and tea, we packed the tools of the trade—cotton bags for potsherds, rubber-tire baskets, brushes, shovels, trowels, string, magnetometer, and survey equipment—into the back of the Land Rover, then climbed aboard this modern "ship of the desert."

Geomorphologist Tatyana Smekalova and I crouched against either wheel well, swathed in blankets against the cold in the open back of the twenty-five-year-old Land Rover which, lacking a muffler, thundered through the still sleeping village of Bashendi.

The only light at this pre-dawn hour beamed from the street

A mother and daughter baking bread in Bashendi

lamps of the villages. These pockets of civilization have been elec-
trified only during the last decade. On the flat horizon of the
desert, they shone like luminescent numerals on a clock face. The
only other motorized vehicles on the road at this hour were half-
ton, Japanese-made trucks roofed with tarpaulins and equipped
with a bench on either side that served as local taxis. They stopped
to pick up groups of schoolgirls, their white headdresses—*shoshes*—glowing against their dark blue school uniforms and the like-
coloured night sky. As the first hint of dawn brushed the horizon,
streaking over the silhouettes of date palms, the first two-
wheeled donkey carts, the most common form of transportation
in the oasis, were being driven by farmers and their families to
their fields.

Cattle egrets, like Desert Fathers robed in white, flocked to
the fields where the farmers were about to build low fires to ward
off the desert chill before starting their round of daily duties. The
overhanging limbs of the tree-lined villages were coming alive with
sparrows, singing, *"Zerzura, zerzura."* On the way, we passed
through Mut, a bustling market town of 15,000 at the centre of the
oasis. Its suburbs are now marked by blocks of modern, cement
high-rise apartment buildings with balconies that always seem to
be flying banners of washing. We then passed through smaller agricultural communities, all built on high ground—barren *gebels*—to
avoid using up arable lowland where it is possible to irrigate and
grow crops. The walled village of Qalamun is perhaps the most pic-
turesque, a tight cluster of mud-brick buildings on a hill that stands
out against the sky like a single earthen dome. Flourishing palms
surround the base of the hill, while just to the west, great sand
dunes rise up in yellow breakers as if to engulf it.

We reached *Ein el-Gezareen* just as the sun topped the horizon.
Its intense pinkish light was reflected off the cliffs of the Plateau,
and in the foreground the prominence of Gebel Edmonstone,

named for the first European to travel to Dakhleh, was burnished for a brief moment by a glowing, cinder-like hue.

Awaiting Mills' arrival, the workmen—*omal*—were standing around an open fire of tamarisk that had burned down to coals. Mills greeted the men in Arabic and they laughed at his good humour.

Mills employs a small crew of local men. The *omal* plod to and fro across the site in a slow-motion dance that might be interpreted as a work-to-rule tactic if this were not Egypt. Two men who carry between them a half-full basket made of rubber tires (the wheelbarrow of Egypt), remove the blanket of sand, shovelfuls at a time. The pace is grindingly slow but perhaps in that seemingly desultory manner lies the secret of Egypt's longevity and preeminence among ancient civilizations. It was with this kind of plodding patience, the laborious moving of one stone after another into place, that those wonders of the desert, the pyramids, took shape.

EIN EL-GEZAREEN MEANS "THE BUTCHER'S SPRING," AND THE site is marked by the sand-filled remains of an abandoned well and long-dry irrigation channels of indeterminate age. It is only one of fifty-one Old Kingdom sites, most of them concentrated in the western end of the oasis near a string of now extinct spring mounds. Mills first identified the site in 1979. Back then, there were tops of walls sticking out of the ground, which was also littered with the usual archaeological bric-a-brac of flints and ceramics. There were also ashy areas, indicating the possibility of well-preserved botanical remains, a key source of information on the eating habits of those who settled here. Besides plant remains, the site was "almost white with bone fragments." The bones would help reconstruct the ecology and economy of the oasis, and tell Mills what wild and domestic animals the Old Kingdomites were eating.

The tops of red mud-brick walls carve the site into rectilinear blocks, a puzzling maze of zigs and zags that must be meticulously

measured and mapped to scale to produce an ever-evolving architectural plan of the 4300-year-old settlement. There are many
small rooms, some with burned areas in the middle where the
cooking was done, and an array of smaller *magazines*, presumably
for storage. Most striking is the thick wall that surrounds this presumed agricultural enclave. Dunes raise their whale backs just to
the south, where there is nothing but desert between here and the
cliffs of the Gilf Kebir, 220 miles away. Green fields enclose the site
on the east and north, where men and women can be seen cutting
fodder for their animals, much as the ancient residents of Ein el-
Gezareen did. Separating the green fields, where they act as sand
catchers, fences of dry palm fronds rustle in the wind, and great
acacia trees spread their generous shade along the irrigation canals.
The haunting song of the desert lark echoes across the site.

Part of the decision to dig at Ein el-Gezareen was to fill in the
huge gap in environmental information for the three millennia
between the late Holocene and the Roman period. The other part
was personal. Mills, who is first and foremost a pharaonic archaeologist, had spent ten years overseeing the conservation of two
Roman Age temples as part of the DOP's mission of monument
preservation. By 1996 he felt a compelling need to return to field
archaeology. "I just about go spare when I can't do archaeology," he
admits. It is not only the intellectual exercise of solving the three-
dimensional puzzle of the past, but the physical aspect of digging
that Mills finds both pleasurable and necessary to his well-being.

Then, too, it was in hopes of studying Pharaonic material that
he had come to Dakhleh in the first place. The reason for focusing
on Ein el-Gezareen was its apparent role as an agricultural community. The information gained there would complement that
being acquired at the ancient capital, where his French colleagues
have chosen to excavate the official parts of the settlement—the
Governor's Palace, tombs and chapels—rather than concentrating

their efforts on the workplaces and residences of the artisans and farmers that supported it.

"I think an archaeologist digs what interests him," says Mills. In his case, it is "the *vie quotidienne*" of the ancient Egyptian population, the mundane matters of daily subsistence rather than the esoteric paraphernalia of temples and tombs that have been the traditional métier of Egyptology.

WHAT MILLS IS DOING AT EIN EL-GEZAREEN FALLS UNDER THE label of settlement archaeology. As a discipline, it is in its infancy in the Valley, as it is in the oasis. Very few ancient Egyptian settlements of any period have survived intact in the Valley, where long ago farmers mined the ancient mudbrick, rich in organics, and spread it on their fields. Other sites have been built over or tilled under, or lost in antiquity to the meanderings and annual inundations of the mighty Nile. Of the few that have survived, even fewer have been excavated and only then when threatened by urban expansion. Ain Aseel, as already noted, is the best preserved Old Kingdom settlement in Egypt.

Until the past thirty years, Egyptologists often dug town sites only to find papyri or other texts. Other archaeological content was often lost or ignored. When they weren't hunting texts, scholars concentrated on the temples and tombs, in pursuit of the ancient Egyptian concept of the afterlife. This focus on monuments and mummies meant that archaeologists came to know a lot more about how ancient Egyptians had died than about how they had lived. The shift to examining their day-to-day lives was stimulated by the Nubian Salvage Campaign, which saw the influx into what Mills calls "the gene pool" of many archaeologists who had had no previous interest in Egypt. Prehistorians, in particular, brought with them expertise in settlement archaeology, rather than a predisposition to study monuments.

"Tombs and temples are really very sexy monuments, which contain interesting information," Mills admits, but he says much of that information is biased. "You cannot tell about daily life from tomb scenes. You know a lot about various industries and activities, but you really don't know how smoky it was indoors or how often you had to eat the same food. So there's a great deal we don't know from the tomb scenes, and there's also everything we don't know from the temples because they're purely religious. They're wonderful to get us into the minds of the Egyptians, their thought processes, but they don't tell you about hunger or flint knapping or anything like that."

The oasis has been spared the kind of development pressure so prevalent in the Valley. At Ein el-Gezareen, Mills was free to examine the neglected matters of everyday life without disturbance—or so he thought. His first step was to lay a thirty-foot square grid over the site with strings. Then a trial square was chosen at random—it was located on the "main mound" at a high elevation and included a rich artifact scatter—and the dig began in earnest. For three days, they trowelled and brushed the earth away in quarter-inch-thick layers, meticulously sieving everything as they went. On the fourth day, they arrived for work to find that the local farmers had dug a huge hole through the test area down to the bedrock, "looking for the treasure," Mills chuckles. Finding none, they never returned. But it meant Mills had to choose another test site.

He began again at the southeastern corner of the site, where, as luck would have it, he exposed a silo structure surrounded by a series of corridors and surprisingly small rooms. One of the corridors, Mills discovered, was "chock full of ash." Ursula Thanheiser sieved the ash to identify what plants the Old Kingdomites were growing or using. To no one's surprise, her analysis revealed two types of wood: acacia and tamarisk used as tinder for fires, as they are today. Both still grow abundantly, acacia near irrigation canals, and tamarisk on the desert fringes, sending out its long roots to distant sources of water.

In one of the adjoining rooms, Mills discovered three "Ali Baba jars," large enough for an adult to hide in, à la The Arabian Nights. These contained grains of emmer wheat, the variety most common to ancient Egypt, and barley. A lack of chaff suggested that the cereals were threshed, winnowed and coarse-sorted elsewhere and then stored in the jars and the silo. "I think you have a bakery," Mills recalls Ursula saying, mimicking her deadpan tone. As if the grain and silo were not evidence enough, Mills also found saddle querns for hand-milling flour and an abundance of bread-baking moulds.

Final confirmation came when he dug to the bottom of one of the rooms, where he found three unbroken bread moulds overturned in the sand. When he picked them up, the sand that filled them held its shape, which, of course, was the exact shape of the ancient loaves of the Old Kingdom—a cone. It was one of those small but satisfying moments of revelation that archaeology occasionally serves up, as if the long-departed baker had been apprehended in the act of creation. Nothing could be more common or more fundamental to daily life than bread.

The bread moulds themselves were made of coarse, porous ceramic. They were filled with dough and then placed directly in small open fires of tamarisk twigs, which, bone-dry, fuelled a short-lived but intense fire. Once they had absorbed the heat, the moulds were removed from the fire and the bread baked as the moulds cooled, probably in about a half-hour. The insides of the moulds were more smoothly finished (though unglazed) to allow easy removal of the cooked loaf.

How did Mills know details of the process? In part, from its depiction on the Fifth Dynasty Tomb of Ti at Saqqara, one of the Tombs of the Nobles particularly rich in "life scenes." Ti married the princess Neferhetepes, and held a fistful of rather affected-sounding titles, including "chief barber of the royal household," as well as "controller of the lakes, farms and cultivated lands." Discovered in 1865, the tomb's architecture and reliefs are considered masterpieces of the funerary art of the Old Kingdom. Besides the obligatory imagery of the afterlife, there are scenes depicting music-making and dancing, as well as autobiographical pictures, such as one recounting a sailing trip made by Ti and his wife—a kind of holiday album. A storeroom where offerings were placed in niches features more domestic scenes of potters, brewers and bakers at work.

Such scenes are crucial sources of information on the economic and, to a degree, the social aspects of life during the period, as Mills himself readily acknowledges. Although Ti's tomb offers insight into the process of baking, and the type of pottery employed, it leaves other aspects of this mundane activity a mystery. It takes the multi-disciplinary approach of the DOP to reveal the ingredients the baker employed, for instance. Thanheiser's analysis of the carbonized plant remains showed that barley was the dominant cereal, with the presence of smaller amounts of emmer wheat. It seems that barley and wheat were both used to bake bread but only barley was used for brewing beer—both considered necessary to a good life in Pharaonic Egypt. Barley may have been a favoured crop because it tolerates drier soils and more salinity than emmer wheat, and those conditions prevail in the oasis to a greater degree than in the Valley. Today, however, oasis farmers mostly grow modern varieties of wheat, having an abundant supply of water from deep wells—at least for now—and a surplus of arable land, should salting ruin existing fields.

Egyptians eat more bread per capita than any people in the world; it is the staple of life in the oasis today. This also seems to have been true in antiquity, as the first Greek writers to visit Egypt gave the Egyptians the nickname *artophagi*, or "eaters of bread." Almost daily, the tantalizing smell of freshly baking bread, heralded by puffs of dark smoke, wafts over the rooftops of Bashendi. The large, dome-shaped bread ovens, decorated with geometric relief, are situated in a corner and dominate the kitchen. Above the oven the ceiling is covered only with palm fronds, allowing the smoke to escape. Grain is stored in waist-high earthen jars atop the roofs, where in this hyperarid climate there is little chance of it getting wet. Women squeeze dollops of dough onto mud platters, letting it rise in the sun while a child stands by with a palm frond whisking away the ubiquitous houseflies. As the bread leavens, the oven is stoked with the readily available fuels of tamarisk, straw and donkey dung, which produce a hot, fast fire. The mud platters are then placed on a shelf above the fire, using a long-handled wooden palette, as in a pizza parlour. The bread cooks in a matter of minutes, producing slightly leavened, delicious loaves, which the archaeologists purchase for their own table.

Bread was just as central to life four thousand years ago. Mills and his crew have found thousands of fragments of bread moulds on and under the surface of the twelve-acre site. Made in their hundreds, the moulds were highly disposable, but, common and utilitarian as they were, these fragments reveal some unexpected insights into the politics of the oasis. Many of the moulds had so-called seal impressions stamped into the clay before it was fired. Mills doesn't yet know what they were intended to denote, whether a weight, size, or quality of the bread, or perhaps the baker himself. Most bear simple geometric designs, or depict whimsical images: for example, a lizard.

All the designs were similar to seals already excavated at Ain Aseel; however, the largest seal found so far at Ein el-Gezareen hints at something more intriguing. Mills describes it as "the size of a quarter" with two winged birds portrayed on either side of a sun disc, with the obligatory enemy underneath. The only matching seal was found on bread moulds in the Governor's

Palace. Mills speculates that the seal may be a quantity or quality registration mark, a tax stamp from a governing office or, by association, it may suggest that high-ranking officials lived at Ein el-Gezareen itself. Mills now wonders if the village might have had some function other than subsistence agriculture.

Most bread mould fragments and other potsherds are not distinguished by any kind of marking. Nevertheless each and every piece of pottery must be collected and examined. I watched Tony Mills' wife Lesley sorting through the seemingly endless piles of sherds the workers unearthed.

She has worked side by side with her husband since she first went to the Sudan in 1964, soon after she and Mills were married. An English nurse, she met Mills in a hospital in Bath, where he underwent surgery. The six weeks of convalescence was time enough for Mills to heal—and for the young couple to fall in love. By winter, they were in the Sudan. "She didn't twitch an eyebrow," Mills says. Lesley recalls the ex-pats in Khartoum betting that this twenty-one-year-old small-town girl wouldn't last two weeks in the primitive conditions of Nubia. How wrong they were. She and Mills continued their fieldwork for seven years, during which time two of their four children were born in the Sudan. "From the age of six weeks onward they were covered in flies and dust, but they seem to have survived," says Mills. "A nurse by training, my wife knew how to look after children. She would wipe their eyes when they got too fly-blown. She could deal with blood."

Lesley allows that field conditions were primitive but the Nubian experience was also, she says emphatically, "lovely." Before the abomination of loudspeakers blaring from minarets became the norm, she remembers when the *muezzin* would climb the closest hill and silhouetted against the rising sun give the call to prayer, a human voice echoing over the river below. Lesley has brought that air of tranquility to camp life in Bashendi. As one long-time member has observed, the DOP is Tony and Lesley's "fifth child." The smooth running of the camp owes a great deal to Lesley, who oversees the operation of the kitchen and other household duties, as well as lending her three decades of field experience. Lesley is at home in Africa and makes other members of the team feel so.

As she sorted through the pottery piles at Ein el-Gezareen, I saw how she kept only the so-called diagnostic pieces. From these rims and bases, the shape and size of the pot can be recreated, at least on paper. Rare pieces that have markings or decorations on them, such as chevrons and triangles, are also kept. "We see all kinds of things here we don't see anywhere else," Lesley told me, "like handles on pots—they're rare elsewhere in the Old Kingdom."

Discards are sorted into two piles: one for bread moulds, another for all other pots. Before these are carted off to a common waste pile, each is weighed and the amount recorded. From these measures, it might be possible to estimate the size and duration of the community.

Despite the tedium of the job, Lesley has never lost the thrill of digging up such common ware. Later that morning, I watched as she gently excavated a pot that emerged from the earth, round and bald, like a baby's head crowning the birth canal. "Lovely, four thousand years old! It gets me every time," she said.

Most days, excavation involves the monotonous repetition of many humdrum tasks. Every once in a while, however, a surprise comes along to rejuvenate the archaeologists' senses and to test their wits. In the second season, one of the *omal* dug up a large red jar, sealed by another jar placed over its mouth. Inside the large jar was a curious miscellany: a Nile oyster shell, beads and amulets of faience, two quartzite rubbing stones, a well-used piece of red ochre (presumably for cosmetic purposes), a small pottery jar with a stopper, two flints, a gazelle horn, and some awls and piercers made from the long bones of goat or gazelle. What was this all about? What significance could it have had? The best explanation, so far, is that it was the kind of random collection of objects that accumulates in a kitchen drawer. Mills feels that such homely artifacts sometimes bring us closer to understanding the individual—and his or her likeness to ourselves—than the most impressive monument or high art on a tomb wall. After all, "Archaeology is the science of Rubbish," as the British archaeologist Stuart Piggott once said.

"I think Ein el-Gezareen is a rich site," says Mills. "It'll produce nice little surprises. You won't find great treasures, all the golden jewellery, rows and rows of pots and so on, simply because what you find here are the things that have been discarded: the rubbish, the broken pottery, the pieces of flint they don't use.

"We hope to get lots and lots of information about the Sixth Dynasty, how people at that time actually lived. What size were their rooms? What kinds of floors did they have? What kinds of foods were they eating, which comes out of this junk we're going through. It's interesting because it's all basic living information."

One of the neglected areas in the study of daily life has been the use of flints to make tools, arrowheads and knives. Discarded tools and the post-production debris such as flakes and cores are found in abundance at Ein el-Gezareen. "One of the exciting bits of this excavation is that the whole technology is represented here," Mills says. "I would like to be able to produce a real description of the technology of flint-knapping in Pharaonic Egypt, at least in the late Old Kingdom, if only to alert my colleagues in Egyptology that they really ought to take notice of the flints they find. It's not just gravel to rake away. It's something to be studied and understood, because it must have been such a common skill."

In the past, such basic household products were largely ignored—in essence, because they did not glitter. Mills sees Ein el-Gezareen as an opportunity to demonstrate just how elaborate the ancient Egyptian flint industry really was. Ancient Egyptians did employ metals and, in fact, began to smelt copper in Predynastic times, acquiring the ore from the Sinai. However, like all metals, it was a scarce resource and the peasantry continued to rely principally on stone implements right through to the Roman period. The Pharaonic flint-knappers demonstrated an uncommon skill, acquired over a lifetime, in fashioning flints into sickles for harvesting grain, for instance, and exquisite ceremonial blades, as well as commonplace choppers and blades. "I think everyone could do this," says Mills. "I don't think there were specialist flint-knappers. They did it because it was a free raw material, a free manufacturing skill because you could do it yourself—you didn't have to smelt something or kill an animal for bone—I think every kid on the block could produce flints."

AS THEY EXCAVATE, ARCHAEOLOGISTS HAVE TO DEAL WITH THE architectural context. As walls begin to appear from their mantle of sand and soil, they must be measured and mapped on the spot, before the winds, which blow unremittingly from the northwest, begin to bury them again, something that happens with alarming speed. Not only does the wind frustrate the archaeologists' efforts, it is a constant source of physical irritation, whipping dust into the eyes, nose and ears, pummelling the skin with its chilling blasts.

In the past, excavating a site involved a large crew of native workers overseen by a cadre of archaeologists and, in many cases, Quftis, the native foremen first trained by Sir Flinders Petrie. For many digs, as at Dakhleh, the Quftis have now priced themselves out of the market. But the grand days of massive excavations are pretty much a thing of the past anyhow, for scientific as well as economic reasons. "I would never think of excavating this whole site," says Mills of Ein el-Gezareen. "We no longer excavate sites with three hundred men and ten archeologists. You can get the same information as before with laboratory techniques—more, really."

One of the more important labour- and money-saving tools now available is the geophysical survey, used to detect subsurface structures and the relative density of artifacts at a site. With this information, the archaeologist can make informed decisions about where to dig. In 1998, the second season of the Ein el-Gezareen dig, Mills contracted the services of Tatyana Smekalova, a geomorphologist from St. Petersburg State University, Russia, and Thomacz Herbich of the Polish Academy of Sciences for such a survey.

Like the discipline she practises, Smekalova, a striking blonde woman with high, sculpted cheekbones, combines an interest in archaeology and physics. A gifted student of mathematics, she first acquired a degree in physical sciences. However, since early child-hood she had had an interest in archaeology and she now began to explore how her training in physics might be applied to her first love. For the last two decades she has been working as a geomor-phologist on digs in northern Europe and in her homeland, con-centrating her efforts on an ancient Greek town in Crimea. Her particular passion was for ancient Roman and Greek archaeology, but when her daughter's interest in Egyptology inspired an excur-sion to Egypt, she immediately perceived the potential for her technique: "I found it exciting because I had never seen sites in such a good state of preservation. It's just a dream for the archaeologist and geophysicist to work here."

Several methods of geophysical prospecting can be applied to archaeology, such as resistivity and acoustic surveying, but Smekalova prefers the more universally applicable method of magnetometry. It is based on the principle that the strength and direction of the Earth's magnetic field, which varies from point to point, is influ-enced by what is underground, or by past human activities that have disturbed the subsoil, such as fire in a hearth. She describes the technique as "a revolution in archaeology," allowing her to see what before was undetectable except by digging.

Smekalova uses what is known as a fluxgate magnetometer, which records the relative magnetism of subsurface structures as either positive (strongly attractive) or negative anomalies. Different structures have different magnetic properties. Iron, for instance, produces its own magnetic field and therefore produces a strong positive anomaly. The most common source of iron at Old Kingdom sites is ceramics, which produce a strong magnetic signal, as the clay contains a small percentage of iron. When the pottery is fired, the iron, which in raw clay occurs in a non-magnetic state, becomes a highly magnetic oxide. The ubiquitous potsherds on the surface create some "background noise," but a structure like a pottery kiln (a common feature in the oasis) is in essence a large mass of clay that has been repeatedly and intensively fired, and therefore shows up as a strong positive anomaly.

That her method could also detect mud-brick walls came as a pleasant surprise to Smekalova, since the fill of the room often contains ashes and pottery sherds that are much more magnetic than the walls themselves. Because so much architecture in Egypt is composed of mud brick, Smekalova believes that her method should have wide application. Vitally, it records architecture and other archaeological features in their original, undisturbed context. "I like this," Smekalova says in her deliberate English. "I can feel what others cannot feel."

Computerized magnetometers designed for archaeology are only a decade old, but have already revolutionized the technique. Previously, all readings had to be noted on site and the maps drawn by hand. But, for all its high-tech wizardry and time-saving efficiency, the method still requires remarkable doggedness and stamina. Each day Smekalova surveys a new 200-by-250-foot square, with her magnetometer, which resembles a metal detector, in hand and her processor strapped on to her back.

First, she divides the area to be surveyed into a three-foot grid, then walks back and forth at a measured pace between her grid lines for eight hours a day under the unforgiving Saharan sun. As she passes each yard marker, she presses a button on her magnetometer to establish co-ordinates for her readings; in between these reference points, the magnetometer records two or three readings at half-second intervals. All of these data points are fed into Smekalova's laptop, digested by a special software program and, at the end of the day, rolled out as a grey scale map, revealing the underlying structure. At the latitude of Egypt, magnetic structures, such as kilns, show as white positive anomalies, with a dark anomaly immediately to the north. The map resembles a black-and-white photograph of the moon but with its enigmatic craters and scar lines revealing human-made structures. It is one the pleasures of camp life when Smekalova emerges from her workroom before supper with the latest version of the site map—an ever-changing and ever more complete picture that gives the impression of showing the growth of the ancient settlement in real time.

Smekalova has a strong sense of responsibility to the archaeologists who will use her maps to plan where best to invest their energies: "I'm always afraid if I make a mistake, then they will start to dig where there is nothing—well, you can imagine it is not very pleasant."

In 1999, her underground map revealed a massive wall, 180 by 330 feet, and varying in thickness from three to five feet, enclosing a puzzling concatenation of inner rooms. Smekalova's discovery radically changed Mills' perception of the Ein el-Gezareen settlement, confirming that he had been right to wonder about its true nature: it was not a simple agricultural community but obviously had a more complicated history. Ain Aseel had had a similar life history, beginning as a fortified city and later growing outside its well-defended walls when the perception of threat had, for whatever reason, disappeared. What the ancient Egyptian immigrants were defending themselves against is not yet clear. "It would seem that the Pharaonic Egyptians doubted the peaceful character of the local Sheikh Muftah," says Mills. "Slowly, as they either became convinced otherwise through peaceful contact or after they had successfully driven the indigenous Sheikh Muftah people out into the desert, they were then able to expand out of their fortified settlements and engage in their usual farming activities." Or perhaps it was, in Mills' words, "just somewhere to shut yourself away in the middle of the night," which would illustrate the psychological stresses of living in a foreign place, of fearing the unknown. We know that the ancient Egyptians were never comfortable living too far away from their Valley homeland.

In the 2000 season, the magnetometer survey and subsequent mapping of the walls revealed another surprise: near the centre of the complex was a symmetrical building with finely constructed walls, plastered on both faces and painted with washes of red and yellow. When Mills faxed the plans to New York, Dieter Arnold, a world expert on Egyptian temple architecture, called back to say, "Congratulations, I think you've got a temple." Part of the problem in identification is that there are simply no other community temples, which Mills compares to a parish church, known from Old Kingdom times. Definitive evidence in the form of religious inscriptions is still needed. "First I have to prove to myself that it is a temple," he says. "I don't want to get burnt." If he can prove it, it will be the first mud-brick temple found within a settlement in Old Kingdom Egypt.

The enclosure wall and the presence of a temple indicate a more substantial role for Ein el-Gezareen than mere agricultural village: it may have served as a kind of satellite capital for a group of Old Kingdom communities in the western half of the oasis. As with any dig, the story evolves with each new season. The changing perspective that new, unexpected results demand is part of what Mills calls "the humility factor in archaeology," which requires enough honesty on the part of the archaeologist to change the story as new evidence comes to light.

ARCHAEOLOGISTS IN DAKHLEH, AS ELSEWHERE IN RURAL EGYPT, have at least one advantage in trying to interpret the past. The timelessness of Egyptian agrarian life offers another window into the world they are trying to resurrect, pot by pot, flint by flint, wall by wall. Climatically, little has changed in the Sahara since the Old Kingdom: each day has dawned in much the same way. "Whatever is causing the local people to do something nowadays was also possibly a cause in the Sixth Dynasty," observes Mills. "It's always dangerous to use this kind of ethnographic parallel to *prove* something, but it helps one to an understanding."

There has always been an ambivalent relationship between anthropology and archaeology. The traditional insularity of Egyptology, with its emphasis on content, especially texts, rather than context, has engendered a particular reluctance to engage in a fertile exchange between the two disciplines. Elsewhere it might indeed be dangerous to rely too much on ethnographic interpretations. In Egypt, however, there has been remarkable continuity in farming methods, despite changes in people's religous beliefs and even in the ethnic origins of the populations themselves.

Mills has observed and absorbed many of the patterns and subtleties of oasis farm life over twenty-five years. As he excavates at Ein el-Gezareen, he can see women in the fields cutting the *berseem* with a short-toothed sickle blade. Today these wooden-handled tools are imported from China, but in design they are similar to the iron sickles used by the Romans and the flint tools used by the ancient Egyptians. Although tractor-driven threshers are becoming more common, most threshing is still done by cattle walking on the grain, as was done in ancient Egypt. Winnowing is done by hand. Donkeys are still the main means of transport for the local farmers, who still raise many of the same animals: ducks, goats, sheep and cattle. The exception is pigs, which ancient Egyptians raised in Ein el-Gezareen but which modern Muslim residents avoid due to an Islamic prohibition on pork.

Local environmental conditions often dictate practices that would seem unusual elsewhere. An uncommon amount of labour seems to be expended upon the animals, for example. Every morning men, women and children work in the fields, harvesting fodder. They squat, straight-backed, harvesting the grass with swift, deliberate strokes of their sickles. Women carry the fodder to carts in reed or rope baskets balanced on their brightly kerchiefed heads, a picture of strength and poise. By late morning families return to their corral, their donkey carts piled high with brilliant green alfalfa for their herds of sheep and goats and the family cow. The reason for this "mollycoddling," Mills points out, is that there is no such thing as a meadow in the oasis. You cannot just put the animals out to graze in a wet, freshly irrigated field—they'd get mired in the mud—though occasionally you see a cow tethered in a field of stubble. In Mills' view, there is no reason to believe farm life in Ein el-Gezareen was not similar to what is seen in the oasis today—a recreation that would simply not be possible from the artifacts alone.

There is no better example of the similarities than the basin irrigation methods used by the oasis dwellers. Although the Nile Valley Egyptians had to learn to deal with many specifically Saharan problems when they came to the oasis—wind, sand, lack of humidity, and isolation—they could easily have applied the farming system they had already practised for hundreds of years to this new frontier.

The earliest record of artificial irrigation in the Valley dates from the end of the Predynastic era (circa 3000 B.C.) when the mace-head of the Scorpion King shows one of the last Predynastic kings ceremonially cutting an irrigation ditch. The annual flooding of the Nile, which occurred in mid-August as monsoonal rains sweeping in from the Indian Ocean recharged the river's highland sources in Ethiopia, inundated the Valley right to its desert edges. It breached the natural banks of the Nile, and the river's natural meanderings created levees, channels and flood basins. The surge of water took four to six weeks to crest, filling the many natural flood basins. As the Nile began to recede, water evaporated, filtered into the alluvial soil, and drained back to the main river channel. By late November, the Nile floodplain had emerged and farmers could sow their winter crops in the damp, fertile alluvial soil.

The earliest settlers of the Valley took advantage of this annual cycle, while building their settlements on the highest levees, out of harm's way. With their intimate knowledge of the river's vicissi-tudes, it was not such a great leap to institute artificial irrigation. By building a system of dikes, or levees, enlarging existing ones, and digging channels and canals, water could be held on the flood plain longer, and then distributed to their fields during the grow-ing season as needed. The fields were laid out in small, manage-able squares surrounded by low dikes, the system we call basin irrigation, and water was fed to the fields or drained from them by temporarily breaching the dike. All that was needed was a hoe and a good eye for land levels. Farmers in Dakhleh lay out their fields in the same way today, using a simple hoe, or *touriyeh*, to heap up the small dikes and to breach them to move water around between their plots.

In Dakhleh, the fundamental difference was that water was not supplied seasonally by flooding but was available year-round from the springs. Spring mounds, however, occupied low ground, so the agriculturists were faced with a new challenge. They had to raise the water for distribution to their fields; otherwise it would simply pool around the spring head, forming swampy ground unsuitable for agriculture. They did not have sophisticated water-lifting devices—just the well sweep, or *shaduf*, essentially a fulcrum with a weight on one end and a bucket on the other; and the shoulder yoke for carrying buckets to transfer water by hand. Essentially, their life-support system depended upon water storage and gravity.

Though he has no archaeological evidence to confirm it, Mills has come up with his own scenario for how the Egyptians might have solved this problem. He guesses that they used the locally available, impermeable clay soils to build a coffer dam around the spring vent to whatever height was required. This volcano-like structure, "like a pyramid with a hole in the top," says Mills, could act as a water storage-area and the spring waters could be raised to whatever height was needed for gravity feeding. Then it was simply a matter of tapping the water from the top of the basin and distributing it by a system of canals. As archaeological theory, the principle virtue of Mills' system is its simplicity and the fact that it was well within the capacity of ancient pyramid builders.

These days, there are only a few free-flowing artesian springs. At least since Roman times, oasis dwellers have hand-dug wells to tap deeper aquifers, and today, drilled wells are sunk more than three thousand feet below the desert floor. Both these methods have gradually lowered the water table, drying up natural springs.

It is no coincidence, therefore, that the Old Kingdom communities were concentrated where natural springs were abundant in the past: near Ain Aseel, near Ein el-Gezareen, and near Mut, at the centre of the oasis, where local residents say the most productive agricultural land in the oasis is found.

The oasis was too far from the Valley to depend upon it for basic foodstuffs: oasis dwellers would have had to produce their own. The expansion of Ain Aseel and satellite communities like Ein el-Gezareen suggests that life there was not merely a matter of subsistence. Tapping the natural springs fuelled a certain prosperity, as no doubt did the desert trade that passed through Dakhleh.

The good life in the oasis, however, would last only for a hundred years. Trouble was brewing in the Valley, and it would soon spill over into the desert.

CHAPTER NINE

A TALE OF WOE

As the French dug down through the layers of Ain Aseel, they uncovered a trail of destruction. There were traces of fire everywhere they looked. The main city gates had been torched; inside, the Governor's Palace had been burnt to the ground and plundered. In the rubble, they found the charred remnants of the Governor's throne. The plunderers never re-occupied or rebuilt the palace, which helped to preserve the artifacts. However, the artifacts do not tell us who the occupying force was, nor what circumstances led to the attack.

At the end of the Old Kingdom, a period of great works in the Valley and of prosperity in the oasis, events took a dramatic turn. Egypt was plunged into chaos for two hundred years, a time known as the First Intermediate Period. How a stable and vital nation state spiralled suddenly into anarchy has long troubled

Late Period ceramic coffins from Ein Tirghi

Egyptologists, and sparked many theories. In particular, fingers have been pointed at the long reign of Pepy II, the boy king who came to the throne at age ten and whose delight at the dancing pygmy we have read about. The reign of Pepy II was the longest in history, according to some historians spanning ninety-four years (2246–2152 B.C.). Others say that he may only have ruled for fifty to seventy years. At any rate, it was too long for the welfare of the Egyptian state. As Pepy II's reign dragged on, some say senility crept in, and the powers of the provincial nomarchs (or Governors) grew steadily. To pacify them, the old king granted them additional lands and special privileges. The local rulers, in effect, set up their own fiefdoms, ultimately undermining the central administration. Pepy II's aggressive foreign policy, particularly his ruthless attempts to suppress Nubia, also weakened his hold on power. While he tried to maintain control there, the Delta was neglected, setting the stage for Egypt's unified state to be torn asunder.

All of these machinations no doubt contributed to the collapse of the orderly rule of the Old Kingdom. However, many Egyptologists now acknowledge that the death blow was probably dealt by environmental change, or as Mills says, "good old Mother Nature." In the early 1970s, Barbara Bell, then at Harvard University, was the first to propose an environmental cause. An unprecedented series of low Niles struck Egypt between 2180 and 2160 B.C., during the senescence of Pepy II's reign. Bell argued that widespread drought and famine led to the breakdown of civil order, a calamity she dubbed "The First Dark Age in Egypt." She also showed that the decline in prosperity and order was not confined to Egypt but also affected a wide swath of the Near East, from Greece to Mesopotamia. "The cause I postulate," she wrote, " . . . is drought—widespread, severe, and prolonged—lasting for several decades and occurring more or less simultaneously over the entire eastern Mediterranean and adjacent lands. This is not to deny the

significance of contemporary political and social factors; it is, however, to assert that a climatic-economic deterioration of sufficient
magnitude can set in motion forces beyond the strength of any
society to withstand."

No ancient culture was more dependent on climatic conditions. The good life Egypt enjoyed depended wholly on a benefi-
cent Nile. Failure of the annual flood could, and did, shake the
riverine civilization to its very foundations. Not only did low Niles
leave crops to wither under the desert sun, they weakened the people's faith in the pharaoh, who as a god-king was thought to exercise magical control over the Nile's life-giving waters.

Although the effects of a low Nile were felt immediately and
acutely along the narrow fertile flood plain, the causes lay far away,
in global climatic forces. The Nile rises in four rivers, two with origins in East Africa and two in Ethiopia. Most of the floodwaters
originate in the Ethiopian highlands, which are fed by monsoonal
rains blowing off the Indian Ocean. The timing and intensity of
these rains depend upon the north-south movements of the
Intertropical Convergence Zone, where the northeast and southwest trade winds converge. If this zone stays farther south and the
persistent low-pressure system that hovers over the Indian Ocean
falters, the monsoonal rains are weak or may fail completely. This
can result in drought in Ethiopia and "a low Nile."

As the Nile flood went, so did the fortunes of ancient Egypt.
Exceptionally high Nile floods occurred at the time the Egyptian
state was unified. Flood levels continued to decline thereafter,
however, and reached critically low levels after 2180 B.C. The consequences for the Egyptian state and for the poor agriculturists of
the Valley were extreme.

A document known as *Admonitions of an Egyptian Sage,* attributed to the First Intermediate Period, records the social chaos and
personal tragedy that ensued after the collapse of the Old Kingdom.

Penned by a man known as Ipuwer, it is a litany of ills and a lament for the loss of royal authority.

> The rabble is elated, and from every city goes up the cry:
> "Come! Let us throw out the aristocrats!" The land is full of
> rioters. When the ploughman goes to work he takes a shield
> with him. The Inundation is disregarded. Agriculture is at a
> standstill. The cattle roam wild. Everywhere the crops rot.
> Men lack clothing, spices, oil. Everything is filthy: there is no
> such thing as clean linen in these days! The dead are thrown
> into the river. People abandon the cities and live in tents.
> Buildings are fired, though the palace still stands. But the
> Pharaoh [unnamed] is kidnaped by the mob . . . Today there is
> no trading with Byblos. No one can get pine wood for coffins,
> funerary materials or the oils for embalming which were once
> brought from as far afield as Crete. There is a gold shortage,
> and raw materials for proper burial are exhausted. Nowadays
> it seems very important that the oasis dwellers should bring
> their caravans of their once despised produce!

The Sage's unflattering reference to the oasis-dwellers' modest produce—mats, plants and poultry—points to an important distinction. Though the Nile was utterly dependent upon the capricious highs and lows of the inundation, the oases were blessed with the unfailing artesian springs. While the Valley was spiralling into famine for want of enough water, the oases had plenty. And since the Sage tells us that oasis produce had become necessary for survival in the Valley, there must have been a surplus for export. Indeed, the community at Ain Aseel seems to have grown and prospered even after the Valley was in a state of riot. But as the French excavations have graphically demonstrated, ultimately even Ain Aseel could not escape the chaos.

Although the oasis was tied into the central administration of the Valley, its remoteness from events there may have bred a kind of complacency. As we have seen, the city had expanded outside the fortified walls. Even if the Sheikh Muftah survived on the fringes of the oasis, they probably did not have the numbers or resources to mount an effective attack. It is also possible, of course, that hostile forces came up from the south, from Yam or Kush, or that the Tjemehu came out of Libya.

What seems more plausible is that the conquering force came from the Valley itself. "I'm sure there was a movement of people from the Valley into the oasis at this time." says Millet. "They could have been friendly: they could have been taking over." But how would the oasis dwellers or their masters incur the wrath of the Valley? One possibility is that the Governor of the Oasis had become too independent, establishing Dakhleh as his own independent fiefdom, over which he ruled with the power of a pharaoh as a self-appointed Lord of the Western Desert. Similar situations had arisen in the Valley with the dissolution of the central authority in Memphis.

Nomarchs who fed their people by carefully controlling irrigation could consolidate their power base. One such was named Khety. A self-congratulatory epistle on his sepulchre reads:

> I nourished my town, I acted as [my own] accountant in regard
> to food (?) and as a giver of water in the middle of the day . . .
> I made a dam for this town, when Upper Egypt was a desert (?),
> when no water could be seen. I made [agricultural] highlands out
> of swamp and caused their inundation to flow over old ruined
> sites . . . all people who were in thirst drank . . . I was rich in
> grain when the land was a sandbank, and nourished my town
> by measuring grain.

Not all nomarchs were as gifted with foresight as Khety, nor did they all take such decisive action. One wonders how those who were not "rich in grain," or in imagination, coped with the famine and unrest. Perhaps one of these less fortunate nomarchs knew of the trade with the oasis, knew of its everlasting springs and the ample supplies of grain in the Governor's granaries. At a time of such desperation, such knowledge might be the only motive needed to lead an expeditionary force to crush this oasis ruler and take what was his.

Or might there have been an opportunistic local uprising? Perhaps the oasis dwellers, like their fellow farmers in the Valley, heeded the cry "to throw out the aristocrats." Perhaps they, too, had fallen on hard times. "The low Niles would have had less impact here," Mills says. "But the economy would suffer because the national economy was suffering. We have no idea how much export there was to the Valley, but the more there was, the greater the impact locally."

Mills and his colleagues cannot yet say whether the overthrow of the Old Kingdom settlements in the oasis was coincidental or connected with events in the Valley. Mills tends to believe it was "climatically based," and more than coincidence that it came at the very end of the Neolithic Wet Phase. The onset of hyper-arid conditions may have had as yet undetected ecological effects. For not only does the ancient Egyptian presence in the oasis dwindle at the end of the Old Kingdom, but the local Sheikh Muftah people also disappear from the archaeological record.

"I still don't know what happened with the Sheikh Muftah, whether the ancient Egyptians lived harmoniously with them, which I'd like to think," says Mills, "or whether they killed them off, in which case we'll find a death pit." For now, Mills and his colleagues lack the information to say whether the Sheikh Muftah were pushed out, died out, or became acculturated, that is, indistinguishable from ancient Egyptians. Such assimilation would be very difficult to detect archaeologically. But if there was a flashpoint between the two groups, most likely it would have been over water. It is conceivable that the Old Kingdomites monopolized the springs, driving the Sheikh Muftah beyond the margins of the oasis, where they would have faced starvation—a version of the competitive exclusion principle applied to humans. What we do know is that all evidence of the Sheikh Muftah vanishes about a hundred years after the arrival of the Old Kingdom pyramid builders.

After the collapse of the Old Kingdom, it is clear that the oasis went into a sharp decline that lasted the better part of a thousand years. "We have a community here, which is represented by a grave or two, a tiny village site, or an inscription here and there, but there is not enough evidence to postulate a really thriving community," says Mills. "I suspect that a lot of people who came out here stayed for a while and then returned to the Valley."

The chaotic First Intermediate Period, chronicled by Ipuwer, was marked by political instability. Records state that there were "seventy kings in seventy days." Although this is surely an exaggeration, no one pharaoh was able to assert authority over the whole country. The monarchs of two competing regions, at Herakleopolis in the Fayum and at Thebes, vied for control of Upper and Lower Egypt, which had broken into fractious regions. During this period of disunity and eventual consolidation in the Valley, Ain Aseel was quickly re-occupied. The sacked palace was never rebuilt, however, and the city never regained its former prosperity.

WHILE THERE IS AN ALMOST EMBARRASSING AMOUNT OF EVIDENCE of Old Kingdomites in the oasis, the opposite is true of the Middle Kingdom (2050–1785 B.C.). Only the scantiest of Middle Kingdom material occurs on the ground, in the form of approximately a hundred tombs, a few scatters of potsherds, personal effects such as sandals, and the odd datable petroglyph and rock inscription. What little we know comes from written records found in the Valley. Often, however, it is difficult to know precisely which oasis they are describing. "We don't know the specific Egyptian name for this place," says Mills. "There are lists of the oases in the valley temples, but unfortunately the lists are damaged at the point of the Dakhleh Oasis." The two oases of Dakhleh and Kharga, though separated by ninety miles, were, for bureaucratic reasons, considered together simply as the "Southern Oasis," or *Kenmet*, but the exact name of the Dakhleh Oasis has been lost. The best guess is that it was *wehat*, which translates as "cauldron" and is the origin of our word "oasis."

We do know that the Middle Kingdom saw a return of prosperity to the Valley, if not to the oasis. However, around 1790 B.C., according to Barbara Bell, Nile floods again fell to lower levels, triggering a gradual slide from prosperity into poverty, disorder and famine. Bell calls this Second Intermediate Period (1785-1567 B.C.), the "Little Dark Age."

In 1987, when Mills first sketched in the Pharaonic history of the oasis for me, he was clearly frustrated by the gaps in the chronology. At the same time, he accepted this as the lot of the archaeologist, who can never know the whole story of a past culture. And for all their ambiguity, the Valley records do give the DOP rare glimpses of events in the oasis for which they have yet to find hard evidence. The records reveal that during the Middle Kingdom the oasis was a kind of desert Devil's Island, where enemies of the state sought refuge and the pharaoh's border patrols hunted them down on the dangerous desert trails. Even during the New Kingdom (1567–1085 B.C.), Dakhleh still seems to have served as a place of exile, either chosen or enforced. Officials who had become *personae non gratae* were banished here. We have one unique record of a Valley resident who fled to the oasis during the

New Kingdom. The papyrus document, written in hieratic script—a cursive form of hieroglyphs written with brush pen—is held in the A.S. Pushkin Museum of Fine Arts in Moscow and is most often referred to as "A Tale of Woe.'" It takes the form of a letter written by one Wermai, a priest in the temple of Re'-Atum in Heliopolis, to a friend, Usima're'nakhte, a scribe in the royal court.

Wermai's tale was written during the great Ramesside period of Egyptian history, between 1300 and 1000 B.C., when Ramses the Great and his successors ruled. It is the first document in world literature to employ epistolary technique to convey a narrative and it is the only Egyptian text to describe the difficult conditions of an isolated rural Egyptian village at that time.

Wermai had been removed from office, stripped of his property, and driven from his hometown. He states his case bitterly: "I was unjustly removed; I was defrauded before anything could be said, and dispossessed, though there was no crime on my part. I was thrown out from my city, and my property was seized; it could not be saved." He accuses his arch-enemies not only of robbing him but of killing women and of imprisoning or kidnapping their children. Wermai is forced to wander the countryside, first by boat, then in his own chariot, which also is eventually stolen from him by his enemies. Continuing on foot, he is treated as a stranger wherever he goes. Finally, his wanderings land him in Kenmet [Dakhleh] in the Western Desert. He compares his desperate condition as an outcast to a dead body: "When flesh and bone are abandoned on the desert-edge, who is going to bury them?" Such would be the worst fate imaginable for someone who believed he needed his body preserved for the afterlife.

Wermai appeals to his friend to bring his plight before his former benefactor, whom he had served loyally and who, in fact, may be the pharaoh himself. Far from his beloved Valley homeland, Wermai finds himself in dire straits, under the thumb of a tyrannical omdah or headman, of the oasis village.

He then outlines the multifarious ills which he and his fellow oasis dwellers suffer: " I am sick at heart; for a month I have been kept away from grain. I and those who are with me ache with hunger.

"The people, among whom I am, their well-to-do are few; the Nile is stopped, and their land in darkness. They cannot escape from dire affliction.

"He who makes a request is turned away from his master, and if he utters a protest the staff uses coaxing with him.

"What they have is fixed, and the staff imposes restrictions on every one of them, not to speak of restrictions on their gleaning and on their wages in salt, natron, onions, reeds and rushes."

Wermai's lament paints a portrait of destitution that seems at odds with other Valley texts which suggest the oasis enjoyed a period of prosperity in the New Kingdom. Perhaps Wermai is expressing in metaphor the homesick sentiments of many Nile Valley residents who feared and loathed the desert. He may also be seeing life for the first time from the unaccustomed perspective of the common man, a condition he was ill prepared to accept. Or perhaps he was an inveterate whiner. Even so, Mills says: "I often use 'A Tale of Woe' as a descriptive model for the type of community you might find out here in the late New Kingdom."

This portrait of the oasis as a place for the destitute and shunned seemed at odds with other documents, however. During the New Kingdom, for the first time since the glory days of the Old Kingdom, supposedly the oasis began to enjoy more frequent contact with the Valley and a renewed prosperity. Nile papyri praise the products of the oases, especially the figs and dates. However, it is the wine of the oasis that receives the loudest praise. A Theban tomb scene from the reign of Tuthmosis III speaks of the "Great ones from the southern [Kharga-Dakhleh] and northern [Bahariya-Farafra] oasis" bringing tribute, including wine. In the tomb of the Governor of the Bahariya Oasis there are scenes depicting the growing of vines and bottling of wine. And during the Nineteenth Dynasty, the time of the great Ramses II, one papyrus lists among the requirements for the Pharaoh's stopover, "1000 grapes of the oasis."

With all of these glowing references, the DOP archaeologists were frustrated by the lack of physical evidence for this wine trade. Mills wondered, "How right are the texts?" If there was wine, there had to be amphorae—but, it seemed, there were none to be found. The DOP ceramicist Colin Hope, who accepted Mills' invitation to work in Dakhleh assuming that he would find lots of New Kingdom pottery, was puzzled. He had been working in the Nile Valley on pottery that contained a cobalt pigment believed to derive from alum deposits in Dakhleh. At Karnak, jar sealings and dockets referring to the Southern Oasis as a source of wine had also been unearthed. However, once in Dakhleh, he searched in vain for evidence. A few New Kingdom vessels did show up in a cemetery, including a blue-painted amphora from the Nineteenth Dynasty. But a single vessel does not an industry make.

Finally, in the late 1990s, the DOP made a breakthrough: physical anthropologist Jennifer Thompson stumbled across a large dump of New Kingdom pottery in the Southeast Basin. More than half of the vessels were amphorae. With these pieces for reference, Hope realized that many previously unidentified pieces might also be of New Kingdom vintage.

He describes these up to four-foot-high vessels unflatteringly as "ugly lumpy things." Examples have been found throughout the Valley, including large deposits from the New Kingdom capital of Akhenaten, Tell el-Amarna, and others from the tomb of Tutankhamun and a large Ramesside tomb now being excavated in the Valley of the Kings. Chemical analysis of "the fabric" of the vessels is needed to positively identify that they are identical to those manufactured in the oasis, but if that can be demonstrated, it will prove, says Hope, that the Southern Oasis, true to its reputation, was a major centre of wine-making.

THE NEW KINGDOM ENDED AS THE OLD AND MIDDLE KINGDOMS had—with the fraying of the fabric of society and state. The peasants again experienced famine, tomb robbers violated royal burials, and the priesthood assumed as much power as the pharaoh. As before, the unified state of Upper and Lower Egypt was divided and the Third Intermediate and Late Periods (1085–332 B.C.) are considered by many a time of decadence in art, architecture and religion, punctuated by a succession of foreign invaders—Libyans, Ethiopians and Persians.

Again, Mills must turn to rare documents to supply the missing pieces of his Pharaonic puzzle. Two stelae found at Mut el-Kharab have thrown some light on this shadowy period. In 1894, Captain (later Sir) Henry Lyons, while on desert patrol against Sudanese raiders, chanced upon the now famous Mut stelae:

> On reaching the village of Mut in Dakhla [sic] Oasis 1st
> January I was shown two stelae; one of limestone and the
> other of sandstone, both of which were said to have been
> found in a mound formed of ruins of ancient buildings a short
> distance S.W. of the Government buildings of that village; I
> could hear of no others from the same place at the time and
> brought these two back to the Nile.

Lyons later donated them to the Ashmolean Museum. One belonged to the Twenty-second Dynasty, when Egypt fell under the rule of Libyan invaders, the other to the Twenty-fifth, when Ethiopians claimed the prize that was Egypt. The latter (sandstone) stela deals with a daily offering of bread to a local temple; the former is of far more interest, as it provides information about irrigation in the oasis. The text on the limestone stela records a trial by oracle, in which the God of the Oasis, Seth, delivers a decision in a dispute over water rights. The trial takes place during the reign of the Libyan prince and soldier Shoshenk, who ruled Egypt between 945 and 924 B.C. He has sent the prince Wayheset to be the new governor of the oasis, who carries among other titles, "overseer of the inundated lands" and "prince of the two lands of the Oasis." The stela tells us that Wayheset's mission was "to restore order in the Oasis-land," which was then in "a state of war and turmoil." His first act was to inspect the wells upon which local prosperity depended. During this inspection, he was petitioned to sort out a dispute about a claim to the water rights of a certain well.

This trial by oracle was staged with ritualistic gravity, with the god Seth being carried from the Holy of Holies, the inner sanctuary, out to the temple's Hypostyle Hall. There the god rested on the shoulders of the priests who jerked upwards or downwards to signal divine assent or dissent to the claims being made—although the litigants must have been fully aware that it was Wayheset himself who was the decision-maker. The final decision was recorded on the stela: "Then said Seth, the great god: 'Nesubast, the son of Pate, is in the right . . .'"

Besides providing a vivid snapshot of the theatre of ancient Egyptian ritual and justice, the stela confirms the crucial importance of the artesian waters. Through all the ups and downs of Pharaonic history, the wells flowed and provided the basis of life in Dakhleh, whoever held nominal power over this desert domain.

The sandstone stela, dated to 726 B.C., identifies a Libyan tribe, the Shain Esdhuti, as living in Dakhleh, but the oasis is under the rule of Ethiopians. The Late Period was also marked by an unexpected invasion from Nubia. An Ethiopian king, Piankhy, commanded a force from the Kingdom of Kush, which had been heavily Egyptianized during the New Kingdom. He moved north-ward along the Nile, eventually driving the Libyan ruler to surrender in the Delta and initiating the sixty-year rule of an Ethiopian dynasty. "The Egyptians weren't xenophobic," says Mills. "They tolerated, if not welcomed, foreign domination."

IRONICALLY, IT IS NOT SO MUCH THE ARTIFACTS OF THE LIVING— a few kilns, badly eroded mud-brick walls, flints and pots—but Dakhleh's dead themselves who provide us with a window on this tumultuous time in Egyptian history. In 1982, field archaeologist Rosa Frey noticed some curious landforms at a place called Ein Tirghi, five miles south of Bashendi. Curving mounds rose several yards above the otherwise featureless plain of red mud and gravel and were pockmarked with depressions indicating that something was buried there. Probing a mound, Frey broke through into a series of tombs. There were hundreds of burials.

A team led by Jerry Melbye, a physical anthropologist from the University of Toronto, set about excavating the cemetery. In 1985, Eldon Molto, Melbye's former student, took his mentor's place as head of the team. Molto is something of a Renaissance man: a former junior hockey star, a folk guitarist who writes his own material, and, with Mary McDonald, the Bashendi camp's other daily jogger, a discipline that maintains his compact, athletic build. His passion, however, is bringing empirical rigour to physical anthropology. He has a talent for crunching numbers, with an uncanny ability to recall the scores in international hockey series—and who scored the goals—as well as to spout statistics on Dakhleh's ancient populations.

Molto's introduction to Dakhleh's dead was dramatic. When he and Peter Sheldrick, a medical doctor and amateur member of the "bone team," opened their first tomb together at Ein Tirghi, they encountered grisly evidence that they were not the first people to invade this sanctuary. The skeleton of a young boy lay on his back in what Molto describes as "a death position," knees bent back, arms splayed, and thorax crushed. Another boy lay beside him. Near them was a coffin with a partially open lid. The young grave robbers had been caught in the act when a portion of the roof collapsed on them, breaking their necks. Their crime—to the victims perhaps nothing more than a boyish prank, a dare—was soon masked by the blowing sands, and it fell to the archaeologists, 2800 years later, to discover their untimely end.

The tombs dug into the brittle clay were indeed prone to collapse, a fact the researchers themselves had to keep in mind so as to avoid the same fate as the unfortunate boys. There were other dangers, too. Once the tombs were opened, they became inviting places for snakes to hide at night. When the researchers returned each morning they took special care where they placed their hands and feet. One morning, Sheldrick found a still-torpid viper curled up beside one of Ein Tirghi's dead. He picked up the thick-bodied, nine-inch-long snake with a long-handled shovel and deposited it in a cotton potsherd bag, which he partially buried, hoping the snake would not revive from its torpid state. At the end of the work day, he carried the bag in "the thickest rubber tire basket" he could find, while the snake jabbed repeatedly in an attempt to free itself. His caution was more than warranted. Sheldrick knew there was no antidote for viper venom and he had heard what the local Egyptians say: "If you are bitten by a viper, you have time to smoke one cigarette." In Bashendi, he popped the snake, bag and all, into the freezer, later preserving the deadly reptile in alcohol as a souvenir. The mummified viper now sits on the mantel in his Ontario home.

"It was a queasy, eerie feeling at first, opening up the tombs and finding all these wrapped bodies," recalls Molto. However, he and his team discovered to their dismay that tomb after tomb at Ein Tirghi revealed the work of grave robbers: the wreckage of smashed wooden and ceramic coffins, a scatter of bones and grinning skulls, and partially unwrapped mummies. Most tombs had been disturbed and coffins were frequently violated and the mummies had been thrown aside in the grave robbers' frantic search for "treasure." Such grave robbing was endemic throughout Egypt. Flinders Petrie deduced that it was often an inside job, requiring the complicity of the cemetery guards and, in the cases of royal burials, perhaps a self-serving priesthood who knew not only what valuables were secreted but how to access them through the series of false doors and traps devised to foil grave robbers. The humble tombs of Ein Tirghi probably yielded little valuable booty, as they were the resting places of peasant farmers as poor, no doubt, as the robbers themselves.

Some had invested in expensive painted, wooden coffins, likely the work of an itinerant coffin painter. But the coffins that had housed most of the linen-wrapped mummies are best described as funerary folk art, probably executed by naive artists. These anthropoid coffins had their origins in the New Kingdom, when sarcophagi, for the first time, began to represent the dead person, becoming mummy-shaped, with a head and rounded shoulders, as opposed to the rectangular coffins of the Old and Middle Kingdoms.

MY INTRODUCTION TO DAKHLEH'S DEAD CAME ON MY FIRST day in the field in 1987, when I accompanied Molto, Sheldrick and Frey to Ein Tirghi. It was late in the day; the sun's last rays created deep wine-red shadows along the folded and eroded façade of the Plateau and lit up the desert with a vivid blood-red hue. I followed my guides toward a depression in the desert floor—an opened tomb. I peered through this window into the earth, at the strange array of dead. Mummies.

My eyes roved, focused, circled, and returned to try and make some sense of this morbid spectacle.

In the centre of the tomb were three ceramic coffins, one of which had been vandalized so that its head portion was completely missing. The broken coffin revealed a mummy wrapped in dirty, time-stained linen, with a wide strip circling the torso as if to hold the arms in place. The mummy was also headless. Beside it were two intact coffins with the visages of their occupants figured in relief. Crosswise at the foot of this trio of sarcophagi was the frame of another sarcophagus, which revealed how it was made of thin slats of wood and then covered with a plaster coat. At one time it would have been elaborately painted, but no colour adhered to it now. At the top of the tomb was a complete skeleton, partially lying on its side, with its head cocked back. It looked as if it had been thrown there but, more likely, it had been disinterred from a coffin. Other skulls, ghastly and grinning, were emerging from the tomb floor as excavation proceeded, along with two large pots, the only grave goods in sight. And to one side was a fully wrapped mummy, its body shape pressing through the shroud.

The crew climbed down into the tomb on an aluminum ladder to continue their work. This house of the dead was like a giant cracked egg curving around us, a mud dome with a hole in the roof. Looking closer at the grisly array, I noticed that the faces of the sarcophagi were grotesque caricatures. They were anthropoid, but not quite human, almost other-worldly. Yet it was obvious that they had been fashioned to portray an individual, however unflatteringly; it was equally obvious that the features had been grossly exaggerated. One mask had a huge Roman-style nose protruding from the forehead between heavily ridged eyebrows; the other had oversize ears projecting at ninety degrees from its moon face. Both figures had slits for mouths and eyes, which were depicted as serenely closed, almost smug, in death. Mid-way down the torsos were a pair of shortened arms which looked more like seal flippers. The artist, it appeared, had mistaken the traditional hair lappets—tresses covering either ear—for arms. The sarcophagi, while Egyptian in origin, were certainly not examples of classical Egyptian funerary art. I beheld them with a mixture of bemusement and dismay.

My attention was diverted from these inept likenesses to where Sheldrick and Molto were now working at the side of the smashed sarcophagi. They were bent over a tiny wooden sarcophagus that, while rough-hewn, was as exquisite as the others were clumsy. It was entirely made of wood and constructed for a newborn. The infant's cherubic, chubby-cheeked face had been carved into the wood and was framed by hair lappets, even though such a child would have been too young to have any hair at all. The coffin-maker had carefully carved the eyes, nose and small mouth of the dead child. The tiny sarcophagus was pieced carefully together at the foot, as the single piece of wood had proved too short to accommodate even the child's small body.

Molto and Sheldrick were speculating that the rare attention given to such a child's coffin might indicate that she—it looked like a girl—was someone of status. Not a queen or princess, but someone of high parentage. But later when they opened the coffin, her pathetic remains were carbonized, the mummy coming apart in their expert hands, so that it could yield little archaeological information.

Later the same evening, I found Molto and Sheldrick in the workroom. Like medieval metaphysicians, they were surrounded by a legion of skulls. Sheldrick had a pair of calipers and was taking precise measurements of each skull, which Molto recorded. It was only Molto's second year in the field. Over the next decade, his careful attention to Dakhleh's dead would reveal much about them as individuals and, moreover, about who the ancient Dakhlans were as a people.

Despite the ravages of grave robbers and time, there were more than enough undisturbed graves and intact mummies for Molto to make a statistically reliable study of the lives and deaths of these Late Period Dakhlans by carefully examining their bones and naturally mummified tissues. Due to the hyper-aridity of the climate, the state of preservation of the Dakhleh mummies is remarkable: 70 percent still have hair clinging to their skulls and, in some cases, tendons still adhere to crooked fingers. Also, even though some skeletons were indiscriminately scattered, it was often possible to reassemble individual burials—a far cry from the situation Molto had encountered as a doctoral student.

At that time, he studied Iroquoian ossuaries, or bone yards of communal burials. The Iroquoian practice was to stay in a village for ten to twelve years. During this time, they buried their dead individually. When it came time to move, however, they held a Feast of the Dead, where they exhumed the bodies and buried them in a common grave pit, to reunite them in the afterlife. "Of course, for a skeletal biologist it's a nightmare, because the head doesn't go with the femur and the femur doesn't go with the tibia. So you end up studying populations of bones," recalls Molto. Having faced this kind of challenge at the beginning of his career, he finds working with individually wrapped mummies cocooned in sarcophagi a special privilege.

Molto completes gross examination of the bones in Egypt, then carries small samples back to his laboratory at Lakehead University in Thunder Bay, Ontario, for biochemical and microscopic analysis. He treats each burial as a distinct human being, bringing to bear a battery of both traditional and cutting-edge techniques to extract as much information from each individual burial as possible. Besides metric data from bone measurements and diagnosis of pathologies, he uses radiocarbon, isotopic and mitochondrial-DNA analyses to determine the sex, age, diet and family and racial lineages of the deceased: "We're interviewing the individual through his skeletal remains."

It is the same method he applies to forensic cases, when bodies turn up in the north woods or lakes of Ontario. "When you study an ancient skeleton, you do all the things you would do in a forensic case: aging, sexing, making sure you're not making any errors in the assessment of normal things before you jump into the realm of pathology and anomalies. What is different about this person? That's what I call osteobiography."

The process begins with a thorough visual examination of the skeleton in the field. "The first thing that jumps out is somebody who carries a unique signature," says Molto, usually some kind of anomaly, some pathology, that sets the individual apart from the rest of the population. It may be a fracture or some traces left on the bones by a disease. Such signatures form the opening chapter of a story told by the bones.

What sets the DOP study apart from much previous mummy research in Egypt is that Molto and his team are studying commoners rather than the glorified remains of royalty and the elite. One key discovery was that virtually every infant and child (94 percent) at Ein Tirghi suffered anemia due to iron deficiency. Anemia was as common among ancient populations as it is today in underdeveloped countries. Even so, the degree of anemia at Dakhleh in the Late Period was unusually high. It expresses itself in a condition known as porotic hyperostosis: in everyday language, "bubbly bone," in which the orbits of the eyes become riddled with tiny pores, as does the cranial vault. It is usually caused by a combination of factors, including dietary deficiencies and infections. Molto's conclusion was that in Dakhleh it was likely caused by gastroenteritis, still the primary health risk in the world's poorest countries and as late as the early twentieth century the major cause of death in the Kharga Oasis. His colleague Peter Sheldrick thinks the culprit might have been malaria, as he believes there was probably more standing water in the oasis at that time. The mosquito-borne pestilence weakens immune systems and opens a door to infection.

Measurement of the bones revealed that the people of Ein Tirghi were of short stature: on average 5'6" for males and 5'1" for females. As well, they were short-lived, average life expectancy being twenty to twenty-six years, with less than 5 percent of the population living beyond the age of fifty-five. (Furthermore, nearly 14 percent of children died at birth.) Short stature and a short life were, most likely, both related to poor diet and the stresses of living in a desert environment, problems addressed in "A Tale of Woe." Molto also noticed a high incidence of genetic diseases, such as spina bifida, possibly as a result of inbreeding, which would not be surprising, given the isolation of the oasis.

By 1991, the DOP team had investigated twenty-nine tombs and studied the lives and deaths of 471 individuals, at which point Molto decided to move his operations to the Roman Age city of Ismant el-Kharab. Radiocarbon dating had shown that the Ein Tirghi cemetery spanned the Third Intermediate and Late Periods, to possibly around 332 B.C. Although the cemetery was used for several hundred years, the community, estimated at five hundred to a thousand individuals, has never been found. Mills believes it is probably hidden under modern cultivation, leading him to wonder how many other "lost cities" there might be in Dakhleh.

THE SANDS OF THE SAHARA CONCEAL AS MUCH AS THEY REVEAL. When I first visited the temple at Deir el-Hagar I noted the carved names of the ill-fated Rohlfs expedition of 1874. They tried to penetrate the Great Sand Sea that lies west of Dakhleh but, encumbered by a large caravan and the unanticipated size and extent of the dunes, after three days they were forced to turn back and take a more northerly route to Siwa. Luckily the expedition encountered a rare phenomenon: "a lasting rain." Finally, after fourteen days, and at the limit of their camel fodder and water supplies, the exhausted party reached Siwa Oasis: "How glad we all were to see human settlements before us again!"

History records that other expeditions were not so fortunate. An invasion by Persians brought the brief period of native Egyptian rule during the Twenty-fifth Dynasty to an abrupt end. It also occasioned the first mention of the oases in Western literature. The writer is Herodotus, the peripatetic Greek whom some praise as the Father of History and others vilify as the Father of Lies. This venerable Near East reporter grew up at Halicarnassus on the rocky shores of the southern Aegean in Asia Minor, now Turkey. His classic tome of reportage, *The Histories,* chronicles the struggles of Athens and neighbouring states against the then-powerful Persians.

One of the events Herodotus recounts is the Persian conquest of Egypt by King Cambyses, who defeated the Egyptian king, Psamtik III, in 525 B.C. in an area that is now in the Suez Canal Zone. It is through the fate of another of Cambyses' armies, however, that Herodotus introduces the oases. Herodotus himself probably never ventured into the Western Desert. More likely, as he often did, he relied on reports from local experts. What he conveys to us is a fascinating tale of military disaster, the details of which scholars and desert travellers have debated ever since.

Upon conquering Egypt, Cambyses, whom Herodotus characterizes as a lunatic despot, quickly set out to subdue the Ethiopians to the south. At Thebes, he also detached an army of 50,000 men to avenge the Ammonians, a Libyan tribe who inhabited the Siwa Oasis. The great army marched west for seven days which, historians say, would have brought them to Kharga. At the time, however, Kharga and Dakhleh were often considered together as The Great Oasis and Herodotus simply mentions the city of "Oasis," calling it the "Island of the Blessed." The army marched through Dakhleh and out into the Great Sand Sea.

The Ammonian version of history, recorded by Herodotus, is that the army made it halfway between Dakhleh and Siwa when, at a mid-day meal, a strong and deadly wind arose from the south— a rare event in a region where the wind blows almost uniformly from the north. This freak and fearsome sandstorm is said to have overwhelmed the army, completely burying them. "Thenceforth," Herodotus declares, "nothing is to be heard of them . . . They never reached the Ammonians, nor ever came back to Egypt."

What really happened? Few who have experienced a desert storm, however fierce, believe that Cambyses' army was buried alive in sand. It is easy to imagine, however, that an ill-equipped army, weakened by the effort of climbing endless dune ridges, lost its way in such a maelstrom and could not find its way back. It is also tempting to wonder if their Egyptian guides betrayed them by leading them into the heart of the Sand Sea and abandoning them, so as to protect the sacred oracle of Ammon from foreign plunder.

We will never know. We know only that they were lost as surely as if they had been at sea. Presumably their bones, weapons and armour still lie under featureless sands where, despite heroic efforts, generations of desert explorers have failed to find them.

Cambyses' successor, Darius, built the magnificent Temple of Hibis in Kharga, employing limestone, cedar wood from Libya, and bronze from Asia. The Persians also constructed an extensive system of underground aqueducts, called *kanats*, which, 2500 years later, still carry water when cleaned. But, despite all this, there is a conspicuous lack of Persian presence in Dakhleh, except for a handful of wooden coffins at Ein Tirghi.

For two centuries, Persians and Egyptians carried on a see-saw battle for control. The last Egyptian pharaoh, Nectanebo II, was crushed by a 300,000-strong Persian army which flooded into the Nile Valley like a human tide in 343 B.C. The second Persian dynasty, even more than the first under Cambyses, looted and terrorized the local populace.

It is not surprising, then, that when the brilliant young general, Alexander the Great, swept through Egypt in 332 B.C., the people offered little resistance. In fact, they welcomed him as the lesser of two evils, compared to the repressive regime of the Persians.

Alexander the Great's conquest brought to an end the Pharaonic
Period and initiated the rule of the Greek Ptolemies.

WITH INGENUITY AND PERSISTENCE, THE DOP HAS STITCHED
together the 2200 years of Pharaonic history in Dakhleh from a
variety of sites and sources, in both the oasis and the Valley. Tomb
inscriptions, stelae, literary works, and excavations of cemeteries
and settlements have contributed to a fuller appreciation of life
under the pharaohs. It is now clear that the oasis filled more than
one role, serving as an entrepot for Saharan trade, a self-sufficient
agricultural enclave, an exporter of fine wines, and a place of banishment and refuge.

Mills' long-term aim is to pull these threads together to create
a more seamless portrait of the evolution of the oasis, and he has
long suspected that the best place to do so is Mut el-Kharab, whose
ancient ruins lie within the modern-day capital of Mut. The pottery
Colin Hope has found here indicates a very long, continuous occupation, perhaps covering the entire Pharaonic Period.

In 2001, Hope returned to Mut el-Kharab to test its potential.
Its location smack-dab in the middle of a busy urban centre makes
it more vulnerable to human disturbance than most other sites in
Dakhleh. Pedestrians regularly cut through the site, as do donkey-
carts and motor vehicles, and animals sometimes graze there. People
have dug pits to dump garbage and dead animals, and residents have
also mined the ruins in search of antiquities.

Despite these depredations, Hope's test trenches revealed
great promise for documenting the many periods that remain
relatively obscure, especially from the New Kingdom to the
Ptolemaic Period. The importance of Mut el-Kharab is proclaimed
by the scale of its standing structures, and Mills and Hope both
believe that from the New Kingdom forward it served as the capital of the oasis, eclipsing Ain Aseel. The temple enclosure, though

much ravaged, is the largest in the oasis and still stands twenty-six feet high in some sections and sixteen feet thick.

In two weeks of digging, Hope unearthed tantalizing evidence, covering almost three thousand years of activity, a broader spectrum than at any other locality within the oasis. He found fragments of Meydum bowls that may predate the Sixth Dynasty. He discovered bronze and carnelian hippopotamus figures and a bronze figure of Seth—"the Lord of the Oasis"—that likely date to the New Kingdom. He also dug out ceramics characteristic of the Late Period, and within the temple excavated a decorated inscribed slab with the figure of Psamtik I, a Twenty-fifth Dynasty pharaoh, making an offering to the gods. In 2002, his first full dig season at the site, he discovered two stone tombs, one containing a massive sandstone sarcophagus.

The whole story of why the ancient Egyptians came to and stayed in the oasis is not yet known. "They took it very seriously, but they didn't tell us why," laughs Mills. Even so, the work of the DOP and their French and German colleagues has ensured that Dakhleh can no longer be considered merely a Pharaonic outpost of marginal interest. It was place of some vital, if still mysterious, importance.

In Valley and desert, Egyptian culture had survived remarkably intact for nearly three thousand years. It was now about to enter its greatest period of change, as it came under the influence of the new western powers in the Mediterranean: Greece and Rome.

PART FIVE

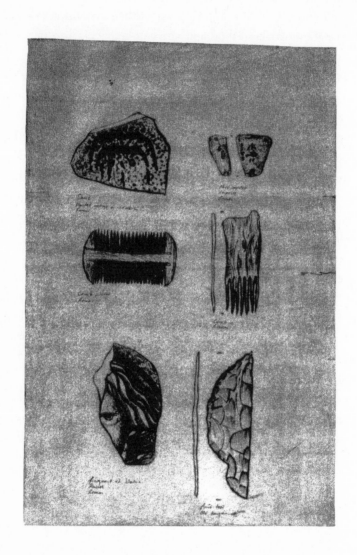

A CURSE OF
SAND AND SALT

332 B.C.-700

Roman Age artifacts from Kellis *(John O'Carroll)*

CHAPTER TEN

THE ROMANS ARE COMING

BEHIND HIS BACK, HIS EGYPTIAN SUBJECTS CALLED ALEXANDER the Great "the Ionian dog," but the young general placated them by paying lip service to their native religion. Soon after his triumphant takeover, he made a difficult pilgrimage along the Mediterranean coast to consult the famous oracle of Ammon in Siwa. The priesthood greeted him as pharaoh, the king of Upper and Lower Egypt, and the oracle, in a politic bit of personal flattery, revealed to him that he was as divine as his Egyptian-born predecessors—a ruse that some historians say he came to believe. Afterwards, he returned to the Nile through the desert, stopping on the way at the oasis of Bahariya, two hundred miles north of Dakhleh. The only temple in Egypt dedicated to him was built there in honour of the occasion.

In 1942, Ahmed Fakhry excavated it as part of his ambitious program to explore all the western oases. The sandstone temple

The Roman Age tomb of Padi-Osiris

sits on a hill, protected by a mud-brick wall. It contains at least forty-five chambers and is surrounded by houses for the temple guards and priests. Fakhry did not guess, however, what riches lay hidden nearby. In 1996, an Egyptian Antiquities Organization guard was crossing the desert plain below the temple on his donkey when suddenly the animal buckled underneath him. The donkey's leg had broken through the desert floor into a hidden vault. It contained one of the most stunning finds in recent Egyptology: thousands—perhaps as many as ten thousand—undisturbed mummies from the Ptolemaic and later Roman periods. It was the largest number ever found at a single site in Egypt. To date, Zahi Hawass, Director of the Pyramids at Giza and the Bahariya Oasis, has exhumed over a hundred of the exquisitely preserved mummies, many in cases decorated with paint and gold leaf. The site, covering some two square miles, has become known as the "Valley of the Golden Mummies." To Hawass, the ostentatious burials are proof that Bahariya was extremely prosperous during the Ptolemaic era of Alexander's successors.

After securing Egypt, Alexander went on to conquer the Persians in their homeland and then advanced as far as India. He died ingloriously in Babylon in 323 B.C., ten days after a prolonged banquet and drinking bout. It is said that his body was brought back to Egypt and buried in a golden coffin (which has never been found) in Alexandria, the city he founded. After much squabbling over the military spoils, his vast empire, stretching from Greece to central Asia, was divided among his generals, Ptolemy Lagos acquiring the prize of Egypt.

Alexander's conquests set the stage for the Hellenization of the Near East. The most important feature of Greek life spread by Alexander's successors was the idea of the Greek city, with its characteristic public buildings such as the temple of the city god or goddess, the town hall, theatre, and gymnasium. Greek social institutions also

became central to life in Egypt, with each city independently supported by the resources of the surrounding countryside. Egypt
became a land of opportunity for Greek immigrants who prospered
in public service or business, or joined the army as mercenaries.

The Ptolemies proved more sympathetic to Egyptian tradition
than the Persians. They built temples and returned temple treasures
to the priesthood. Under Ptolemaic rule, however, Egypt ceased to
benefit the great mass of Egyptians. The peasant Egyptians—the *fellahin*—went on as before, cultivating the rich soil of the Nile and
the oasis lands, but they did so, not for Egyptian nobles but for the
urban Greeks who took over the country estates. The Greeks practised a kind of cultural apartheid, based on Hellenistic manners and
speech. If an Egyptian wanted to succeed, he had to speak Greek
and dress like a Greek. Even if he exchanged his loincloth for the
loose tunic of Greek fashion and adopted a Greek name, he could
expect to find work only in the lower echelons of the Greek administration. The only Egyptians who maintained their status were the
white-robed, shaven-headed priests, who continued to be accorded
the dignity of aristocrats, at least by their countrymen and -women.

Although the Greeks and Macedonians considered themselves
superior to their Egyptian neighbours, they could not help but be
impressed by the antiquity of their religion, which, like their own,
worshipped many gods. However, a Greek proverb poked fun at the
practice of animal worship: "Like an Egyptian temple, magnificent to
look at, and inside a priest singing a hymn to a cat or crocodile."

The xenophobic, conquering Greeks lived separately from the
mass of the Egyptian population in three main cities: Ptolemais in
Upper Egypt, and Naucratis and Alexandria in the Delta. The latter became, under the early Ptolemies, a major Mediterranean
port and the cultural centre of the post-classical Greek world. It
was home to an estimated one million people and to one of the
wonders of the ancient world: the great Pharos, or lighthouse. The

Ptolemies' primary interest in Egypt was profit. They sought to bring as much fertile land into production as possible, designating large portions "Royal Land." They had no compunction about pressing the native population into building and maintaining dikes. In the midst of plenty, the Egyptians sank into dire poverty.

According to Hawass, early in their reign the Ptolemies expanded irrigation systems in Bahariya and established military outposts to guard the trade routes between Egypt, Libya and the Sudan, routes that had to pass through the other Egyptian oases, including Dakhleh. Eventually they took control of the whole Western Desert, as well as Libya.

Mills and his team have been surprised and frustrated, therefore, by the apparent lack of evidence of a prominent Ptolemaic presence in Dakhleh. They suspect it lies buried under later Roman material, or beneath modern cultivation—or they have not yet dug in the right places. But they have found enough to confirm that the Ptolemies had a stake in Dakhleh.

In Bashendi, an impressive stone tomb marks the burial place of a prominent person named Kitinos. Oddly, there are no titles or epitaphs to tell us who exactly this Ptolemaic worthy was, though the funerary text suggests his father may have been a Hellenized Egyptian and his mother a Libyan. And, based on the artwork, Mills has been able to date the tomb of Kitinos to just before Cleopatra ascended the throne in the first century B.C.

The tomb was built above ground, mausoleum-style, and when Mills first established the DOP headquarters in Bashendi, people were still living in a house built on top of it. They were using the tomb itself as a storeroom or cellar. The Egyptian Antiquities Organization (now the Supreme Council of Antiquities) asked Mills to clean up and restore the tomb to make it attractive to visitors. The removal of the house, the structural repairs and the cleaning of the fragile sandstone took two years. The superstructure measures thirty by thirty feet; the inside consists of six rooms. When Mills first saw it, all the walls were blackened with soot from the former residents' cooking fires. Parts were also filled with debris and dung, as it had once been used as a donkey stable. But the artwork had remained intact.

A sun disc adorns the lintel at the entrance to the tomb. Inside, only one of the chambers is decorated. The figures of the traditional funerary gods have been carved into the sandstone walls: Anubis, the jackal-headed god of mummification, and Osiris, the god of resurrection. There is also a magnificent carved relief of a lion. The quality of the art suggests an artist was probably commissioned from the Nile Valley, where similar tombs have been found. These finely wrought figures would originally have been painted, but only a few flecks of colour have survived.

Restoring the tomb yielded one of Mills' *Raiders of the Lost Ark* stories. During the reconstruction phase, he wanted to salvage several stones from an adjacent first century Roman tomb, where a local holy man had later been buried. However, when Mills began to move the free stones, six old women who had been sitting against a wall stoically watching the proceedings admonished him, saying that it was a holy place and he should not touch them. Mills protested, explaining that he needed the stones to shore up the Tomb of Kitinos. When he lifted the first stone, there was a large scorpion under it. "They all looked at each other as if to say, 'We told you so.'" Mills promptly returned the stone to its original place.

When he had finished refurbishing the tomb, the Antiquities Organization, which had long ago forbidden foreigners to remove antiquities from the country, took the rare step of allowing Mills to make a latex mould of the inside. "It was like painting your bathroom, forty times," says Mills of the tedious process. Today, a perfect replica of the tomb—a cast made from the latex mould—resides in the Royal Ontario Museum.

Mills found another tantalizing bit of Ptolemaic architecture in the medieval city of El-Qasr, at the western end of the oasis. There, foundation stones of a Ptolemaic temple dedicated to the ibis-headed god Thoth (whose image also appears in Bahariya) had been incorporated into the door jambs of one of the multi-storey mud-brick residences, as Arab conquerors built on the ruins of previous structures.

But the most compelling evidence of the Ptolemaic period was a series of tombs cut into the base of a hill northwest of Ismant el-Kharab. Eldon Molto and Peter Sheldrick began excavating the cemetery in the early 1990s. Many of the mummies they found lay in elaborately decorated *cartonnage* coffins, indicating that they belonged to a population of high status. Cartonnage was made by soaking strips of linen in plaster, which hardened to form a material much like a modern medical cast. Embalmers then moulded the *cartonnage* as closely as possible to the face and sometimes the whole body. A face was painted on the mask—often, a yellow face to imitate gold—in the likeness of the deceased. The linen shroud was dyed blood-red, a colour associated with Osiris, the mummiform god who represented all people in death, and the body cartonnage was covered with figures of the funerary gods and goddesses, to provide guidance and protection for the deceased in the afterlife. Several of these mummies have been carbon-dated to 200–230 B.C., dates confirmed by the handful of Ptolemaic pots also discovered in one tomb.

In all, Mills's team has turned up seventeen Ptolemaic sites (out of over seven hundred sites for all periods in Dakhleh), including three possible buried settlements. Much more evidence must lie under the sands, fertile fields and villages in the oasis, and perhaps it will take a case of serendipity, such as uncovered the riches in the Valley of the Golden Mummies, to discover it. Colin Hope, however, thinks he knows where to look first—under the ruins of the Roman Age city Ismant el-Kharab, where pieces of Ptolemaic pottery have already turned up, as well as at Mut el-Kharab and at Amheida, a city in the western half of the oasis.

THE PTOLEMAIC RUINS PRESUMABLY LIE UNDER THOSE OF THEIR conquerors: such is the hierarchy of history. After three centuries, the Ptolemies were replaced by their Mediterranean rivals, the Romans. In fact, for the last two centuries under Greek rule, Egypt was little more than a protectorate, or plaything, of Roman politics, as the Romans expanded their influence in the Mediterranean. The formal takeover centred on Cleopatra and her political and amorous machinations, first with Julius Caesar, then his protegé and successor Mark Antony.

After Caesar's assassination in 44 B.C., Mark Antony and Caesar's adopted son, Octavian, brought the eastern Mediterranean under the Roman standard by defeating the armies of Brutus and Cassius in battle at Phillipi in 42 B.C., while Cleopatra stood by, cannily awaiting the outcome of the power struggle. Like his mentor before him, Mark Antony became involved with Cleopatra, and their relationship lasted for twelve years; they had three children: twins (a boy and a girl) and another daughter. Through this liason, Mark Antony effectively controlled the Eastern Mediterranean, while Octavian, his former ally and brother-in-law, consolidated power in the west. Their inevitable showdown came in a naval battle off Actium in western Greece in 31 B.C., where Antony and Cleopatra's fleet was soundly defeated. In 27 B.C., Octavian assumed the name Augustus and became the first of the Roman emperors with absolute power over the entire Roman world.

AUGUSTUS, AN ABLE ADMINISTRATOR AS WELL AS SOLDIER, SET ABOUT reorganizing and revitalizing a country whose economy had foundered under a succession of weak and ineffective late Ptolemaic leaders. Central to his plan was to make Egypt the breadbasket of Rome by assigning it the responsibility of supplying one-third of the grain supply for the capital city. As before, this burden was born by the *fellahin,* whom the occupying Romans, like the Greeks before them, treated as less than human. They were not even granted Roman citizenship until 212, when everyone in the Empire was given that privilege. This prejudicial attitude may have stemmed in part from the long civil war. To deflect attention from troubles at home, Roman rulers often demonized foreigners, singling out oriental cultures for particular scorn. The normally moderate poet Horace, for instance, had called Cleopatra "the mad queen, the deadly monster," and claimed she was intent on destroying the Empire.

Despite this, Egypt benefited from the huge market of the Roman Empire now open to its produce. Dakhleh experienced an unprecedented boom. "There's all the signs of prosperity: a burgeoning population, great cities, temples and tombs. You name it and we've got it," says Mills. "Everyone gets their house painted, and a new porch put on and a new car—all the things that happen when the good times are around." He realized the extent of the Roman involvement during the survey, when he found that nearly a third of all the sites, and more than half the sites in the western part of the oasis, were Roman. They ranged in size and purpose from isolated farmsteads, industrial pottery kilns, and cemeteries, to entire cities, such as Kellis (Ismant el-Kharab) and Amheida.

Mills could explain the size and range of the sites only by assuming that in the first century the Romans aggressively promoted a major agricultural expansion scheme in western Dakhleh. Opening up previously undeveloped land and digging new wells to support the influx of farmers, the Roman rulers were determined to push back the edges of the desert. Farmsteads sprang up across the western oasis, where many still stand today, their immaculate brickwork remarkably well preserved.

IN 2000, I TRAVELLED WITH MILLS TO THE WESTERN END OF THE oasis on a Friday, the Muslim Holy Day, when archaeologists have their one day off and are free to do as they like. Mills seemed particularly happy to leave camp, briefly escaping the unending administrative burden of filing reports and filling out permits. "I'm not very bureaucratic," he confessed. "It pains my ass but you have to do it."

The farther west we went, the more pervasive the sand dunes. In places, the road had been built right over their whalebacks. Underneath were other buried roads for a future generation of archaeologists to dig up.

We stopped at a barren plain, stripped of sand, and wandered off toward a Roman farmstead a quarter mile away. "They're all pretty much built to the same basic plan," Mills observed. "And all probably from the same time, around the first century." This bureaucratic stamp of uniformity has further convinced Mills that government must have been behind the project. Most farmsteads, like this one, consisted of two rooms on the ground floor with vaulted ceilings, and a second storey reserved as a pigeon loft. Visibile in the second storey were rows of small holes—dovecotes. The wooden nest boxes set into the mudbrick walls showed remarkably little wear. Such a house design was called a *columbarium* (*columba* is Latin for pigeon). Each dovecote could house approximately fifty nesting pigeons, each pair producing two unfledged nestlings, or squab, per month. Young pigeons were an important source of protein in Roman Egypt. "You can imagine how quickly you could get tired of eating pigeon," quipped Mills. Regardless, pigeons would have provided a reliable source of protein while the new immigrants got their operations up and running. The new farmers would have planted wheat for bread, perhaps vines for wine production, and likely olive trees—all products high in value in Rome and its provinces. The farms could also feed the local population, fuelling the good times not only of far-away Rome, but of the towns and cities in the oasis. In the distance I could see several more farmsteads, now isolated in the desert.

The distribution of farmsteads suggests to Mills that land use and probably population was greater during the Roman period than at any other time before the present, with as many as 40,000 local residents.

Mills believes the push to develop the oasis may, in part, have been spurred by crop failures in the Fayum. As production there fell off, farmers were given incentives to emigrate to the oasis—perhaps provided with implements, seed, and draft animals, perhaps even given a monetary incentive.

WHEN MILLS FIRST SAW THE FARMSTEADS, HE WONDERED WHAT town or towns they fed. The answer lay close by, at Amheida. The ruins of Amheida proclaim immediately that this was once a grand place, perhaps the greatest of the Roman cities in the oasis. Known as Trimithis in the Roman period, today it is largely blanketed by sand. A few walls of one large institutional building, perhaps a temple or a fort, stand out starkly on the high ground, but it is the necropolis of prominent citizens that dominates the present landscape, ravaged tomb vaults stretching off for a quarter mile or more toward the dunes to the south. Eroded so that they now look like keyholes, these vaults were passages to the afterlife. The most ostentatious of them is a massive pyramidal structure, a family tomb that is almost twenty feet square and towers twenty-six feet high. When the city was occupied, this imposing landmark must have signalled to the visitor that even here, at the far reaches of the Roman Empire, lived citizens of stature.

At Amheida, masses of pottery sherds mask the sand, as if a banquet for the ages had been staged here and the guests had left their tableware scattered on the ground. When he passed this way in the 1870s, Rohlfs commented on the "huge mounds, almost mountains" of potsherds—so many that he speculated that perhaps the houses themselves, like modern-day pigeon lofts, had been mostly constructed of pots. This abundance partly relates to the length of time Amheida was occupied. Colin Hope has found pottery spanning nearly the entire historical period of the oasis, from the Old Kingdom through to the Byzantine, or Christian era, as late as the sixth and possibly seventh centuries. Its golden age, however, coincided with the Roman occupation.

During the initial survey, Mills, Freeman and others had taken time to dig a test trench to probe the richness of this ruined metropolis. Luck was on their side: they had dug only inches deep when they came upon a beautiful fresco in a remarkable domed room. It depicted a woman with what looked like a halo radiating from her serene visage. Mills thought at first that they had dug into a Coptic church and that the scene was of Mary Magdalene washing Christ's feet. This idea was quickly abandoned when, a little further down, he came upon a procession of pagan gods— Dionysus, Helios and Poseidon—and an image of Polis, the embodiment of a Roman city.

It turned out to be not a church but an ostentatious villa, consisting of some fifteen rooms. On the north side was a peristyle court with coloured columns made of pie-shaped bricks that were visible at the surface. The owners would have used this area as a wind-catcher during the blazing summer heat. The frescoes Mills had found were in a square room, fifteen feet on all sides, in the southeast corner, no doubt a place where the family gathered during the cool winter days and nights, enveloped in classical imagery.

To the left of the doorway on the north wall is a vividly executed fresco depicting the legend of Perseus and Andromeda. Perseus holds the serpent-coiffed head of Medusa, while he rescues

Andromeda from being sacrificed to the sea serpent lurking at the bottom of the painting. To the right is a scene in which a man, seated on a fleece-covered stool, is having his feet washed by a serving woman, while a noblewoman—indicated by the halo—looks on. Mills soon realized that the scene was not Christ with Mary Magdalen, but Odysseus, returning home from his twenty-year voyage. Washing of the feet was a traditional welcoming gesture in the eastern Mediterranean. The image is a striking example of the Hellenistic influence brought to Egypt by the Greeks and emulated in turn by the Romans.

The most dramatic of these mythologically-inspired scenes decorates the east wall: the adultery of Aphrodite and Ares. A group of gods—Poseidon, Dionysus, Apollo, Heracles and Helios—has assembled to bear witness for the outraged cuckold, Hephaistos. Besides these classical scenes, there are a number of finely executed decorative elements, including fields with grass and shrubs and small geometric panels framing faces and birds.

"To find such lively paintings in a country where local artistic traditions are so strongly conservative was a great surprise, but to find them so far from a major centre was an even greater thrill," says Mills. No classical paintings to rival these have ever been found in Egypt. In fact, you have to travel to Pompeii to find something comparable. Mills' elation, however, was tinged with regret and frustration. After photographing the walls, he was forced to bury the room in order to preserve the paintings from the sun and vandalism.

At that time of the survey, funds were simply not available to excavate a city the size of Amheida. Only in the 2000 season could the DOP begin to map small parts of this sprawling metropolis. But, in the coming years, a Columbia University team headed by Roger Bagnall and Lynn Meskell will undertake the monumental task of excavating Amheida, under the direction of the DOP. "It is an absolutely unique situation in Egypt," says Roman-era expert

Bagnall, brimming with excitement, "to have three thousand years of settlement history with nothing built or growing on top of it." He believes that the riches of Amheida will rival those of the famous Roman city of Karanis in the Fayum. He plans to saw the frescoes from the villa walls and preserve them in a museum on site—the first of many such treasures likely to be discovered and preserved over the coming decades.

MILLS AND HIS SURVEY TEAM FOUND OTHER DRAMATIC SYMBOLS of the Roman boom near Amheida, at *el-Muzzawaka*, or "The Painted Rock." Honeycombing the rock of a *gebel* are hundreds of tombs, all plundered. When the archaeologist Herbert Winlock visited here in 1908 he found broken fragments of mummified human remains strewn at the entrance. Remains of rams, both adult and young, lay scattered about, their legs folded under their bodies and tied with strips of cloth—no doubt embalmed sacred animals of the ram-headed god Amon. Fortunately, the grave robbers had left the art in two of these rock-cut tombs pretty well untouched, probably because they could not carry it away. Like the frescoes at Amheida, they show a marked classical, or Hellenistic, influence. The tomb of a nobleman, Padi-Osiris, combines typical Egyptian funerary art with decidedly un-Egyptian imagery. To Mills, it was obvious that two painters had decorated the tomb, one practised in producing flat-sided, two-dimensional figures, the stock-in-trade of Egyptian iconography, and another familiar with the three-dimensional figures of the Graeco-Roman tradition.

The Egyptian wall panels are rich in traditional funerary imagery, as Winlock pointed out:

> Females with stars on their heads pull a bark with the ram-
> headed Amon holding a serpent which arches canopy-like
> over his head, two mummies in front, and Horus steering.

The bark is followed by genii with knives, the last of which is an ape . . . a female offering bearer facing Isis and Nephthys mourning at a bier tended by Anubis, on which lies a mummy with its soul hovering above.

On the ceiling are the signs of the Roman zodiac, decorated with female heads, sun barks, scarabs and apes.

The Greco-Roman panel depicts a toga-clad figure, Padi-Osiris himself, holding a scroll in his left hand. Above him, his soul is depicted as a human-headed *ba* bird, one of a trio of non-material aspects of the deceased that includes the *ka* and the *akh*. While noting the religious symbols, Mills was most intrigued by the environmental information that could be gleaned from this earthly scene. A tiny servant offers oasis food and drink to Padi-Osiris: grapes for wine, olives, grain and dates—prized since Pharaonic times—and the by-then ubiquitous pigeons. "This kind of art shows marvellous connections with the rest of the Roman Empire," says Mills, that are connections not only cultural but also commercial. Prominent citizens of Amheida, like Padi-Osiris and the anonymous villa owner, undoubtedly maintained trading contacts with Alexandria. The wealth on display in the artistry of the tomb and the frescoes demonstrates that, far from being marginalized, the local gentry of Dakhleh apparently enjoyed all the privileges of well-to-do citizens anywhere in the Empire.

AFTER VIEWING THE FARMSTEAD, MILLS AND I DROVE TO THE extreme western end of the oasis to inspect the restorative work he had supervised on Deir el-Hagar, literally, "The Stone Convent," although the site was a pagan temple rather than a church.

As at my first visit, the first-century farmsteads still stood like ruined sandcastles on the Plain of Sio'h, and on the far horizon the aqueducts, still plunged under the dunes, writhing away into the distance. The temple, however, had undergone a facelift. It was now surrounded by a sand-catching palm frond fence and a rebuilt mud-brick *temenos* wall. As we drove up the hill, from which the temple has a commanding view of the plain, I could see that the pale sandstone structure looked more whole, as if many of the centuries since its construction had been reversed and its decay had been arrested.

A good measure of the welfare of a community in ancient Egypt is the number of temples. Temples like Deir el-Hagar were economic pillars in the community. They depended on the community for food offerings and sacrificial animals, and part of their livelihood stemmed from the production of amulets and the saying of prayers for people. There are no fewer than twenty-five Roman Age temples in the oasis, their ruins potent reminders of Roman boom times.

"This whole plain was in agriculture," Mills reminded me as we walked toward the temple. "The farmsteads in this district are all part of the urban area that belonged to Deir el-Hagar."

When Mills and conservator Adam Zielinski first inspected Deir el-Hagar in 1978, Mills says, "It was a lovely Roberts ruin," referring to the Scottish artist David Roberts, who produced a romantic series of lithographs on the monuments of Egypt and Nubia in the 1830s. The main gate was in a critical stage of decay, the massive sandstone lintel weakened by a deep vertical gash that threatened to bring it crashing down. Inside, the sands had buried the long line of columns that marked the Processional Way. The main body of the temple had seemingly imploded: a jumble of roof stones filled the sanctuary. A single intact column, its capital flared out in imitation of the papyrus plant, stood erect at the entrance to the sanctuary, bearing the carved names of nineteenth-century explorers, that in 1987 were almost at eye level but that now, with the removal of the sand fill from the temple floor, were ten feet above my head.

In the early 1990s, the DOP, with the aid of the Egyptian Antiquities Organization, the British government and the Canadian International Development Agency, carried out a partial restoration of the temple. The object was, as much as possible, to restore it to its original look while making it safe for tourists. For the sake of authenticity, however, they decided not to include any new stone work.

The most difficult part was rebuilding the northern wall of the Hypostyle Hall and the Hall of Offerings, which had collapsed outward from the pressure of the sand that had filled the temple. Mills and his team carefully mapped the position of each fallen block, numbering it before it was removed to a storage area. They were helped in reassembling the walls by the methods of the original builders, who had used blocks of different height for each course; as well, the stonemasons had scratched a centring line on the upper surface of each block. Mills's team, aided by local workers, refitted the blocks by hand, stone by stone, much as the original builders must have done. They were able to reconstruct the walls to window height using a lime mortar, as the original masons did, rather than cement.

This restoration effort was the latest in a long line of attempts to excavate and explore what is, despite its ravages, the most intact stone temple in the oasis. The first Westerner known to have visited Dakhleh, Sir Archibald Edmonstone, in 1819, was led by local guides to Deir el-Hagar, which he described as "a temple in tolerable preservation." The next day, he and a local crew set about trying to clear the interior of the temple which at that time was half-filled with sand. After half a day his enthusiasm flagged, and he settled for measuring the dimensions of the temple. He noted "the winged globe encompassed by a serpent, the emblem of eternity," carved over the door to the sanctuary, and that the walls were covered with hieroglyphics, but "much blackened by the lamps used in the service of the temple."

A more ambitious effort was undertaken in 1873 by the photographer of the Rohlfs Expedition, Phillip Remelé. Lured by the occult hieroglyphics and figures visible above the sands, Remelé undertook to clear the temple with the aid of a locally hired crew. The greatest challenge they faced was moving the great ceiling blocks that had fallen into the interior. Using long ropes made of palm fibre, they attempted to remove the colossal stones, each weighing more than a ton. The ropes, however, kept breaking, and in the end Remelé had no choice but to break the blocks in half in order to move them. "As soon as the workers realized that the sandstone could be easily split lengthwise, they began to break it into pieces," he reported. As they removed the sand with hoes and straw baskets, they sang work songs, repeating the choruses in a monotonous refrain as many as fifty times, much to Remelé's distress. What Remelé discovered when the ceiling blocks were overturned was an astronomical motif unique to Egypt. However, his workforce dwindled from forty to ten when no "treasure" was found and, like his predecessor, he abandoned his efforts.

The first archaeologist to examine the hieroglyphics seriously was Herbert Winlock, who journeyed by camel in 1908 from neighbouring Kharga Oasis, where he was excavating the Persian temple of Hibis for the Egyptian Expedition of the Metropolitan Museum of Art in New York. Unfortunately, Winlock did not have a permit to dig; however, he did a remarkable amount of work in his fortnight in the oasis. By examining the cartouches inscribed in the temple, he was able to deduce that it had been built during the reign of Emperor Nero (54–68), with additions made under Vespasian, Titus and finally Domitian (81–96), during the same time that the Empire's most magnificent building, Rome's Colosseum, was under construction. After Domitian's rule, it seems, all work on the temple ceased.

Despite the long-standing fascination of travellers with Deir el-Hagar, the full story of its construction, short life, and demise has only been recently unravelled by the DOP. Hidden in its arcane reliefs and hieroglyphics is a story of imperial ambition and of ancient gods on a collision course with nature.

It now appears that it was used throughout its short life in an unfinished condition, with decorations only on the doorways and the walls facing the Processional Way, while the remaining walls were left roughly dressed, with chisel marks still visible and mortar left running out between the joints. Mills describes its construction as "jury-rigged," thrown up in a hurry, presumably to satisfy a rapidly expanding population during the early days of the Roman boom.

To enter an Egyptian temple is to enter into a dream-like world of animal-headed gods and goddesses engaged in mysterious rituals, speaking words that are, themselves, living things. The artwork in Deir el-Hagar is remarkably well preserved, and even flecks of the original colours—the royal reds and blues, the hints of gold—still adhere to the plaster reliefs. Everywhere around, on the walls, door jambs and ceilings, are the ancient beliefs, incarnate, in the form of hieroglyphics. While to the non-scholar it is a phantasmagoria of cryptic imagery and indecipherable language, to the expert it is a feast of meaning.

Mills needed a full-time epigrapher to make sense of the panoply of gods and goddesses and their hieroglyphic incantations. He found a brilliant one in Olaf Kaper of the Humboldt Foundation in Berlin. The Dutch-born Kaper's love of Egyptian culture began in childhood when he kept a scrapbook of newspaper clippings on ancient Egypt. Ginger-bearded and blue-eyed, he has retained a childlike wonder concerning the ancient Egyptian language, displaying an unabashed joy as he goes about his daily duties, balanced acrobatically on ladders and scaffolding as he carefully traces the ancient symbols and figures.

Epigraphy is a fundamental Egyptological science: interpreting temple and tomb inscriptions is one of the few ways, besides papyrology, to know the thoughts of ancient Egyptians, though the language of the temples is not that of the street or the home. The language of the temple reflects not the farming class—the *fellahin*—but their more privileged contemporaries: the priestly order and the urbanized elite.

"The fascination for me," says Kaper, who describes himself as not a very religious person, "is to try to see the oasis with the eyes of the people in antiquity, to try to see what they were thinking about and how they would perceive the landscape, how they would perceive the environment and how it would influence them." He characterizes his pursuit as the creation of "an ancient mental map of the Dakhleh Oasis."

In the Valley, Kaper would likely be restricted to working on a single temple, or even one section of a temple. His work amongst the twenty-five Roman Age temples in the oasis has given him a broader context, and has revealed not only a continuity between Nile Valley and oasis beliefs, which would be expected, but surprising clashes between the priestly orders of the river and the desert.

Kaper began in 1988 by studying the gateway to the Ein Birbiyeh temple, near Bashendi. "It had been known since the last century that there was something here, but it had been largely dismissed as the remains of a Roman fort or the foundation of a temple, and in fact, Winlock didn't bother to come to look at it, it had such a bad press," says Mills. "When we came across it again in 1982, we scratched around, as we do at all the sites, and suddenly realized that what we were looking at were ceiling blocks, not foundation blocks." Beneath their feet was the first intact temple discovered in Egypt since the nineteenth century. It had been built in the time of Augustus, during the initial Roman boom.

Mills began by excavating the gateway. There, guarding the entrance, he exposed a huge, winged, falcon-headed figure in a striding pose, spearing a Libyan enemy who is being trodden underfoot and "tasted by a lion," the god's ally. Mills thinks the oasis residents would have needed a very strong god because they felt vulnerable living in this frontier land. The headdress and wings of this resplendent figure had at one time been outlined in coloured glass, "like a gigantic cloisonné." His name was Amon-nakht, meaning "mighty" or "victorious" Amon.

To Kaper he was a remarkable revelation. "To find a new god to whom a whole temple is dedicated is a novelty," he says. Even more intriguing, in terms of picking up the spread of ideas from the Valley to the oasis, and vice versa, was the discovery that the old god Seth, who had been reviled and blacklisted by the Nile priesthood, was alive and well in the oasis. Kaper's deciphering of the iconography and inscriptions associated with the new god Amon-nakht exposed a heated priestly feud. Seth, who from the New Kingdom forward had been outlawed in the Valley, continued to be venerated in Dakhleh where, in fact, he was considered Lord of the Oasis. Amon-nakht, Kaper decided, was an official creation of the Nile priesthood to counteract the worship of Seth. This theological intrigue was precisely the kind of information that Mills hoped could be teased out of the writings, clearly demonstrating the similarities and differences between mainstream Nile Valley culture and its offshoot in the oasis.

There were other riddles for Kaper to solve that bore even more directly on the oasis-dwellers' unique perception of their environment. In most respects the temple reliefs reflected the usual exchanges where the pharaoh makes offerings to the gods, beseeching their blessings, and in return the gods promise to defeat his enemies and give him a long life and an afterlife. But here at Ein Birbiyeh, and elsewhere in Dakhleh, the gods also promised "a good inundation." Such a divine promise was habitual in the Valley but seemed nonsensical when applied to the desert.

"I thought it was ridiculous when I first read it," Kaper recalls. "It sounds so incongruous. We're here in the oasis. This has nothing to do with the Nile, but still you find the same answer." Kaper decided to take this apparent incongruity seriously and not simply assume the oasis priesthood was copying by rote the patterns used in Nile Valley temples.

At temples throughout the oasis, local gods repeated the same promise. At Ein Birbiyeh, Amon-nakht says: "I give you the inundation, it comes on time, and it overflows the fertile earth." This desert god was not only promising the inundation, but that it would come at a certain time, just as in the Valley. In the doorway to the Hypostyle Hall at Deir el-Hagar, the relief depicts the gods Khnum-Re and Sothis, the "Lord and Mistress of Elephantine," who controlled the mythical sources of the Nile at the First Cataract, near present-day Aswan. (It was here, on Elephantine Island, that the nilometer was placed to measure the height of the annual inundation.) The principal god who controlled the Nile waters everywhere in Egypt was Osiris and on the relief in the outer gateway at Ein Birbiyeh, he is pictured with water "from Elephantine."

Kaper recognized this could only mean that the waters at Dakhleh were thought to be dependent upon the Nile inundation. In fact, there are still some geologists who hold to the theory that the artesian waters of the Western Desert are in part derived from seepage from the Nile, despite a preponderance of evidence to the contrary. To the ancients, however, such a notion would have seemed entirely logical. They believed the Nile inundation was derived from an ocean underlying the flat earth, a primal water source known as Nun, and that it was the gods' responsibility to ensure that the flood came on time and at the proper height. It followed that the waters bubbling up through the desert floor also originated in Nun. The inhabitants simply perceived the oasis as being in a perpetual state of inundation, a kind of blessed state. "It's a nice thought," Kaper reflects, "that they say, 'We're drinking the same water.'"

Celebrations at Deir el-Hagar reinforced this promise of a bounteous water supply and harvest. Normally a temple was located at the centre of a village, where daily the priesthood administered to the needs of the god's cult statue in the sanctuary. The very isolation of Deir el-Hagar suggests that it was not used specifically for such daily rituals. Also, its mud-brick enclosure wall is furnished with six side doors and two more doors on either side of the main gateway. Temples usually had only a single gate, set into a great wall that went around the entire outside, a layout designed to keep the public out, to protect the sanctity of the god. Deir el-Hagar seems to have been designed for quite the opposite purpose, which suggests to Kaper that its primary function was as a festival temple. The doorways were a means of crowd control, letting people come and go more or less at will. In fact, Kaper has found graffiti scribbled on the side doors and on the walls indicating the date for an annual festival.

Such events were enormously popular in rural Egypt, attracting people from all around the countryside. It is not difficult to imagine farmers gathering to watch the spectacle, crowds surging through the side doors into the large forecourt to get a peek at the golden god as he was carried aloft by the priests on a sacred boat. Those fortunate enough to be in the front row could approach and ask the god their most urgent questions. Hard-working farmers could relax and kick up their heels, singing, dancing and clapping hands. Dancers, wearing diaphanous costumes and masks to play the role of the gods, performed high-kicking routines. A carnival atmosphere prevailed, and wine flowed liberally. So did libations of oil, it seems, since the sanctuary of the temple is covered with a mysterious black residue—Mills calls it "gunk"—which preliminary analysis indicates is olive oil, perhaps mixed with animal blood.

Regardless of the frivolity, such festivals always had an underlying religious function—to ensure the fertility of the land. At Deir el-Hagar the god Amon-Re was given the epithets, "Ruler of Plants" and "Lord of the Fields." When the god was paraded throughout the countryside, his benevolence was thought to radiate over the surrounding land. The procession that followed the god would have flowed out of the temple and over the hills to Amheida, the year-round home of the priesthood.

Greek inscriptions indicate that Deir el-Hagar was last used at the end of the third century, which means it may have been sporadically active for more than two centuries. Mills, however, observed that the farmsteads on the Plain of Sio'h showed very little wear and tear. The most likely reason for the failure of the farms was that the water supply was exhausted, forcing the immigrant farmers to move on and leave the temple unfinished.

THE SURREAL SPECTACLE OF AQUEDUCTS MATERIALIZING OUT OF THE planet's largest body of sand underscores the optimism and hubris of the Romans. They came here believing that they could conquer the desert as they had conquered the other lands circling the Mediterranean. The Sahara, however, proved more resistant to their intentions than mere nations.

Even though Amheida continued to flourish into Byzantine times, the Roman heyday seems to have been short-lived for the farmers in the western part of the oasis. As the wells failed and the aqueducts ran dry, the immigrant farmers must have packed up their implements, constructed cages of palm for their pigeons and poultry, and headed down the road, looking for greener pastures.

It must have seemed that the old gods had failed to keep their part of the bargain. The mental map of the priesthood had given the ancient residents a false sense of security about the abundance of water and the bounty of the land.

However, the Roman boom continued in other parts of the oasis for three more centuries. In the eastern oasis, the DOP has been excavating the ancient city of Kellis for fifteen years. Buried in sand 1700 years ago, its monuments, houses and artifacts reveal a vivid portrait of daily life in Dakhleh's golden age.

CHAPTER ELEVEN

A DESERT POMPEII

NOTHING BRINGS HOME THE EPHEMERAL NATURE OF THE HUMAN enterprise better than finding a buried city. Nothing states with more surety that good times will be followed by bad, that the daily rituals we take for granted cannot last forever. Archaeology underscores the frailty of the human project in the face of the ravages of time and the supremacy of nature. At the same time, it is an optimistic science. It preserves some vestiges of our past ambitions and dreams, and passes them on to the future. It states by its acts of conservation and its passionate quest to discover what our ancestors thought, believed in and cherished, that the human experience is not totally obliterated by the passage of time. These were some of my thoughts when I first laid eyes on the buried city of Ismant el-Kharab—Ismant-the-Ruined.

Ismant, or ancient Kellis—its name during its life under Roman rule from the first to the fourth centuries C.E.—is located east of

A pot beside the Kellis *codices*, the world's oldest books

Mut, at the edge of a desolate section of desert that divides Dakhleh into halves, east and west. Nothing prepared me for the first encounter with this ancient city as we drove off-road across the rolling topography of the desert plain. Suddenly, over a hillock, there rose up on the horizon a ragged skyline of mud-brick ruins, vividly red against the pale Saharan sands.

The Romans had a penchant for pomp and ceremony, and something of this is preserved even today. The modern access runs past the still imposing tombs of Kellis's rich and mighty. The façades are much ravaged, although the vaults are remarkably well preserved. Here lie the elite of this desert metropolis. The tomb closest to the city centre still stands largely intact and, by its size and placement, must have been reserved for the highest and mightiest of Kellis's citizens.

It is a stunning experience to see an ancient city unfold before you; however, on my first visit to Ismant in 1987, I found it difficult initially to make visual sense of the congeries of ruined mud-brick façades and vaults carving the sky. That, of course, is the job of the archaeological architect, and on the Dakhleh Oasis project that person is Jim Knudstad, who has spent his adult life performing just that task throughout the Middle East, from the Sudan to Turkey and Egypt to Iran. Knudstad first met Tony Mills when they worked together on the Nubian Salvage Campaign and today they are still the best of friends as well as neighbours in Cornwall, England. Knudstad met me in the village square for a cursory tour of the streets and monuments of ancient Kellis. Silver-haired and bearded, his face, it seemed, was permanently sun-burned from the years of exposure to the desert sun, his blue eyes faded from so much intense scrutiny of the paled past.

Even for Knudstad, the prospect of reviving the city plan, that imaginative act of the archaeological architect, was daunting at first. "I can envision it in my head now because I've seen it on paper and I've worked it out on the ground," he told me. "But when I first walked out here, I said, 'Oh my God, what is this lunar landscape, you know, these big chunks of stuff? What do I do with them? I might draw them but they won't go together to mean anything.'"

The reality was far more rewarding, once he got down to the business of tracing walls and streets. The tops of walls were exposed simply by brushing aside surface sherds and an inch or two of sand. "It was a high for that season in '82; two of us came out here and realized that there was composition just under our feet," he recalled. "You had a sense of a growing place and you wanted to know what was around every corner. And I'm still in that kind of mood about the place."

His partner that season was the Canadian archaeologist Rosa Frey. Like Mary McDonald, Frey was a farm girl from rural Ontario who had held to her ambition to be an archaeologist since elementary school. A student of Mills, sitting in the audience when Fakhry gave his inspirational speech to the Society, she was a member of the original survey team. "It was bliss, just bliss," she remembers of that season when Kellis first came to life. Knudstad and Frey met in Dakhleh and their partnership has been something of an archaeological romance, evolving from a professional to a personal relationship among the desert sands. They are now married and still work together in the field as Knudstad travels between assignments throughout the Middle East.

Knudstad and I were standing in what seemed to be the city square, where two major streets met, one lined with the tombs and the other overlooked by an imposing structure that Knudstad has dubbed "The Governor's Palace." In fact, Knudstad does not understand the formal function of this, the largest building in the city, nor do any of his colleagues. The L-shaped structure measures 302 feet north-south by 312 feet east-west, a massive building by the standards of any age. Given that it was still standing several yards above the desert plain, it must have been extremely well built. Inside, there was decorative brickwork, the remains of a winding staircases, and fragments of painted plaster still clinging to the walls. In all, it boasted 220 rooms. The erstwhile "palace"—now known by the less inspiring name "Large Unidentified Structure"—reflected the pretensions of this desert outpost, albeit a pale imitation of the splendour that was Rome.

"This is derivative of real Roman work," Knudstad said, as we stood admiring the monumental ruin. "It's provincial, and it's mud-brick of course, but it's first-class mud-brick work, indicative of a real professionalism, a real tradition."

Though much of the city was blanketed by sand, large chunks of architecture poked through, as if thrust up tectonically. Besides the standing ruins, I had now begun to notice another remarkable feature of the site as we walked along. The ground was literally paved with potsherds. In fact, the boundaries of the city, which cover nearly 250 acres, were defined by the limits of these smashed pots. Knudstad explained that it was common practice for the Romans to mix sherds into mud-brick, but that many of the sherds were used as chinking to create the vaults and domes that Roman-Age architects were so fond of. As the wind eroded the mud-brick—the grains of sand acting like a pillaging army—the sherds fell to the ground, mantling it.

A great deal of the architecture, however, has been preserved. The sand has acted not only as a destroyer but also as a preserver of these antiquities.

As I toured the ruins with Knudstad, he casually pointed out the main features. Here was an Egyptian temple, its gateway marked by a few limestone blocks gleaming in the strong light. Looming ahead was the most conspicuous feature of the cityscape, a massive section of mud-brick wall that still stood, fortress-like, twenty-five feet above ground level. Such a *temenos* wall had once completely surrounded the temple complex, shielding it from the prying eyes of the commoners. Just past the wall, we turned left onto what Knudstad jokingly referred to as "Church Street." It had now become clear to me that we were walking on ancient streets, marked by the tops of walls, with thin lines of plaster outlining the limits of the rooms on either side of the street. As we made the corner, Knudstad pointed to his right to an unprepossessing ruin: "That's a Roman bath." No self-respecting Roman town would be without one. Knudstad has found semicircular niches inside the rubble where tubs had presumably been fitted, and vertical flues of ceramic pipe that transported hot air through the floors. Located in the centre of the city, it must have been a popular place, welcome after a day in the dusty fields.

At the end of the street, we came to a large structure marked by two rows of columns. I hardly needed to be told that this was the church.

We now backtracked to examine the excavation-in-progress of a house. To get there, we walked over the roofs of other houses. In some cases, I could look down and see domed rooms.

Finally we descended into a large room in the excavated interior of the house, several feet below ground level. "Come into the living room," Knudstad said. Such a north-facing room was typical of hot countries, Knudstad explained, serving as a wind-catcher.

"This house doesn't show much use," he continued. "There's not been much deterioration in this place since it was buried in sand. So you're pretty much looking at it as it was abandoned."

We walked to the south end of the house, passing through the kitchen, where there was a mud-brick dome-shaped oven, not unlike those found in oasis houses today. At the end of a narrow hallway, we entered a bedroom, where the handprints of a child were clearly visible on the white plaster walls. A shelf still clung to one wall. On the floor, the archaeologists had found the remains of a bed, a slipper and an amphora. Sixteen hundred years ago, a family had taken what they could put in a bundle on a donkey's back and bade farewell to this home—and their city.

THE DECISION TO DIG AT KELLIS WAS TAKEN PRIMARILY BECAUSE it seemed so little disturbed. A test pit had determined that structures extended at least two storeys underground, where houses had been buried to their rooftops when sand overwhelmed this once-proud provincial town. With such depth of occupation, Kellis also was one of the few places in the oasis where the DOP could record the orderly march of time.

The director of the Kellis dig is Colin Hope, Director of the Centre for Archaeology and Ancient History, Monash University, in Melbourne. Hope describes Kellis as "a desert Pompeii." Although the scale is different, the degree of preservation is comparable at Kellis because of its rapid burial in sand and the almost complete lack of rain in the last two thousand years.

Digging up a city requires many hands, a constant scramble for funding, and a consuming dedication. An original member of the DOP, Hope could hardly have imagined what he was getting himself into when he accepted Mills' off-hand original invitation. After three years of working in Luxor on an American dig, he had found himself tiring of the Valley, where security concerns and tourists were a constant distraction. It was then that he serendipitously met Mills and a senior official of the Egyptian Antiquities Organization in an elevator, in what he describes as "a really cheap hotel in Cairo." The official knew both men and made the introductions.

"Oh, you're Colin Hope," said Mills. "I was going to write to you because it's been recommended that you might like to come and join this project I'm starting."

"Oh, yes," Hope rejoined. "Where is it?"

"Dakhleh Oasis," Mills replied. Then he said, "Would you be available next January, then?"

"Oh, yes, I think I'll be free."

"Good," Mills drawled. "Then I'll tell my wife."

"So, I thought, this man sounds amusing to work with," Hope now recalls. The next season, in 1978, he was in Dakhleh for the initial survey.

Then twenty-eight, Hope did not expect to find himself still in Dakhleh twenty-three years later, with no end in sight. His hair and beard have thinned and greyed. Now, however, he cannot imagine working anywhere else. At the same time, he admits, "I would never, ever be so stupid again as to take on a whole city." When he started, he thought he could finish in a decade. But excavating the first two houses took five years: three years of digging and two seasons just to study the artifacts that came to light. Every year since, his team has unearthed a similar trove from the temples, tombs, houses, churches and cemeteries. Kellis has produced a wealth of information on Roman Age Egypt, but even more important than the quantity of material is the fact that so much of it is novel. "Sometimes it's rather like running through a list of firsts," says Hope. "It gets a bit ho-hummy."

One suspects Hope is being somewhat disingenuous, for Egypt has been his passion since elementary schooldays in England. While majoring in Egyptology at the University of Liverpool, he spent summers digging in Jordan, where he learned the true value of ceramics, his stock-in-trade. He did his Ph.D. on a particular type of New Kingdom ceramics used extensively for dating sites. It was a lesson in how ceramics can often yield dates more accurately than carbon-14 methods. "Wherever you go to an archaeological site, you are struck by the amount of ceramic lying around," says Hope. "People now realize that if you can get a handle on the pottery, you can get a great deal of information on your site without even excavating."

EXCAVATION OF KELLIS HAD JUST BEGUN WHEN I VISITED IN 1987, and I was anxious to see what had emerged in the thirteen years since. The tombs still stood along the road, much as I remembered them. But a great deal of the rest of the city had now taken shape. Near the town square, the Australians had erected a fieldhouse to deal with the wealth of material that was coming out of the ground daily. Instead of a team of two architects and a small local work-force, the site was bustling with eighty local *omal* and twenty archaeologists, many of them Hope's graduate students. The scale of the dig hearkened back to the excavations of the early part of the century. Hope himself seemed to have taken on the identity of that romantic era, having donned khakis and a pith helmet like a latter-day Flinders Petrie. He exercises tight control over his workmen and students, demanding no less from them than he does from himself. "It is an exhausting routine of rising at 5:30 a.m. every day, six days a week."

The unrelenting effort has been worth it, however. In Hope's opinion, the tombs and public buildings, temples and churches, are the equal of anything found outside Alexandria and attest to the level of affluence in Kellis. Despite this, Hope made a deliberate decision to excavate the houses first, in order to begin compiling a picture of everyday life as Mills has done at Ein el-Gezareen. "When you excavate the houses you get so much material that is of daily use—sandals, baskets, linens. Then you really get a sense of the people," says Hope. "And when you excavate a series of these houses you get a sense of the density of the settlement and what it must have been like to be there. And, of course, living in a place like Bashendi, you can transpose that experience to the ancient setting, and you know exactly the hustle, the bustle, the noise, the lack of privacy, everything that must have been."

Not a single tree stands near the ruins of Kellis today, but once there would have been groves surrounding the city. The chattering of tree sparrows would have filled the air, accompanied by the hollow, trisyllabic love-sick plaint of hoopoes perched on the domed roofs of tombs and houses. It is easy to imagine shaggy-tailed brown and black goats being herded through the streets, adding their bleating to the bustle of the city; donkeys braying, ducks splashing in the irrigation canals, chickens flapping and clucking through the streets; women grinding grain on rooftops or sitting out on their mastabas as they do today; camels, brought to Egypt by the Persians during the Late Period, growling and grumbling in protest as their owners loaded their backs. Camel herders would have saddled caravans of camels in the city square with amphorae, containing olive oil or Dakhleh's famed wine (Augustus is thought to have had a personal vineyard here), bound for the Nile Valley or Libyan coast via Siwa, or to Kufra.

Kellis drew its lifeblood from the farmers' fields, the ghostly checkerboard pattern of which can still be glimpsed in the surrounding desert. But Kellis was also home to artisans, the clack of the weaver's loom, the whirr of the potter's wheel, the clang of the blacksmith's anvil, the whistle of the glass blower offering a counterpoint to the bucolic cacophony.

Numerous spindles, spindle whorls, beating combs, loom weights and fragments of unspun wool discovered in the houses attest to the weaver's craft. Linen, usually in unbleached form, was the most common yarn used; it ranged in texture from very coarse, heavy-weight fabric to an extremely fine, almost transparent, cloth. Sheep's wool was woven into garments for decoration or used in embroidery; a vine motif was popular. Papyri found in the houses tell us that there were rag-workers' guilds where old garments were cut into pieces and sewn into blankets and heavy outer garments.

Judging from the cloth fragments, purple appears to have been the most common dye, although greens, blues, yellows, oranges and reds were also employed, and were sometimes woven into plaids and checks. Men wore *galabiyas,* one-piece full-length cloaks, and a child's cape has been found, all similar to what people still wear here. The inhabitants wore sandals of palm fibres or leather as they shuffled through the narrow, crowded streets and alleyways. Like the garments, the baskets and boxes used two thousand years ago have changed little in their form and function. As a result, whenever Hope's crew find something they cannot identify, they ask the workmen, who usually know what it is. In the first house they excavated they found a basket of the same kind used today for carrying eggs.

Tatyana Smekalova has applied her magnetometry wizardry to identify a large number of commercial kilns as well as a black-smith's shop in Kellis. The sheer mass of sherds still on the ground reveals the enormous amount of pottery that rolled off the local potters' wheels—pottery being the plastics of the ancient world. More than a thousand different kinds of vessels have been identi-fied: small and large, plain and ornate. In all likelihood, glass was also produced locally. Among a large horde of glass found in House 4 were two conical glass lamps which either stood in a tripod or hung from the ceiling. They had been placed in a basket, presum-ably to protect them, since even in the fourth century, glass was still a precious commodity. Household glass objects included bowls, jugs and flasks with handles and spouts, and beakers and drinking cups. The strangest glass object, a so-called *lacrimarium,* was found not in a house but a tomb. Mourners used this tall-necked flask of very fine glass to collect their tears shed for their beloved, an offer-ing thought to comfort the deceased in the afterlife.

Each and every artifact—indeed, every fragment, however humble—is recorded and adds to the store of knowledge. Excavation of the first house yielded typical domestic debris: large jars, fine-ware cooking vessels, bowls, a strainer, handled flasks, a bread dish, a small basket, a pottery lamp, a broad-bladed knife, a grinding stone, and an elaborate wooden key—the same kind oasis people still carry concealed in their gowns.

What Hope found on January 20, 1988, however, as he was busily digging down through the sand in House 2, was the kind of discovery that usually comes only once in a career. The original house had eight rooms and a courtyard. The two main living areas were flat-roofed, while the remaining rooms were barrel-vaulted. Hope and an assistant, Jessica Hallet, were digging in the kitchen, which had been added at a later date and was apparently open to the sky. Sand had filled it nearly to the top of its seven-foot-high walls. After several days, they had reached the top of the oven, which was set in one corner. Hallet, a student volunteer from Cairo, continued to excavate around the oven until she found a large storage jar lying on its side next to the oven. It was her first dig, so even finding something as commonplace as a pot was thrilling. She worked around the jar, diligently brushing away the sand until she reached the bottom of the largely intact vessel. There, next to the jar, emerging from under her brush, were pieces of rectangular wood.

"We've got some wood," she called out. "I think it's got writing on it." Slightly bemused, Hope politely responded by having a closer look for himself, thinking it was probably just a scrap of wood the occupants had dropped or deliberately left behind. As he bent down, his own interest was piqued. The rectangular pieces of wood did appear to have writing on them, and he began to carefully brush away the sifting sand that still obscured the words. More writing appeared on separate pieces. As he continued to brush away the sand, it became obvious that the pieces of thin wood had been drilled with four tiny holes, two each at the top and bottom, and bound by string. The string had loosened so that the boards on top had slid sideways like a carelessly laid down deck of cards. There was now no question what the wooden thing was: it was a book. One book would have been remarkable enough, but Hope found a second, completely intact, under the first. "Amazing!" he recalls thinking. Just how amazing was soon to be trumpeted in the world press.

"Aristotle text in desert documents," reported the *Times* of London. Of the hundred and fifty named works that Aristotle allegedly wrote, fewer than thirty have survived in fragmentary form, and it seemed that Kellis might have preserved one of these lost works. Mills and Hope were circumspect, however, and on more careful reading by the papyrologists, the texts proved to have been written, not by the great philosopher himself, but by his contemporary, Isocrates. There was still reason for dancing in scholarly circles, since this version of the three essays on kingship, concerning Nikokles, the Cypriot King of Salamis, copied onto the wooden boards in a tiny but extremely clear hand, pre-dated the earliest complete manuscript by six centuries. Scholars could now compare the tenth-century manuscript held in the Vatican Library with the fourth-century Kellis text and ferret out the errors that six hundred years of copying by scribes must have inevitably introduced.

The greatest excitement for the DOP, however, was generated by the second book, which lay under the Isocrates text with its binding still intact. It was written by an anonymous tax collector for an estate owner named Faustianos. His account—nearly 1800 lines worth—gave a record for four consecutive years in the mid-fourth century of the goods and services provided by the tenant farmers of Kellis. A priceless source of new information, it was a godsend for the DOP's study of the relationship between human activity and the environment. The Kellis Agricultural Account Book, as it has become known, records the crops grown and live-stock raised. A careful reading of its accounts has done much to fill in the economy and life history of ancient Kellis.

The paper-thin boards tied together with string are the oldest books of modern style—consisting of pages written on both sides and bound at the spine—in the archaeological record. In basic structure they were the prototype for all the numberless books that were to follow. These ancient examples of the book trade are called *codices* from the Greek word *codex,* meaning wood. (Eventually, the *codex* would replace the papyrus scroll.) Unbound wooden boards with writing on them subsequently discovered in Kellis also contained fragments of great literary texts such as Homer's *Iliad,* and, by themselves, doubled the number of fragmentary *codices* previously found in Egypt.

What was important about the Isocrates essays was that this was the earliest complete copy, in book form, of an ancient work ever found. In short, it was the world's oldest book, a landmark discovery warranting the flurry of worldwide press it received, despite the initial disappointment that it was not one of Aristotle's lost works.

When he heard the news, John Sharpe, the Curator of Rare Books at Duke University, could hardly contain his excitement. As soon as he could, he was on a plane bound for Dakhleh to inspect the books. What he saw there was the eight-leafed signature, the basic unit of today's book: "We're looking at the modern book in formation," he says. Sharpe's detailed analysis of the books, leaf by leaf, allows us to recreate this earliest example of the book-making process.

ACCORDING TO SHARPE, THE BOOKMAKER CAST A DISCRIMINATING eye around his workshop and selected a block of acacia. Measuring off a Roman foot (approximately twelve inches), he cut the wood to length. Then he set the rectangular block on its side and proceeded to saw it into eight leaves, taking pleasure in the ease with which the freshly sharpened blade bit across the grain and filled the workshop with the familiar aroma of worked wood. However, as he was making the last cut, for leaf eight, the saw slipped, gouging the wood. Perhaps he cursed. He finished the cut, calculating that this last leaf should be somewhat thicker than the others and would serve as the cover of the book. Next he took his plane and smoothed the leaves to less than a tenth of an inch in thickness. Where his saw had slipped, he made finishing touches with a drawknife, the reddish-brown shavings curling under his steady hands. He probably smiled with satisfaction, believing the slip of his hand would hardly be noticed.

He now reached for his pumice stone and began burnishing each leaf to a polished smoothness. His job was not quite done, however, and what remained was a ticklish task. He lashed the cut boards to his workbench. Straddling it, he began to drill two sets of two holes—one near the top, one near the bottom—using a bow and drill. Again, the sweet smell of wood heated by the friction rose from the book, as the spoon-shaped bit bored through all eight leaves. He again took his pumice stone and smoothed the edges of the holes, leafed through the pages, making sure that they met with his approval, then stacked them to be sure the holes lined up.

Now he applied a coat of gum arabic to make the scribe's ink adhere better, left the book to dry, and returned a few hours later with a length of linen, probably spun by his wife. He threaded the single length of string through the holes, beginning at the top.

There was one last detail to complete. He balanced the book on its side and cut a pair of shallow notches on the spine, in a V-shape, to help the leaves lie flat and help the owner reassemble the book if it came unbound. Finally, he took the remaining string and wrapped it around the book, binding it securely together.

Amazingly, 1600 years later when the Kellis Account Book emerged from the sands of the Sahara, the string still held, a

246

testament to the bookmaker's skill and the remarkable degree
of preservation at Kellis.

THE BOOKS WERE NOT THE ONLY DOCUMENTS OF IMPORTANCE TO
emerge from House 2. Hope exposed an archive of papyrus fragments, several wooden tablets, and various *ostraca* (potsherds with
writing on them). This cache was only a harbinger of what was to
come. Over the next twelve years, the largest cache of papyri discovered in Egypt in sixty years, well over 10,000 pieces, has turned
up in Kellis, and more are being discovered all the time.

Ironically, *Cyperus papyrus,* the plant that furnished papyrus
(and incidentally our English word "paper"), no longer grows wild
in Egypt; it only survives in the marshy upper reaches of the Nile
in Sudan. It is a kind of sedge that grows to luxuriant heights of
eight to nine and a half feet. To prepare a papyrus, Egyptian scroll-
makers first stripped the outer covering off the plant, revealing
several layers of a whitish papery fibre, running vertically parallel
to the stem. The sheets, or rolls, of papyrus were made of two
layers, the outer layer running vertically, the backing layer in
horizontal strips. The two were stuck, or glued, together with gum
arabic and polished using a pumice stone or shells. Sheets varied
in size, normally around nine inches in width and up to eleven
inches in height. These were attached, one below the other, to make
scrolls, which, for official documents, reached gargantuan proportions. The Great Harris Papyrus in the British Museum measures
16.5 inches wide and 133 feet in length. But for everyday use, most
papyri were of much more modest proportions. It was common to
write first on the side on which the fibres ran horizontally, the so-
called *recto* side. But due to the cost of papyrus, it was also common to use the *verso* side, sometimes for a completely different
document. In late Egyptian times, the scribe used a thick reed
cut like a quill pen, and ink made of lamp-black or powdered

charcoal, mixed with water and, often, a gum. The writing could easily be washed off and the papyrus re-used. Kept dry, the papyrus was remarkably durable.

Within Egypt, caches of papyrus have been limited to the places with the driest environments: the desert edges along the Nile, the oases, and the Fayum. These records give us the richest portrait of both public and private life in the Greco-Roman periods.

Papyri became all the rage in Europe in the nineteenth century, for practical if dubious reasons: they were simply the most convenient "antika" for travellers or traders to smuggle out of Egypt. Their popularity was undiminished by the inconvenience of not being able to read the hieroglyphic writing—which was the case until 1822, when Jean-Francois Champollion finally managed to decipher the Rosetta Stone.

The first papyrus to emerge in Europe was acquired under compromising circumstances. In 1778, an Italian merchant travelling in Egypt encountered a group of *fellahin* in the Fayum who tried to sell him fifty scrolls they had accidentally dug out of a rubbish heap. (Ever since, rubbish heaps have proven to be the most fertile ground for papyrus hunters.) When the merchant found the price too high, the peasants began to smoke the scrolls like Havana cigars, claiming they liked the aroma. As they smoked one after another, the price, however, remained the same, until there was only one scroll left, which the befuddled merchant purchased at the original price.

Subsequently, the Western appetite for papyri fuelled much of the early pillaging of Egypt's treasures, with the loss to archaeology of any objects that got in the way. Perhaps the most lurid account of a papyrus hunt is given by a master grave robber and former carnival circus man, Giovani Battista Belzoni, who, during the early 1800s, made a living as a collector of antiquities. In his *Narrative of the Operations and Recent Discoveries in Egypt and Nubia*, published in

1820, he wrote of his travail in a tomb: "I sunk altogether among the broken mummies, with a crash of bones and rags, and wooden cases, which raised such a dust as kept me motionless for a quarter of an hour . . . I could not pass without putting my face in contact with that of some decayed Egyptian; but as the passage inclined downwards, my own weight helped me on; however, I could not avoid being covered with bones, legs, arms and heads rolling from above . . . The purpose of my researches was to rob the Egyptians of their papyri; of which I found a few hidden in their breasts, under their arms, in the space above their knees, or on their legs, and covered by the numerous folds of cloth, that envelop the mummy."

Papyrology came into its own as a legitimate branch of Egyptology in the late nineteenth century, through the efforts of the London-based Egypt Exploration Society. Two of its young members, B. P. Grenfell and A. S. Hunt, made what must be considered the most exotic discovery in the annals of what is surely an exotic science. While excavating in Tebtunis, in the Fayum, they came across a crocodile cemetery. The crocodiles, which were considered sacred animals in that part of Egypt, had been wrapped in *cartonnage*. As the workmen dug into burial after burial in the hope of finding a human sarcophagus, only to find yet another mummified crocodile, tension mounted. Finally one workman vented his frustration, smashing one of the glorified reptiles into pieces, only to discover that the crocodile *cartonnage* had been fashioned from papyri. To everyone's surprise, papyrus scrolls had also been stuffed into the animals' mouths and body cavities. From this bizarre source came some of the first documents relating to the administration during the late Ptolemaic period.

In 1895, the Egypt Exploration Society mounted the first deliberate expedition to search for papyri. Hunt and Grenfell combed the ruins of Oxyrhynchus, one hundred miles upstream of Cairo. Grenfell wrote home to the Society to share his excitement: "The flow of papyri soon became a torrent which it was difficult to cope with . . . We engaged two men to make tin boxes for storing the papyri, but for the next ten weeks they could hardly keep pace with us." To date nearly 3500 papyrus rolls and fragments have been published in the forty-eight volumes of *The Oxyrhynchus Papers*, with many more planned. This is still the largest cache of papyri ever to be unearthed.

The second-largest hoard came from the Roman city of Karanis, excavated mostly from rubbish dumps by the University of Michigan between 1924 and 1934. The third-largest has come from Kellis. Prior to 1988, the Western Desert remained a blank on most maps of important Roman sites. Now Kellis, with its yield of papyri, *ostraca* and *codices*, conspicuously occupies that former blank spot. Not only are there a great many papyri but, even better, they have been found in context rather than in a garbage dump.

As more papyri emerged from the houses—the largest cache coming from House 3—Colin Hope became acutely aware of the need for a papyrologist to begin decoding this growing archive of "sand papers."

Klaas Worp of the University of Amsterdam is a child of war-torn Holland, who remembers riding on the handlebars of his parents' bicycles as they fled before the invading Nazis. He admits that he was skeptical when approached to serve as the DOP's papyrologist. He had never even heard of Kellis. Worp was reluctant to accept the assignment on two other counts. On his first visit to Egypt in the early seventies, he was rewarded with an egregious bout of Pharaoh's revenge. "It was no fun to spend a week of your two-week vacation on the loo. I swore an oath to myself never to return," he recalls. Also, Hope's invitation mentioned a cache of five thousand papyri, which, to Worp, seemed like "a staggering number," and he wondered whether the fragments were all the size of his fingernail. Finally persuaded, he has been gladly returning every year since 1993, with no end in sight.

Hope says Worp reads ancient Greek with the ease of anyone else reading the newspaper. Worp, in fact, follows contemporary news with equal enthusiasm. In remote Dakhleh, Worp gets his daily fix of world news by tuning into various shortwave bands early in the morning and reports breaking stories to his colleagues over breakfast. He then makes his way up the narrow, eroded staircase to the workroom, where he begins the task of deciphering and translating words set down by a scribe nearly two millennia ago.

Daily he is found perched on a high stool, hunched over his glass plates, half-glasses pushed down his nose—the very picture of a scholar at work. Worp's heavy build, ruddy, sun-tanned face and grey moustache, however, make him look more like a rugby coach than the bookish man he is. Like a field archaeologist, he does work that is mostly large measures of tedium, relieved by Eureka moments when he is able to "make a join," putting fragments together in some intelligible way.

Papyrus rarely comes out of the ground the way it went in, in discrete scrolls that can be unrolled and read in their entirety. Most of the papyri found in Kellis emerge in pieces, sometimes with fragments of a single text found in more than one house. Before the houses were completely buried, these so-called "wandering fragments" were scattered by the wind, or sometimes carried by rats, creating special challenges for the papyrologist in his quest for coherence.

Fragments from any one area are first collected in plastic bags, on the assumption that they belong to the same document or set of documents. Before they are passed on to the papyrologist, they are placed briefly in a humidifier to conserve them; otherwise, they would be so brittle that they could not be handled. A conservator then brushes away any sand or other contaminants, such as salt, and places the fragments between glass panes, ready for reading.

The critical faculty for the papyrologist, according to Worp, is "a very extended visual memory." At any given time, Worp is faced with a cryptic jigsaw puzzle: multiple plates that he must manipulate and match. "They pass before your eyes like a kind of microfilm and all of a sudden you say, 'I've seen that type of handwriting before—where was it?'—so you go back until you stumble across the other plate and then it may be, yeah, you've had success and the combination is spot on. But it could be that your memory was garbled and it doesn't match," he says. "Well, okay, it's a kind of Sisyphean labour trying to bring all the frames together."

The fragments are like a conversation only half overheard. "It's quite simple," says Worp. "If you do not get any sensible notion out of the text, well okay, then it's your fault. It's not the fault of the people who wrote these texts. But it also must be said, they sometimes make great efforts to make life difficult for the modern transcriber."

Reunited by Worp's eye, memory and scholarship, the papyri reveal as no other artifacts can the private thoughts and actions of Kellis's residents. The documents touch upon every sphere of human concern: personal, political, religous and economic. There are bureaucratic memos, judicial proceedings and, inevitably, records of tax collections—an activity at which the Romans excelled, much to the grief of their subjects. Many documents also relate to private loans of money, products manufactured, and crops grown. The most revealing are the many private letters that offer glimpses into people's daily lives.

WHEN HOPE AND HIS TEAM REACHED FLOOR LEVEL IN HOUSE 3, they found some two hundred pots in the central room. It was sickeningly obvious that most had been intact but that they had been standing on them and their weight had smashed the whole lot. What was for Hope a ceramicist's nightmare, was for Worp a papyrologist's dream. More than three thousand fragments of papyrus stored in the pots fanned out onto the floor, in Worp's words: "a virtual torrent of documents." The pots held a family archive, spanning five generations, beginning with Aurelius Pamour in the late third century. Unlike many small, sometimes disjointed fragments, this cache formed a discrete, largely intact record with a stable cast of characters.

Worp eagerly delved into the correspondence, learning that the patriarch Aurelius Pamour and his sons and grandsons operated a transportation system, a kind of parcel service between the oasis and the Valley. The profession of *dromedarios* is mentioned, signifying that they used camels. The letters reveal a wide range of goods the Pamours transported, not surprisingly dominated by agricultural produce: dried figs, dried grapes, olive oil, and probably dates, still much prized in the Valley. But there are also references to more exotic items, including a bronze object, which Worp speculates may have been used for cult purposes, and statues destined for Alexandria. Statues seem a most unlikely product of the oasis, as there are no known quarries nearby, and they would seem to be too bulky and costly to transport across the desert and then upriver to the capital. One possible explanation is that they were specialized statues made of bronze rather than stone. Hope's team has shown that metal-working was part of local industrial activity.

The Pamour clan also owned a house in the Valley, in the appealingly named town of Aphrodite. Probably it was a resting station for the family after their arduous two-hundred-mile trek. No specific references are made to what they brought back from the Valley, but back-hauls likely included bundles of papyrus, as the oasis did not have the marshy conditions required for its growth. Excavations at Kellis have also revealed the presence of luxury items such as glass from Alexandria and North African red slipware from Cyrenaica in Libya, implying trade to the north and west via Siwa, as well as east to the Nile.

Though they seem to have prospered, the Pamours were not without their troubles in Kellis, where the family was singled out for some rough treatment. In one letter Aurelius petitions an official to have a powerful citizen from the capital city of Mothis (Mut el-Kharab) make restitution for the theft of a donkey. He claims that the accused had taken it from him "forcefully and acting like a tyrant, while . . . I was still an adolescent." A more egregious act against his wife is detailed in a petition to the former magistrate of Mothis:

> Now Sois son of Akoutis, *comarch* of the same village of Kellis, who is constantly plotting against me, [is harassing?] me every day in violation of everything, stirring up the locally present soldiers and *officiales* and *expunctores* against my wife, and being a constant pain in the neck to me. For yesterday, during my absence, he burst the . . . door open with an axe, went in with the son of Psenamounis, the carpenter from Pmoun Pamo, though being neither a liturgist nor happening to be a [fellow?] villager of mine, he assaulted my wife with a club and he beat her up with blows so that these are visible on her body, as if they are not subject to the laws.

Such stories appear in local newspapers every day, or are retold in soap operas. What his discipline has taught him, says Worp, is that over two millennia little has changed. The letters reflect the basic needs of people in all ages: Do I have enough to eat? A place to live? Do I have to pay all my taxes or can I dodge some?

Taken together, the papyri and *codices* paint a picture of Kellis as a stratified society, with tenant farmers, landlords and various tradespeople. The letters refer to a broad range of occupations: coppersmiths, potters, weavers, camel drivers, bath-house attendants, letter couriers, court-room lawyers, a church-reader, a cobbler, a honey seller, religious officials, magistrates and the Governor and

Chief Accountant. The Isocrates *codex* was a schoolmaster's copy. There are also references to carpenters (*tectones*), some of whom had a sideline making books. One request for a book from outside, probably from the Valley, indicates that this was a well-known specialty of Kellis craftsmen. "Send a well-proportioned and nicely executed ten-page notebook for your brother Ision. For he has become a user of Greek and a comprehensive reader," says one mid-fourth-century letter.

The papyri explode any preconceptions about the role of women in oasis society, which apparently differed from that in Egypt-at-large. For its day, Dakhleh seems to have been in the vanguard of equality. Under Greco-Roman law, women were required to have a guardian when they concluded agreements with another party or when they addressed authorities. Exceptions to this law included women with three or more children (alive or dead) and women of high station. The picture presented by the Kellis letters is far more liberal. Women in Kellis ignored the need for a guardian and apparently were not forced by authorities to observe this rule. In one case a woman receiving a loan of money is assisted by another woman. Such independent action harks back to the rights of women several centuries earlier, when they could act on their own without the legal restrictions imposed by their Greek and Roman conquerors. The isolation of the oasis—despite the trade with the Valley—may have helped maintain their old legal rights. The persistence of native cultural traditions is underlined by the fact that Kellis letter writers often refer to the Nile Valley as "Egypt," as if to say they and their traditions were not part of it.

WHILE KELLIS HAS PRODUCED A WONDERFUL ARRAY OF MATERIAL, Hope acknowledges that many of the artifacts are aesthetically "tacky kitsch and Hollywood stuff." The 2000 digging season, however, produced a precious object second in value only to the priceless books. Its discovery underscores the unpredictability of archaeology. Hope had uncovered a heavy trap-door of acacia wood, sealing a crypt just inside the outer gate of the temple. Jokes circulated about his having discovered the Well of Souls and that the Ark of the Covenant itself might be buried there. Joking aside, anticipation ran high for what Hope might find—perhaps a golden god statue buried by the priesthood for safe-keeping.

Hope was in the midst of carefully excavating the crypt when he was called to an adjacent site in a nearby cemetery, where a wall had collapsed in antiquity. That morning a local worker had been digging through the wall debris, testing for any burials concealed underneath. Suddenly, his *touriyeh* exposed glass: he immediately stopped digging and called the archaeologists.

Freelance Sydney archaeologist Dan Tuck then began carefully working the glass fragments free from a stubborn matrix of sand and mud-brick cemented together with salt crystals. The first piece he extracted was a nearly complete goblet of lime-green, translucent glass in the form of a chubby-cheeked child with curly hair. Then the sides of a larger painted vessel began to emerge. Tuck immediately recognized the rarity of the object and called in Hope.

Hope hurried to the site just as a sandstorm began sweeping across the barren plain, whipping sand into the archaeologists' eyes. He held a piece of plywood in one hand to shield Tuck as he painstakingly pried loose each piece, handing them to Hope who cradled them with his other hand in a plastic tray. As more and more pieces came to light, it was obvious how special this item was. The pigments were bold and rich and perfectly preserved, as if they had just been brushed on by the artist's sure hand. "This is a wonderful piece," Hope enthused, adding with undertaker's wit, "—it makes up for the lack of things with these dead bodies." Even before it was completely out of the ground, he recognized that it was a "museum piece."

In the following days, the DOP's conservator Laurence Blondaux cleverly pieced the fragments together with masking tape, to determine which pieces were missing (in fact, very few) and for photographing. It was a tall vessel (ten inches) of enamelled glass called an *oinochos*. Its temporary reconstruction revealed a gladiatorial scene, with two pairs of gladiators in combat being urged on by toga-clad patrons who held palm fronds in their hands. One gladiator wields a trident and a dagger and has brought to his knees his opponent, who is defending himself with a shield. It is a dramatic and beautifully executed scene.

Obviously the artist knew about, or had seen, gladiatorial combat. There is no direct evidence that such spectacles actually took place in Kellis, although one of the skeletons exhumed from Kellis belonged to a six-foot-tall individual—the largest yet found in Dakhleh—who, Molto believes, may have been a Roman centurion, or even a gladiator. His foot bones exhibited a painful case of gout. "He was an elitist kind of guy," says Molto, expanding on his osteobiography, "who came into the oasis drinking lots of wine and eating rich foods—your mind can run amuck."

Fragments of similar vessels have been found from one end of the Roman Empire to the other, from Edinburgh to Afghanistan. Hope believes, however, that the Kellis *oinochos* is the only virtually complete one in existence that preserves an entire gladiatorial scene. Such painted glass was a luxury item and may have originated in Alexandria, well known for the production of elaborate glass vessels. Fragments of such glass have also been found in Kharga, Oxyrhynchus and Karanis. Hope wonders, however, whether this vessel may have been manufactured in Dakhleh itself, as there is clear evidence of glass-making in the city and a floral motif that decorates the gladiatorial scene has been found on other glassware from the shrine of the temple.

Hope still shudders when he thinks of how easily the *oinochos* might have been destroyed. For twenty years, the archaeologists had walked over the rubble of the collapsed wall, which had formed a convenient footpath for workers between the field house and the temple. Ironically, when he returned to finish excavating the mysterious and tantalizing crypt, he found only a few coins, a couple of pots, and a fragment of low-grade emerald from the Red Sea. If it had ever held anything of greater value, it was now gone.

ALTHOUGH EXTRAORDINARY ITEMS SUCH AS THE OINOCHOS AND the *codices* are few and far between, every artifact, however commonplace, yields important information about its makers and users. The humble houses of Kellis have yielded much of the most valuable and poignant information. "You get the feeling that these people just left—and they left so much," Hope says.

Not all signs of the past residents are tangible, however. As Hope walks inside the houses, he gets a feeling for what proportions and features people wanted in their homes. Many of the rooms were roofed with barrel vaults to expand the interior space. Bands of whitewash ran across the ceilings and the walls which, illuminated by a small oil lamp, would have brightened the rooms in a flickering light.

The most poignant touchstone for me was the set of handprints by a child left on the white plaster walls of the bedroom in House 1. These fragile prints may be the only sign left of this person who lived nearly 1700 years ago. Did the child grow up? die young or old? fall in love? raise children? What changes might this person have witnessed during a lifetime in Kellis? How did that lifetime end?

In the last decade, answers to many such questions are emerging from the extensive rock-cut tombs and graveyards in and around Kellis. Lying within are thousands of mummies and unadorned skeletal remains which are only now giving up their secrets. Nearly 1700 years later, the oasis dwellers' own bones are telling the stories of their lives.

CHAPTER TWELVE

SKIN OF THE GODS

Tomb 10 had been dug, like most of the others, into the red clay at the base of the sandstone hills west of Kellis. The entrance was framed by roughly squared sandstone jambs and a lintel. In the past, a grave robber had pushed aside the blocking stone. On November 23, 1993, when Peter Sheldrick and his assistant, Abdul Ghani, crawled through the cramped entrance and inched across the loose sand on their knees, they found themselves inside a rectangular chamber. Even as Sheldrick knelt, the four-foot-high ceiling scraped his head. The space was claustrophobic and hot, oppressive with dead air. Six mummies, wrapped in linen and enveloped in a patina of dust, lay in a baleful row.

Later that morning, Sheldrick stepped outside momentarily and removed his dust mask to take a few breaths of fresh air, only to hear Ghani shout, "Mabruk—congratulations!" Sheldrick quickly

A golden mummy mask

scrambled back inside, where he found Ghani gently brushing centuries-old dust from a mummy's face. Sheldrick knelt in thrilled silence as gold leaf shone through the gloom and the features of the mask came to light. Heavy gilding had been applied to the head. Large black irises stared serenely up at him. The golden lips held a trace of a knowing smile. Further brushing revealed that the *cartonnage* covering the upper body depicted seated deities before offering stands, their heads mounted with solar discs, and sphinxes with mummiform figures on their backs. Here was the thing Egyptologists dream of: a golden mummy. The skin of the gods.

Nothing has fascinated Egyptologists more than the trappings that accompanied death. The preparations were more elaborate than those of other ancient civilizations. The golden mask of the boy-king Tutankhamun staring regally at us out of the remote past is an icon not only of ancient Egypt, but of humankind's universal wish for a life beyond the grave.

Sheldrick, a mild-mannered, fiftyish doctor from Chatham, Ontario, arranges an annual locum for his general practice so that he can join the Dakhleh team. On occasion, he is called upon to exercise his vocational role as physician in the village, attending to minor maladies and injuries of the villagers and DOP crew. He is happy with the bargain he has made with life, which allows him to pursue his hobby without the financial insecurity so many Egyptologists now face. The pleasure of working on the DOP, he says, is that something of significance is found every day. "Getting up in the morning, I can hardly wait to get in the truck to see what we're going to find," he says. "I can't say that about my vocation." Sheldrick's early fascination with ancient Egypt has never dimmed since his first trip to the Land of the Pharaohs in 1969, and today he is the only SSEA member still active in the field, carrying on Freeman's legacy of amateur contribution. Now balding, with a thin, grizzled beard, he has returned to Dakhleh every winter since 1979, driven by what he describes as "an inexplicable attraction" to Egypt and its antiquities: "The idea of looking in the face of a mummy of somebody who lived two thousand years ago, and wondering what they thought, who they loved and who they hated, and how they died; or even picking up any object that was made by a human being so long ago. I have still not lost the thrill of seeing something and bringing it to light for the first time in so long." For him, the golden mummy has been the high point so far of his experiences as part of the team headed by Eldon Molto.

Molto and Sheldrick have become not only good friends but co-investigators, systematically exploring the burials of Dakhleh together over the last fifteen years. Molto readily acknowledges that Sheldrick's first-hand medical experience has been an invaluable complement to his own expertise. Previously they had found scraps of gold foil, including on two bodies where the gilding had been applied directly to the hands, arms, and faces. But grave robbers had torn the skeletons limb from limb in an attempt to remove the gold. The mummy of Tomb 10, however, had somehow escaped these ravages and was nearly intact.

In the Old Kingdom, the use of gold to adorn the mummy was specifically reserved for the pharaoh. In later periods, however, when the pharaoh no longer wielded absolute power, lavish burials became more common among the privileged, including minor members of the royal family, high priests, court scribes, army generals and provincial governors. By the Roman period, such honours might be accorded to other members of the upper or even middle classes. The papyri told Sheldrick and Molto that amongst the citizens of Kellis were retired magistrates and other high officials who might well have been able to afford the best burial money could buy. Indeed, several other "golden mummies" have since been discovered at Kellis. However, for the "bone team" the archaeological pay-off

is not so much in the gold as it is the bodies—the mummies—
themselves.

The physical anthropology team has access to three large cemeteries spanning some 1200 years. At Ein Tirghi, near Bashendi, the
team has unearthed mummies—or rather wrapped burials, as they
are not embalmed—dating from approximately 800 B.C. to 332
B.C. Then, near Kellis, are two large cemeteries, known simply as
Kellis 1 and 2. Kellis 1 has yielded mummies and skeletonized
remains from the Ptolemaic Period, circa 300 B.C.–36 B.C., that
Hope believes represent a high-status population, as with the
golden mummy. Kellis 2 is a later cemetery (100 B.C.–300) and,
besides embalmed and decorated mummies, includes classic,
unadorned Christian burials. In all, there are at least three thousand burials, of which Molto, Sheldrick and team have been able to
analyze only 450 so far.

In 1993, Molto asked Art Aufderheide to join his team to carry
out autopsies on the mummified remains. A professor at the
University of Minnesota's Medical School in Duluth, he is best
known as one of the fathers of modern mummy research, having,
in the last three decades, examined nearly eight hundred mummies
in far-flung places around the world. He was quick to accept
Molto's invitation to work in the Egyptian desert, where mummification reached the level of high art.

I first met this sprightly septuagenarian at the DOP's Third
International Symposium held in Melbourne, Australia, in August
2000. An unassuming man, Aufderheide has nevertheless been
dancing to his own drummer for the last three decades. Bored by
the routine of laboratory work, in his early forties he set off with
three friends to raft down the 1200-mile-long MacKenzie River
which outlets into the Arctic Ocean. Thus began his infatuation
with the North. He followed his MacKenzie odyssey by living for a
year on the land with the last Inuit hunter-gatherers of Bathurst Inlet

in Canada's High Arctic, and returned there to make a highly acclaimed documentary film on their last season in the wild before they were resettled to permanent communities—and Aufderheide himself settled into academia. Long interested in the history of disease, he made world headlines with his revelation that the ancient Romans had six times as much lead in their bones as modern North Americans. The reason? Romans lined their aqueducts with lead, kept wine in lead containers and even sweetened it with lead acetate. He suggested lead poisoning could account for the madness of the Roman emperor Caligula.

However, his major interest was in soft tissues, and for that he needed mummies, which he joked "were in short supply in Minnesota." Using what he ruefully refers to as the "Mary and Art Aufderheide retirement fund," he bankrolled his own research on the mummies of the Canary Islands, and followed that with an exhaustive study of the natural mummies of the Andean Atacama Desert, where it has not rained in recorded history. From a perfectly preserved thousand-year-old Peruvian mummy, he extracted the DNA for the tuberculosis bacillus, thus exonerating Columbus of being the carrier of this devastating disease to the New World. It seemed inevitable that he should eventually make his way to Egypt.

In Dakhleh, Aufderheide employs a simple tool kit to disassemble the dead: a Swiss Army knife, a chisel and a hacksaw. He is unsentimental about the mortal remains, viewing them, he says, as "a broken-down car." He has another natural attribute that aids him in carrying out his morbid science without wincing: he has almost no sense of smell, a virtue when you are cutting into two-thousand-year-old bundles of human flesh, albeit mummified.

For all his experience, Aufderheide has been surprised by some of the bizarre forms of mummification used in Dakhleh. In the classic Nile Valley method, first described by Herodotus, the embalmers made an incision on the left side of the abdomen with a ceremonial flint knife and, reaching a hand in, ripped out the stomach and intestines. The abdomen was washed out, then the diaphragm was punctured and the chest contents removed, except for the heart, which, rather than the brain, was considered the seat of intelligence and the will. The corpse was then covered with heaps of natron (a naturally occuring mixture of sodium bicarbonate and various salts) and left to dessicate for forty days. By then it had lost most of its moisture and was a shrivelled effigy of its former self. To compensate, the embalmers stuffed its cavities with resin-soaked linen to give it a more lifelike appearance. They then painted the entire body with a molten resin before carefully wrapping it and placing the mummy mask over the head. But what Aufderheide found in Dakhleh rarely conformed to this pattern.

Here, many of the so-called mummies had simply been preserved by natural means due to the hyper-aridity of the region. Especially in summer, when temperatures soar above 100°F, the sun can do a more than adequate job of mummification, sucking moisture from the tissues. In such cases, a relative or embalmer sometimes applied a thin, almost transparent, coat of resin to the body, which, while doing nothing to preserve the internal organs, at least had an antibiotic effect on the outer surface. Despite this slipshod attempt at preservation, Aufderheide found that nearly all of the Dakhleh mummies had been elaborately wrapped in several layers of linen. Perhaps the resin was applied simply to make the wrapping in linen more convenient. First, the embalmers laid two or three sheets down the back of the corpse, then folded them over to cover the face. Then they individually wrapped the neck, arms, torso and legs in horizontal bands, to make a tight package. No attention was paid to the internal organs, except for the brain, which was invariably removed. Based on Herodotus's description, Egyptologists had always believed that the embalmer used an iron hook inserted into the nostrils to pull out the brain. Aufderheide's practical experience as a clinical pathologist suggests otherwise to him. The brain, he points out, has the consistency of half-set jelly. After a body has sat in summer heat for three or four days, it is possible, and easier, simply to pour the brain out.

Even when an actual embalmer practised his art in Dakhleh, the methods were still puzzling. In some cases he made a crude incision above the clavicle or hacked a hole in the back and poured hot resin directly into the body cavity, as if it was an industrial mould. These were not the only portals employed: in one individual the right eye was plucked out, in another a crude hole was punched into the cranium and later plugged with resin-soaked linen. Even more bizarre were instances where the mummies were tied to a rack made of palm ribs bound with palm-fibre twine or cloth. In one case, the mummy had been made up from parts of four different bodies: the head of a thirty-five-year-old woman, the spine of a fifty-year-old woman, the left leg of a three-year-old child, and the right leg of a five-year-old. In other cases, a palm rib had been inserted in the spinal column and passed into the skull to stabilize the bodies. Was there a strange death cult being practised in Dakhleh? More likely, Aufderheide thinks, relatives were attempting to counter the repeated depredations to corpses by tomb robbers and simply got the body parts mixed up.

Only a few mummies showed a high degree of professional care and treatment. Here, all the viscera were removed, rolls of resin-coated linen inserted to replace them, and a thick layer of resin applied to the outside. Often the resin included a mixture of asphalt from the Dead Sea, where the bitumen bubbles to the surface in great globs, and resin from the so-called cedars of Lebanon (actually juniper trees). Mixing in asphalt, or bitumen, was an economizing measure to mitigate the cost of the labour-intensive process of extracting and distilling the resin.

The amateurish efforts displayed in many of the mummies indicated to Aufderheide that the oasis did not have a resident embalmer. The bereaved may have had to rely on an itinerant embalmer from the Valley or on their own unpractised hands. The varying treatment may also reflect the varying socio-economic status of the bereaved. As Herodotus tells us, there were three methods available—for royalty, for the rich, and for the poor. But in Dakhleh, it seems, many of the bodies were not even accorded the most basic dignities.

Despite the often crude efforts to preserve the flesh, their bones have yielded a remarkable amount of new information on the challenges of life in a Saharan oasis.

As each body is disinterred, the bones are individually wrapped in toilet paper, placed carefully in a tin box, and transported back to Bashendi for closer inspection. Most evenings, Molto and Sheldrick are to be found working side by side in the second-storey workroom. When Molto looks up from his workbench, he can imagine the ancient people of Kellis alive and well, people with families and jobs, talking, laughing and telling jokes while they walked the streets. His challenge is to retrieve as much personal history as possible from the bones, and with new techniques he is garnering more information than was feasible even at the time he joined the project in 1985.

Every dead person has a story to tell, and Molto believes he has a responsibility to the dead to tell as much of it as he can. However, the limitations on the study of ancient burials are not only technical but increasingly ethical as well. Do archaeologists have the right to disturb the dead in the name of science? In North America, some native groups have challenged that right, on grounds that it is desecration of their ancestors. They have prevented further excavations in some locations, and have obtained the return of certain bones from universities and museums for proper re-burial. Molto respects these arguments but counters by pointing out that many of us, himself included, would be glad to have our story told two thousand years from now. As long as the bones are treated with reverence, Molto feels there is no sacrilege. In his mind, an osteo-biography is a kind of immortality. Not everyone would agree, but to date he has not had to face the kind of outrage directed at some of his colleagues in North America. In Egypt, few of the modern Islamic inhabitants consider the ancient Egyptians their direct ances-tors. For now, the bones remain in their metal boxes for future study, though one day they will be returned to their original tombs.

Molto's professional care and personal compassion stand in sharp contrast to the treatment accorded mummies throughout most of history. In *The Mummy Congress*, Heather Pringle chronicles the various crackpot and generally unpleasant uses of mummy flesh. During the Renaissance, Europeans, desperate for panaceas and often suffering as much at the hands of their doctors as from their diseases, hit upon mummy powder, or, as it was then known, *mumiya*. Convinced of its efficacy, Europe's privileged classes, it seems, would stop at nothing to obtain it. In 1586, Sir John Anderson travelled to Egypt, where he plundered an ancient burial ground near the Pyramids, bringing home six hundred pounds of mummified corpses and turning a tidy profit by pulverizing the remains of ancient human beings. Mummies were even used for purely aesthetic purposes, being ground into dust to make a bitumen-like powder that Victorian painters thought lent a lovely amber varnish to their works.

The greatest destruction, however, was wrought by collectors, both private and public, who wished to display the wizened, tanned bodies as museum attractions or as domestic conversation pieces. Owning a mummy became all the rage in Europe after Napoleon's savants published the monumental *Description de l'Egypte*. Private travellers set out for the Nile with the goal of smuggling a mummy home. The first Western traveller to Dakhleh, Sir Archibald

Edmonstone, purchased a mummy near Thebes (Luxor) and on returning to England, oversaw its dissection. While in Dakhleh, Edmonstone also entertained the notion of carrying off mummy parts, which he found strewn around the rock-cut tomb at *el-Muzzawaka*. "Our Arabs, however, looked upon [the mummies] with a degree of religious horror; for upon our pretending that we would carry one away with us, they unanimously declared they would desert us."

Few Arabs or Europeans showed such scruples. Long after the Egyptian government outlawed the export of antiquities in 1835, Europeans continued to slip by authorities with mummies stowed away in their luggage. Getting a whole mummy out of Egypt was a challenge. As it was impossible to cram a whole mummy into most steamer trunks, observes Pringle, collectors often settled for mummy parts: heads, hands and feet. Such dismembered mummies became valuable Victorian keepsakes which today are lost or mouldering away in attics. Most museums also have a collection of mummy parts, which are only now receiving scientific attention, although much of their value has been forfeited, since their origin is unknown.

IN MOLTO'S EXPERIENCE, EACH CASE OF SKELETAL PATHOLOGY becomes a course in itself, involving hours and sometimes years spent poring through the literature and consulting with other experts to arrive at the correct diagnosis. Molto has found Sheldrick's medical knowledge invaluable. In 1997 in Kellis, they excavated the skeleton of a young child whose frail bones were horribly riddled with pockmarks. They had never seen a skeleton so ravaged. They brought it back to the field camp and decided to think about it overnight. Both men spent a sleepless night. In the morning they met in the manner of two clinicians case-conferencing a living patient.

"Leukemia," said one. The other nodded.

It is not surprising that they were initially puzzled, because, if they are right, this is the earliest known case of childhood leukemia. Five years later, five experts are still working on this unique case, trying to decide which type of cancer the child suffered from: nephroblastoma, neuroblastoma or, as Molto believes, acute lymphocytic leukemia.

Although Molto relishes the detective work, and takes an understandable professional pride in solving such medical mysteries, the process is, for him, much more than academic. His emotional investment is more like that of a coroner trying to catch a killer.

In the case of the child with leukemia, his compassion has been honed by life in Bashendi, where a death in the community brings the whole village to a standstill. For three days, plaintive prayers ring out from the mosque, for the loss of any member of this tight-knit community is deeply felt. However, children are especially valued in Egyptian culture. "Imagine this child who had this hideous form of cancer," says Molto. "I think the whole community would have suffered along with the family."

FOR ALL ITS EMPHASIS ON THE INDIVIDUAL, MOLTO's "INTERVIEWING" techniques have also revealed a wealth of new information on the population in Dakhleh as a whole. By carefully studying the bones found in the Ein Tirghi and Kellis cemeteries, Molto is able to determine not only such basic parameters as stature, life expectancy and diet, but also more subtle information such as lifestyle, beliefs, vulnerability to disease, and the stresses of the desert climate. There are subtle differences between the two populations. As we have seen, people at Ein Tirghi were short in stature and lived short lives. Although the gene pool changed very little between the Late Pharaonic Period and the Roman Age, people were slightly taller during the Roman boom times, perhaps reflecting a better diet. And the elite, who could afford more lavish burials, were taller yet, presumably indicating privileged access to choice foods. What seems strange, however, is that infant mortality was much higher in Kellis. Rather than indicating that times were leaner, Molto feels it proves the opposite. Better nutrition during Roman times probably boosted fertility. However, given the difficulties attending childbirth, this would mean more deaths. Molto has detected two cases of birth trauma, one male, one female. Both displayed deformities of their arms, whose growth plates—the area of active bone development—were damaged at birth when the babies were pulled into the world hands first.

Those Dakhlans who died in childhood probably did so from gastro-intestinal disease as a result of poor sanitary conditions. In the oasis, this would not have been caused by contaminated water, since it runs clean at its source, but more likely transmitted by the houseflies that constantly light in the eyes, on the lips, and in the nose—because that's where the water is. Today, residents are so inured to these pests that they hardly bother to brush them away.

If people did survive into adulthood, they might expect to live into their mid-thirties or early forties, and many survived into their seventies. Women were three to four times more likely to live into old age than men, suggesting that the men, overall, lived a more stressful existence, perhaps occupation-related.

Molto has found a remarkable lack of violence among the population. Dakhleh, he says, was a relatively peaceable kingdom, although the violence recorded by the Pamours in the Kellis papyri show that this was not always so. Of those who came to a bad end, most were young males, "awash in testosterone." One young man had clearly been stabbed between the ribs with a dagger, which the killer then twisted to finish the job. Cross-examined in a courtroom, Molto says, he would have to conclude there had been, in forensic lingo, "malintent." Another skull displays two depression fractures, "a double whammy," according to Molto, who suspects

that altercations might have been sparked by the perennial skir-
mishes over water rights. He has himself seen hoes raised in threat-
ening gestures at Dakhleh in disagreements over irrigation canals.
What the true cause was, of course, we will never know. But Molto
is fairly sure that oasis men were not engaged in warfare. He also
observed a conspicuous absence of trauma in children, indicating
little or no child abuse in ancient Dakhleh—which might also be
inferred from its apparent absence today.

People were, however, prone to occupational hazards and
domestic accidents. Falls down stairs or off roofs are still common
causes of injury and death here. One burial revealed two individuals with "a pile of fractures"—broken legs and a crushed rib cage
among them—which Molto attributes to a house collapse. Such
deaths occur even today, when old mud-brick gives way.

To TEASE OUT PATTERNS, MOLTO LOOKS AT COHORTS, SEGREGATED
by age and gender, as well as at the population as a whole. By doing
so he is able to address more specific questions: What was it like to
be a child in Dakhleh? A young man? An old woman? Women, for
example, show a remarkably low rate of fractures until they reach
their mid-forties and the onset of menopause, when forearm fractures and hip fractures, typical of osteoporosis, show a significant
jump. Molto has also detected signs of occupational stresses suffered by women, especially arthritis in the neck region. From a very
young age, women no doubt carried large loads on their heads.
Even now, every day women carry jugs of water, or heaping bags of
rice and grain, or baskets filled to overflowing with fodder or firewood on their heads. Straight-backed, they seem to glide under the
burden. "I don't know how they do it," Molto marvels. "Even little
girls do it, but certainly over time it's going to show up."

What most surprised Molto was the remarkable degree of
healing many skeletons showed, given the severity of some of their

injuries. In one case, a man's rib cage had been "flailed" (all the ribs fractured in at least one place), a condition that, even with modern medical techniques, often proves fatal. Yet his ribs, and his shoulder and hip, all healed without sign of any infection. Furthermore, the whole population displayed an almost total absence of bone infection.

Such pervasive immunity confounded Molto. The explanation only came when he consistently found traces of the naturally occurring antibiotic tetracycline in the bones. Tetracycline is produced by a fungus, *Streptomyces*, which Molto traced to its source in the grains these Dakhlans used to make their daily staples of bread and beer. In times of plenty, when the granaries were full, fungi flourished at the bottom of grain bins where there was more moisture, or in the fermentation process for beer, conferring immunity on the adult population.

Diet in the Roman period, however, was not always advantageous. Just as in Ein Tirghi, the Kellis population suffered from "bubbly bone" caused by iron-deficiency anemia. A thorough study of the Coptic Christian community resident in the Kharga Oasis in 1909 noted widespead anemia, manifested in a sickly appearance, listlessness, and lack of energy and vitality. Molto cannot be sure of the cause, but he can make some educated guesses. He believes that the primary cause of the iron-deficiency anemia was gastro-enteritis, though malaria, which leaves its victims vulnerable to infections of the gastro-intestinal tract, may also have been a contributing factor.

Molto pursued this particular medical mystery by delving into both modern and ancient texts, including the Kellis Agricultural Account Book. For iron to be absorbed in the body, he knew, the diet must include folic acid, which is amply available in mother's milk. The second-century Roman physician, Soranus, approved of maternal breastfeeding, but not until three weeks after birth, to allow the mother to regain her strength. He recommended the services of a wet nurse but, failing that, honey diluted with water or goat's milk. We now know that infants started on goat's milk suffer severe anemia due to folic-acid deficiency. And Molto knew from the account book that honey, which can also compromise children's health as a source of botulism, was produced in Dakhleh.

Any one or combination of these dietary or infectious factors could have ultimately caused the death of these infants. In later life, such symptoms seem to have abated, with the bubbly-bone condition disappearing in adolescence. The Roman population seems to have suffered less than the Ein Tirghi people, suggesting a difference in diet or some other environmental factor. Molto suspects the earlier population may have been more subject to malaria. To prove it, he plans to scrape out the pulp from sample teeth and test it for the DNA of *Plasmodium malaria*.

For his part, Aufderheide is also looking for malaria, as well as shistosomiasis, the latter being an extremely common parasitic disease in the Valley today. The shistosome parasite is hosted by a snail that lives in the Nile and in irrigation canals, and malaria, too, is carried by a water-borne mosquito. The presence of either disease in Dakhleh would tend to indicate a wetter climate in Roman times than prevails today in the oasis, where both diseases are absent.

Aufderheide is searching for shistosomiasis and malaria DNA in the preserved mummy tissue rather than the bones, using specific antibody tests. Besides indicating wetter conditions during the Roman Period—a possibility the archaeologists regard with skepticism—shistosomiasis or malaria antigens in the mummies could also indicate contact with the Valley, a fact already amply supported by the papyri. Unfortunately, Aufderheide has discovered that much of this testing is difficult, or in many cases impossible, because the soft tissue was contaminated when the embalmers poured hot resin into the bodies.

Molto is also following the trail of another pathological condition that has been linked to folic-acid deficiency, spina bifida, in which the neural arch of the spine fails to fuse. Although there are sometimes no debilitating effects, many Roman Age Dakhlans who were victims of the condition died in their late twenties and early thirties, suggesting that the defect could be contributing to shortened lifespans. Even today, such neural tube defects are relatively common in Egypt and elsewhere in the Middle East. The medical community is still debating whether dietary factors or genetic predisposition are more responsible. The very high incidence in Dakhleh, where roughly 25 percent of the Ein Tirghi adults had the condition and almost that many at Kellis, suggests to Molto an inbred population, an hypothesis he will test by DNA analysis.

ONE OF MOLTO'S OBJECTIVES WHEN HE JOINED THE DOP WAS to refine and develop new ways of working with old bones. Since only so much can be deduced from even microscopic inspection of the bones or soft tissues, Molto has turned increasingly to the latest biochemical techniques, including isotopic and DNA analysis of bone tissue.

"People come back to where their roots are," Molto says of his undertaking. "As a kid I was fascinated with genetics, much to my parents' chagrin." The twelve-year-old Molto had fifteen aquaria. His local tropical fish dealer had black angel fish, which the young Molto admired but which the dealer would not sell him. Undeterred, Molto borrowed genetics books from the library and tried to produce the first all-black guppy instead. He managed to produce "an almost black strain" but the fish became so inbred they could no longer reproduce. "I'm now getting into the same question I had when I studied guppies, of intragroup genetics," he says philosophically.

DNA was first recovered from a 2400-year-old Egyptian mummy in 1985, a development that created a great buzz in both archaeological and anthropological circles. This breakthrough created the potential to profile the genetic composition of ancient populations and shed light on such issues as population movements in antiquity, specific group associations within a population, and familial structure. Soon after this, Molto became aware of the potential for extracting DNA from the Dakhleh bones when histological analysis revealed well-preserved collagen, a fibrous protein that binds bone cells together. In her lab at Port Huron Hospital in Michigan, Megan Cook was able to extract amino acids—the building blocks of DNA—from this ancient connective tissue, opening the door to this new line of inquiry. Not only will this allow Molto to address population questions concerning the ancient Dakhlans themselves, it also creates the exciting possibility of recovering the DNA of pathogens, such as the malaria protozoan, and making a definitive diagnosis of ancient diseases.

In the mid-1990s, Molto became eager to apply the latest molecular biology techniques when he realized that cloning, DNA sequencing and, in particular, the perfection of the Polymerase Chain Reaction Technique (PCR)—which he describes as "a Xerox machine for making lots of copies of DNA without worrying about destroying your original"—could greatly expand his knowledge of the Dakhleh population. There was a catch, however, as there were no fee-for-service laboratories in North America that he could hire to do the testing. He decided to build his own. Molto, who is most at ease in sneakers, jeans and a hockey jersey, put on his business suit and shoes, which he admits wore thin at times, and began knocking on doors in the corporate community. Due to the publicity from "DNA fingerprinting" in high-profile legal cases, he found more sponsors willing to bankroll his vision than he had anticipated. In 1996, he opened his Paleo-DNA laboratory in a small house on the campus of Lakehead University, and his researchers began processing bones from Dakhleh. By 2000, the $1.23 million project had moved into a new high-tech, climate-controlled building in Thunder Bay.

This lab is one of the first in the world to apply DNA analysis to the genetic material of ancient bones and teeth. Dr. Ryan Parr, a Mormon from Salt Lake City, who honed his skills at the University of Utah, oversees the half-dozen staff who carry out the finicky analysis. The process requires extreme levels of contamination control to ensure that modern DNA does not mix with the ancient material, which can happen by merely handling a sample without gloves.

Because of its density, bone is a particularly rich DNA archive, and recovering DNA encased in bone is a relatively simple procedure, says Parr. He needs less than a gram of bone for analysis. He first sandblasts the surface, then exposes it to ultraviolet light or soaks it in bleach for twenty minutes to decontaminate it. The sample is then washed with sterile water to remove any trace of bleach and placed in a sterile enclosure to dry. After drying, the sample is ground to fine powder—recalling the apothecaries' production of *mumiya*—and the powder dissolved in a special reagent that releases the DNA. The DNA is then purified and replicated by the PCR process. Finally, the order of the genetic alphabet, comprised of four amino acids, is read by separating the fragments of DNA in a gel.

The ancient DNA that Molto's team works with is mitochondrial DNA, rather than the nuclear or chromosomal DNA found on the chromosomes. It is found in respiratory organelles, mitochondria, which function as the power plants for the cell, providing energy for all its vital functions. There are a number of advantages to working with mitochondrial instead of nuclear DNA. Foremost, there are thousands of mitochondria in each cell, but only one nucleus. Since researchers are working with minute quantities of ancient DNA at best, and since with nuclear DNA there is only one shot at success, the probability of extracting DNA from mitochondria is hundreds to thousands of times more likely. With the PCR technique it is then possible to amplify a single DNA molecule into millions, even billions, of copies. In addition, the entire mitochondrial DNA genome (the complete set of genetic material), which consists of 16,000 amino acid pairs, was described in 1981, so it is much better known than the nuclear genome, which consists of some three billion pairs and was only recently mapped by the Human Genome Project.

Mitochondrial DNA is inherited maternally rather than from both parents, as is the case of nuclear DNA, which means that all siblings have the identical mitochondrial genome. This allows researchers to establish matrilineal relationships. Using mitochondrial DNA, Molto's researchers can also detect differences between modern and ancient populations, pinpoint how long ago the change occurred, and determine the origin of a population. For this purpose, they zero in on the hypervariable region of the mitochondrial genome, where the mutation rate is much faster than on the rest of the molecule. (This is the same area used for genetic fingerprinting in forensic cases.) Also found there are continent-specific markers. Three in particular occur with much higher frequency in the sub-Saharan African population than in the Eurasian population, and it is these markers that Molto's team has been investigating to determine whether Dakhleh's population came from south or north of the oasis.

So far, results are preliminary, but they are highly suggestive. Not one of the sub-Saharan markers has shown up in the burials from Kellis or Ein Tirghi. As Molto points out, "this does not answer the question of who the ancient Egyptians were, but it tells you who they were not." Nevertheless, it strongly points to these ancient Dakhlans being "North Africans," of Eurasian extraction.

The testing has also revealed a greater diversity of matrilineal lines than expected, confirming once again that Dakhleh was less isolated than one might have guessed. It is obvious that women were entering the population from outside, probably from the Valley, given the documents translated by Worp that indicate a bustling trade between there and the oasis.

The Kellis population has also been compared to the modern residents of Bashendi, using hair samples and throat swabs collected from schoolboys. The tests show significant differences. Since Roman times it appears that the maternal gene flow has reversed, south to north, as the modern population has a fifty-fifty split between northern genes, and southern ones, the latter similar to those observed in northern Sudan or historic Nubia.

Molto next plans to study ancient populations from the Nile to see how they compare with those in the oasis. Much to his surprise, his DNA profile of the ancient Dakhlans is the first such population study ever done in Egypt, despite long-standing debates over who the pyramid builders were. By dint of Molto's work, all such studies in Egypt in the future are likely to use the Dakhleh population as the benchmark.

WITHIN THE KELLIS CEMETERIES, ALONGSIDE THE DESCENDANTS of the pyramid builders with their elaborate death trappings, Molto found more simply buried bodies. These skeletonized remains lay in an east-west orientation without grave goods (save the odd pot) or ornamentation of any kind, let alone gold. A new faith was sweeping across Egypt, replacing the three-thousand-year-old native religion and its old gods. By the mid-fourth century, the embalming trade itself had died out. People had exchanged the glory of gold and the preservation of the body for another concept of immortality.

CHAPTER THIRTEEN

SIGNS OF THE CROSS

DURING THE INITIAL SURVEY, JIM KNUDSTAD WAS HARDLY SURPRISED
to find the remains of a large Egyptian temple near the centre of
Kellis. What did surprise him and his colleagues was also finding
three Christian churches, especially the basilica-style Large East
Church, capable of accommodating a sizable congregation of
believers. The co-existence of a polytheistic temple and monothe-
istic churches down the street from one another suggested a complex community. It proved that the great social changes sweeping
through the Nile Valley had spread across the Saharan sands and
found fertile ground in Dakhleh.

Before the rise of Christianity, Egypt was a land in which the
gods of three cultures—native Egyptian, Greek, and Roman—
lived comfortably side by side. Even the names of gods were used
interchangeably, so that a Roman citizen might worship the Greek

---

A fourth-century basilica, the oldest church in Egypt

279

goddess Demeter, who to a native Egyptian was known as Isis, the giver of life. Some Romans, including the poet Juvenal, demonstrated an open contempt for Egyptian religion, calling Egypt a "demented land" where people worshipped animals. For the most part, however, religious tolerance prevailed. In a world of many gods, it seems, there was always room for one more, and it was in this atmosphere of live-and-let-live that early Christianity first took root in Egypt. Acceptance of the new religion was made easier by the fact that, in many respects, it differed very little from the old religion. As Sir E. A. Wallis Budge wrote, it "in all essentials so closely resembled that which was the outcome of the worship of Osiris, Isis, and Horus that popular opposition was entirely disarmed."

IN 1991, COLIN HOPE TURNED HIS ATTENTION TO THE MAIN TEMPLE in Kellis, which was built around the reign of Hadrian (117–138), whose cartouche graces the gateway. Hope found the temple in a generally poor state of preservation, much of the precious stone having been looted. However, among the rubble he found fragments of gilded barques decorated with the figures of various deities flanked by goddesses with their wings outstretched. In 1994, he uncovered a painted panel hidden in a cupboard underneath several pottery vessels. The face staring back at him was that of the goddess Isis. According to Herodotus, Isis and Osiris were the most universally worshipped gods in Egypt. Even so, very few painted images of Isis on wood had ever been found. To Hope's delight, Kellis had yielded yet another rare and beautiful object.

The painting is rendered in tempera on a wash similar to that found on the *codices*. With her large eyes, Isis looks out from a blue background. She wears a golden disk and horn crown, painted in red and yellow, with a rearing cobra on the front of the disk. Tight curls outline her forehead, and her long locks fall to her shoulders. Her pale pink face is long and serious, with a narrow nose and a small mouth with full lips. Even today, the fashion industry would mark her as a beauty, an object of secular worship. The closest comparable painted image of Isis is a triptych held in the Getty Museum. Dating of the Kellis painting has proved difficult, but Hope's best guess places it in the mid-second century. Hope also found fragments of plaster sculptures of the much-beloved Isis, which would have lined the walls of the temple.

The greatest trove of religious artwork had yet to be uncovered, however. It lay buried in sand at the back of the temple, in an adjacent shrine called the *mammisi,* or birth house of the god. Once the sand was removed, Olaf Kaper set to work interpreting the hieroglyphics and artwork and determined that the temple and shrine were dedicated to a god with the whimsical-sounding name of Tutu. Significantly, this was yet another Kellis first: it is the only temple in Egypt dedicated solely to this oddball god who seems to have become a favourite in Ptolemaic and Roman Periods. Tutu first appeared in the Delta as a minor god, in the Late Period. Ironically, he was the son of Neith, a Delta goddess and one of the most ancient of the Egyptian deities: "She gives a very late birth," Kaper quips.

Tutu's formal title was "The Master of Demons." He is portrayed as a walking sphinx, indicating his active nature and his readiness to come to his worshippers' rescue against illness and the forces of evil in the world. He is well armed for the job and in many ways resembles the kind of chimera common to fantasy comic books, like some superhero of antiquity. He is blue-skinned and two-faced, with a bearded man's face in front and a lion's face at the back. A crocodile protrudes from his chest, and he has a cobra for a tail to fend off any attack from the rear.

The 2000 dig season ended with a stellar find, a *stela* or stone slab dedicated to Tutu. It was uncovered in rooms under the temple where it had been used as a lid on a large, empty pot. Carved on white limestone, pieces of inlaid glass had been preserved, including a blue eye of the crocodile. It was only the second Tutu stela found in context in Egypt, the other having been excavated by Howard Carter in the early part of the century. Some sixty others are housed in private collections and museums worldwide, but all were smuggled out of Egypt on the black market, still a thriving business in Egypt, and sold at art auctions in London. Therefore, their provenance was unknown. Similarly, golden masks and decorated cartonnage from Dakhleh mummies have mysteriously appeared on the market in recent years.

The discovery was marked in camp by Mills presenting Kaper with a small plastic purple sphinx, a child's toy, that he had picked up at the Metropolitan Museum of Art in New York—it seemed for just such an occasion. There was back-slapping and a round of before-dinner toasts in the courtyard.

Kaper hopes that the rich imagery adorning Tutu's shrine will yield new insights into the dying days of the old religion. "One of my ideals," says Kaper, "is to bring back the wealth of religious ideas that developed in antiquity, and make them available again. That's the task of the archaeologist, to bring them back."

This was easier said than done, as the once-vaulted roof had collapsed in antiquity. Kaper has spent a decade reconstructing the complex reliefs, a task as rewarding as it is tedious. The roof contained three thematic panels, or registers, on either side, each forty feet long. In classic Egyptian style, every available inch of space was covered with figures and inscriptions painted on the plaster. When the roof came crashing down, the crumbly plaster shattered into smithereens. Kaper's challenge was to put the thousands of pieces of this room-sized jigsaw puzzle back together again.

The DOP conservators came up with a simple but ingenious method. In the field, they cut away the mud-brick, leaving only the plaster. They applied gauze backing to each plaster fragment to hold it together, then treated it with transparent resin to preserve the colour. They gave each block a number and collected all the fragments under and around it. Each block and fragments were then placed together in a tray for piecing together at the field-house. The ability to connect the black-line figures of the artwork helped in this painstaking manual process, but Kaper's encyclope-dic knowledge of the panoply of Egyptian gods was critical to the identification and placement of the figures.

When Kaper returns to Bashendi at the end of each day, some-one is sure to ask: "Did you find any new gods today?" Often, his answer is "Yes." The great number of gods stems from the *mam-misi*'s major theme, "the counting of time"—a ritual necessary for the cyclical rebirth of the god Tutu. So far, Kaper has identified nearly four hundred different gods, including local ones such as Amon-nakht and Tapshay, the consort of Tutu and a goddess unique to Dakhleh. Kaper thinks that she may have been a local "saint" raised to the level of deity by the Kellis priesthood, who were clearly well versed in the mainstream Egyptian religion, but also not afraid to create their own traditions.

Although physical reconstruction of the vault was not possible, Kaper has been able to work out its design on paper. The DOP is now applying the latest computer technology to try to reconstruct the temple and its shrine as a virtual reality. Increasingly, the archaeologist carries a trowel in one hand and a laptop computer in the other. This is particularly true of a bright new generation of computer-literate archaeologists such as Caroline MacGregor, a doctoral student at Monash University who is generating the virtual reconstruction of Tutu's temple.

MacGregor fully recognizes that any virtual reconstruction must be based on sound data, which can only be obtained by the application of good old "elbow grease"—the careful measuring, sieving, sorting and recording that have always been the underpinning of modern archaeology. "You can't do away with the old techniques, because they are absolutely imperative," she says, "but there is room to bring in some new techniques. That's always the case in any discipline and if it doesn't happen, that's when you start to run into trouble, because it stagnates."

Essentially, she uses 3-D animation software, similar to, though less sophisticated than, that employed in movie animation. She compares her virtual reconstructions to working with papier mâché. The computer builds a wire frame for the ancient building. McGregor then applies textures over the top like strips of papier mâché. Using photographs of the painted decoration, she then applies the patterns and colours, just like wallpaper. By specifying a camera track, it is then possible for someone on the Internet to take a walk through the virtual temple, and even see how the light would have filtered into the sacred precinct.

As Kaper and his crew dug deeper, they uncovered confounding images on the still-standing walls. There was a hapless line of Libyans bound together by their necks with a rope, for example. Although the parading of the pharaoh's enemies before him is a stock image in temple art, Kaper found the depiction of the multicoloured Libyans (red, brown and green) strangely out of place, given that Roman Egypt, including Dakhleh, carried on a brisk trade with Libya. Below the Libyans were rectangular panels—grape vines, local birds, and Medusa heads—which showed the strong influence of Greco-Roman themes.

When the DOP cleared the last of the sand away in the *mammisi* they found a thick layer of manure on the floor. By the late fourth century, the shrine was obviously being used as a stable. On the north wall, they found a Coptic graffito left by a literate gooseherd, in which he tells how he and his companion kept the flock there on one night in the month of Paone. When the iconography in the temple was created, the religious tradition that had served the population for three millennia was alive and well. But in retrospect the conversion of the birth-house of the Egyptian god Tutu to a humble stable seems symbolic of the larger conversion to Christianity taking place in the fourth century.

THE DECLINE OF THE ANCIENT RELIGION WAS DUE TO A COMBINATION of official neglect and the juggernaut of Christianity. The first Roman Emperor, Augustus, generously supported the Egyptian priesthood and the upkeep and construction of temples. His cartouche appears on temples throughout Egypt, including the largest stone temple in Dakhleh, Ein Birbiyeh. Augustus privately professed contempt for the native religion, but his public support was a politic move to further his civic plan to reorganize and revitalize the country. Later emperors withdrew their support, slowly starving the temple cults to death by seizing their large land holdings and converting the temples themselves to other uses, including fortresses for Roman legions.

Christianity came early to Egypt. Many Egyptian Christians, or Copts, date the founding of their church to the Apostle Mark, the author of the oldest Gospels, who, according to legend, came to Alexandria between 41 and 44, and returned twenty years later to preach and proselytize. He found his first converts among the Jewish community and the new religion soon spread down the Nile. By 200, Alexandria had become the centre of Christian thought, with the founding of a catechetical school.

At first, Roman officials and the populace regarded Christians as a zany cult of the nonconformist Jewish community. However, the early Christians attracted negative attention by their own intolerance, refusing to pay homage to the Roman gods, including the Emperor himself. Such behaviour was seen as socially disruptive and an affront to the Empire. Even so, given the accommodating

Egyptian attitude, the new faith developed pretty much unmolested until 249, when Emperor Decius issued an imperial order requiring every person to participate in pagan worship in the presence of local officials. Christians could get themselves off the hook if they agreed to offer incense at a Roman altar, but those who refused were imprisoned, tortured, or, in some cases, thrown to wild animals in the Colosseum. The official attitude hardened further under the rule of Diocletian, and 303 saw the beginning of the period known as the Great Persecution, a last-ditch effort to stamp out the increasingly influential faith. Diocletian perceived Christians "as enemies of the gods" and had countless numbers tortured, banished, put to death, or worked to death in the mines of the Sinai. At an early Christian site in the Fayum, half of all skulls examined, including those of women, have unhealed fractures. Apparently, they had been blugeoned to death.

In the face of ever-present danger, many Christians sought refuge in the remote reaches of the Eastern and Western Deserts, where they began a monastic tradition early in the fourth century. Dakhleh possesses both a hermit's cave, home to some anonymous Desert Father, as well as a monastery. Under Roman rule, increasingly intolerable tax burdens were also causing many Egyptians to seek sanctuary within a Christian community. Besides providing some protection from the heavy hand of government, the early Christian community practised what it preached, offering charity, clothing and food to the downtrodden in society—the ill, widows, and orphans.

The persecutions came to an abrupt halt when Emperor Constantine (306–337) converted to Christianity. He issued an Edict of Toleration in 313, opening the way for the widespread public practice of Christianity. By then, however, there were already ninety to a hundred bishoprics in Libya and Egypt, with a concentration around Alexandria. The last mention of a pagan priest in the Kellis papyri, one Stonios, is made in 335, though it is not known whether he had merely retained this inherited title or whether he was still officiating. Curiously, it is the same year the first reference is made to a Christian priest in Kellis.

THANKS TO THE TORRENT OF PAPYRI UNEARTHED IN THE KELLIS houses, there is ample new documentation of the transition in values that accompanied the Christian conversion. Many of the letters were set to paper, or papyrus, by a professional scribe in the business *lingua franca* of the Empire, Greek. But there are also many documents written in Coptic, the language of the early Christian church in Egypt and also of the street and the home. Many residents would have been bilingual, and the documents clearly reveal they were multi-cultural as well.

In addition to those who called themselves Christians, another group in Kellis was revealed to Hope in the papyri. They were Manichaeans, who also considered themselves followers of Christ. This gnostic faith that believed in the duality of good and evil was launched in the third century by the Persian prophet Mani, who combined elements of both eastern and western religious thought. Known to his followers as "Illuminator," Mani thought of himself as a latter-day Apostle, the last in a line of prophets that included Buddha, Zoroaster and Jesus. The basic tenet of the faith is that the soul is fallen in this world of matter and can only be saved by transcendence of the spirit. Manichaeism was an evangelical and charismatic sect, which spread quickly west, reaching Egypt by 260. By the turn of the third century, both the state and the Bishops of Alexandria were watching its rapid growth with a jaundiced eye.

Iain Gardner is the Manichaean specialist on the DOP team. I met him at the Melbourne Symposium, where he reported to colleagues on his progress in translating Manichaean and Coptic documents from Kellis. With self-deprecating humour, he told me that Manichaean scholars are "either philologists or they're mad, and quite a few of them are both." Gardner is certainly not the latter; trim and prematurely grey, he has an air of calm sanity about him. He did his Ph.D. on Manichaeism at Manchester and then took a position in Australia at Edith Cowan University, Perth, in 1986. At the time, Gardner admits, there wasn't much call for a Manichaean expert in Australia and he had started to turn his attention to other matters—until the spectacular Manichaean documents at Kellis were discovered and, in turn, Colin Hope discovered he had an expert practically on his doorstep.

From the documents, it appears there were more Manichaeans in Kellis than regular Christians. In Gardner's opinion, Manichaean evangelists may have deliberately sought out isolated places like Dakhleh to sow the seeds of their radical faith, a safe distance from state and church authorities, who considered it heresy. Among the literary texts found are nineteen separate psalms of Mani, which suggested to Gardner that the community enjoyed "a vibrant faith focused on praise and conversion." The Manichaean church was divided, possibly on the Buddhist model, between the catechumens, lay believers who could marry and work, and ascetic professionals, the elect who dedicated themselves to a life of prayer and study. Most Kellis believers were catechumens.

Manichaean texts elsewhere in Egypt have come mostly from rubbish dumps or the black market. Kellis provides the first opportunity to study the gnostic sect in a well-dated social context. Within the oasis, it would seem that Manichaeans and Christians lived as neighbours without tension. It may be that, in some instances, they lived in the same house, as documents professing both faiths have been found in House 4.

The Kellis finds, consisting of 120 letters written in Coptic, have quadrupled the number of extant Manichaean personal texts and demonstrated that the community placed a high value on literacy. One letter written by a father to his daughter, asking that she send him wheat and oil with her brother, begins with this fervent salutation: "Our beloved daughter, the daughter of the holy church, the catechumen of the faith; the good tree whose fruit never withers, which is your love that emits radiance every day . . . I am your father who writes to you in God. Greetings."

To Gardner, these rich and varied fourth-century letters from a provincial village demonstrate that written Coptic was alive and well at a much earlier stage than experts previously believed. Indeed, on the basis of the Kellis letters, Gardner has taken the radical position that the development of Coptic (which reached its zenith in the sixth and seventh centuries) was not driven by an urban and monastic elite but adopted by the Christian Church for the purpose of proselytizing.

By the mid-fourth century, if not earlier, Christians and Manicheans had become the dominant community in Kellis, although there were a few hangers-on of the old Egyptian cults. The letters, in fact, reveal an interesting marriage of Christian and Greco-Roman beliefs, apparently without conflict or any sense of personal hypocrisy. One document on the manumission of a female slave by her master, a former magistrate of the city of Mothis, begins: "I acknowledge that I have set you free because of my exceptional Christianity, under Zeus, Earth and Sun." Obviously, the writer had no scruples about invoking the power of the greatest of the gods in the Greek pantheon, while proclaiming his qualifications as a Christian. Worp has also turned up a number of amulets, both Christian and pagan, to ward off illness or evil spirits. One Manichaean amulet was intended as protection against snakebite. These formulae and magic symbols were written on small pieces of papyrus and worn on the body of the person they were intended to protect. Rather than adhering to any strict orthodoxy of beliefs, it seems early Christians were quite content to borrow from earlier traditions if it suited their purpose.

THE CHRISTIAN BURIALS AT KELLIS HAVE ADDED THEIR OWN intriguing chapter to this story. Kellis 2, the later cemetery (c. 100–300), is where individuals were laid out in mud-brick tombs in the classic Christian position, with the head to the west. They are identifiable as Christians not only by this orientation, but by the lack of grave goods. Neither have the Christian bodies been mummified, a practice abhorred by the early Christians, but, in some cases, they are wrapped in linen. While the Christian burials do not yield archaeological treasures—gold masks, pots, and *cartonnage*—the bones have revealed the most intriguing of Kellis's osteobiographies.

Some bone signatures tell a story not only of the individual but of the history of a disease itself. Such was the case when Molto and Sheldrick exhumed burials number 6 and 16 in Kellis 2. Despite having studied nearly four hundred burials from the two grave-yards, they had not seen anything quite like these two.

Peering into the nasal cavities, Molto saw the ravages wreaked there by the bacterium *Mycobacterium leprae,* the organism that caused the ancient scourge of leprosy. The cartilage that forms the septum was completely destroyed. "That's the anchor for the nose and when that goes, it's like losing the prop for your tent," says Molto. The effect is a hideous deformation known as "drop nose," which starts a chain reaction, resulting in the loss of the teeth, as well as changes to the eyes. The infection then travels through the bloodstream and lodges at the roots of peripheral nerves supplying the hands and feet. The bacilli cause inflammation that, over time, breaks down the insulation of the nerves, anesthetizing the feet and hands. The skeletons displayed the tell-tale claw-hand deformity of leprosy and deterioration of the bones in the feet. The loss of feeling in the feet and hands often leads to mutilation or to the loss of fingers and toes, as the leper is unaware of injuring himself. It is a cascading litany of ills, and the Kellis skeletons had all the classic symptoms. When Molto presented his diagnosis to a forum of international pathologists there was not a single dissenting voice. (Molto has since provided definitive proof by isolating leprosy bacterium—DNA from the nasal passages.)

These were not the first cases of leprosy diagnosed in Dakhleh. The French team had excavated four lepers from Ain Aseel, and dated them on the basis of artifacts to the late Ptolemaic Period. The French believed that Dakhleh was perhaps still a place of banishment and that the individuals were elite Greeks sent to Dakhleh, as to a leper colony, to quarantine the much-feared disease. Molto, however, has brought to bear empirical methods on his lepers to test this hypothesis and has put together an entirely different, but no less intriguing, story.

Both leprosy victims were men in their late twenties and they were buried within six feet of each other, which at first made him think that they might have been related. DNA analysis indicated otherwise, showing that the two had different mothers. However, genetic comparisons to other individuals also showed that these two were not outsiders, but belonged to the oasis population.

Wanting to extract as much information as possible, Molto sent bone samples to Tosha Dupras of the University of Central Florida, who was then studying the diet of the Roman Age residents of Kellis. Part of her work involved analyzing nitrogen isotopes in the collagen, since the amount of a certain isotope in the bone tissue is dictated by what the person ate.

Isotope analysis also makes it possible to glean other information, including the type of climatic conditions where the individuals lived. Dupras analyzed the ratio of nitrogen-15 to nitrogen-14 in the bones, a ratio influenced by the amount of rainfall. The body's response to extremely dry environments is to conserve water. This so-called "drought effect" turns on automatically, whether or not ample drinking water is available. Molto points out that after a few days in Dakhleh you sweat and urinate less. In the latter case, this concentrates urea, which is rich in nitrogen-15, in the urine and ultimately in your bones.

When he sent the bone samples to Dupras, he attached numbers only, giving her no other information on the individuals which might bias her readings—what, in science, is known as a "blind test." When she finished her analysis, she immediately phoned Molto to convey some unexplained results: she had two "outliers" that didn't seem to fit the rest of the population. These two had significantly less nitrogen-15 in their bones. They were the lepers.

Molto now had to account for the unexpected difference. Obviously the lepers had spent time in a wetter environment than the Western Desert. Also, since they had retained relatively low nitrogen-15 values they must have returned to the oasis relatively recently, before the arid climate could cause an increase in their levels. "They may well have been young males who left town and contracted the disease elsewhere," says Molto. "We don't know this. We do the osteobiography first before we go to the higher level of 'What does this mean?'"

The logical assumption was that the two young men had recently been in the Nile Valley, which is a more humid, if still rainless, environment. The papyri clearly showed that the people of Kellis had regular contact with the Valley. On the basis of the DNA and isotope work, Molto could not conclude that the men had contracted the disease in the Valley, but he could say, with some surety, that they had moved away to the Valley, then come back to the oasis and died there. In fact, the number of lepers—four others have since emerged from the Kellis burials—suggests to him that the disease might have been endemic to the oasis.

Finding leprosy at Dakhleh raised an even larger question in Molto's mind about the genesis of the disease itself. The Dakhleh lepers represent the oldest cases in the archaeological record.

Older medical texts in China and India describe a skin disease of the face that many authorities have accepted as being leprosy, though Molto suspects it was a disease called glanders that produces very similar lesions. These texts had led to the currently accepted notion that the disease evolved in the Far East and that the armies of Alexander the Great may have brought it back, spreading it throughout the Middle East and the Mediterranean.

There was nothing wrong with this rather epic scenario, as far as it went. The first unequivocal cases of skeletal leprosy were those from 230 B.C. in Ain Aseel, well after Alexander's reign. The Kellis lepers were dated at the end of the fourth century. By contrast, there were no confirmed cases from Asia that early in the archaeological record. All the skeletal evidence suggested that North Africa, not the Far East, was the "hot spot" for the disease. "Why are we getting all of these cases in northern Africa and nothing in between?" Molto asked himself.

There were other reasons for Molto rejecting the Alexander-the-Great hypothesis. The bacterium that causes leprosy lives in tropical soils and is usually transmitted to children at a young age. It has been called a "household disease," because families living together will spread the disease from member to member. Even so, it is surprisingly difficult to contract the disease; married couples may co-habit for many years without spreading the infection from one to the other. It seems the young are most susceptible, because their immune systems are not yet fully developed. "The other thing that has always bothered me about the interpretation with Alexander the Great was that he's got all these men who have travelled these great distances," Molto reasons. "Now what do you do? Do you send weaklings to war, or do you take healthy young men? And usually you get leprosy when you're exposed to it in childhood, and there's a long latency period. So I have my doubts." Even if an immunologically compromised individual did pick up leprosy, say in India, Molto would not bet on him surviving the trek back to the Middle East.

Not everyone at the DOP buys Molto's story, among them Colin Hope. "To me it is not convincing at all," he says. "Is El aware of the fact that thousands of Greeks returned to their homeland after Alexander's death, with their wives and children?" Earlier, in 324 B.C., faced with mutiny, Alexander declared that all Greek exiles could return to their native cities, including ten thousand of his soldiers who were sent home with a hefty bonus. "Even if we do not have early dated examples from the Far East," says Hope, "the few from Kellis do not show an alternative origin for the disease."

Besides addressing this larger controversial question, Molto wanted to know why the Kellis lepers had returned to the oasis from their sojourn in a wetter climate. Here, he turned to the work of his archaeological colleagues to put the finishing touches on a plausible plot, which he calls "A Tale of Two Lepers." The churches and the papyri reveal a largely Christian community in place when the two native sons—it is tempting to say prodigal sons—came home. Certainly, leprosy—thought of by many as a "biblical disease" —is strongly associated with Christ's teachings of charity for and tolerance of the downtrodden and less fortunate. Few could be considered more unfortunate than the victims of such a disfiguring and wasting disease, and lepers in the ancient world, as was true until recent times, were pariahs.

Christ, however, was not afraid to touch a leper in carrying out his ministry of healing and Molto now believes there might have been a similar spirit of tolerance among the Christian community at Kellis: "I'm thinking of this Kellis story: 'My son's coming back from the Nile and he's bringing an old friend with him, and by the way they both have leprosy and I hope our community opens its arms to them'"—a plea for Christian charity that might have been spoken by a biological father, or by a spiritual father.

Some might have remembered the young men when they had left

the village, healthy and strong. Now they had returned, disfigured and dying. Even those with no prior experience of leprosy might well have feared these unfortunate men who were suffering from facial disfiguration, claw-hands and a limping gait. Molto questions whether it was a level of tolerance in the Kellis Christian community that allowed the young men to return and live out their last days there or was there just less intolerance than in the Valley. A final fact to consider: the lepers were buried in the common cemetery, which was reserved for Copts and the Manichaeans. To Molto, it is significant that these two graves were not disturbed by grave robbers, unlike most of their neighbours. It may be that the lepers were feared in death as in life.

In a spirit of collegial skepticism—a spirit alive and well in the multi-disciplinary DOP—Hope also takes issue with this notion that early Christians were necessarily more accepting of society's pariahs than their pagan contemporaries. "This interpretation undermines non-Christian values," he argues. "Remember how uncharitable Christians have been at times."

WHAT IS BEYOND DISPUTE IS THE PRESENCE OF A WELL-ESTABLISHED Christian community. The burning question was when this new religion had taken hold. Determining the date first required a careful excavation of the churches, undertaken in 1996 under the direction of Gillian Bowen, a vibrantly energetic woman who, after raising a family, did her Ph.D. at Monash University, where she is now a lecturer. "It was something I wanted to do since I was eight," she says of her delayed career.

Bowen had received a scholarship to study Roman-Jewish relations, but when the chance to work at Kellis came up, she rationalized that in the beginning Christianity was merely a sect of Judaism. Despite the rapid growth of Christianity in Egypt, none of the known churches had been built during the faith's formative phase. Bowen wondered whether the Kellis churches might fill that gap. Other supposed early churches, including two in Kharga, were converted public buildings, but excavation revealed that the Large East Church and the West Church in Kellis were "purpose-built" for Christian worship. How early might the Kellis churches be?

In 1987, when I first visited the sand-entombed Large East Church, there was just a feeling of being "in church." In 2000, visiting with Bowen and seeing its apse and colonnades now fully exposed, their white plaster shining in the full blast of desert light, there could be no doubt I was standing in a basilica. It was an impressive structure, sixty-six feet long by fifty-five feet wide, with a flat roof supported on palm beams over the main space, some of which were found in the debris when the sand was cleared away. The absence of the roof, in a way, heightened the power of the place, open to the purest blue of desert sky. The eroded columns once had capitals that flared out at the top at the four corners, Bowen told me, simulating the shape of palm leaves.

We were standing at the front edge of the apse, at the eastern end of the Large East Church. It was easy to imagine the spiritual power of the living church, the flicker of candlelight reaching into its dark corners and playing off the devout faces of the faithful. At one time the apse was roofed with a semi-circular dome, painted in maroon and deep yellow and decorated with scroll or vine motifs. The bema—or sanctuary—was directly in front, with two steps on either side for access. It had been screened from the congregation and it was here that the portable altar would have been placed. "What you've got here is oil," Bowen said, pointing to dark stains at my feet. "You can see at three points they had been lighting lamps and the oil had dripped down."

During excavation, Bowen had also found fragments of thin, flat-painted glass in the rubble of the bema that proved to be wonderful relics. When reassembled, they were identified as painted panels that would have been set in wooden frames. They appear to depict biblical scenes, including one of "a child swathed," apparently, she says, a Nativity scene.

Abutting the basilica on the south side is what Bowen calls the Small East Church, measuring a modest twenty-eight feet by eighteen feet. Though much smaller, its layout mimics its larger neighbour, with the apse to the east. "The theory is the little church is the earliest," said Bowen, her words tumbling over each other as we slid down the sandbank into the little church. It had been excavated down to floor level since my first visit. "It makes sense they would build small before erecting the basilica next door," she explained. If that theory is correct, the little church is what was known as a *domus ecclesia,* or house of the church. It was common practice among early Christians to meet in a private home, as a matter of safety, and to later convert it into a formal house of worship when the community had been accepted. As the congregation grew, they purposely built the basilica, which could easily have held two hundred worshippers.

We stepped forward to admire the decoration of the apse, which had been wonderfully preserved. There were geometric designs painted in the dark ochre and mustard yellow tones that are still the common house colours in the oasis. In sharp contrast to the elaborate, sometimes baroque, imagery of the pagan temple, with its four hundred gods and goddesses, bound enemies, and Medusa heads, the only image in the small East Church was a group of three pointed acanthus leaves rendered in a free-hand, provincial style. A pilaster was placed slightly off-centre at the back of the apse. Niches were set in the side walls and under them was a decorative painted square with a small *crux ansata* at the centre. "This cross is the only element of Christian iconography in the church," noted Bowen.

To determine the earliest date Christians showed up at Kellis, Bowen has had to collect circumstantial evidence, by tracing the use of Christian names in the papyri, a method known as onomastics.

Although no papyri have been found in the churches, the wealth of material from the nearby houses has provided a paper trail. The preeminent scholar of Roman Egypt, Roger Bagnall, who recently joined the DOP, has worked out an onomastic system of dating the establishment of Christianity based on the assumption that a person with a Christian name is likely to have had Christian parents. In this way, you can trace back the advent of the Christian faith in an area by at least one and possibly two generations. Bagnall has estimated that 20 percent of the Egyptian population were Christians when Constantine's rule began in 306 and a majority by his death in 337.

A case in point from Kellis is a contract dated to 308, which mentions a certain Timotheos, the Greek form of the Christian name Timothy, who is identified as coming from Kellis, where presumably his parents were also born. The formal use "in God" in the contract confirms its Christian context. Assuming Timothy was at least twenty years old, this pushes back the origin of Christianity in the community to approximately 280. And if you have Christians, then you need a church.

To date the churches themselves, Bowen used numismatics, a complex method of dating old coinage. Roman coins bear the portraits of the issuing emperor and it is known when specific issues were struck. The problem is in determining how long dated coins have been in circulation. "If you look in your pocket," says Bowen, "you will probably find coins that have circulated for forty or more years." In the Roman era, some coins might circulate for a century.

The first step for Bowen was to analyze coins from those Kellis houses that were already firmly dated to the late third and early fourth centuries. She examined them for signs of wear and analyzed the relative proportions of coins of different dates, to give herself an idea of the rate of coin loss. She then compared them to large hoards of coins from the Nile Valley and Cyrenaica to confirm which coins were in circulation during the period under study, as well as how long they had stayed in the currency pool. These two sets of coins (one local, one national) were then compared to those found in the churches themselves, where presumably the congregation had accidentally dropped them. Only 175 coins were found in the Large East Church, ranging in date from the late third century to a single coin from the reign of Theodosius (378–83). Two types of coins—*tetradrachms* and *sol invictus*—were particularly critical to establishing the time frame. The *tetradrachms* were withdrawn from circulation by the Christian-persecuting Diocletian in 296 and disappeared approximately two decades later. The *sol invictus* do not appear in any Egyptian hoards after the 340s. Employing this range of dates, Bowen cautiously points to the founding of the church during the reign of Constantine, sometime between 323 and 337, if not earlier.

Bowen's detective work has produced yet another first for the DOP: the churches in Kellis are the oldest in Egypt. They are, in fact, the only fourth-century churches in Egypt that can be dated by archaeological and textual evidence. Large Christian churches would have existed throughout Egypt at the same time, but they have either been destroyed or no one has yet been able to find them. Dakhleh's isolation and the Saharan sands had preserved these two.

Kellis was obviously a hotbed of Christian activity at the beginning of the fourth century and had a large and well-to-do congregation in place by late in the century. While this conversion was gathering force, another dramatic change was overtaking the community. Bowen has found no coins, nor any papyrus documents, from the fifth century. To Hope and his colleagues, it looked more and more as if Kellis had become a ghost town at the end of the fourth century, forcing the faithful to make a pilgrimage elsewhere. Now the archaeologists had to account for this calamity. Was it an act of God or Nature? And did the parishioners play a part in the demise of Kellis?

CHAPTER FOURTEEN

A CURSE OF SAND AND SALT

As COLIN HOPE AND HIS TEAM EXCAVATED THE KELLIS HOUSES, they noted signs that the residents were fighting a losing battle with sand and growing increasingly desperate. One family had built a semi-circular wall outside their front door. They then had been forced to raise the sill of the door by three feet and build a set of steps down into their house. Door sills were also raised three feet at the two-hundred-room administrative building, which stood directly in the path of the prevailing winds—and blowing sand. The residents of Kellis were obviously trying to keep themselves above ground.

When Jim Knudstad first showed me House 1, he observed that it did not show signs of much use: "You can put as much wear-and-tear on an expedition house in a couple of seasons as you see here." Other houses also showed very little wear-and-tear, suggesting a

---

An ox-driven Persian water wheel, or *saqia*

rapid acceleration in the build-up of sand and leading Hope to conclude that the residents had been forced to abandon their homes
soon after they were built.

Eventually, the city was buried to the rooftops. But it struck the
archaeologists as odd that today there were no major sand dunes in
sight. When Kellis was buried in sand, where did the sand come
from? And where did it go?

To the north, the Libyan Plateau forms the horizon and in
many places along this shining limestone landmark, yellow sands
cascade over the rim like golden, dry Niagaras. Today, the effect of
this constant immigration of sand is most evident in the western
half of the oasis, where huge dunes are migrating southward, burying fields and even villages as they move. Between El-Qasr and
Mahoub, the dunes have swallowed the main road repeatedly.
Officials have stoically rebuilt the road over their crescent-shaped
backs. Beside the road, telephone poles, buried nearly to their
cross-trees, project from the sand like grave markers.

At the time Kellis was buried, Hope thinks sand might have
been channelled more through the eastern part of the oasis, putting Kellis directly in harm's way. The sheer weight of the dunes
would have crushed roofs and sand would have poured in, filling
the interiors of the houses to the tops.

Working in the Western Desert in the 1930s, Major Ralph
Bagnold of the British Royal Signals was the first to understand
how dunes formed and moved across the vast reaches of the
Sahara. "Dunes are mobile heaps of sand whose existence is independent of either ground form or fixed wind obstruction," he
wrote in 1933. "They appear to retain their shape and identity
indefinitely, and so have an interesting life of their own." Barchan
dunes are shaped like a crescent, with the inside of the "C" facing
downwind. He described them as having a single summit and a col-
lapsing front, so that "the sand gives the impression of having been

swept up in the dune heap with a broom." Perhaps the most remarkable characteristic of a dune—and the reason Bagnold said it had a life of its own—is the tenacity with which it holds its shape even when confronted with formidable obstacles such as rocky prominences or villages. Sixteen hundred years ago, just such a dune may have migrated over Kellis, smothering the houses, temples, and churches, then continued its inexorable journey so that today it is nowhere to be seen.

However relentlessly they may migrate, dunes do so slowly. Rediscovering a dune in northwestern Sudan studied by Bagnold in 1930—Bagnold's fuel and food tins were still exposed on the surface—Vance Haynes of the University of Arizona in Tucson calculated that the dune had advanced southward at a rate of 24.6 feet per year over the intervening fifty years. Over the four centuries Kellis was occupied, such a dune could have migrated nearly two miles; in the 1600 years since, it could have moved a further seven miles southward. There are lots of dunes south of the oasis.

Obviously, such a geological snail's pace would not have caused the community to pick up and leave overnight. It was utterly unlike Vesuvius covering Pompeii to a depth of eight to fifteen feet in a hellish rain of volcanic ash in a mere two days. The burying of Kellis might have gone almost unnoticed at first—a sifting of sand under the door that had to be swept away in the morning. And again the next morning, and the next, until you had to raise the sill, and finally abandon your home.

Clearly an enormous amount of sand eventually drifted over the area. Even now, with no dunes bearing down on the city, six inches of sand can accumulate on the site between field seasons. Sand is always shifting from one part of the oasis to another, causing farmers to abandon some fields and, in extreme cases, relocate whole villages. On a windy day, so much sand is whipped into the air that it is impossible to see the 1600-foot-high Plateau. There is always enough circulating in the oasis environment to bury a city, given sufficient time, with or without the spectre of a monumental dune marching over the desert floor like a malevolent living thing.

HOWEVER, IT IS UNLIKELY THAT THE ABANDONMENT OF KELLIS was due to sand alone. A host of political, environmental and social factors also contributed to the downfall of Kellis, and indeed Rome. As Mills' team has shown, the prosperity that flowed into Dakhleh as a satellite of the Roman Empire lasted for nearly four hundred years in Kellis, but perhaps as few as fifty years in places like the Plain of Sio'h. The decline, when it came, was triggered by the splitting of the Empire, with inevitable consequences for crop exports. Over Kellis's lifetime, power and wealth were shifting from Rome and Italy to the outlying provinces. The armies were now made up of and controlled by the very tribes the Roman legions had once held in check. Non-Roman emperors rose through the ranks, including Septimus Severus of Libya, the first African-born ruler. So-called barbarians constantly tested the fragile frontiers. At the end of the fourth century, after two centuries of peace and prosperity, the Empire was beginning to experience poverty, famine and decline. First Diocletian and then Constantine tried to halt the disintegration by increasing taxes and imposing the supremacy of the central state, creating a virtual caste system, in which a person was tied to a job, and a village, for life. Rather than sustaining its citizens, the state now became a financial as well as a spiritual burden. The flip-flop from Diocletian's persecution of Christians to Constantine's embrace of the new faith would have done little to reassure citizens that the situation was improving. When Constantine established the capital of his new Christian Empire far to the east at Byzantium, which he renamed Constantinople, it sounded the death knell of Rome's all-encompassing power in the Mediterranean. The dissolution of the Empire naturally affected marginal areas first and most, and Dakhleh was at its very southern limit.

Local agricultural practice also had an effect, though this, too, can be linked to overreaching imperial ambition. Agricultural development throughout Egypt was driven by the needs of Rome, whose interest in Egypt was purely extractive. In the third century, however, Egypt was no longer required to produce grain for Rome's daily bread. Colin Hope wondered what other foodstuffs they might be sending abroad.

He found the answer in the Kellis Agricultural Account Book. It contains, in the opinion of its translator, Roger Bagnall, "the most extensive and well-preserved set of accounts for an agricultural entity to survive from the fourth century. Indeed, it is exceptional even for the entirety of the thousand years from which we have Greek papyrological texts from Egypt." Its nearest counterpart is a set of wooden tablets from Hadrian's Wall. As it turns out, it tells us not only about the agricultural ecology of Dakhleh, but about how Roman power shaped the lives of the people living on the fringes of the Empire, for better and worse. It also provides new clues as to how Kellis spiralled into decline.

The document itself is rather forbidding at first glance, even to Bagnall, one of the world's foremost papyrologists. He explained its contents to me in Melbourne. Bespectacled, decked out in blue blazer, slacks and neck tie, he seemed the very image of a scholarly Ivy Leaguer. It consists, he told me, of 1734 lines, many of them entries recording how much was due to the estate and how much had been received, as well as expenditures paid by tenant farmers to their landlord in commodities. It was a daily journal which the keeper of the book probably kept tucked into his *galabiya* as he made the rounds of his master's estate. Later he would have transferred the record to papyrus for reckoning. The owner of the estate, Faustianos, appears to have been an absentee landlord living in Hibis, in the Kharga Oasis. Our record-keeper was just one of ten managers of the estate, which seems to have reached into virtually every corner of the Dakhleh Oasis, a little empire within the larger Roman Empire. He makes frequent mention of a female donkey, which we assume was his mode of transport, just as it is for many modern oasis dwellers. We can easily picture him riding far back on the rump of the donkey if he was in a hurry, urging his diminutive steed on with a stick. His arrival must have been an unwelcome sight to the hard-done-by tenant farmers. Bagnall knows nothing about this tax collector, except that he was probably a Christian, since a Christian symbol appears in large letters at the head of the accounts. (There are also several references to "the bishop" and "the church" as well as to a "monastery" in Dakhleh.) Beyond that, the account book offers no clues as to its keeper's identity. He remains as faceless as the fictional functionaries in a modern-day revenue department.

In Roman Egypt, taxes were collected in fifteen-year cycles, of which the account constitutes a record of years five through eight. Based on well-documented prices for commodities in the mid-fourth century, it could refer to either the period 361–364, or the period 376–379. Various commodities, as well as cash in talents, were used as payment. Wheat, barley and wine accounted for just over half the rent crops. Chaff, or straw used as fuel, hay, and green fodder—the *berseem* still grown in the oasis today—were important crops, as were beans. Turnips, fenugreek, safflower and sesame are also mentioned, as are onions and vetch. Chickens were raised, mostly for eggs it seems, as the abundant poultry bones analyzed by Rufus Churcher show few roosters. Pigs were the predominant meat source, verified by a preponderance of pig bones unearthed at Kellis. Other food products included butter, cheese, porridge and *stagma,* a drink made of wine-must and honey. Something called *oregmos* was a word Bagnall had never encountered before—literally it means "bruised beans" and may refer to the fava or broad beans used today in falafel. There is also something called *tiphagion*, which remains a mystery, as it is a word known only from the oasis.

Cotton, a relatively minor crop along the Nile in antiquity, was also grown in Roman Dakhleh. In addition to it, figs, dates, olives, olive oil and jujubes (the fruit of the *Zizyphus* tree still found in Dakhleh) accounted for 40 percent of Faustianos's rent crops.

Ursula Thanheiser has corroborated the existence of many of the crops mentioned and found many more. Most of the plant remains are dried, not carbonized like the Neolithic material, which makes her job much easier. She was surprised at the broad range of the agricultural economy: "I thought in Roman times, in an oasis, in the middle of the desert, in the middle of nowhere, at the edge of the known world, it must be a very poor life. And what we then found was that they had everything that they could wish to have. They had a very varied diet." Their staple crops were bread wheat, hard wheat and barley, supplemented by lentils and broad beans, but they also grew a variety of fruits, vegetables and spices, including cumin, anise, coriander and rosemary. Thanheiser has found apples, citron, peaches, apricots and pomegranates and, to her delight, a single artichoke. "So I think they lived very well," says Thanheiser. "They had almost everything known in the ancient world." As today, almost all of the food eaten was produced locally, except for pine nuts, hazelnuts and walnuts, which must have been imported.

Despite this cornucopia of local produce, wealthy landowners such as Faustianos were not interested in developing the oasis for the good of the resident population. Their estates had to furnish income by producing a surplus of an exportable commodity. The answer, Bagnall found, was olives.

Thanheiser has counted thousands of olive pits under her microscope, as well as the leaves, twigs and roots of olive trees.

Based on the amounts and values of olives in the Account Book, Bagnall believes that olives, in fact, formed the major cash crop in Kellis, accounting for four-fifths of the value of all crops. The only products that could be shipped across two hundred miles of desert economically were high-value, low-bulk, non-perishable products. Olive oil fit the bill perfectly.

Olive trees do not like to be flooded, and too much watering ruins the taste of the oil. For proper cultivation, you need either just enough rainfall or the ability to irrigate. The Valley, with its summer inundation, was not prime olive-growing country, and the geographer Strabo, visiting Egypt in the time of Augustus, commented scathingly on the poor quality of its oil. The poet Juvenal, whose poison-pen satire of Emperor Domitian had seen him banished to Oasis Major (Dakhleh and Kharga) in 96, also disparaged African olive oil.

Wealthy Egyptians saw that Dakhleh, with its perennial water supply, could easily be adapted for the commercial production of olives. Recent research elsewhere in North Africa leads Bagnall to believe that olive oil was an important engine of the Roman economy. Much like petrochemicals today, it permeated every facet of life then. It was the prime lighting fuel and the primary ingredient in a variety of medicaments, soaps, skin oils, perfumes and cosmetics. Furthermore, it was a basic foodstuff, with traditional peasants depending upon it for up to a third of their calories. Roman archaeologists estimate an average person consumed at least five gallons of olive oil per year. If this is true, the total annual consumption in the Mediterranean heartland would have been 500,000 to 1,000,000 tons. Such a colossal scale of production would have had major implications for trade, labour, and land use throughout the Roman world.

Olives were not a major product of the oasis in earlier Pharaonic times, nor are they today, though some are still grown.

During Roman times, however, there was an enormous expansion of olive cultivation in many agriculturally marginal areas, including Spain, Tunisia and Libya. In some places, olive groves extended into the semi-desert. In Tunisia, great orchards—whose ghostly tree pits, twenty to an acre, can still be detected in aerial photos—were cultivated right at the edge of the Sahel. Around Leptis Magna in Libya, there was an olive press every mile and that area alone produced five million gallons a year, mostly for export. However, there was environmental cost. These once-prosperous North African provinces are now surrounded vast deserts, a grim reminder of the environmental damage brought about by the once booming agribusiness.

Olive trees in Dakhleh may well have financed the fine villas, public buildings and grand tombs of Amheida and Kellis, but, ultimately, decisions made in Rome or Alexandria to promote olive oil production came with a price for the common people. Growing olives on marginal lands depletes the soils, robbing them of more nutrients than it returns. In other regions of the Empire, olive cultivation led to serious ecological stress. "If the olive oil hypothesis is correct," says Bagnall, "we see an economy under considerable pressure to export high-value crops. And the pressure may have led to the export of products people would have been happy to consume but for which there was a market willing to pay more somewhere else."

In Bagnall's opinion, the olive-growers of Dakhleh may even have half-starved themselves in order to meet the export demands of their urban landlords. This situation may have applied equally to Dakhleh's famous dates, which today form the oasis's only substantial export. Bagnall's reading of the Account Book has convinced him that some of the nutritional stress, especially anemia, Molto has detected may have been caused by pressure to export dates, an important source of iron. Profit for the landlords thus appeared as a debit to tenant farmers' health. On the other hand,

Bagnall's conclusion seems to contradict Thanheiser's observation that Roman period Dakhlans ate well. But as Molto has shown, the village elite were taller on average, suggesting that they enjoyed a better diet, perhaps eating artichokes and imported pine nuts while the tenant farmers ate beans and bread. For a time, at least, all strata of Kellis society may have benefited from the booming olive oil trade—but they were living on borrowed time.

HOPE AND HIS TEAM HAVE DISCOVERED TELL-TALE SIGNS THAT THIS drive to overproduction may have played a major role in Kellis's demise. Isotopic analysis of the botanical remains and comparison to modern plants suggest that towards the end of the Roman Age the fields surrounding the city were becoming laden with salt, probably due to the poor irrigation practices of the resident farmers. The remains of an irrigation canal lead from a large dry well toward the city. Near the well lie abandoned fields, the checkerboard pattern created by the dikes still faintly visible beneath the enveloping sands.

Salinization is always a problem with irrigation in arid climates. But Roman practices made it more so. In Dakhleh, the exploitive design was focused on pushing back the edge of the desert. Unlike their predecessors, who depended on natural spring flow, the Romans had the technology to carry out their plan, in the form of the *saqia,* or Persian waterwheel, which they introduced into Egypt. (It was to be a long-lasting innovation: the last *saqia* was still in operation in Bashendi in the 1990s.) It consisted of a chain of ceramic buckets tied by ropes on to a vertical wheel. A pair of oxen walked in endless circles to lower the buckets into the well and to lift them out, laden with water. With this simple but effective device the Romans could tap deeper sources of water. In a twelve-hour day, 0.3 inches of water could be delivered to a one-acre plot—about double the daily evaporation rate in summer and eight times that in winter. To supply the enormous aqueducts near Deir el-Hagar, numerous *saqia* must have been harnessed, to pump more than a trickle of water to these massive conduits. By such means, the Romans brought into production three times as much land as is currently farmed.

Local environmental factors also played a major role. Seventy million years ago, as we have seen, the Tethys Sea lapped up against the latitude where Dakhleh now lies. As a result, there is a great deal of salt in the underlying geological structure—the limestone, shale, and clay soils. To make matters worse, the cultivable soils are clay, so drainage is very poor. Water seeps into the soils slowly and if too much water floods onto the land, it stands and can only be dissipated by evaporation. Basically, the Saharan sun boils away the excess water, leaving behind the salts. More irrigation merely leaches out more salts, which are brought to the surface by capillary action, making the problem worse. Massive irrigation sediments from the Roman Age are still visible today as ridges of compacted clay, up to sixteen feet high in some cases, covering several square miles. This land was eventually abandoned, due to salting.

Modern irrigation practices have had the same result in the low-lying central area around Mut, where over-irrigated fields are white with salt and today wheat will not grow and rice withers and turns yellow. For these fields to be viable again, the salt would have to be flushed from the fields (a challenge where fields are poorly drained) or blown away by the wind, a process that can take centuries.

In the recent past, local farmers coped with the build-up of salt by leaving fields fallow in regular rotation. In the Roman period, however, government policy exhorted farmers to always produce more—first wheat, then olives. Fallowing became impossible and eventually the Roman Age farmers overwhelmed the capacity of the land both to produce and to recover.

So, did the Roman Period end with a whimper or a bang? In the Plain of Sio'h it seems to have ended abruptly. To supply the great aqueducts, the *saqias* quickly lowered the water table, until they could no longer draw water to the surface. Farmers had to abandon their new *columbaria* and make another start elsewhere in the oasis. As time went on, however, and more wells were exhausted, people began to leave the Island of the Blessed, most likely returning to the Nile Valley.

During the initial survey, Mills had already concluded from the tally of Roman era versus Christian, or Byzantine, sites that a major decline occurred after the Roman boom. Fully a third of all sites in Dakhleh date to the Roman Period. There are only half as many Christian sites, and only six churches, compared to twenty-five Roman temples. "I think that's a very nice proportional reflection of the size of the settlement and its prosperity," he says.

We might also guess that the oasis was already in decline, because later Roman rulers passed a law designating the oases as "receptacles for state delinquents," who were banished to the desert for six months to a year. The Christian heretic Nestorius, the patriarch of Constantinople who emphasized the human nature of Christ, was banished to a city called "Oasis," probably Kharga, where he spent several years before being rescued by a barbarian tribe, the Belemmyes.

Amheida and Mut seem to have survived into the sixth and perhaps seventh century. But Hope now thinks that Kellis was abandoned over a twenty-year period around the end of the fourth century. A number of lines of evidence support Hope's conclusion. The cemeteries also show a declining population, as there are simply not enough burials in the late fourth century for the number of people who should have been living in Kellis if it was fully occupied. In one of the excavated houses a few coins and documents postdate 370; in another, there are records that it was occupied until the

390s. Hope dates the probable end of the village by a horoscope found on a wooden board. It was written in the 108th regnal year of the Era of Diocletian (the Era of the Martyrs), which dates the composition of the horoscope to 392–393. After that, not another word is heard from the residents of Kellis.

In Mills' mind, what played out was a "Dust Bowl" scenario—a kind of Roman *Grapes of Wrath*: "It is a real natural disaster—man-induced, but nevertheless it becomes a natural disaster."

People obviously recognized what was happening and had time to react. Before bidding farewell to Kellis, they removed most of the salvageable wood, a rare and valuable commodity in the oasis. They ripped out the doors and the door- and window-frames from the temples, churches and houses. As they did so, the integrity of the structures was weakened; roofs and fancy domes collapsed as sand began to overwhelm the town. What did the residents think as they bundled their few precious belongings on the back of the family donkey and headed down the road? Did those who had converted think the old gods had taken revenge for their treachery? Was the new religion not strong enough to shield them from the malicious desert? Or were they just repeating a familiar pattern that had played out before? Perhaps the last to leave looked back at the once-grand city—the red domes and vaults carving the skyline into fanciful arabesques, the white stone of the temple, and the West Tomb, with its grand columns and Medusa capitals—and saw a dead city now wreathed in yellow sands, its streets choked and its once verdant fields smothered.

The desert went on to reclaim other far-flung fields and homesteads, the places where the Roman landlords, in their greed and hubris, had for a short time made the Sahara bloom. The two dozen Roman temples were abandoned to the wind and sand. Squatters and herders occupied them for a time. The six churches served the dwindling number of Christian diehards. "I think the hardship must have been enormous in Egypt in the fourth and fifth centuries, just at a time, of course, when you have a new religion forming," says Mills. He believes that part of the appeal of the new Christian faith was its inherent stoicism, which helped the oasis dwellers to endure earthly suffering in the hope of a reward in heaven.

It would take another wave of religious zealots to revive the fortunes of the Island of the Blessed. In the mid-seventh century, they would arrive with the fury of the *khamsim,* the Fifty Days' Wind.

PART SIX

THE LOST OASIS

700–

Amon-nakht *(John O'Carroll)*

CHAPTER FIFTEEN

THE LOST OASIS

EVERY MORNING IN DAKHLEH, I WAS WAKENED BY THE HAUNTING sound of the *muezzin* piercing the predawn darkness and echoing over the rooftops. For the last 1300 years, every day has begun in much the same way in the Island of the Blessed. It is no longer the unadulterated sound of a human voice but an electronically amplified, if live, broadcast. The intent, however, is the same as it has always been: to praise Allah and to call the faithful to prayer. Five times a day between dusk and dawn, the *muezzin* mounts his minaret and makes his call, in Dakhleh as everywhere across the Muslim world.

At the call of the *muezzin*, the archaeologists muster for another day's fieldwork, while village men converge at one of two mosques in Bashendi, one venerable, the other a new, blazing white structure with squat minarets at the corners. The faithful kneel on their prayer

A street in the walled, medieval Islamic city of El-Qasr

mats, bowing to the east, then return to their homes for something to eat before heading out to their fields and fruit groves.

The daily rhythms of subsistence agriculture have dictated the pattern of life in Dakhleh since the Pharaonic period. Adherence to Islamic tenets, including the ritual of prayer, was introduced only in the mid-seventh century, when a Muslim force swept out of Arabia and across North Africa, overwhelming the settled farmers in the Nile Valley and the oases of the Western Desert. Since at least the tenth century, there has been travel in the other direction, toward Mecca. Today colourful murals of, for example, a large-bodied commercial plane soaring over the Great Mosque, decorate the walls of houses, depicting the modern-day pilgrimage, a trip every Muslim family hopes to make once in a lifetime. During *Ramadan*, the month of fasting, the archaeologists marvel at how their workers carry out their duties without food or water during the heat of the day, and without complaint. Outside most villages, the white, domed tombs of sheikhs and local holy men shine in the desert, symbols of devotion to Islam.

ARAB IS A SEMITIC TERM MEANING SIMPLY "DESERT DWELLER." Prior to the rise of the unifying influence of Islam, the various tribes, with their fiercely loyal members, were centred in the Arabian Peninsula. The nomadic Arabs, or Bedouin, were perfectly adapted to life in the desert, living in tents and moving with their herds of sheep, goats and camels from one green pasture to another, one step ahead of the constant threat of thirst and starvation that stalked them in a parched country. In their freedom they considered themselves superior to the settled peasants who worked the land. In reality, both groups were dependent on each other. The Bedouin pastoralists could not produce all of their own food and relied on settled people to supply them with cereals and dates; in turn, the settled Arabs needed the meat, hides and wool of the animals kept by the Bedouin.

The camel was the Arabs' most prized possession: they drank its milk, burned its dung for cooking, and when it was no longer able to travel, they killed and ate it, using its hide to make their tents. The camel was also essential to the mercantile success of the Arabs, carrying raw materials and manufactured goods over convoluted caravan routes while surviving on little fodder and even less water for days in the desert. Arab tribes, who started out as spice traders, profited greatly from the trade they brokered between the empires of the Persians and the Romans: incense from southern Arabia, cloth and silks from China, pearls from the Persian Gulf, and exotic goods from India. The Arabs who occupied big cities such as Petra and Palmyra grew rich supplying luxury goods to the leisure-loving Romans. The caravan city of Mecca controlled much of the flow of these commodities. It was here in 571 that the Prophet Mohammed was born into a powerful clan of merchants, the Quraysh. Mohammed proved himself a successful trader. But his destiny lay elsewhere.

In 612, he heard the voice of the angel Gabriel, exhorting him to spread the word of the One True God and specifically to convert the Quraysh, who, like other Arabs, were polytheists. At first, his mission was scorned. Driven from his birthplace to Medina, Mohammed waged an extended battle of words with his former tribesmen. His converts grew, and eventually he handed the Quraysh a military defeat. Many Arabs now converted to the new faith, which Mohammed called Islam, the Arabic word for submission to God.

When Muhammad died in 631, the Prophet's successors (the caliphs) expanded their authority with further military action. By 644, the whole of Arabia, part of Persia and the Syrian and Egyptian provinces of the Byzantine Empire had been conquered. Some historians have attributed Islam's extraordinary success solely to religious zeal. Others, however, believe that population pressure and hunger were also driving the Arabs to conquer more fertile lands.

In any case, the Byzantine Empire was already in decline due to barbarian invasions, failure to maintain its agricultural works, including aqueducts, and a shrinking urban market. In the desert lands the Arabs also had the technical advantage of the camel. By the end of the seventh century they had reached Morocco and soon afterwards crossed into Spain.

It is hard to imagine the poor farmers of the oasis offering much resistance to a militia of hardened soldiers mounted on swift camels. Islam might not even have seemed alien at first to Coptic Christian converts, who also were monotheists. Life probably went on much as before, with the proud soldiers unwilling to stoop to common labour. As Molto's DNA analyses have shown, however, the population that was in the oasis at the end of the Roman period was replaced over time, presumably by people from different quarters of the Arab world.

The Arabian Empire became the largest in world history, stretching from Morocco and the Pyrenees to the Red Sea and eastward to Mongolia. However, this colossal empire, which eclipsed even Alexander's, was unstable: it contracted and expanded repeatedly. Various clan-based dynasties ruled in succession, the empire prospering under their founders and just as often foundering under less able successors, success depending to a considerable extent on the charisma and genius of individual leaders. Egypt became the cultural centre of the Islamic faith, and ever since, Dakhleh has been part of the Islamic world.

DURING THE SURVEY, MILLS FOUND RELATIVELY FEW ISLAMIC sites for the entire period starting circa 700 C.E. and continuing to the present. The ones he did find seemed to be small farming communities, much like the ones that dot the landscape today. One site, discovered in the first year, consisted of severely eroded mud-brick farmhouses which had at one time been set in palm gardens, long since obliterated by the desert's advance. Sherds of glazed pottery, a few bronze coins, and glass bangle bracelets were the only arti-facts. Outside the houses, Mills found burned earth within the mud-brick remains of ovens and a pottery kiln. During the second field season, he noted that many of the Islamic sites were perched precariously at the southern edge of the oasis. To Mills they seemed small and poor. Drifting sand had probably buried other villages, as it had Kellis. Mills also suspected that much of the medieval Islamic record lay buried under modern cultivation.

The small number of Islamic sites—they have found fifty-five—suggested that the intensive farming during the Roman period had sucked the oasis dry of easily accessible water supplies. During the Byzantine period, Mills believes Dakhleh was unable to provide more than a subsistence living for a greatly reduced and declining population. Judging by the paucity and the poverty of settlements, the decline in oasis fortunes persisted through the early part of the Islamic period.

In his 1909 book, *A Libyan Oasis,* British geologist Hugh J. Beadnell recounts a picture of wilful neglect. After the Mohammedan conquest, he says, "decay set in . . . the aqueducts choked, the fields were neglected, and malarial fever invaded a district [Kharga-Dakhleh] which had at one time been regarded as a health resort." The records of Arabian geographers, he says, indicate that the oases of the Western Desert became depopulated between the eleventh and fifteenth centuries, though he doubts whether either Kharga or Dakhleh became entirely uninhabited.

What actually happened in Dakhleh during this formative peri-od of Islam is obscure. There are no tangible remains predating the end of the Fatimid period in 1171. The writer Al-Bakhri tells us Dakhleh was on "the old road to Egypt" from Ghana, which was engulfed in sand after the tenth century. So Dakhleh would have been strategically located as the entry point into Egypt both from the Lake Chad Basin via the Libyan oasis of Kufra and from western Sudan. However, Mills has faced serious challenges in finding archaeological evidence of any such commerce.

"Unless you have trade actually going on here, you're not going to find artifactual remains," Mills says. What may have happened instead was that caravans passed through Dakhleh, paid their customs dues or tribute, and then hurried on to the great market of the Nile Valley. The offloading of goods may not have taken place in Dakhleh, leaving little evidence of the caravans' passing. Even so, Mills' team has found beautifully carved ivory combs and it is a reasonable bet that there was also trade in gold, slaves and other West African goods during this time.

Albert Hourani tells us in *A History of the Arab Peoples* that by the end of the tenth century an Islamic world had come into existence that was united by a common religion and language, and by the bonds forged through trade, migration and pilgrimage. Despite its cultural cohesion, politically it was divided by three rulers who claimed the title of caliph, in Baghdad, Cairo and Cordoba.

A chain of great cities stretched across the Islamic Empire and became magnets for Islamic scholars such as the famous traveller Ibn Batutta (1304–1377) who made a pilgrimage from his native city of Tangiers, in Morocco, to China. The city of Cairo boasted a quarter of a million residents by the fourteenth century. Merchants were the most powerful city elite, controlling the importation of food and raw materials from the countryside as well as long-distance trade in spices and other precious goods.

At the heart of the city lay the main congregational mosque and the central marketplace, or *suq*. The population clustered around these meeting places, often segregated into quarters where people were linked by geographical, ethnic, or religious origin, or by kinship. Although there were no ghettos *per se*, Jews and Christians often lived separately from their Muslim neighbours.

Although much of the record of the early Islamic Period in Dakhleh seems lost, by the fifteenth century—a thousand years after the Roman collapse—the fortunes of the oasis were revived and a period of prosperity followed. Under the rule of the mercenary Mamluks (1250–1517), the medieval walled city of El-Qasr grew up. When Mills first entered its gates in 1977, El-Qasr was still a vibrant, working city with blacksmiths, weavers and potters plying their crafts. But he also immediately recognized that it was a major archaeological site. Home to Dakhleh people for eight hundred years or more, it provided an opportunity to study "archaeology in action."

Located close to the Plateau, which forms an intensely white, dramatic backdrop, the walled city has an *Arabian Nights* charm. The road to the city gate wends through a palm grove, above which soar the roofs of medieval mud-brick high-rises that might be embodiments of verses in the Arabic poem, *The Seven Odes*: "A house with a high roof has been built for us, and the young and the old alike try to reach its height." Towering above them all is the cone-shaped minaret of the old mosque, reinforced by great beams that project from its sides like spokes from a wagon wheel.

On my first trip to the oasis, I followed Mills inside the walls, where the streets conspire to create a labyrinth. We watched weavers plaiting local reeds into floor mats, a blacksmith hammering at his mud-brick forge, and potters producing the distinctive Dakhleh water barrels called *fantas*, torpedo-shaped vessels pointed at both ends with a stubby rim on top for pouring. Unglazed and often hung in trees, they are designed to keep water cool in the searing heat. The houses of El-Qasr are all connected, one to another, and dwarf those of the other oasis villages. Sometimes reaching six storeys high, these medieval skyscrapers are so tall that little light reaches the narrow, dark alleys that thread between them. Enclosed walkways overhang sections of the streets, adding another dimension to the city's mysterious warren. "I invariably crack my head in El-Qasr,"

Mills observed. Even during the hottest part of the day, the streets were deep pools of cooling shade. Little light penetrated the houses, either; the windows were battened with acacia shutters, carved into elaborate patterns known as *mashrabiyya*. This claustrophobic architecture has the advantage of shielding those inside from both the probing rays of the sun and from the prying eyes of outsiders. Inside these great houses was the domain of the *harim*, where the women of wealthy families spent most of their lives. A fourteenth-century jurist, Ibn el-Hajj, declared that a woman should only leave her home when she is escorted to the bridegroom's house, when her parents die and when she herself is buried. In reality, according to Hourani's *History*, women met each other on other occasions, such as the birth of children and the celebrations of marriages, frequented public bath-houses reserved for them at certain hours, and maintained a culture of their own.

Some 190 house doors are decorated with intricately carved lintels, bearing the names of the builder, the carpenter, the date of construction, and verses from the Qur'an, rendered in florid Arabic script. The sills of the doorways have sunk below the street level, which has been built up by centuries of life's grubby leavings. Heavy acacia gates divide the city into neighbourhoods, each of which would have been the precinct of a tribe-based clan. The gates were locked at night, as were the main city gates, against the threat of raids, which continued into the nineteenth century.

DURING THE INITIAL SURVEY, MILLS ENGAGED EDWARD KEALL, an Islamic historian from the Royal Ontario Museum, to begin scratching around El-Qasr to see what he could find out about the ancient city's origins and chronology. As with other periods, pottery is the best dating tool. Keall's job was made more difficult, however, by the fact that Islamic pottery traditions did not change greatly through the medieval period. Although he found nothing from the Fatimid period, from the Mamluk era he turned up three thirteenth-century sherds, enough to suggest that the city may have begun its life two centuries before the fifteenth-century houses that now grace it. Mills himself discovered that one doorway was supported on the foundation of a Ptolemaic temple dedicated to Thoth, making it obvious that El-Qasr rose over layers of older cultures. Much of that prior history will have to remain hidden, however, as the city has been declared a national monument and digging under the existing houses is no longer an option.

Keall also found the typical black-under-blue pottery that was common across the Arabian sphere of trading; it told him that Dakhlan traders had been to ports on the Red Sea. Such links suggested relative prosperity during the fifteenth century. Keall doesn't know which products were traded, though the most coveted items from Sudan, all of which would certainly have passed through the oases, were gum arabic, ivory, ostrich feathers, and, of course, gold and slaves. In its heydey, El-Qasr offered all the amenities of an important Islamic city: a Qu'ranic school (*madrasa*) and a court-house, along with a marketplace and bath-house, all of which remain to be documented in detail.

The prosperity of the early Mamluk period came at a price, however. Like the Romans, the Mamluks extracted as much revenue from the land as possible, with little concern for the long-term consequences for the residents or the productivity of the land itself. "The imprint that Mamluk culture left on the land was as long-lasting as that left by the Romans," says Keall.

By the end of the fifteenth century, the Mamluk influence in the Red Sea area was declining. Around that time, two Arab clans, the Quraysh and the Shorbag/Shorfa/Ashrif, took possession of the oasis lands. It is the names of these two clans that adorn the lintels of houses in El-Qasr that date from between 1495 and 1698, a period that saw the Ottomans, a Turkish dynasty, take over from the Mamluks as the rulers of the Arabic empire. The Quraysh clan is thought to have moved into the oasis in the mid-fifteenth century and bought many of the springs and lands in the western part of the oasis. It was the Shorbagees of Qalamun, however, who took power and actually governed the oasis. They date from the time of Sultan Selim, also known as Selim the Grim, who, backed by the Ottoman Turks, seized Cairo in 1517, initiating the Ottoman Empire.

In a pattern repeated throughout world history, the first dozen Ottoman sultans governed the Arab lands in an enlightened manner, but were eventually succeeded by a series of incompetents. Agriculture in particular suffered under Ottoman rule. Absentee landlords neglected their holdings, so that by the mid-seventeenth century, many of the once-prosperous farming areas had eroded and turned to deserts. While Mills has not found any direct evidence of Ottoman mismanagement during this period, perhaps it is telling that the last great houses were built at the end of the seventeenth century, indicating that El-Qasr's star was no longer ascendant after that time.

BY THE EIGHTEENTH CENTURY, THE EUROPEAN STATES, ESPECIALLY France and Britain, had gained control of much of the world's trade through their merchants and shipowners, making overland routes less important and thus weakening the Ottoman Empire.

The first flurry of Europeans arrived at the Nile in the wake of a French expeditionary force commanded by Napoleon, which occupied Egypt for three years beginning in 1798, until the British navy destroyed Napoleon's fleet at Alexandria. Herodotus had kept the wonders of ancient Egypt alive in the Western mind, and the French Revolution had fanned the flames of scientific enlightenment. The scientists, scholars, and engineers who accompanied Napoleon's army set about producing a thirty-six-volume set of books—twelve volumes of text and twenty-four of plates—depicting and describing Egypt's incomparably rich collection of antiquities. *Description de l'Egypte* has been described as almost comparable in scale and grandeur to the monuments themselves. When it was published, it lit a fire under a new class of European adventurer-travellers.

Although they were most interested in the Nile corridor, the Europeans soon began looking beyond to the desert country. In chronicling their exploits, these early travellers have provided the DOP with invaluable and rare glimpses of the oasis in the nineteenth century.

The first European to visit Dakhleh was a Scottish baronet, Sir Archibald Edmonstone. He landed in Egypt in late 1818 with the primary purpose of exploring the "stupendous grandeur of the ruins" along the Nile. The oases, however, had also been strongly recommended to him—by whom he doesn't say—as "objects of curiosity."

He departed Cairo on January 14, 1819, accompanied by two friends and travelling by *fellucca*, the cargo boat native to the Nile, with its characteristic raked, single sail. Winds were unfavourable, however, and progress slow. After three weeks, they were only a third of the way to Aswan. While on the river, Edmonstone's party had a chance meeting with the muscled and mustachioed Giovanni Battista Belzoni, who strongly encouraged a trip to the oases, saying there were two, and that only one, Kharga ("The Outer One"), had been explored. The deciding factor for Edmonstone was learning that Chevalier Bernardo Drovetti, the French Consul-General in Egypt, was about to go in search of the rumoured second oasis (Dakhleh, "The Inner One").

The race for the honour of European "discoverer" of the inner oasis was on. After a mere day's delay, and carrying a letter of introduction from the governor of Asyut to "the sheikh of the Bedouins," Edmonstone set out with his "baggage packed on three camels, and ourselves mounted on three asses." Edmonstone, whose feet nearly touched the ground, marvelled at the strength of these small draft animals. He must have cut a somewhat comical figure in his coarse silk waistcoat, "an immense pair of cloth trousers," red slippers, and white turban, with a Turkish sabre slung over his shoulder.

He commented on the singular lack of life in the desert: "Nothing was to be seen but a vast immeasurable plain of sand, extending in all directions." The carcasses of camels that littered the desert road, their long necks curved back in death agony so that their skulls lay on their spines, assured him that at least he was on the right track. His account records his anxiety about the loyalty of his guides, who, he thought, might desert him, but his fears proved unfounded. The party marched thirteen hours a day, following the Darb el-Tawil. With water running short, they completed the last leg of the journey under moonlight, arriving in the village of Balat five days after they set out.

"Our object," Edmonstone says in *A Journey to Two of the Oases of Upper Egypt*, "was 'Old Buildings.'" Not only does he give us the first Western view of Dakhleh's ruins, but also the first Western portrait of life in the oasis country. He speaks of the springs "strongly impregnated with iron and sulphur, and hot at their sources." He notes that there are no conventional dug wells in the oasis—but that the inhabitants are absolutely dependent upon the artesian springs, which flow all year. The pungent waters support crops of corn, barley and rice, as well as dates, which are exported to the Valley. Citrus fruits grow in the gardens of this "blessed isle." Edmonstone speculates that the inhabitants are Bedouins, but notes that they are exposed to raids from Barbary Arabs from the Mediterranean coast. Just three years earlier, a band of four hundred Libyan Arabs had plundered Dakhleh, killing many and "carrying off much booty." After only four days in the oasis,

Edmonstone beat a hasty return to the Nile by way of Kharga, meeting his bested rival Drovetti on the way.

French mineralogist Frederic Cailliaud visited each of the Egyptian oases of the Western Desert between 1818 and 1820. One of the things he witnessed was the large-scale trade in human beings. Slaves from sub-Saharan Africa were brought north to cultivate the land in Upper Egypt and the oases of the Sahara—work that the Bedouin considered beneath them. Many of the women became domestic servants and concubines in the cities, and some men were installed as eunuchs. At Asyut, the terminus of the famed Darb el-Arbain, Cailliuad witnessed the arrival of a caravan of 16,000 individuals, 6000 of whom were slaves—men, women, and children. "They had been two months travelling in the deserts," he observes, "in the most intense heat of the year; meagre, exhausted, and the aspect of death on their countenances, the spectacle strongly excited compassion."

Five years later, in 1825, the pioneer Egyptologist John Gardner Wilkinson made the first survey of the ruins in Dakhleh. He estimated that between 1200 and 1500 people then lived in El-Qasr. Although he found the ancient ruins impressive, he vehemently disagreed with Herodotus' description of the oasis as "the blessed isle." In a letter dated January 15, 1833, he wrote: " . . . of all the places on earth I do think the oases the most miserable. People used to talk of fortunate & blessed islands & other similar nonsense—it was a pity that they were not forced to live there."

After Wilkinson's visit, a half-century passed before another European retinue filed into Dakhleh. This was the ill-fated Rohlfs expedition of 1874, sponsored by the Egyptian Court. One of its primary goals was to investigate whether a legendary old riverbed of the Nile existed in the desert (it did not) and could be used for irrigation development—a perennial dream of Egyptian rulers that continues to this day. The expedition was the first multi-disciplinary group to study the oases; it included a topographer, a botanist, and a geologist, but no archaeologist.

The Rohlfs expedition stayed in El-Qasr, the large retinue of a hundred men occupying one of its great houses. An experienced Saharan traveller, Rohlfs noted how well it was built "for an oasis town," and was struck by the industriousness he saw everywhere around him. There were village carpenters, cobblers, potters, several millers (three large mills driven by oxen), two blacksmiths, a weapons- and tool-smith, and a distiller "who made bad liquor from bad dates in bad alembics." Women cleaned cotton in the narrow streets.

THE BRITISH OCCUPIED EGYPT IN 1882, PRIMARILY TO PROTECT their cotton plantations, and virtually ruled the country until the nationalist government of Gamal Abdel Nasser ousted them in 1952. In 1909 they passed the Relegation Law, which gave the government the power to deport dissidents without trial to specially created penal colonies in the Kharga Oasis, reviving the pharaonic role of the Western oases as desert Devil's Islands. Meanwhile, during those seventy years, British explorers had the run of the country, so in 1909 the famous explorer J. Harding King was dispatched by the Royal Geographical Society to study sand dunes and to fill in some of the "humiliating blanks" on the map of the Western Desert, perhaps the least explored region of Africa at that time. King, however, was frustrated in his efforts by his native guide, who belonged to the Senussi sect, an order of Islamic dervishes centred in Kufra, but which had adherents throughout North Africa, including Dakhleh. The Senussi were sworn to keep the secrets of the desert and were often openly hostile to Europeans. After two seasons of blundering about south of Dakhleh, misled by his guide, who one time left him for dead without water, a frustrated King "left the romantic desert" and what he called "the heated atmosphere of the *Arabian Nights*."

Although King did little to fill in the blanks on the map, he did offer some insights into the customs of the oasis in *Mysteries of the Libyan Desert*. Many of these, he believed, resembled those of the Nile Valley, while others were peculiar to Dakhleh. Among the latter was the procession of the bride to the bridegroom's house, or *Zeffet el Arusa*. The procession was led by a jester "who had tied the end of the long leaf of a palm to his waist in front and then passed the other end through his legs and up his back, so that it had very much the appearance of a bushy tail. He carried a staff in each hand, and hopped about on these in a most grotesque manner."

There followed a man beating a drum, a blind man clashing cymbals, and the crowd of the bride's friends and family. The bride trailed behind, wearing an everyday dress and a red shawl on her head, while behind her, raised on cross-lashed sticks for all to see, was her wedding dress.

At the same time as King was exploring the mysteries of the desert, his countryman Hugh J. Beadnell was plumbing its hidden water resources. Many of the wells in Dakhleh, he noted, dated back to Roman times. He did not know what tools the well-borers had used, for there were none to be found. But he observed that in all cases the bores had been lined to a considerable depth with wooden casing, manufactured from the local sources of the doum-palm, date-palm or acacia. The acacia wood had proved particularly durable and, even two thousand years later, many of the wells were discharging several hundred gallons a minute "by day and by night." (Such old wells in Dakhleh are still called *romani*, says Mills.) Inevitably, in some cases, the wood had rotted, causing the shaft to collapse and choking off the flow. When this happened an improbable class of desert men called *gattasan*, or divers, were employed to replace the well casing and dig out the sludge that had accumulated at the bottom of the well.

Beadnell watched these men at work near the Dakhleh village of Hindaw. Each man descended into the well six or seven times a day, remaining submerged for two to two and half minutes each time. The diver made his descent feet first, hand over hand down a rope. Working underwater, he placed the excavated material in baskets which were drawn up by hand, and when the diver wished to return to the surface he signalled to the men at the top with a tug of the rope. They then quickly pulled him to safety. The divers were paid a shilling a day and given their food for this dangerous task. Work had been in progress on the well for four years, showing Beadnell the value of these old wells to their owners.

During the nineteenth century many new wells had been dug. Modern boring methods were introduced by Hassan Effendi, a servant of a French engineer who was sent to Dakhleh by the Egyptian government in 1832. The local residents quickly learned the technique, drilling wells to a depth of 500 feet with primitive hand-boring rigs operated by several men pulling on a palm-beam fulcrum that drove the casing. Beadnell lamented that they had set about "promiscuously" sinking a great number of new wells, with no regard for the effects on old wells. As a result, large areas of the oasis had suffered a general lowering of the water table, and in some cases, older wells had stopped flowing, with dire consequences for the palm groves and cultivated fields dependent upon them. It was a harbinger of the challenges faced by modern oasis dwellers who have to drill wells to depths of 2500 to 4000 feet or more, to sustain agricultural production.

Between the World Wars a bevy of explorers—Egyptian princes, European counts, and other jet-setters of the Jazz Age, as well as a small number of trained archaeologists—penetrated to the remotest corners of Egypt. They were British, German,

Hungarian and Egyptian, among other nationalities, all joined in the common cause of exploring the mysteries of the Western Desert. Hassanein Bey explored the desert by camel, but his successors flew over the Sahara in fragile biplanes and crossed the Great Sand Sea in trucks outfitted with caterpillar tracks. So little was known about this sector that one of its explorers, Dr. Richard Bermann, wrote of his 1933 expedition: "As the expedition's official chronicler I was in charge of our travelling library, which, I am sorry to state, mainly consisted of one book: the *Histories* of old Herodotus, the best Baedecker of the Libyan [Western] desert still existing."

Count Ladislaus de Almasy, made famous by Michael Ondaatje's *The English Patient*, undertook a prolonged search for the legendary oasis of *Zerzura*, "The Oasis of Little Birds" that supposedly lay five or six days west of Dakhleh. Racing car driver, pilot and born adventurer, he was described in his obituary as a man "out of his element in civilization." In 1932 and 1933, Almasy discovered three *wadis* in the Gilf Kebir where the Tibu pastured their cattle after rain fell—every seven years or so—and believed that he had found *Zerzura*. Not everyone agreed.

All these intrepid travellers in their searches laid the foundations for the later systematic study of human prehistory and history in the region, but ironically, most of them used Dakhleh only as a jumping-off point, ignoring the archaeological treasures under their noses in their haste to venture out into the desert. It remained for the DOP archaeologists to tackle the 400,000 years of human occupation in the oasis.

IT IS IRONIC THAT MILLS AND THE DOP KNOW LESS ABOUT THE Islamic period—closest to them in time and firsthand experience—than any other. The DOP has not neglected the Islamic period and, in this respect, differs from most other archaeological

332

digs, which usually concentrate on civilizations of earlier periods in lands that converted to Islam.

One of the reasons the DOP has not focused more attention on the Islamic period is simply that the Egyptian Antiquities Organization (EAO) itself has taken on much of the responsibility for investigating Coptic and Islamic sites, including El-Qasr. Until recently, the town retained much of its busy character, being home to potters, blacksmiths and weavers, and hundreds of residents. Starting in the mid-1970s, however, after the EAO declared El-Qasr a national monument, residents began to move out rather than be told what renovations they could or could not make. "It mummified the place," says Mills. As a result, the abandoned homes are quickly deteriorating—the very thing the EAO wished to avoid.

On my return to the oasis, I found the once-vital city eerily silent. Outside the old city walls a small group of children met me, showing their wares of baskets and trivets woven from palm fibre and decorated with bright hanks of red and blue cloth. An eager guide led me inside through the now-deserted streets, pointing skyward to the darkened windows of the *harim*. On my first visit, I had been conscious of eyes looking back; now I knew there were just the blind patterns of the arabesques. My guide proudly led me up the narrow, twisting staircase that climbed the three storeys of the *madrasa*. From the rooftop I surveyed the crumbling skyline. Goats gambolled along the rooftops like their wild mountain cousins. A single family occupied a nearby dwelling, marking their place with a line of washing. Their neighbours had moved down the hill to the modern community. The craftspeople who had given the place a sense of purpose and vitality had also left the city.

This abandonment after at least six centuries of continuous occupation is emblematic of the rapid pace of change now sweeping the oasis—a change Mills is determined to document, as the DOP has done for all previous periods. To that end, a Dutch research team

333

from Groningen University has joined the DOP to study El-Qasr's demography and the history of its fascinating architecture, and also to collect stories and analyze the local dialects. Mills believes such ethnographic research will add a critical anthropological perspective.

Linguist Manfred Woidich of the University of Amsterdam has already spent several seasons in the oasis, interviewing local residents of Bashendi and El-Qasr. He began by trying to collect fairy tales and common folk poetry. In the beginning, he found people reluctant. "'We used to have them long ago,' they would explain to me," he says, "'but now, with radio and television, nobody cares any longer for tales and poems, and we have forgotten them.'" Later, when he had made friends in the oasis and was no longer viewed as a "foreigner," he realized that people had not felt free to share their stories and songs. He believes they were also reluctant because of religious turmoil within the community. In recent years there has been an ongoing dispute between those villagers who wish to practise traditional popular Islam and some zealous young men who are promoting their ideas about orthodox Islam, which has strong support in Middle Egypt. To them, there is no place for singing and dancing or veneration of the local sheikhs, and they have persuaded some families to abandon traditional weddings, which were always an occasion for music, singing and dancing.

After four years, Woidich managed to collect 120 specimens of poetry: verses sung during daily work such as harvesting, threshing and grinding; nursery rhymes and songs; songs sung while crossing the desert alone after collecting firewood; and wedding songs, to name a few. He observed that drums, flutes and hand-clapping accompany the many wedding songs. Women sit in a separate room and sing their own songs. Women and men also dance separately, the men performing a kind of stick dance, popular in Upper Egypt and believed to have had its origins in Pharaonic culture. Some songs are intended to give structure to the wedding feast, while

334

others are for entertainment only. One song collected by Woidich was intended as a farewell:

An evening and one of the finest!
Strangers are we and go home!
A shout of delight, O friends,
And a farewell to you!

Much to his surprise, Woidich discovered such songs are very localized, even differing between the eastern and western parts of the oasis.

WITH THE ARCHAEOLOGICAL TEAM IN THE OASIS FOR SIX MONTHS every year, there is an inevitable cultural exchange between the visitors and the locals. The relationship is friendly and respectful. Some of the archaeologists "go native": women dye their hair with henna; men wear *galabiyas*. Local people tutor the visiting archaeologists in Arabic, and the archaeologists reciprocate with English lessons.

One night, Mills invited a local band from Mut to entertain at the compound in Bashendi. The young village boys arrived first, followed by girls dressed head to toe in kerchiefs, sweaters and long dresses. The lead singer was a tall, striking Bedouin decked out in a bright orange shirt unbuttoned to his waist, tight black pants and pointed black shoes, with his jet black hair slicked back. He cut quite a figure, a sort of Elvis of the Oasis. But he was also a talented percussionist and singer, and a mesmerizing dancer, his quick, suggestive hip gyrations keeping perfect time with the complex syncopations of the drums. Only men dance publicly in the oasis, with each other or alone, sometimes with a ceremonial cane called a *nabut* as their surrogate partner. The band leader danced with the *nabut*, performing an athletic limbo. Suddenly, another band member jumped into the circle. Suspending the *nabut*

335

between their midriffs, they circled in unison, faster and faster, as the rhythm of the drums and flutes reached a feverish pitch. Then yet another band member abandoned his instrument and became a dervish, crossing and uncrossing his legs in a rapid scissoring motion as he circled round and round the courtyard, kicking up dust that laid a yellow veil around the full moon. Boys and girls stood apart, clapping in time to the beat, and answering the lead singer in choral rounds. As he danced, the band leader dangled a cigarette from his lip, then with a flip of his head, seemed to swallow it, to the wide-eyed amazement and gasps of the children. Then, after dramatic pause, his mouth opened and the cigarette appeared again on his lip, as if by magic, accompanied by thick clouds of exhaled smoke—and the children's delight.

When female archaeologists joined in the dancing, the band played on, only varying its rhythms and speeds to allow musicians and dancers to catch their breath. Men dressed in traditional *galabiyas* looked on approvingly. The village guard, the tallest man in the village and Woidich's main source of indigenous songs, joined the watchers, his ever-present, antique-looking carbine slung over his back, a weapon he fires only at feral cats, stray dogs and desert foxes. As the night wore on, village women appeared, one by one, to retrieve their children. When the band finally stopped playing, the courtyard cleared and there was a potent silence interrupted only by the barking of the village dogs, white phantom creatures that during the day are camouflaged by the wan background of the desert.

WOIDICH'S IS THE FIRST FORMAL EFFORT TO DOCUMENT DAKHLEH folklore and oral literature, and he feels like a man working against time, trying to record what he can of the indigenous culture and language before it is too late. He began his work in the Western Desert some two decades ago while collaborating on an Egyptian dialect atlas. He concluded then that the "strangest dialects spoken in Egypt are found in the Western Desert." Apparently, from the eleventh century on, speakers of different dialects of Egyptian, Maghrebinian and Bedouin origin came into contact in the Western Desert and created a unique mixture of Eastern and Western Arabic. As well, a formerly Berber-speaking segment of the population from the mountains of the Maghreb and Sahara contributed some of the more unusual variations detected by Woidich. Within the oasis itself, there are at least three distinct dialect groups: western, central and eastern.

Woidich believes that this rich stew of languages was brought together by the Arab conquest and later enriched by trade, migration of nomadic pastoralists, and the annual pilgrimage to Mecca. His interpretation has been corroborated by genetic analysis, bringing together two poles of the DOP's multi-disciplinary team.

RETURNING TO DAKHLEH AFTER AN ABSENCE OF FIFTEEN YEARS, Woidich has observed a host of changes in the cultural and material life of the oasis. Dakhleh's languages and its lifestyle are increasingly influenced by the outside world, especially the mainstream Egyptian culture of the Nile Valley. Perhaps the most potent force of change is television, which was introduced in the late 1980s. At night a telling blue glow emanates anachronistically from the windows of many mud-brick homes in Bashendi and other oasis villages. The younger generation tends to use "the television language," standard Egyptian as spoken in Cairo.

Formal education, while positive in itself, is another factor affecting the indigenous culture. All oasis children now attend the village school and, although teachers come from local villages, they often receive their higher education in the Valley and, according to Woidich, inevitably pick up "linguistic habits" there. Also, as part of the government's New Valley development scheme, many new settlers, workers and traders have emigrated from the overcrowded Valley. These emigrants largely control the oasis trade, selling garments, vegetables, fruit, meat, even fish, from cars while broad-casting their wares from loudspeakers as they drive through the villages. As well, many men from the oasis spend time in the Valley, where they trade in fava beans or find work as garbage collectors in Cairo, their donkey-drawn wagons piled high with pyramids of refuse a familiar sight. Most eventually return to their villages, bringing with them aspects of mainstream Egyptian culture.

ALWAYS SENSITIVE TO LOCAL CULTURE AND THE PROCESS OF change, Mills has developed a training program for Dakhleh residents to conserve and preserve their own cultural heritage. The Royal Netherlands Embassy has funded the construction of a new conservation centre where the DOP will provide training for local people in artifact conservation and recording techniques. Mills does not believe that oasis residents should, or would want to, live in a museum, just that it is to their benefit to know about their past.

Electricity is the most significant factor driving change in Dakhleh, especially farming methods. Farmers are turning away from the use of traditional agricultural tools such as waterwheels (*saqia*), *shadufs*, stonemills and handmills. Threshing is now done mainly by machine. "The days are gone," says Woidich, "when everywhere you could see rows of cows and donkeys turning in circles around the threshing ground." Farmers require electrically driven pumps to bring water from deeper underground. This, in turn, has lowered the water table to below thirty feet, making the traditional *saqia* obsolete. "The farmers complain that they have to go deeper and deeper to strike water," says Woidich.

I REMEMBER MY CHANCE MEETING IN 1987 WITH A 15-YEAR-OLD boy with the familiar name Muhammad. He was dressed in white slacks, a golf shirt, and plastic sandals. We fell into casual conversation as we walked through the narrow lanes between the fruit groves behind Bashendi. Like many oasis young people, he was anxious to practise his English. "I like the English very much on television, they are the best," he flattered me politely. He also was familiar with pop culture figures from the radio, rhyming off "Michael Jackson, Knight Rider, Presley." His values about farming also seemed to be borrowed from a North American model.

"The farms in Canada are big, good," he asserted.

Not always, I tried to explain. He seemed dejected by my apparent rejection of his opinion. For a while, he led me silently along a narrow path flanked by mud corrals that were fringed at the top with palm fronds. Shy, chattering girls dressed in long pink and lime green gowns, with baskets full of firewood on their heads, followed behind us

After a few minutes we came to a field of alfalfa, perhaps 150 feet by 50 feet, surrounded by a small irrigation canal, of the kind used continuously in the oasis since the Old Kingdom Egyptians arrived here 4500 years ago. Muhammad leaned down and showed me how a farmer like his father must irrigate the land by hand, opening and closing the small dikes with his *touriyeh* to move water where he wants it to go. His gestures were obviously intended as an object lesson, since he then reiterated his earlier opinion. "Canadian farms big but good," he insisted.

Muhammad's wishes have since become reality. With government incentives under the New Valley Project and modern heavy machinery, local farmers are opening up large fields that have not been worked since Roman times. Most of the new production is going into cereals, a vital commodity to support the growing population both in the oasis and the Valley. DOP archaeologists cannot help but compare what is happening to the Roman boom. The lessons of the past about the fragile relationship between humankind and the oasis environment have taken on new and urgent meaning in light of this latest effort to push back the edges of the desert.

CHAPTER SIXTEEN

THE NEW VALLEY

I RETURNED TO DAKHLEH IN JANUARY OF 2000, OPTING THIS TIME
to fly rather than risk again the nerve-wracking drive down the
ever more crowded Nile Valley. In the pre-dawn darkness, amidst
the constant chaos that is Cairo airport at any hour, I met up with
a group of DOP scientists from far-flung spots on the globe—
British Columbia, St. Petersburg and Vienna—assembled for the
once-a-week flight to Dakhleh. As we took off the sun was rising in
a crimson blaze over the purple peaks of the Eastern Desert, but
we were headed west.

"Do you want to sit in my seat?" asked a courteous young
Egyptian who was, in fact, sitting in my assigned window seat.

"Yes," I confessed.

"It is only desert," he observed apologetically, as he relin-
quished the seat and joined an acquaintance seated behind me. He

A woman carrying water jars

seemed to echo the prejudice of the ancient Egyptians who called the Nile Valley "The Land of the Living," and the surrounding desert "The Land of the Dead."

ONLY DESERT? UNFOLDING BELOW ME WAS THE WORLD'S grandest and most pitiless desert, the Sahara. We flew over earth-toned sands, here and there veined with dry *wadis*. As we veered west, we passed over limestone tracts of the Libyan Plateau that looked disconcertingly like banks of snow. After an hour, we suddenly dropped over the lip of the escarpment and began a steady descent over a long line of dunes, the great *Abu Moharik* dune belt, which stretches unbroken for hundreds of miles, forming the western border of the Kharga Oasis and, by degrees, overwhelming it. As we descended further, I could make out the rectangular, ghostly tracings of abandoned fields now under sand. Then, the improbable greens of the Kharga Oasis came into view: the bright unblemished greens of the crops, the dusty greens of the date palms, the still more muted greens of the sand-catching tamarisk. More improbable still were the blues of the tiny lakes that had accumulated from the overflow of artesian wells. Around these lakes were rings of white salt, left behind, poisoning the soil, as the water rapidly evaporated under the desert sun.

After a short stop, during which an armed guard marched a visiting dignitary to the plane with much pomp and ceremony, we set out on the last, short leg of our flight to Dakhleh. We skirted the edge of the Plateau, deeply incised by ancient stream beds that no longer held water, only the cooling, mauve shadows of early morning. Soon the faint greens of the Dakhleh Oasis shimmered against the golden sands.

MILLS LIKES TO MAINTAIN THAT IF OASIS LIFE TODAY WERE TO BE depicted on the walls of a tomb, in its essentials it would not look much different from images of the Pharaonic period: farmers harvesting their wheat with hand scythes, picking their famed dates, weaving mats, and raising poultry, cattle, sheep and goats. The donkey is still the primary form of transportation for the subsistence farmers, who make up 90 percent of the population. Boarding their two-wheeled donkey carts—the family vans of the oasis—the farmers perch high atop their seats and urge their small donkeys toward the fields and fruit groves. To protect themselves from the Saharan sun, they wear homemade wide-brimmed straw hats trimmed with brightly coloured cloth, a headgear unique to Egypt. Beside them are their wives, fellow farm workers who wear brightly coloured gowns and headdresses. Together, with help from their children, they produce the food needed to sustain themselves: bread wheat in winter, rice in summer, fruit from their groves, and vegetables from their gardens. When Mills first came to Dakhleh in 1977, he was quickly given a lesson in subsistence economy when he discovered that he could not buy eggs for the expedition, because the farmers produced only enough for their own families. "Everything here is either food, fuel or building material," he says. Of course, the oasis dwellers need money for items they don't produce themselves, such as sugar, tea, tobacco and cloth. For income, they grow dates, apricots and olives for export to the Valley.

Surrounded by one of the harshest environments on the planet, the oasis dwellers have not only adapted to the Sahara but manage to live comfortably on the fruits of their own labour and the gift of artesian waters that lies under the Western Desert. However, a closer look, beyond the timeless tableaux of agrarian life, reveals changes that are rapidly drawing this once remote outpost into the sphere of the global village.

Upon my return it was immediately obvious that the forces of modernity were bearing down on oasis life. A newly dug trench along the main road now carried fibre-optic cables. Rows of concrete

apartment buildings had grown up on the outskirts of Mut, as utilitarian and faceless as those around any modern urban centre.
There were new Qu'ranic schools in the villages, and on the outskirts, concrete soccer fields with night lighting. Electrical towers
strode across the desert from the Nile Valley with the imperious-
ness of a pharaoh. Stainless-steel light standards now appeared
incongruously above mud-brick walls, threadbare wires snaked
along the mud plaster like vines, and primitive TV aerials sprouted
from the roofs. Thirteen years before, electricity was furnished for
only a few hours a day by diesel generator; now it was available
around the clock at a flick of the switch.

The one thing that had not changed, and will not, is the
dependence of life on the waters under the desert. In the past, the
waters flowed freely under artesian pressure. Now they must be
pumped to the surface from great depths. Once at the surface, as
Mills says, the farmers channel them to their fields in much the
same way as the Pharaonic Egyptians did 4500 years ago. However,
if those waters are ever exhausted, life will not be possible in
Dakhleh. Unfortunately, Dakhlans face this grim prospect at the
beginning of the twenty-first century.

TODAY EGYPT IS A COUNTRY CAUGHT IN A WATER CRUNCH, HELD IN
the vice-like grip of the desert on either side. The Nile can no longer
meet the needs of its burgeoning population. Currently, 96 percent
of Egypt's 65 million people live on 4 percent of the land, crowded
into the narrow, green corridor of the river valley and the Delta
where the Nile fans out to meet the Mediterranean in the shape of a
lotus flower. The population is expected to double in the next thirty-
five years, raising the question: Where will the water come from to
sustain such dramatic growth, if not from the Nile?

Egypt is the country furthest downstream from the Nile's
sources and already it is using its maximum quota of Nile water

under an uneasy agreement, negotiated in 1959, with the eight countries upriver. Of these, Sudan and Ethiopia are the two with the most to gain or lose. Sudan gets 650 billion cubic feet of the Nile's waters, while Egypt is entitled to 1.942 trillion cubic feet. In 1990, the water-stressed country was managing to squeeze out 2.242 trillion by recycling. Demand, however, had surpassed 2.401 trillion feet by 1998 and was still rising. Although Egypt signed a deal with the new Ethiopian government in 1993, in which each country agreed not to do anything to the Nile that would endanger the other, Egypt is in a poor bargaining position, since 86 percent of the Nile's waters arise in Ethiopia. Naturally, Ethiopia wants a larger share to spark its own development and, to that end, has built a series of small dams on branches of the Blue Nile. If Ethiopia ever decided to construct the four major hydro-electric dams on the Blue Nile that the U.S. Bureau of Reclamation devised in 1964, it could reduce the Nile's volume downstream by 140 to 280 billion cubic feet a year—a prospect that alarms Egyptians. By its own admission, Egypt's national security is in the hands of other African countries, a precarious position that prompted former President Sadat to declare, "The next war in the region will be over the waters of the Nile." Despite this sabre-rattling, Egypt, Sudan and Ethiopia continue to hold talks on the division of its life-giving waters.

Control of the waters of the Nile and the desert oases has been a centrepiece of national policy and pride in Egypt since Pharaonic times. By the time of the Twelfth Dynasty of the Middle Kingdom (circa 1985 B.C.E.) a canal system already linked the Fayum to the Nile. The system was still functioning during the rule of the Ptolemies in the three centuries before the time of Christ and could have continued to do so if the Romans had not neglected it.

The system of basin irrigation, aided only by the simple water-lifting devices of *shaduf* and *saqia*, was able to sustain the Egyptians until the early nineteenth century, when the population began to explode. Before that, the population had probably peaked at five million during the first century, when the Romans aggressively developed the countryside as Rome's breadbasket. By 1850, however, the traditional method of capturing and distributing the waters from the Nile's annual flood, which allowed for crop production for only a third of the year, was being rapidly outstripped by the growing number of mouths to feed.

In 1860, Muhammad Ali, Egypt's Ottoman ruler, built a series of dams across the Nile at the head of the Delta and diverted water into canals, primarily to boost cotton production for export. In 1902, British engineers built the first Aswan Dam in Upper Egypt; it was enlarged twice by 1934. These dams allowed for crop production on a year-round basis, but dam building did not address the fundamental problem of overpopulation. By 1966, the population had burgeoned to 30 million and, in a desperate bid for a solution, President Gamal Abdel Nasser initiated the building of the Aswan High Dam. With nationalist fervour, he compared this Soviet-aided project to "pyramids for the living." The massive new dam displaced 50,000 Nubians in northern Sudan and drowned much of Nubia's archaeological heritage, but it could hold back two years' worth of Nile floodwaters compared to a mere 10 percent of the annual average flow held by earlier dams. The water reserves were used not only to boost food production and nourish water-hungry export crops such as cotton, but to generate electricity for industrial development.

True to predictions, the perennial irrigation made possible by the dam led to water-logging and salt build-up (salinisation), and the retention of silt behind the dam has caused a loss of natural fertility downstream. But, whatever its long-term drawbacks, droughts in the early 1970s and mid-1980s seemed to more than justify the investment.

However, as the population continued to grow, it became obvious that the High Dam in itself was not enough to sustain Egypt's economy and social needs. Without new initiatives, Egypt faced a bleak future.

Like the Pharaohs before him, Nasser looked west to the oases, with their seemingly endless supply of artesian water. By the 1970s, his successor, Anwar Sadat, had developed a plan he called the El-Wadi El-Gedid, or New Valley Project. The idea was to tap the motherlode of water under the Western Desert oases and create a New Valley running parallel to the Nile. The development would both relieve population pressure in the overcrowded Valley and boost the nation's food production, without drawing further on the Nile, which was already being exploited to the maximum.

Before carrying out the ambitious scheme, Sadat's scientists first had to answer a number of questions about this wondrous water supply: where was the water in the oases coming from, how old was it, and how much was left? In 1909, British geologist Hugh J. Beadnell had first speculated on the sources of artesian waters held under pressure in the porous sandstones. He posited a number of sources: the Nubian reaches of the Nile, the great marsh regions of the Sudan, or direct from the rains in the Ethiopian highlands. According to this last theory, these artesian waters sealed in the sandstone beds by impermeable clays near the surface and granite bedrock at the base, seeped northward by gravity—like underground rivers—through the beds of sandstone that tilt from south to north. As well, Beadnell identified a fourth possible source: water absorbed into the sandstone from regional lakes during previous rainy periods. At the rate that water was being extracted in the 1920s, Beadnell believed it might take as long as 3000 to 4000 years for the oasis waters to be sucked dry.

John Ball, then Director of the Desert Surveys, and Beadnell's boss, disagreed as to the source. He believed that the waters underlying the oasis were being recharged not from the Nile region but from rainfall on the highlands to the southwest of Dakhleh. Ball felt sure, in fact, that the water was being replaced as quickly as it was being used.

Fifty years later, in 1974, a government feasibility study reached the same conclusion—that the aquifer was being recharged from present-day rainfall in the Tibesti and Ennedi mountains near the rim of the Lake Chad Basin and from the huge storage reservoir of the Nubian sandstone in the Western Desert itself. Government officials admitted, however, that the recharge was not great enough to allow for economic development without depleting groundwater resources. Sadat's own science advisor, Farouk El-Baz, believed there might only be enough water to sustain expanded agriculture for a hundred years, yet still thought the New Valley Project might be worth it, if it relieved population pressure in the Valley and alleviated hunger in the country.

Further studies have overturned the sanguine assumptions of Beadnell, Ball and the Egyptian New Valley hydrologists, showing that there is very little present-day recharge of the Western Desert aquifers. The southern and southwestern frontiers of the Western Desert are underlain by impermeable rocks which prevent further water from seeping in, except a minuscule amount of local rainfall. Sadly, Beadnell's fourth option was correct: the vast majority of the water is so-called "fossil water," dating to previous humid periods. Establishing just when those waters collected is difficult, because the rain waters in the aquifer have obviously since mixed together, so, on average, all of the water in the basin is over 40,000 years old, and therefore beyond the range of radiocarbon dating. Some of the rain would have fallen during the Pleistocene period and some during the Holocene. Water not only collected under Dakhleh during these periods, but stayed there, because the geological contour rings close around the oasis, creating a self-contained, subterranean reservoir. But this gift from the past also means that the future supply of water is finite.

THE HISTORY OF WATER EXPLOITATION IN DAKHLEH SHOWS THAT there are no easy solutions. Until the late nineteenth century, shallow hand-dug wells tapped waters in the uppermost layer of the water-bearing rocks, at a depth of 100 to 500 feet. More recent wells, drilled using steam- and diesel-driven equipment, plumb depths to 4000 feet. The water from all levels flows at bathtub temperatures of 80° to 105° Fahrenheit and at the end of each day, the DOP crew bathe in the pungent, spa-like waters as they flow through a cistern, and then out by irrigation canals to the farmers' fields. However, very few wells now run freely under natural artesian pressure. Instead, pumps must be used to raise the water to the surface.

The vulnerability of the water supply was clearly demonstrated when, in the 1960s and 1970s, a hundred deep wells, ranging in depth from 2500 to 4000 feet, were sunk in Dakhleh, doubling the total water production to a eighteen million cubic feet per day. "Water gushed to the surface under artesian pressure, feeding large canals backhoed geometrically across the level areas of Dakhleh's lowland," observes Ian Brookes, a York University professor and DOP's former geologist. "Large cones of depression formed around these wells, cutting off water from traditional shallow ones and forcing abandonment of land and some smaller settlements." Shallow wells dropped in their production by a quarter and the water table was lowered overall. Further testing has proven that the rate at which the water table has fallen is directly linked to the number of wells that have been drilled. "The evidence is incontrovertible," says current DOP geologist Bob Giegengack, "they're mining the water." Water depletion in neighbouring Kharga has been even more dramatic, calling into question the feasibility of the New Valley Project as a whole.

Despite this, new wells are being drilled all the time, both to replace old wells that have run dry and to develop agriculture in new areas. Over the last twenty-five years, Dakhleh's population has grown from 45,000 to 75,000 people. However, the initial headlong rush to implement Sadat's New Valley Project has slowed for a number of reasons: few Egyptians have wanted to leave their beloved Valley for life in the desert; the expense of drilling deep wells has also discouraged full-scale development; and the falling water table has raised alarms.

More recently, President Hosni Mubarak has initiated a water project of his own, which he calls the New Delta Project, or, as it is better known, the Toshka Project. Like the New Valley Project—to which it will be connected—it is designed to get people out of the overcrowded Nile Valley and to meet the country's ever growing food demands.

Mubarak officially inaugurated the project on January 9, 1997. The plan calls for drawing off 194 billion cubic feet of Nile water each year from Lake Nasser—equivalent to ten percent of Egypt's quota. The world's largest pumping station, slated for partial completion in October 2002 by an Anglo-Norwegian company at a cost of $400 million U.S. will raise the water 69 to 174 feet and deliver it to a forty-mile-long canal that leads into the Toshka Depression, 110 miles south of Aswan. The channel is called the Sheikh Zayad Canal, after the president of the United Arab Emirates, who is providing financial backing for this phase of the project. The first water flowed through the Canal in 2001. In total, the project is expected to cost $2 billion U.S. If all goes according to plan, the open canal will be extended 220 miles northward to Kharga and Dakhleh by 2017, since it is now obvious that the underground waters there could be depleted in the next fifty years.

The ultimate goal is to develop some 750,000 acres of land for farming in southern Egypt around the tiny village of Toshka and further east at Uweinat, and an additional 250,000 acres in Kharga, Dakhleh and Farafra—making five times as much land suitable for settlement than is the case now. Mubarak has hailed the project as opening a new era in Egypt—"the era when we go out of the confines of the narrow Nile Valley." He hopes to resettle some six million Egyptians from the Nile Valley to southern Egypt and the oases, where they will produce wheat, cotton and foodstuffs, and find employment in light manufacturing.

Outside Egypt the project has many critics. Tony Allan, of the University of London's School of Oriental and African Studies, has called the project "preposterous, a national fantasy." He points out that both Sudan and Ethiopia are planning to build impoundments on the Nile and therefore Egypt is going to have less, not more, water in the future. Farouk El-Baz, now Director of the Center for Remote Sensing, Boston University, and former science advisor to Sadat, worries that much of the slow-moving water in the open canal will evaporate and that it could easily be clogged with sand blowing in from the surrounding dunes. He has also warned that the new scheme will likely result in poor drainage and waterlogged fields, which can only lead to salinisation. Furthermore, he says the canal will become a breeding ground for the parasite that causes shistosomiasis, not to mention mosquitoes and malaria. But, as with the Aswan High Dam, others might ask what choice Egypt has, faced with a population that is expected to double to 120 million within thirty-five years.

Craig Anderson, head of agricultural policy at the Egyptian branch of the U.S. Agency for International Development, claims the authorities could learn to make existing water supplies go further. He believes Egypt could save enough water to offset the need for the Toshka Project by improving irrigation methods, reusing water more efficiently, and giving up such water-guzzling crops as rice and cane sugar.

Water conservation measures are being explored, including irrigating areas still undeveloped in the Valley and developing more efficient irrigation systems in the desert that do not rely on wasteful flooding techniques. Israel has been a leader in desert agriculture. In 1995, Israel teamed up with its Jordanian and Palestinian neighbours in devising a fifteen-year, $400 million plan to conserve water and fight desertification. They have developed closed irrigation systems, introduced water treatment and solar-powered energy systems that exploit radiation and heat from the sun, promoted cultivation of desert-adapted crops, reforested denuded land and implemented conservation measures for grazing lands. Egypt, too, is experimenting with desert technology through the American University in Cairo's Desert Development Center. The Center is testing drip irrigation systems, the efficacy of soil treatment to decrease water infiltration and wind erosion, growing of salt- and drought-resistant plants, and the use of shelter belts to conserve soil and water. The challenge in the Western Desert is far greater, however, as it receives virtually no rain, while Israel receives nearly eight inches per year.

WHILE EGYPT PUSHES AHEAD WITH THE TOSHKA AND NEW VALLEY Projects, many water experts have conceded that the answer to the world's looming water shortage does not seem to be to build more dams, canals and reservoirs, which have already destroyed the ecosystems of countless rivers, streams and lakes and displaced millions of local people, often without improving their lives. The answer seems obvious: to use the water we have more efficiently. This approach applies especially to irrigation practices. Most irrigated land is watered by flooding fields or channelling water between rows and letting gravity move the water to where it is needed. Basin irrigation as practiced in Dakhleh is a version of this simple technique. Not only does it waste water, it leads to salinisation and destruction of the soil. Two new options are now available. The drip system delivers water at low pressure through a network of perforated plastic tubing directly to the plants. Studies in India, Israel, Jordan, Spain, and the U.S. have shown that drip irrigation reduces water use by 30 to 70 percent and, at the same time, boosts crop yield by 20 to 90 percent. Low-energy sprinklers that deliver water in small doses through nozzles positioned just above the ground perform nearly as well as the drip method. Currently, however, sprinklers only water 10 to 15 percent of the world's irrigated fields, and drip systems a little over 1 percent.

Installing such water-saving systems is beyond the means of some poorer countries in Africa and Asia. Meanwhile, today's existing economic and institutional structures—water distributors, dam builders and governments—still encourage the wasting of water and the destruction of ecosystems. Addressing the world's water shortage, therefore, will not only depend upon technological innovation but will require fundamental changes in how we think about water.

The old ways die hard, especially in traditional cultures such as survive in Dakhleh. It seems unlikely that local farmers will be quick to abandon the methods that their predecessors have used successfully for 4500 years. Some progress has been made, however, toward conservation. In the mid-1980s the pumps from the deep wells worked continuously, day and night—a flagrantly wasteful practice. Now, at least, the pumps are shut down at the end of each workday and started again in the morning, "if for no better reason than that diesel fuel is now too expensive," says Mills.

The New Valley scheme, however, raised local people's hopes for a bright future. I listened as a local official grilled DOP's Bob Giegengack about future water supplies: "Everybody has high hopes for Toshka. There will be cultivation of 500,000 *feddans* [acres] and people will come here."

"It is futile," said Giegengack.

The official, who remembered springs flowing naturally when he was a child, was insistent. "Is there not an ancient Nile under the desert?"

"No."

"Can you not make artificial rain? Can you not change the climate?" he asked, each query becoming more desperate as Giegengack patiently explained why these alternatives were not practical.

"Will the crocodiles and hippos not come again to the desert?"

"Unfortunately, not in our time."

Even though the pace of the New Valley Project has slowed, the oasis is currently capable of producing more food and supporting a larger population than the current 75,000 and there is unquestionably another boom underway. But is history poised to repeat itself? "Most of these new agricultural areas are pretty short-lived," says Mills. "They sink a bore and out comes the water for five or six years, and then they go find another well and piece of ground. They're really drying it up."

At the present rate of consumption, there may be as few as fifty years of water left in the aquifers. The DOP archaeologists are acutely aware of the modern megaproject's similarity to one undertaken in Roman times and of the prolonged bust that resulted. The Romans, however, were only able to tap the upper layers of the aquifer with the *saqia*, or Persian water wheel. Present deep-drilling techniques reach the very bottom of the aquifer, meaning that all of the water secreted under the oasis could eventually be brought to the surface. If that happens, and if the Toshka Canal fails, the oasis will cease to exist.

Mills' earnest hope is that authorities will listen to the lessons he has gleaned from the DOP's study of booms and busts during

Dakhleh's panoramic past: "I think there are lessons from the Roman period that may have some pertinence to the New Valley scheme," he says. "I wouldn't want to say whether bringing all this land under cultivation is the best use for the oasis in economic, sociological or agricultural terms. But we know what happened in the past. Maybe we should watch it and learn from it."

At Dakhleh, the developers must decide whether to manage the non-renewable resource of fossil water—the legacy of past ages—for short-term gain or for the longer term. What they decide will affect the fate of the oldest continuously inhabited community on the planet.

CHAPTER SEVENTEEN

HISTORY'S LESSONS

Two images of Dakhleh had been etched in my mind, compelling me to return. Each graphically symbolizes the age-old folly of human arrogance in relating to the environment. One was the surreal spectacle of Roman aqueducts emerging from under the dunes of the planet's largest body of sand. The other was Lake Mut.

A few miles west of the capital of Mut, the mirage-like image of a deep blue lake appears in the desert. It is no illusion. Rafts of several hundred waterbirds, including coots and several duck species, float on and dive into the glassy waters. Migrating flocks of grey herons fish in the shallows, stabbing freshwater fish called *tilapia* that were introduced into this artificial lake, and long-legged stilts strut along the waterline plucking brine shrimp from the salty waters. Windrows of dead fish wash onto the shore, perhaps overcome by the growing salinity of the water. Spent shotgun

---

Drowned palm trees in artificial Lake Mut

shells left by hunters also litter the dikes overlooking the lake.

This is wasted water from irrigation in the surrounding district. It has been drained from the fields to prevent more of the salinisation that has already turned large tracts of land around Mut snowy white. Several backhoes and tall cranes shore up the dikes to store the growing volume of waste water, and a pumping station adds daily to the reservoir. At the eastern and southern ends of the lake, the tops of drowned palm trees seem to float above the still water, reminders that this was once dry land. Meanwhile the sun beats down, evaporating the water and making it too salty to recycle.

Looking at Lake Mut, it would be easy to think that the problem in the oasis was too much water, not too little. But this lake is really just part of the much larger lake—the underground aquifer—that is in danger of being mined to extinction. In the modern context, Lake Mut is as incongruous as the Roman aqueducts on the Plain of Sio'h. It is a stark symbol of human shortsightedness in trying to push production in the oasis far beyond the level of sustainability.

ON HIS TOUR OF VARIOUS DIGS IN THE OASIS, MILLS OFTEN STOPS at Lake Mut, an appropriate place to contemplate not only the DOP but the future of the oasis itself. In Mills' opinion, there have been three high points in oasis history. The first came during the Mid-Holocene, the time of the hut-building Bashendi. Dakhleh then supported several hundred hunter-gatherers, who made the technical and cultural leap to become pastoralists. As we have seen, many of these innovative desert peoples were driven by the great drought of six thousand years ago as "environmental refugees" to the Nile Valley, where they helped to found the great Pharaonic civilization. The second high point was the Roman Period, which Mills calls "the original New Valley scheme." But the development of nearly all available land in the oasis with the aid of the *saqia* had disastrous consequences. It took another thousand years for the oasis to recover a reasonable level of prosperity under Arab rule. The third high point, says Mills, is the present, when long-abandoned Roman lands are once again being developed under the impetus of the New Valley and New Delta Projects.

Throughout the twenty-five years of the project, Mills has been guided by the need to come to an understanding of how the oasis functioned under different climatic conditions and successive cultural groups. He now feels that the boom-and-bust patterns he has uncovered in Dakhleh are applicable not only to other oases in the Sahara, such as Kufra, but elsewhere in the world where similar conditions prevail.

"Whatever we learn here can be of interest to governments and developers who need to come to a realization of how delicate the environment is in these areas," he says. "You can't monkey with it too hard, too fast, otherwise there will be real, longer-term problems created.

"One of the things I'm hoping our study will eventually do is give developers an idea of what has happened in the past and how to avoid it."

Other countries that rely on underground aquifers for water are also mining those resources to extinction. Perhaps the most dramatic example is the Ogallalla Aquifer that lies beneath 225,000 square miles of the Great Plains of the United States. Not exactly desert, this vast region, covering eight states, is nevertheless characterized by poor soils and low rainfall. In the Dirty Thirties, the Oklahoma Dust Bowl carried off much of the topsoil when drought and winds followed upon poor farm practices that failed to provide adequate ground cover and wind-breaks. In the wake of this disaster, as much human-made as natural, government and farmers began mining the underground lake sequestered since the last Ice Age underneath the plains.

Pumps powered by cheap electricity from the Hoover Dam and Texas oil began to bring this reserve to the surface, creating a breadbasket in America's heartland. By the 1980s, however, there were ominous signs that the Ogallalla Aquifer was being depleted. The annual drawdown was equal to the flow of the Colorado River and it was not being replaced. A 1982 government report made the gloomy prediction that the water would probably run out by 2020. Conservation might extend that forecast, but eventually the water will be exhausted, foreclosing the agricultural industry in the six states—Texas, Oklahoma, Kansas, Colorado, Nebraska and South Dakota—that now produce much of the United States' grain exports and half of its beef. When this day comes, there will be another migration of farm people off the land, another *Grapes of Wrath*.

A similar scenario is being played out in Libya. While drilling for oil in the 1970s, drillers struck a massive aquifer near the Kufra Oasis. Libya, like Egypt, is mostly desert, but it does not have a Nile River. Coastal aquifers were already overdrawn, which officials admitted left the country facing "disastrous environmental and socioeconomic impacts." The Kufra aquifer was seen as Libya's saviour. Colonel Gadhafi funnelled Libya's abundant oil money into the Great Man-Made River Project to bring the Kufra water to the coast along a 1200-mile pipeline. The prognosis, however, is hardly reassuring: the water is expected to run out in fifty years.

What all these governments are buying is not so much water as time, in the hope that more water might be found. But in the case of aquifers under the Sahara, the supply is finite. When the last drop has been mined, it is gone for good—until the next Ice Age and the rains return, a prospect that provides cold comfort indeed.

A MAJOR PROBLEM PLANNERS FACE IN FULLY DEVELOPING THE New Valley Project is salinisation, as has been the case around Mut. Historically, other societies dependent on irrigation that pushed beyond the limits of sustainability have collapsed. Sandra Postel, Director of the Global Water Policy Project, has stated: "It is impossible to talk about the history of human civilization without talking about water." She goes on to observe that "the overriding lesson from history is that most irrigation-based civilizations fail," and asks: "Will ours be any different?"

Up to the present, Egypt has been the most successful of all irrigation-based societies. By adapting to the natural hydrological cycle of the Nile River for most of their history, rather than transforming it, as they recently chose to do with the Aswan High Dam, the Egyptians have been able to practise agriculture continuously for five thousand years, longer than any other agrarian culture. Other great civilizations have not been so fortunate.

The first irrigation society arose on the plains between the Tigris and Euphrates rivers in modern-day Iraq. In the 1950s, the Iraqi government wanted to learn from past environmental problems in planning their agricultural development. They engaged the prestigious Oriental Institute of Chicago to study the early irrigation societies of the southern Mesopotamian plains to see what, if any, lessons the past had to teach them.

Peoples from the northern highlands, where farming first took root in the Middle East, moved into the southern part of the country six thousand years ago. By digging ditches to divert some river water for use during the dry season, they were able to grow an extra crop and for the first time produce surplus food. This freed up a portion of the population to concentrate on other activities, resulting in the development of writing and architecture, metallurgy and mathematics. By 3000 B.C., irrigation had became the foundation of the first great civilization of the ancient world—Sumer.

For a further five hundred years, things went well, but irrigation technology also had profound effects on the land. Evaporation of the impounded waters during the dry season left behind salts that gradually poisoned the root systems of the plants, undermining the foundations of the civilization.

Around 2200 B.C. the thriving Sumerian Empire suddenly collapsed. The Chicago scientists concluded that the collapse was triggered by a three-hundred-year-long drought. Lack of rain in the wheat-producing region in the north sent a stream of "environmental refugees" into the southern cities. In the south, the river, robbed of water, dropped more silt, clogging irrigation canals and water channels. Standing water led to a build-up of salt. This combination of ecological events resulted in the collapse of a seemingly stable, resourceful society.

Then, around 700, the Assyrians built a network of channels that criss-crossed the Mesopotamian plain at right angles between the Tigris and Euphrates rivers. Water accumulated in the channels, again causing salt to build up. Salinisation led to desperate measures: 15,000 slaves were forced to peel off the salty upper layers to get at the fertile soil beneath—a brutal exercise in futility that ended in revolt. A third major episode of salinisation occurred near Baghdad sometime after 1200.

By the sixteenth century the once-fertile crescent of Mesopotamia had been transformed into a salty wasteland.

Even today, half of Iraq's irrigated land is affected by salinisation and waterlogging, largely due to the development of the Greater Mussayib Irrigation Project. Established in the 1953–1956 period, just prior to the Chicago study, it used water from the Euphrates to irrigate the alluvial plains south of Baghdad. Within ten years, it was declared a failure due to poor drainage, increasing soil salinity and excessive silting. In the case of Iraq, the lessons of history were learned too late.

Environmental disasters were not limited to the Old World. Central Mexico, coastal Peru, and the American southwest each saw a similar rise and fall of highly developed cultures dependent upon irrigation. One of these was the Hohokam, who lived along the Gila River in present-day Arizona. Alone among New World culture, they engineered a hydraulic technology as sophisticated as any developed in Mesopotamia and ancient Rome. They built hundreds of miles of irrigation canals reaching into the desert on either side of the Gila. As their culture prospered, they built monumental buildings such as the three-storey Casa Grande, a possible observatory erected around 1300, and enjoyed a comfortable material lifestyle. As in Mesopotamia, however, this high culture eventually succumbed to salt. Their cities were abandoned to snakes and this once-prosperous people seemed to disappear into the landscape—like the farmers of Sio'h.

WHAT DOES HISTORY—AND PARTICULARLY THE HISTORY OF Dakhleh—have to show modern irrigation cultures? A great deal, as it turns out. A greater proportion of the population in the modern world is dependent upon irrigation than was ever the case in the ancient world. In addition to Egypt, countries such as China, India, Indonesia and Pakistan rely on irrigation for more than half their food production. Irrigated soils now grow 40 percent of the world's food and account for 17 percent of global cropland. The fact that farmers who can irrigate can often grow two or three crops every year has been critical to a tripling of world grain production since the 1950s—and therefore to the feeding of the human race. Irrigated lands are also expected to produce most of the additional food needed in the future. However, this green revolution is threatened by irrigation practices that not only waste water—almost half of the water diverted for agriculture never produces any food—but degrade the soil, primarily through salinisation. Currently irrigation accounts for two-thirds of water used worldwide and as much as nine-tenths in developing countries. Most of the world's rivers that can be economically exploited to provide water for agricultural, domestic and industrial use already have been. To feed the estimated eight billion people expected to be around in 2025, farmers are going to require an additional volume of water equal nearly to ten times the annual flow of the Nile. And no one knows where they are going to get that much additional water while still ensuring future supplies.

If the water resources of the oasis are exhausted, and the Toshka Canal fails to efficiently deliver Nile waters to the oases, in Egypt the desert wins. The problem of desertification, in fact, is worldwide, afflicting not only the Sahel-Sahara region, but also significant portions of China, southern Africa and Pakistan, as well as parts of Australia, North America and the former USSR. Arid and semi-arid lands occupy a third of the planet and are home to 700 million people. In the past, shifting cultivation and nomadic practices avoided widespread ecological damage. In the last half century, the trend toward more permanent cultivation and settled herding has rendered much once-productive land worthless. At least 230 million people are threatened by desertification, and every year 52 million acres are transformed into desert, largely by human activity.

As we have seen, the human use of fire may have kick-started the desert-making process. That process accelerated dramatically when people became pastoralists and farmers. Overgrazing, especially by goats, is a major factor in the advance of deserts. Removal of vegetation has an "albedo effect," increasing the reflectivity of the land, which, in turn, decreases the likelihood of rainfall. The cutting of timber—half the world's daily harvest is for fuel for cooking and heating—also exposes the topsoil to erosion, further impoverishing the land and impairing its ability to recover. During the drought of 1969–1974, between 70 and 220 million tons of soil were lost from the Sahara annually, blown into the Atlantic Ocean.

There has been an ongoing debate over whether humans were responsible for creating the Sahara in the first place. It seems that global atmospheric factors originally led to the drying up of North Africa, but there is little doubt that human actions have caused the desert to expand into the Sahel region. The response of human societies to drought has created a vicious feedback loop. In years of heavy rainfall, herds and human populations increase. Then, when drought comes, as it inevitably does, animals over-graze the vegetation and people must forage more widely for firewood. The growing of cash crops like groundnuts for export instead of native, drought-resistant crops like millet has only made matters worse. The tragedy repeats itself as it did in 1984 without, it seems, governments and people learning the necessary lessons.

The sustainability of a culture depends not just on the innate qualities of its people but in large measure upon a delicate balance between its technology and its native environment. Whether peoples survive and prosper is a global lottery, as Jared Diamond points out in *Guns, Germs, and Steel*. Unfortunately the Fertile Crescent and eastern Mediterranean societies did not hold a winning ticket. They arose in ecologically fragile environments and, according to Diamond, committed "ecological suicide" by squandering their once productive alluvial soils. As a result, power shifted westward.

When the pyramid builders emigrated to the oasis, their Nile-based agricultural technology of basin irrigation began the process of transforming the natural habitat into a human-engineered environment—or, put another way, of turning an ecosystem into an agro-system. However, there were never enough ancient Egyptians in the oasis to fully develop its lands and water—nor enough time before environmental change in the form of low Niles dealt a death-blow to the Old Kingdom. Before its demise, however, the imperial Egyptians either wiped out or pushed out the surviving oasis pastoralists, the Sheikh Muftah. In the twentieth century, pastoralist people in the Sahel have suffered a similar fate at the hands of colonial powers. As Brian Fagan observes in *Floods,*

Famines, and Emperors, the developed world has marginalized millions and killed thousands in the Sahel by imposing western-style economic and political institutions on traditional drought-adapted herder socities.

The triple threat that Egypt faces of too many people, too little fertile land, and too little water is not unique, and in the future it will become the norm for more nations. In many cases, global climate change will amplify the stark realities of growing populations and shrinking resources, notably fresh water. In light of these dire global predictions, preservation of productive areas like oases is ever more important.

No one can say precisely how irrigation agriculture will be affected by global warming. However, engineers are designing dams based on past trends that may not hold true in the future as the climate warms up. The implications for agriculture, ecosystem survival, and settlement patterns are enormous, if uncertain.

Like it or not, we are engaged in a game of global brinkmanship. Climate change has been compared to "the joker in a game of cards"—no one knows when it will be played or under what circumstances. Climate models agree on global-scale changes but are not yet fine-tuned enough to predict what will happen on a regional or local scale. Average global temperature is projected to increase by 9° Fahrenheit over the next thirty years, with higher latitudes experiencing a greater temperature rise. Such global warming would cause increased flooding in some areas (already the case in the United States, where heavy rain events have increased by 20 percent since 1900) and drought leading to desertification in others.

Climate analysis has shown conclusively that the dramatic increase in famine in North Africa—especially in Ethiopia, the Sudan and Somalia—coincides with a prolonged shift in rainfall patterns. After a relatively wet episode, the precipitation in Northern Africa and the Middle East has declined dramatically over the last forty years, while at the same time rainfall has increased proportionately in Europe. Researchers who carried out the study worry that this forty-year trend is an early effect of global warming and may indicate more extreme climate changes to come if global warming continues.

A group of Australian and Canadian scientists (Commonwealth Scientific and Industrial Research Organization, or CSIRO) released a study in August 2002, implicating pollution from industrial nations as the cause of the drought in North Africa that between 1970 and 1985 resulted in death by starvation of 1.2 million people. Tiny particles of sulphur dioxide—aerosols—spewed into the atmosphere by factories and power plants in North America, Europe and Asia altered the physics of cloud formation and reduced rainfall in Africa thousands of miles away. Some atmospheric scientists have questioned the validity of the computer-generated climate model employed by the CSIRO group, arguing that El Niño and overgrazing are more likely causes. However, CSIRO scientists point out that rainfall returned to the Sahel in the 1990s, when laws in the industrial West reduced aerosol pollution.

Lamentably, historical memory is often short and people assume life will continue as it has in the very recent past. The archaeological and geological perspective provided by the DOP makes it clear that massive changes in the oasis have always required human adaptation, as when the slow but inexorable drying of the Sahara forced early hunter-gatherers to experiment with domestication and ultimately adopt pastoralism as a more secure lifestyle. Such adaptability is one of the hallmarks of humanity, demonstrating our ability to transcend negative circumstances. But with increased technological sophistication, our strategy seems to have changed from adaptation to control of nature, with the now-familiar costs to the environment and ourselves. Roman efforts to transform the desert were as remarkable for their ingenuity as they were ill-advised. Today we find ourselves again faced with fluctuations in climate, this time on a global scale, due in large measure to our own actions, prodding us to ask: can we change our behaviour in time to avert disaster?

TONY MILLS REMAINS A REALIST, IF NOT A CYNIC, ABOUT PRESENT political facts. He has never been motivated by ideological considerations, and certainly wouldn't describe himself as an environmentalist. "It was really my curiosity about how people lived in the past that brought in this whole environmental aspect," he avers. Nevertheless, his and Freeman's decision to place as much emphasis on environmental aspects as on the cultural story has made the DOP a model for environmental archaeology. Of course, there are other digs that interpret cultural changes in an environmental context. What distinguishes the DOP is that it covers a whole suite of cultures in this way, over nearly a half-million years, and it remains the only regional archaeological study in North Africa.

The DOP's free-ranging intellectual approach has already paid, and will continue to pay, dividends to the science of archaeology. Mills is convinced more than ever that it is vital to study a region rather than a single archaeological site. The rise and fall of Kellis, for instance, is far more telling when considered in the context of the natural environment, local agricultural practices, and the fate of the Roman Empire.

Archaeology is often considered a "luxury science"—another way of saying that it has little practical application in the contemporary world. Even though projects like the DOP have demonstrated that this is far from true, fund-raising remains a perennial problem. Ever since the five-year survey period, Mills has had to look to the private sector for support. The lion's share of Mills' time in the off-season is spent in a never-ending round of fund-raising—networking and knocking on corporate and private donors' doors in Britain and the United States—under the aegis of the Dakhleh Oasis Foundation. It is, he admits, "an arduous, boring, but essential task." It takes a minimum of $250,000 annually to sustain the project, of which $100,000 is needed merely to cover airfares. Fortunately, many academics are paid by their institutions while in the field and bring with them research grants to cover other costs, such as room and board. Lab services, like those performed by Eldon Molto's laboratory, are also provided at no cost to the DOP and would otherwise be unaffordable. On the outskirts of Mut, a much-needed new dig house is under construction, adjacent to the Dakhleh Oasis Training and Archaeological Conservation Centre. At the same time, the twenty-three-year-old Land Rovers are wearing out and the constant repairs to keep them roadworthy also "keep us poor," says Mills. He compares the DOP's economic state, as well as his own personal economy, to that of local farmers, calling it "subsistence only."

Archaeologically, Mills feels, "the future is as good as the past." There is as much to discover at Dakhleh as has been unearthed to date, so much, in fact, that he doubts whether any of the present DOP members will ever complete what they set out to do. Much of the residential area of Kellis—which already has yielded the most important documents found in Egypt since before the Second World War—remains unexplored. Excavation of the much larger Roman Age city of Amheida is just beginning. So is exploration of Mut el-Kharab, likely the capital in late Pharaonic times. Given their size and longevity, these ancient cities are expected to yield even greater archaeological riches than Kellis. The prehistorians, Kleindienst and McDonald, and their protégés, will continue to make forays into the desert to document the prehistoric cultures that have made Dakhleh the "everlasting oasis." McDonald hopes to date the rock art using a technique pioneered on aboriginal petroglyphs in Australia. Similarly, Kleindienst wants to apply the new dating technique of optically stimulated luminescence to her much older artifacts. Churcher and Molto also plan to apply isotopic analysis to bones to determine the source of the people and animals—whether they were native or migrated to the oasis. And there is a younger generation of archaeologists, such as those being trained by Colin Hope at Monash University, who are bringing a battery of sophisticated and new computer laboratory techniques to bear on the questions traditional archaeology tackled with a brush and a trowel.

The DOP has grown from six original members to more than eighty scientists, who come and go from around the globe for varying periods over the six-month field season. The DOP has become so large, in fact, that it now holds an international symposium every three years (the next one will be held at the Poznan Archaeological Museum, Poland, in July 2003) so that its far-flung members can share their latest discoveries and exchange ideas in person. In addition, the project has initiated a publishing program with Oxbow Books to issue monographs on the various aspects of the research. Ten volumes have been issued, with others in progress. As well, the DOP, with funding from the Royal Ontario Museum, has created a permanent display of the prehistory of the Dakhleh-Kharga region for the New Valley Museum at Kharga, where the Kellis *codices* are on view. At Amheida, Roger Bagnall hopes to establish a museum reconstruction of an ancient building in which to display artifacts in their original context. Already more tourists are travelling outside the Nile Valley to the desert and such attractions should increase that traffic.

The people, the scenery, the smell and noise of Dakhleh and the contrasting tranquillity of the desert have become an indelible part of the lives of Mills and other DOP members. Mills no longer considers himself essential to the project, but he does feel the project is essential to his own well-being. "I'm totally committed," he says. "I love it here. I'm fascinated by what we find every year, in fact, every day. And I'd rather not be doing anything else. I still very much enjoy doing fieldwork. And I very much enjoy living out here in all this dust and grime—that suits me just fine."

Originally conceived as a twenty-five-year project, the DOP marks its twenty-fifth field season in 2003. There is probably another fifty to one hundred years' worth of investigation to be carried out. Even then, the whole story of Dakhleh will not have been told. "Patience is a great archaeological virtue," says Mills. "It's a bit like a 1000-piece jigsaw puzzle when you haven't got the picture on the box. And then you realize you've only got six and a half pieces inside the box, and you have to speculate on what the picture is. Maybe in two years, you get another piece or the second half of the broken piece, and so it goes. But every time you get a piece, your idea of what the picture is probably changes. The humility factor is very large in archaeology, or at least it should be."

Perhaps Mills is too humble, or modest, to state the obvious: He has been not only patient but prescient with his focus on the human-environment question. Looking at the wasted water in Lake Mut, however, Mills cannot help but worry about the long-term future of both the oasis and the DOP. "I wouldn't like to put a number on the life that's left out here," he says. "I hope we get through the archaeology before the place completely dries up. But I wouldn't want to guarantee it."

My return trip to Dakhleh had reinforced my belief not only in the ingenuity of the DOP's mission, but the pressing need to heed the lessons the archaeologists and natural scientists had pieced together from the multifarious pieces of the puzzle—the stones, plants, bones, mummies, *codices*, papyri, hieroglyphics, domestic bric-a-brac, art and architecture—left behind by an unbroken cycle of cultures, both primitive and civilized. It is a message modern society seems loathe to hear, with their seemingly unshakeable faith in gross national product and technology. Farmers in the Plain of Sio'h must have been as confident in the promises of their gods and the brute force of the *saqia*. They would not have countenanced the notion that the "everlasting oasis" could turn to dust, undoing their dreams.

Dakhleh's story is an environmental parable for our times. An oasis is a place of refuge, even plenty, in an otherwise hostile environment; life is possible there, while all around there is danger. An oasis, however, is also an island, a place with definite borders and finite resources. Survival depends upon wise management of those resources, for there is no way off this island. The need for us to recognize that these limits apply to the planet as a whole becomes more urgent every day. Earth, too, is an Island of the Blessed whose resources—of which water is the most essential—must be protected if the human experiment is to continue, if we are to have a chance to adapt to changing conditions brought about by natural climatic fluctuations and our own actions. As we have seen, highly successful civilizations have collapsed for failing to do so.

EPILOGUE

Before leaving the oasis for the second and perhaps last time, I returned to the Plain of Sio'h, drawn by an irresistible need to see where those aqueducts led. Within view of the refurbished temple of Deir el-Hagar, I passed a large well-drilling rig driving its casing through the sandstone in search of new veins of water hundreds, sometimes thousands of feet below. Shifting into four-wheel drive, I steered the aging Land Rover off the road and rattled across the plain, by-passing the wind-blasted remains of *columbaria* and the plundered, open tombs of long-departed farmers dug into a nearby *gebel,* before pulling up beside the aqueducts.

Following an aqueduct, I walked toward the horizon, that "infinite space of mystery and terror," where the limpid blue of the cloudless sky and the blinding yellow sands meet. Eventually the aqueduct disappeared under a dune, but in the trough of the dune

Roman aqueducts in the Great Sand Sea

I found remnants of it, and could see more sections emerging ahead, as well as pieces of others that had once funnelled water to the Plain below.

As I climbed the ever-higher dune hills, I remembered something Tony Mills had said to me about the Roman boom time in Dakhleh: "I blame them for their prosperity." It had struck me then as a curious statement, but I now realized how applicable it was to our own time. The prosperity of the developed countries, unparalleled in human history, is dependent upon a level of exploitation which takes no account of future needs. Like the waters underneath Dakhleh, many of those resources are finite and at present rates of consumption will not be there to support the survival of future generations. Our boom will be our children's and their children's bust if we do not temper our use of the resources that remain.

And as I crested another hill, I also remembered the great microbiologist René Dubois saying that our species might best be described as "desert-makers." Before me lay a vision of a ruined world, a post-human world in which our artifacts, such as the aqueducts that once promised so much, lie buried or weathering away to grains of sand.

On the crest of yet another great dune I saw a further swath of red, another remnant of aqueduct, leading to a long-extinct well, perhaps a good half mile away, that probably ran dry nearly two thousand years ago.

It was getting late and I decided to turn back. The wind was now blowing harder, raising wisps of yellow sand along the ridges of the dunes. Shells tumbled across the sands and a round bowl of the long-departed peoples of the Plain of Sio'h rolled by.

Like so many "crossers of the sand" before me, I turned my back on the desert and set my sights, with a mixture of hope and apprehension, on Dakhleh, Island of the Blessed.

BIBLIOGRAPHY

I. ISLAND OF THE BLESSED

Churcher, C.S. and A.J. Mills, eds. *Reports from the Survey of the Dakhleh Oasis, Western Desert of Egypt, 1977-1987*. Oxford: Oxbow Books.

Cloudsley-Thompson, J.L. ed. 1984. *Sahara Desert*. New York: Pergamon Press.

Fagan, B.M. 1975. *The Rape of the Nile: tombs, tourists and archaeologists*. New York: Scribners.

Fakhry, A. 1974. *The Oases of Egypt, II, Bahariyah and Farafra Oases*. Cairo: The American University in Cairo Press.

Herodotus. 1976. *The Histories*. Aubrey de Selincourt, trans. Harmondsworth: Penguin

Weaver, K.F. The Search for Our Ancestors. *National Geographic*, November 1985, 561-623.

Williams, M.A.J. and H. Faure, ed. 1980. *The Sahara and the Nile: Quaternary environments and prehistoric occupation in northern Africa*. Rotterdam: A.A. Balkema.

Winlock, H.E. ed. 1936. *Dakhleh Oasis, Journal of a Camel Trip Made in 1908*. New York: The Metropolitan Museum of Art.

II. THE GARDEN

Butzer, K.W. 1971. *Environment and Archaeology: An Ecological Approach to Prehistory*. Chicago: Aldine-Atherton.

An *omal* drinking water

373

Caton-Thompson, G. 1983. *Mixed Memoirs*. Gateshead, Tyne and Wear: Paradigm Press.

Caton-Thomspon, G. and E. W. Gardner. 1932. The Prehistoric Geography of Kharga Oasis. *The Geographical Journal* 80: 369-406.

Churcher, C.S., M.R. Kleindienst, and H.P. Schwarcz. 1999. Faunal remains from a Middle Pleistocene lacustrine marl in Dakhleh Oasis, Egypt: paleoenvironmental reconstructions. *Palaeogeography, Palaeoclimatology, Palaeoecology* 154: 301-312.

Clark, J.D. 1980. Human populations and cultural adaptations in the Sahara and the Nile during prehistoric times, 572-582. *In* Williams, M.A.J. and H. Faure, ed. *The Sahara and The Nile*. Rotterdam: A.A. Balkema.

Cole, S. 1964. *The Prehistory of East Africa*. London: Weidenfeld and Nicolson.

Hawkins, A.L. 2000. Getting a handle on tangs. Ph.D. thesis (unpublished), Toronto: University of Toronto.

Hawkins, A.L. 2001. Aterian, 23-45. *In* Peregrine, P.N. ed. *Encyclopedia of Prehistory*. New York: Kluwer Academic.

Hoffman, M.A. 1979. *Egypt Before The Pharaohs: The Prehistoric Foundations of Egyptian Civilization*. New York: Knopf.

Kleindienst, M.R. et al. (in manuscript) Water in the Desert: First report on Uranium-series Dating of Caton-Thompson's and Gardner's "classic" Pleistocene sequence at Refuf Pass, Kharga Oasis.

Kleindienst, M.R. 2001. What is Aterian? The view from the Dakhleh Oasis and the Western Desert, Egypt. *In* Marlow, M. ed. *Oasis Papers: Proceedings of the First International Symposium of the Dakhleh Oasis Project*. Oxford: Oxbow Books.

Kleindienst, M.R. 2000. On the Nile Corridor and Out-of-Africa Model. *Current Anthropology*. February 2000 Volume 41, Number 1: 107-109.

Kleindienst, M.R. et al. 1999. Geography, geology, geochronology and geoarchaeology of the Dakhleh Oasis region: an interim report. *In* Mills, A.J. and C.S. Churcher, ed. *Reports from the Survey of the Dakhleh Oasis 1977-87*. Oxford: Oxbow Books.

Kleindienst, M.R. 1999. Pleistocene archaeology and geoarchaeology of the Dakhleh Oasis: a status report. *In* Mills, A.J. and C.S. Churcher, ed. *Reports from the Survey of the Dakhleh Oasis 1977-87*. Oxford: Oxbow Books.

McBrearty, J. and A.S. Brooks. 2000. The Revolution That Wasn't: a New Interpretation of the Origin of Modern Human Behavior. *Journal of Human Evolution*. November, 2000. Vol. 39, No. 5, 453-563. Academic Press.

McBurney, C.B.M. 1960. *The Stone Age of Northern Africa*. Harmondsworth, Middlesex: Penguin Books.

Nicoll, K., R. Giegengack, and M. Kleindienst. 1999. Petrogenesis of Artifact-bearing Fossil-spring tufa deposits from Kharga Oasis, Egypt. *Geoarchaeology: An International Journal*. Vol. 14, No. 8: 849-863.

Phillipson, D.W. 1985. *African Archaeology*. New York: Cambridge University Press.

Tattersall, I. 2000. Once we were not alone. *Scientific American*. January, 2000, 56-62.

Tattersall, I. 1997. Out of Africa again and again. *Scientific American*. April 1997, 60-67.

Van Peer, P. 1998. The Nile Corridor and the Out-of-Africa model, an Examination of the Archaeological Record. *Current Anthropology*. June 1998: Volume 39 supplement, 115-140.

Wendorf, F. and Schild, R. 1980. *Prehistory of the Eastern Sahara*. New York: Academic Press.

Wendorf, F., Schild, R. and Issawi, B. 1976. *Prehistory of the Nile Valley*. New York: Academic Press. Wendorf, F. et al. 1976. The Prehistory of the Egyptian Sahara. *Science*. 193: 103-114.

Wiseman, M.F. 2001. Problems in the Prehistory of the Late Upper Pleistocene of the Dakhleh Oasis. *In* Marlow, M. ed. *Oasis Papers: Proceedings of the First International Symposium of the Dakhleh Oasis Project*. Oxford: Oxbow Books.

Wiseman, M.F. 1999. Late Pleistocene Prehistory in the Dakhleh Oasis. In *Reports From the Survey of the Dakhleh Oasis 1977-87*. Mills, A.J. and C.S. Churcher, ed. Oxford: Oxbow Books.

Wiseman, M. 1999. Kharga oasis, prehistoric sites, 408-411. *In* Bard, K.A., ed. *Encyclopedia of the Archaeology of Ancient Egypt*. London and New York: Routledge.

Wiseman, M.F. A 'retro-tech' Approach to Dating the Llater Late Pleistocene in the Dakhleh Oasis. *In* Technological Perspectives on Prehistory: a conference in honour of M.R. Kleindienst and H.B. Shroeder, University of Toronto, May 17th 1998.

Wiseman, M. 1993. The Dakhleh Oasis During the Terminal Pleistocene: Is Anyone Home? 283-285. *In* Jamieson, R.W. et al., ed. *Culture and Environment: A Fragile Co-existence, Proceedings of the Twenty-Fourth Annual Conference of the Archaeological Association of the University of Calgary*. The University of Calgary Archaeological Association.

III. CROSSERS OF THE SAND

Banks, K.M. 1984. *Climate, Cultures and Cattle: The Holocene Archaeology of the Eastern Sahara*. Dallas: Department of Anthropology, Institute for the Study of Earth and Man, Southern Methodist University.

Bey, A.M.H. 1924. Through Kufra to Darfur. *The Geographical Journal*. November, 1924. Vol. 64, No. 5.

Braidwood, R.J. 1958. Near Eastern Prehistory. *Science*, 20 June 1958. Vol. 127: 1419-1430.

Brookes, I.A. 1989. Early Holocene Basinal Sediments of the Dakhleh Oasis Region, South Central Egypt. *Quaternary Research*. 32: 139-152.

Close, A.E. 2002. Tides of the Desert. In *Contributions to the Archaeology and Environmental History of Africa in Honour of Rudolph Kuper*. Koln: Heinrich Barth Institute.

Cook, G. 2002. Topography and the Pyramids. *Boston Globe*. In *The Chronicle Herald*. January 1, 2002.

El-Baz, F. 2001. Gifts of the Desert. *Archaeology*. March/April 2001: 42-45.

El-Baz, F. 1981. Desert Builders Knew a Good Thing When They Saw it. *Smithsonian*. Vol. 12, No.1: 116-122.

Goudie, A. 1993. *The Human Impact on the Natural Environment*. Oxford: Blackwell Publishers.

Grayson, D.K. 1993. *The Desert's Past, A Natural History of the Great Basin*. Washington: Smithsonian Institution Press.

Hassan, F.A. 1986. Desert Environment and Origins of Agriculture in Egypt. *Norwegian Archaeological Review, 19: 63-76*.

Krzyzaniak, K. 1990. Petroglyphs and the Research on the Development of the Cultural Attitude Towards Animals in the Dakhleh Oasis (Egypt). *Sahara* 3/1990: 95-97.

Krzyzaniak, L. and Kroeper, K. 1991. A Face-mask in the Prehistoric Rock Art of the Dakhleh Oasis? *Archeo-Nil, Bulletin de la societe pour l'etude des cultures prepharaoniques de la vallee du Nil*. May, 1991: 59-61.

Krzyzaniak, L. and Kobusiewick, M. ed. 1989. *Late Prehistory of the Nile Basin and the Sahara*. Poznan: Poznan Archaeological Museum.

Krzyzaniak, L. 1981. Origin and Early Development of Food-producing Cultures in Northeastern Africa. *Current Anthropology*. December 1981. Vol. 22, No. 6: 693-694.

Kuper, R. 1999. On the Tracks of Early Herdsmen. *Archaeologie in Deutschland*. Heft 2, April–June: 12–17.

McDonald, M.M.A. 1999. Neolithic Cultural Units and Adaptations in the Dakhleh Oasis. *In* Mills, A.J. and C.S. Churcher, ed.*Reports from the Survey of the Dakhleh Oasis 1977-87*. Oxford: Oxbow Books.

McDonald, M.M.A. and K. Walker. 1999. Holocene Prehistory: Interim Report on the 1992 Season. *In* Hope, C.A. and A.J. Mills, ed. *Dakhleh Oasis Project: Preliminary Reports on the 1992-1993 and 1993-94 Field Seasons*. Oxford: Oxbow Books.

McDonald, M.M.A. 1999. Holocene Prehistory: Interim Report on the 1993 Season. *In* Hope, C.A. and A.J. Mills, ed. *Dakhleh Oasis Project: Preliminary Reports on the 1992-1993 and 1993-94 Field Seasons*. Oxford: Oxbow Books.

McDonald, M.M.A. 1998. Adaptive Variability in the Eastern Sahara during the Early Holocene. 127-136 *In* di Leria, S. and G. Manzi, ed. *Before Food Production in North Africa*. A.B.A.C.O. Edzioni.

McDonald, M.M.A. 1998. Early African Pastoralism: View from Dakhleh Oasis (South Central Egypt). *Journal of Anthropological Archaeology*. 17: 124-142.

McDonald, M.M.A. 1996. Relations between Dakhleh Oasis and the Nile Valley in the Mid-Holocene: A Discussion. In *Interregional Contacts in the Later prehistory of Northeastern North Africa*. Poznan: Poznan Archaeological Museum.

McDonald, M.M.A. 1993. Cultural Adaptations in Dakhleh Oasis, Egypt, in the Early to Mid-Holocene. 199-209. *In* Krzyaniak, L., M. Kobusiewicz, and J. Alexander, eds. *Environmental Change and Human Culture in the Nile Basin and Northern Africa until the Second Millennium B.C.* Poznan: Polish Academy of Sciences.

McDonald, M.M.A. Neoltihic of Sudanese Tradition or Saharo-sudanese Neolithic? The View from Dakhla Oasis, South Central Egypt, 51-70. *In* Sterner, J. and N. David, ed. *An African Commitment: Papers in Honour of Peter Louis Shinnie.* Calgary: University of Calgary Press.

McDonald, M.M.A. 1991. Origins of the Neolithic in the Nile Valley as Seen from Dakhleh Oasis in the Egyptian Western Desert. *Sahara.* 4: 41-52.

McDonald, M.M.A. 1991. Technological Organization and Sedentism in the Epipaleolithic of Dakhleh Oasis, Egypt. *The African Archaeological Review.* 9: 81-109.

Millet, N.B. 1975. Valley and Desert: The Two Worlds of the Egyptian. 27-48. *In* Levine, L.D. ed. *Man in Nature.* Toronto: Royal Ontario Museum.

Muzzolini, A. 1993. L'Origine des Chevres et Moutons Domestiques en Afrique. Reconsideration de la these Diffusioniste Traditionnaelle. In *Extrait de Empuires*, t. 38-50, 2: 160-171.

Thompson, J.L. Neolithic burials at Sheikh Muftah, Dakhleh Oasis, Egypt: A Preliminary Report. *In* manuscript: Department of Anthropology and Ethnic Studies, University of Nevada, Las Vegas.

Thompson, J.L. Mss. Neolithic Dental Remains from Sheikh Muftah, Dakhleh Oasis: A Preliminary Report. *In* manuscript: Department of Anthropology and Ethnic Studies, University of Nevada, Las Vegas.

Winkler, H.A. *Rock Drawings of Southern Egypt I* (1938) and *II* (1939). London: Egypt Exploration Society.

Winkler, H.A. 1939. Rock-pictures at 'Uweinat. 307-310. *In* Bagnold, Major R.A. An Expedition to the Gilf Kebir and 'Uweinat, 1938. *The Geographical Journal.* April 1939: Vol XCIII, No 4.

Winkler, H.A. 1938. Rock-drawings of Southern Upper Egypt (including 'Uweinat). In *Sir Robert Mond Desert Expedition, Preliminary Report.*

IV. LORDS OF THE WEST

Bell, B. 1971. The Dark Ages in Ancient History: The First Dark Age in Egypt. *American Journal of Archaeology*, 1971, 75: 1-26.

Bell, B. 1975. Climate and History of Egypt: The Middle Kingdom. *American Journal of Archaeology*, 1975, 79: 223-269.

Butzer, K.W. 1976. *Early Hydraulic Civilization in Egypt.* Chicago: University of Chicago Press.

Caminos, A.R. 1977. *A Tale of Woe.* Oxford: Ashmolean Museum.

Emery, W.B. *Archaic Egypt.* Harmandsworth: Penguin.

Fagan, B. 1999. *Floods, Famines and Emperors: El Nino and the fate of civilizations.* New York: Basic Books.

Gardiner, A.H. 1933. The Dakhleh Stela. *Journal of Egyptian Archaeology*. 19: 19-30.
Giddy, L.L. 1987. *Egyptian Oases*. Warminster: Aris & Phillips.
Grimal, N. 1997. *A History of Ancient Egypt*. Ian Shaw, trans. Oxford: Blackwell.
Hassan, F.A. 1988. The Predynastic of Egypt. *Journal of World Prehistory*. 1988. Vol. 2, No. 2: 135-185.
Kamil, J. 1984. *The Ancient Egyptians, A Popular Introduction to Life in the Pyramid Age*. Cairo: The American University in Cairo Press.
Kaper, O.E. and H. Willlems. 2001. Examining the Desert: Old Kingdom Activity Around the Dakhleh Oasis. *In* Marlow, M. ed. *Oasis Papers: Proceedings of the First International Symposium of the Dakhleh Oasis Project*. Oxford: Oxbow Books.
Kees, H. 1977. *Ancient Egypt, a Cultural Topography*. Chicago: University of Chicago Press.
Mertz, B. 1978. *Red Land, Black Land, Daily Life in Ancient Egypt*. New York: Dodd, Mead & Company.
Mills, A.J. 1999. Pharaonic Egyptians in the Dakhleh Oasis. *In* Mills, A.J. and C.S. Churcher, ed. *Reports from the Survey of the Dakhleh Oasis 1977-87*. Oxford: Oxbow Books.
Redford, D.B. 1976. The Oases in Egyptian History to Classical times, to 2100 B.C. *Journal of the Society for the Study of Egyptian Antiquities*. 7: 7-10.
Shaw, I. ed. 2000. *The Oxford History of Ancient Egypt*. Oxford: Oxford University Press.
Wilson, J.A. 1968. *The Culture of Ancient Egypt*. Chicago: The University of Chicago Press.

V. A CURSE OF SAND AND SALT

Abley, M. The Sand Papers. *The Gazette*. July 24, 1988.
Associated Press. 1988. ROM's Archaeologists Find Aristotelian Text in Egyptian Excavation. *The Globe & Mail*, April 9, 1988.
Bagnall, R.S. 1997. *The Kellis Agricultural Account Book*. Oxford: Oxbow Books.
Bagnall, R.S. 1993. *Egypt in Late Antiquity*. Princeton, New Jersey: Princeton University Press.
Barrow, R.H. *The Romans*. Harmondsworth: Penguin.
Belzoni, G.B. 1820. *Narrative of the Operations and Recent Discoveries in Egypt and Nubia*. London: John Murray.
Bevan, E. 1968 (2nd ed.). *A History of Egypt under the Ptolemaic Dynasty*. Chicago: Argonaut Inc. Publishers.
Birrell, M. 1999. Excavations in the Cemeteries of Ismant el-Kharab. *In* Hope, C.A. and A.J. Mills, ed, *Dakhleh Oasis Project: Preliminary Reports on the 1992-1993 and 1993-94 Field Seasons*. Oxford: Oxbow Books.
Bowen, G.E. 2001. The Fourth-century Churches at Ismant el-Kharab. *In* Marlow, M. ed. *Oasis Papers: Proceedings of the First International Symposium of the Dakhleh Oasis Project*. Oxford: Oxbow Books.

Bowen, G.E. 1999. Textiles from Ismant el-Kharab. *Bulletin of the Australian Centre for Egyptology*. Vol. 10: 7-12.

Bowen, G.E. 1999. The Coinage: A Preliminary Report. *In* Hope, C.A. and A.J. Mills, ed, *Dakhleh Oasis Project: Preliminary Reports on the 1992-1993 and 1993-94 Field Seasons*. Oxford: Oxbow Books.

Bowen, G.E. The Spread of Early Christianity in Egypt. (unpublished in manuscript) Melbourne: Monash University.

Dupras, T.L., H.P. Schwarcz, and S.I. Fairgrieve. 2002. Infant Feeding and Weaning Practices in Roman Egypt. *American Journal of Physical Anthropology*, 115: 204-212.

Dupras, T.L. and H.P. Schwarcz. 2001. Strangers in a Strange Land: Stable Isotope Evidence for Human Migration in the Dakhleh Oasis, Egypt. *Journal of Archaeological Science*, 28: 1199-1208.

Dupras, T.L., H.P. Schwarcz, and S.I. Fairgrieve.. 2000. Stable Isotope Analysis of Botanical Remains: Possible Evidence for Site Abandonment in Egypt. *Ecologia* in review.

Dupras, T.L. 1999. Dining in the Dakhleh Oasis, Egypt: Determination of Diet Using Documents and Stable Isotope Analysis. (unpublished in manuscript) Hamilton: McMaster University.

Fairgreve, S.I. and J.E. Molto. 2000. Cribra Orbitalia in Two Temporally Disjunct Population Samples From the Dakhleh Oasis, Egypt. *American Journal of Physical Anthropology* 111: 319-31.

Freeman, C. 1999. *Egypt, Greece and Rome, Civilizations of the Ancient Mediterranean*. Oxford: Oxford University Press.

Gardner, I., ed. 1996. *Kellis Literary Texts I*. Oxford: Oxbow Books.

Gardner, I. 1999. Progress on the Coptic Texts from Ismant el-Kharab. *In* Hope, C.A. and A.J. Mills, ed. *Dakhleh Oasis Project: Preliminary Reports on the 1992-1993 and 1993-94 Field Seasons*. Oxford: Oxbow Books.

Graver, A.M. et al. 2001. Mitochondrial DNA Research in the Dakhleh Oasis, Egypt: A Preliminary Report. *Ancient Biomolecules*, Vol. 3: 239-253.

Gray, M. No word from Aristotle. *Maclean's*. May 2, 1988: 60-61.

Hamilton-Patterson, J. and C. Andrews. 1978. *Mummies, Life and Death in Ancient Egypt*. Harmondsworth: Penguin.

Hawass, Z. 2000. *Valley of the Golden Mummies*. New York: Harry N. Abrams.

Hawass, Z. 1999. Oasis of the Dead. *Archaeology*. September/October 1999. Vol. 52, No. 5.

Haynes, C.V. 1989. Bagnold's barchan: A 57-yr Record of Dune Movement in the Eastern Sahara and Implications for Dune Origin and Paleoclimate since Neolithic Times. *Qarternary Research*, 1989. 32: 132-157.

Hill, G. 1988. 'Aristotle Text' in Desert Documents. *The Times*. April 8, 1988.

Hill, G. 1988. Scholars View Lost Greek Text. *The Times*. April 12, 1988.

Hope, C.A. 1999. Pottery Manufacture in the Dakhleh Oasis. *In* Mills, A.J. and C.S. Churcher, ed. *Reports from the Survey of the Dakhleh Oasis 1977-87.* Oxford: Oxbow Books.

Hope, C.A. and J. McKenzie. 1999. Interim Report on the West Tombs. *In* Hope, C.A. and A.J. Mills, ed. *Dakhleh Oasis Project: Preliminary Reports on the 1992-1993 and 1993-94 Field Seasons.* Oxford: Oxbow Books.

Hope, C.A. 1987. Dakhleh Oasis Project: Report on the 1986 Excavations at Ismant el-Gharab. (Unpublished in manuscript)

Hrdlick, A. 1912. *The Natives of Kharga Oasis, Egypt.* Smithsonian Miscellaneous Collections, Vo. 59, No. 1. Washington: The Smithsonian Institution.

Kaper, O.E. 1997. *Temples and Gods in Roman Dakhleh: Studies in the Indigenous Cults of an Egyptian Oasis.* Ph.D. thesis: Rijksuniversiteit Groningen.

Kaper, O.E. 1999. Epigraphy at Ismant el-Kharab: Interim Observations. *In* Hope, C.A. and A.J. Mills, ed, *Dakhleh Oasis Project: Preliminary Reports on the 1992-1993 and 1993-94 Field Seasons.* Oxford: Oxbow Books.

Knudstad, J.E. and R.A. Frey. 1999. Kellis, The Architectural Survey of the Romano-Byzantine Town of Ismant El-Kharab. In *Reports from the Survey of the Dakhleh Oasis 1977-87.* Mills, A.J. and C.S. Churcher, ed. Oxford: Oxbow Books.

Lewis, N. 1986. *Greeks in Ptolemaic Egypt.* Oxford. Clarendon Press.

Lewis, N. 1985. *Life in Egypt under Roman Rule.* Oxford: Clarendon Press.

Marchini, C. 1999. Glass From the 1993 Excavations at Ismant el-Kharab. *In* Hope, C.A. and A.J. Mills, ed, *Dakhleh Oasis Project: Preliminary Reports on the 1992-1993 and 1993-94 Field Seasons.* Oxford: Oxbow Books.

Marlow, M. ed. *The Oasis Papers: Proceedings of the First International Symposium on the Dakhleh Oasis Project.* Oxford: Oxbow Books.

Maslen, G. 1990. History books. *The Globe and Mail.* March 3, 1990.

Mattingly, D.J. 1988. Oil For Export? A Comparison of Libyan, Spanish and Tunisian Olive Production in the Roman Empire. *Journal of Roman Archaeology.* 1988, 1: 33-56.

Mills, A.J. 1980. Lively Paintings: Roman Frescoes in the Dakhleh Oasis. *Rotunda.* 13: 18-25.

Mills, A.J. 1999. 'Ein Birbiyeh. *In* Hope, C.A. and A.J. Mills, ed, *Dakhleh Oasis Project: Preliminary Reports on the 1992-1993 and 1993-94 Field Seasons.* Oxford: Oxbow Books.

Mills, A.J. 1999. Deir el-Haggar. *In* Hope, C.A. and A.J. Mills, ed, *Dakhleh Oasis Project: Preliminary Reports on the 1992-1993 and 1993-94 Field Seasons.* Oxford: Oxbow Books.

Molto, J.E. Leprosy in Roman Period skeletons from Kellis 2, Dakhleh, Egypt. *Leprosy: Past and Present.* Roberts, C. and M.K. Manchester, ed. *BAR.*

Molto, J.E. 2000. Humerus Varus Deformity in Two Roman Burials from Kellis 2, Dakhleh, Egypt. *American Journal of Physical Anthropology* 113: 103-109.

Molto, J.E. 2001. The Comparative Skeletal Biology and Paleoepidemiology of the People From Ein Tirghi And Kellis, Dakhleh, Egypt. *In* Marlow, M. ed,

The Oasis Papers: Proceedings of the First International Symposium of the Dahkleh Oasis Project. Oxford: Oxbow Books.

Pringle, H. 2001. *The Mummy Congress: Science, Obsession, and the Everlasting Dead.* Toronto: Penguin Canada/Viking.

Pringle, H. 1999. In this Eternal Land. *Equinox.* June/July 1999.

Reid, T.R. 1997. The Power and the Glory of the Roman Empire. *National Geographic.* July, 1997.

Reid, T.R. 1997. The World According to Rome. *National Geographic.* August, 1997.

Schwarcz, H., T.L. Dupras and S.I. Fairgrieve. 1999. ^{15}N Enrichment in the Sahara: In Search of a Global Relationship. *Journal of Archaeological Science.* 1999, 26: 629-636.

Shaw, R.L. 1995. Something Old, Something New: The Deir el-Haggar Visitor Centre. *Archaeological Newsletter.* Series II, No. 58, May 1995.

Thanheiser, U. 1999. Plant Remains from Kellis: First results. *In* Hope, C.A. and A.J. Mills, ed, *Dakhleh Oasis Project: Preliminary Reports on the 1992-1993 and 1993-94 Field Seasons.* Oxford: Oxbow Books.

Webster, D. 1999. Valley of the Mummies. *National Geographic.* October 1999.

Whitehouse, H. and C.A. Hope. A Painted Panel of Isis. *In* Hope, C.A. and A.J. Mills, ed, *Dakhleh Oasis Project: Preliminary Reports on the 1992-1993 and 1993-94 Field Seasons.* Oxford: Oxbow Books.

Winlock, H.E. 1936. *Ed Dakhleh Oasis, Journal of a Camel Trip Made in 1908.* The Metropolitan Museum of Art, New York.

Worp, K.A. and A. Rijksbaron, ed. 1997. *The Kellis Isocrates Codex.* Oxford: Oxbow Books.

Worp, K.A. ed. 1995. *Greek Papyri from Kellis: I.* Oxford: Oxbow Books.

VI. THE LOST OASIS

AUC Desert Development Center. *1985 Report.* Cairo: The American University in Cairo.

Bagnold, R.A. 1939. An Expedition to the Gilf Kebir and 'Uwenait, 1938. *Geographical Journal.* April 1939: 13-39.

Bagnold, R.A. 1933. A Further Journey Through the Libyan Desert. *Geographical Journal.* 82: 103-129, 211-235.

Bagnold, R.A. Journeys in the Libyan Desert 1929 and 1930: A Paper Read at the Evening Meeting of the Society on 20 April 1931. *Geographical Journal.* 78: 13-39.

Baker, M.M. 1997. Mubarak: Toshka Project Opens Way Towards New Civilization in Egypt. *The Executive Intelligence Review.* December 1997.

Ball, J. 1927. Problems of the Libyan Desert. *Geographical Journal.* 70: 21-28, 105-108, 209-224.

Beadnell, H.J.L. 1909. *An Egyptian Oasis: An Account of the Oasis of Kharga in the Libyan Desert with Special Reference to its History, Physical Geography and Water Supply.* London: John Murray

Bermann, R.A. 1934. Historic Problems of the Libyan Desert: A Paper Read

With the Preceding at the Evening Meeting of the Society on 8 January 1934. *The Geographical Journal.* Vol. 83, No. 6: 30-39.

Brookes, I.A. 1989. Above the Salt: Sediment Accretion and Irrigation Agriculture in an Egyptian Oasis. *Journal of Arid Environments.* 17, 335-348.

Cloudsley-Thomson, J.L. 1974. *The Ecology of Oases.* Watford: Merrow Publishing.

de Villiers, M. 2000. *Water.* Toronto: Stoddart.

Diamond, J.M. 1998. *Guns, Germs, and Steel: The Fates of Human Societies.* New York: W.W. Norton.

El-Baz, F. 1982. Egypt's Desert of Promise. *National Geographic.* February, 1982.

Edmonstone, Sir. A. 1822. *A Journey to Two of the Oases of Upper Egypt.* London: John Murray.

Ezzat, M.A. 1974. Exploitation of Groundwater in El-wadi El-gedid. Ministry of Agriculture and Land Reclamation, ARA. March 1974.

Gladman, A. 1997. Massive Nile River Diversions Planned. *World Rivers Review.* June 1997, Vol. 12, No. 3.

Glantz, M.H., ed. 1977. *Desertification, Environmental Degradation in and Around Arid Lands.* Boulder: Westview Press.

Gleick, P.H. 2001. Making Every Drop Count. *Scientific American.* February 2001: 41-45.

Gore, A. 1992. *Earth in the Balance: Ecology and the Human Spirit.* New York: Houghton Mifflin.

Gore, R. 1979. The Desert: An Age-Old Problem Grows. *National Geographic.* July 1979: 594-639.

Gore, R. 2000. Just A Mirage? *Gulf Business.* Volume 4, Issue 10. February 2000.

Haynes, V. 1982. Great Sand Sea and Selima Sand Sheet, Eastern Sahara: Geochronology of Desertification. *Science.* Vol. 217, 13 August 1982: 629-633.

Himida, I.H. 1970. The Nubian Artesian Basin, its Regional Hydrogeological Aspects and Paeleohydrogeological Reconstruction. *Journal of Hydrology (N.Z.).* Vol. 9, No. 2: 89-116.

Hourani, A.H. 1991. *A History of the Arab Peoples.* Cambridge: Harvard University Press.

Keall, E. 1981. Some Observations on the Islamic Remains of the Dakhleh Oasis. *Journal of the Society for the Study of Egyptian Antiquities.* 11: 213-223.

King, W.J.H. 1925. *Mysteries of the Libyan Desert.* London: Seeley, Service & Company.

Kunzig, R. 2000. Exit from Eden. *Discover.* January 2000: 85-91.

Manion, A.M. 1991. *Global Environmental Change: A Natural and Cultural Environmental History.* Burnt Mill: Longman Group UK.

Mitchell, A. 2001. The World's 'Single Biggest Threat'. *The Globe and Mail.* Monday, June 4, 2001: A8-A9.

Negus, S. 2002. Toshka, Egypt's New Desert Gamble. *Arab Chat.* January 14, 2002.

Ondaatje, M. 1993. *The English Patient.* Toronto: Vintage Books.

Penderel, H.W.G. 1934. The Gilf Kebir: A Paper Read With the Following at
the Evening Meeting of the Society on 8 January 1934. *Geographical
Journal*. June 1934, Vol. 83, No. 6: 29-30.

Pointing, C. 1991. *A Green History of the World: The Environment and the Collapse of
Great Civilizations*. New York: Penguin.

Postel, S. 2001. Growing More Food With Less Water. *Scientific American*.
February 2001: 46-51.

Postel, S. 1999. *Pillar Of Sand: Can the Irrigation Miracle Last?* New York: W.W. Norton.

Rotstayn, L. D. and U. Lohmann. Tropical rainfall trends and the indirect
aerosol effect. *Journal of Climate*. Vol. 15, No. 15: 2103-2116.

Stevens, W.K. 1999. *The Change in the Weather: People, Weather and the Science of
Climate*. New York: Dell Publishing.

Warren, A. 1984. The Problems of desertification *In* Cloudsley-Thompson,
J.L. ed. 1984. *Sahara Desert*. New York: Pergamon Press.

Wells, G.H. and D.R. Haragan, ed. 1983. *Origin and Evolution of Deserts*.
Albuquerque: University of New Mexico Press.

Woidich, M. 2001. Gi ca's ["wedding songs"] from Il-Bashandi, Dakhla. *In*
manuscript: University of Amsterdam.

Woidich, M. 2000. The Arabic Dialect of il-Bashandi at Dakhla Oasis. *In* M.
Mifsud, ed.*Proceedings of the 3rd International Conference AIDA Malta, 29
March-2 April, 1998*. Malta 2000: 113-118.

Young, E. 1999. Just A Mirage? *New Scientist*. 18 December 1999.

THE DAKHLEH OASIS PROJECT MONOGRAPHS AND REPORTS

1. *Ceramics From Dakhleh Oasis: Preliminary Studies.* by W.I. Edwards, C.A. Hope,
and E.R. Segnit.

2. *Reports From the Survey of the Dakhleh Oasis 1977-87.* edited by A.J. Mills and
C.S. Churcher

3. *Greek Papyri from Kellis 1.* edited by K.A. Worp

4. *Kellis Literary Texts, Volume 1.* edited by Iain Gardner

5. *The Kellis Isocrates Codex.* edited by K.A. Worp and A. Rijksbaron

6. *The Oasis papers: Proceedings from the First International Symposium of the Dakhleh
Oasis Project.* edited by Mandy Marlow.

7. *The Kellis Agricultural Account Book.* edited by Roger Bagnall

8. *Dakhleh Oasis Project: Preliminary Reports on the 1992-1993 and 1993-1994
Field Seasons.* edited by C.A. Hope and A.J. Mills.

9. *Coptic Documentary Texts: Volume 1.* edited by Iain Gardner, Anthony Alcock
and Wolf-Peter Funk.

10. *Dakhleh Oasis Project: Preliminary Reports on the 1994-1995 to 1998-1999
Field Seasons.* edited by Colin Hope and Gillian Bowen.

All published by Oxbow Books, Park End Place, Oxford OX1 1HN
Available in North America from The David Brown Book Company,
P.O. Box 511, Oakville, CT 06779.

INDEX

Abu Ballas, 157
Abu Moharik, 341
Abydos, 146
acacia, 37, 245
Acheuleans, 35, 38, 41, 45, 54
Actium, 216
Admonitions of an Egyptian Sage, 185
A History of the Arab Peoples, 321
Ain Aseel, 140-143, 150-152, 154, 160, 165, 176, 181-183, 186, 189, 206, 291
A Journey to Two of the Oases of Upper Egypt, 327
akh, 223
Akhenaten, 193
Al-Bakhri, 320
"albedo effect", 362
Alexander the Great, 205-206, 210-211, 293-294, 319
Alexandria, 211-212, 223, 240, 253, 257, 285-287, 308, 325
alhagi, 49
al-Hajir, 49
A Libyan Oasis, 320
Allan, Tony, 350
Amheida, 27, 216-217, 219-222, 232, 308, 311, 368
Ammon, 210
Ammonians, 204-205
Amon-nakht, 229-230
Amon-Re, 231
Amratian, 131
Andean Atacama Desert, 263
Anderson, Craig, 350
Anderson, Sir John, 267
Andromeda, 220-221
Antony, Mark, 216
Anubis, 102, 214
Aphrodite, 221, 253
Apollo, 221
Apostle Mark, 285
Ares, 221
Aristotle, 244-245
Arkenu, 95
Ark of the Covenant, 256
Arnold, Dieter, 177
artophagi, 168
Aseel Spring. *See* Ain Aseel
A.S. Pushkin Museum of Fine Arts, 191
Aswan, 143, 153, 230, 326, 345, 349-350
Aswan High Dam, 23
Asyut, 326, 328
Aterian, 59-62
Aufderheide, Art, 262-266, 273
Augustus, 285, 307
   See also Octavian

Babylon, 211
Badarians, 131
Bagnall, Roger, 222, 298, 304, 306-309, 368
Bagnold, Major Ralph, 109, 301-302
Bahariya oasis, 8, 19, 192, 210–11, 213, 215
Bailey, Lady, 42
Balat, 51, 108, 140, 156, 327
Ball, Dr. John, 156, 346-347
Barchan dunes, 301
Barich, Barbara, 118
Barth, Heinrich, 155-156
Bashendi, 15-16, 35, 76, 80-81, 85, 114, 117, 120, 123, 131, 134, 157, 161, 169-170, 196, 228, 262, 266, 269, 278, 283, 309, 316, 334-335, 337, 338, 355
   culture, 86-88, 93-107, 110, 114, 117, 129
battikh, 44
Batutta, Ibn, 321
Beadnell, Hugh J., 320, 330-331, 346-347
Belemmyes, 311
Bell, Barbara, 184, 190
Belzoni, Giovanni Battista, 248, 326
Bergmann, Carlo, 158
Berlin Museum of Archaeology, 85
Bermann, Dr. Richard, 332
berseem, 178, 305
Bey, Hassanein, 94-95, 332
Bir Sahara, 62, 64
Bir Tarfawi, 62, 64, 153
Blondaux, Laurence, 256-257
Boston University, 118
Bowen, Gillian, 295-299
Braidwood, Robert, 73, 82
Brookes, Ian, 48, 84, 348
Brutus, 216
Buddha, 287
Budge, Sir E. A. Wallis, 280
Byblos, 152
Byzantium, 303

Caesar, Julius, 216
Cairo University, 19
Caligula, 263
Cailliaud, Frederic, 328
Cambyses, King, 204, 205
Canadian Institute in Egypt, 8
Canadian International Development Agency, 225
Carter, Howard, 282
cartonnage, 249, 260, 290
cartonnage coffins, 215
Cassius, 216
Caton-Thompson, Gertrude, 40-46, 53, 62
   "Khargan Industry", 65
   Wendorf's theory, 63
Champollion, Jean-Francois, 248
Churcher, Rufus, 10, 27, 46-52, 62, 64, 78, 87, 103-110, 121, 122, 124, 130, 136, 305, 368
Clark, J.D., 61
Cleopatra, 213, 216-217
Cloudsley-Thompson, J.L., 63
codex, 245, 255
codices, 245, 250, 254, 258, 280, 368-369
columbaria, 371
columbarium, 218
Columbia University, 221
Commonwealth Scientific and Industrial Research Organization. *See* CSIRO
Constantine, 286, 298, 303
Constantinople, 303, 311
Cook, Megan, 275
Coptic, 287-289, 319, 333
Coptic graffito, 284
Copts, 285, 295
crux ansata, 297
CSIRO, 365
"CSS", 48-49, 52
Currelly, C.T., 24
Cyperus papyrus, 247

Dakhleh oasis
   agriculture, 17, 27, 122-123, 305-306, 338
   appearance of early man, 54-55

art, 51, 149-150
artifacts, 114, 129, 170-173, 178
bones, 24, 104, 106, 110, 125, 127-128
cattle, 7, 93-94, 99, 100, 102, 106, 110
dark age, 72
deforestation, 63-64
early food, 54, 78-79, 168-169, 305-306
early tools, 53-54, 57-58, 87
early vegetation, 49-50, 79-80, 82, 90
early wildlife, 15, 37, 49-51, 90, 105-110, 121-
    122, 179
history, 6-15, 17, 27
inhabitants, 60-65
irrigation, 179-181
location, 1, 8
meaning, 8
people movement, 116
religion, 317-325
rock art, 94, 95, 96, 97, 98, 99, 100, 101,
    103, 104, 105, 147
slavery, 328
structures, 76-77, 326-327
women, 322-323
Dakhleh Oasis Project, *See* DOP
Darb el-Arbain, 152, 328
Darb el-Gubari, 48, 150, 155
Darb el-Tawil, 94, 130, 154, 327
debitage, 75
Deir el-Hagar, 1, 27, 203, 223-227, 230-232,
    310, 371
Demeter, 280
Description de l'Egypte, 267, 326
Diocletian, 286, 303, 312
Dionysus, 220-221
Djoser, Pharaoh, 146
DNA analysis, 128
Domitian, 226, 307
domus ecclesia, 297
DOP, 22, 75, 78, 84, 86, 94, 97-99, 125, 142, 147-
    148, 164, 168, 171, 190, 193, 202-203, 206-
    207, 213, 221, 226, 232, 238, 244, 250, 256,
    260, 274, 282-284, 287, 294-295, 298-299, 326,
    332-334, 337-338, 340, 348, 353, 356, 365-369
dromedarios, 253
Drovetti, Chevalier Bernardo, 326, 328
Dubois, Rene, 372
Dungul oasis, 68
Dupras, Tosha, 291-292

Edict of Toleration, 286
Edmonstone, Sir Archibald, 225, 267-268, 326-328
Effendi, Hassan, 331
Egyptian Antiquities Organization, 21, 211, 213,
    225, 238, 333
Egyptian Expedition of the Metropolitan
    Museum of Art, 226
Ein Birbiyeh, 27, 228-230, 285
Ein el-Gezareen, 162-166, 169-174, 176-177,
    179, 181-182, 240
Ein Tirghi, 196-198, 202-203, 205, 262, 269,
    272-274, 277
El Guettar, 59
el-Muzzawaka, 222, 268
El Niño 365
El-Qasr, 21, 215, 301, 322-325, 328-329, 333
El-Wadi El-Gedid, 346-347, 349, 351, 353, 356
Emery, Walter Bryan, 112
Ennedi, 347
"Everlasting Oasis", 34

Fagan, Brian, 363, 364
Fakhry, Ahmed, 19-20, 141-142, 146, 154, 210-211, 235
falafel, 306
fantas, 322
Farafra oasis, 8, 118, 153, 192, 350
Farouk El-Baz, 118-119, 132, 347, 350
Fayum, 189, 219, 222, 248-249, 286
feddans, 353
fellahin, 212, 217, 228, 248
felluca, 326
Fertile Crescent of Mesopotamia, 83
Flood, Famines and Emperors, 363-364
Freeman, Geoffrey, 17-22, 142, 220, 366
French Institute of Oriental Archaeology, 21, 142
Frey, Rosa, 24, 196, 198, 235

Gadhafi, Colonel, 148, 358
galabiya, 242, 304, 335-336
Gardner, Elinor, 41, 62
Gardner, Iain, 287-289
Gareet el-Afreets, 60
gattasan, 330
gebel, 49, 109, 162, 222
Gerzean period, 131
"Getting a Handle on Tangs", 58
Ghani, Abdul, 259, 260
Giegengack, Robert, 51, 348, 352-353
Gilf Kebir, 95, 105, 113, 157-158, 164, 332
Glaser, Alfred, 81
Greater Mussayib Irrigation Project, 360
Great Harris Papyrus, 247
Great Sand Sea, 1, 2, 156, 159, 203, 332
Grenfell, B.P., 249
Grimal, Nicholas, 154
Groningen University, 334
Guns, Germs and Steel, 363

Hadrian, 280
Hadrian's Wall, 304
halfa, 108
Halfat el-Bir, 155
Halicarnassus, 204
Halim, Hussein Abdel, 40
Hallet, Jessica, 243
Hall of Offerings, 225
Harkhuf, 153-154
Harvard University, 184
Hassan, Fekri, 131
Hawass, Zahi, 211
Hawkins, Alicia, 58, 59, 60
Haynes, Vance, 302
Heinrich Barth Institute, 155
Heliopolis, 191
Helios, 220-221
Hephaistos, 221
Heracles, 221
Herakleopolis, 189
Herodotus, 204-205, 263-264, 280, 325, 328, 332
Hibis, 226, 305
Hindaw, 331
Holocene period, 63, 76
Homo Erectus, 14, 46, 54
Homo habilis, 13
Homo sapiens, 34, 45, 54-55
Homo sapiens sapiens, 54, 59
Hope, Colin, 193-194, 206-207, 215, 220, 238-
    240, 243-244, 247, 250-252, 256-258, 280-281,
    287-288, 294-295, 299-301, 304, 312, 368

Horace, 217
Horus, 280
Hourani, Albert, 321, 323
Human Genome Project, 277
Hunt, A.S., 249
"Hyena Hill," 108, 109
Hypostyle Hall, 195, 225, 230

Ibn el-Hajj, 323
Ice Age, 14, 37, 39
Iliad, 245
Intertropical Convergence Zone, 185
Ipuwer, 186, 189
iridium, 159
Iron Balls Spring, 52
Isimila, 35
Isis, 149, 280
Ismant el-Kharab, 27, 104, 140, 203, 215-217, 233-234
Isocrates, 245, 255

jerd, 94
Juvenal, 280

Kakashnikovs, 8
Kalambo Falls, 35
kanats, 205
Kaper, Olaf, 148-153, 227-231, 281-284
Karanis, 222, 250, 257
Karnak, 19
Keall, Edward, 323-324
Kellis, 51, 232-234, 238-242, 244-247, 250, 252-255, 257-259, 263-262, 266, 268-270, 272, 274, 277-281, 283, 286-293, 295-304, 307-309, 311-312, 320, 366-368
Kemal el Din, Prince, 157, 190-191
khamsin, 151, 313
Kharga, 8, 19, 39, 41-43, 45, 48, 53, 57, 60, 118, 121, 127, 130, 141, 150, 153, 202, 204-205, 226, 257, 272, 296, 305, 311, 320, 326, 328-329, 341, 348-350, 368
Khety, 187-188
Khnum-Re, 230
Kila' el-Debba, 141-142, 147
King, J. Harding, 329-330
Kitinos, 213-214
Kleindienst, Maxine, 34-35, 40-53, 125, 127, 148, 367
    Dakhleh's evolution, 56
    explaining artifacts, 54
    on archaeology, 69
    Wendorfs theory, 64
    working with other archaeologists, 41-53
Knudstad, Jim, 234, 236-237, 279, 300
Kroeper, Karla, 84-85
Krzyzaniak, Lech, 80, 84, 88, 97-101-103
Kufra Oasis, 153, 158, 241, 321, 329, 357-358
Kuper, Rudolph, 155-159
Kurkur Oasis, 68
Kush, 187, 195

lacrimarium, 242
Ladislaus de Almasy, Count, 95, 109, 157, 332
Lakehead University, 201, 276
Lake Mut, 355, 356, 369
Lake Nasser, 23
Late Pleistocene, 45
Leakey, Mary, 38, 64
Leptis Magna, 308
Levallois, 65
Levant, 83, 117

Libyan glass, 159
Limnae stagnatus, 50
lingua franca, 287
Locus V, 43
Luxor, 19, 24, 42, 238, 268
    See also Thebes
Lyons, Sir Henry, 194

MacArthur, Robert, 107
McDonald, Mary, 27, 34, 65, 73-74, 98-100, 103-106, 110, 112, 114, 117-118, 120-122, 124, 128, 130, 132, 136, 196, 235, 367
    in Egypt, 73-92
    in Iran, 73-74
MacGregor, Caroline, 283-284
McMaster University, 40
madrasa, 324, 333
Maghreb, 57
Mahoub, 301
Mamluks, 322, 324, 325
mammisi, 281, 283, 284
Mani, 287, 288
Manichaeans, 287, 288, 289, 295
Man in Nature, 133
Masara, 75, 76, 78, 86, 93, 105
mashrabiyya, 323
mastabas, 16, 141, 146
mazbut, 22, 85
Medusa, 220
Melbye, Jerry, 196
Memphis, 146, 187
Merenre, 152-153
Meskell, Lynn, 221
Meydum bowls, 207
Middle Pleistocene, 45
Millet, Nick, 20, 30, 133, 187
Mills, Lesley, 170, 171
Mills, Tony, 16, 20-22, 28, 84, 97-98, 117, 129, 142-143, 147, 150, 152, 160-170, 172-174, 176-179, 181, 184, 188-190, 192-194, 196, 203, 206-207, 213-215, 217-225, 227-228, 231-232, 234-235, 238-240, 244, 282, 303, 311-313, 319-325, 330, 332-335, 338, 341-343, 352-353, 355-356, 366-369, 372
Miosi, Frank T., 18
Mitochondrial DNA, 277
Mixed Memoirs, 42
Molto, Eldon, 196-203, 215, 257, 261-262, 266-278, 290-295, 309, 319, 367-368
Monash University, 283, 295, 368
Mothis. *See* Mut el-Kharab
Mrj, 158
Mubarak, Hosni, 349-350
muezzin, 170, 316
Muhammad, 338-339
Muhammad Ali, 345
Mumford, Greg, 76, 84
mumiya, 267, 276
Mut, 22, 162, 181, 206, 234, 310-311, 335, 343, 355, 358
Mut el-Kharab, 140, 194, 206, 216, 254, 289, 367
Mycobacterium leprae, 290
Mysteries of the Libyan Desert, 330

Nabta Playa, 88, 118
nabut, 335
nageurs, 96
Naqada, 130
Narrative of the Operations and Recent Discoveries in

Egypt and Nubia, 248
Nasser, Gamal Abdel, 329, 345-346
Naucratis, 212
Nectanebo II, 205
Neferhetepes, Princess, 167
Neith, 281
Neolithic Revolution, 73, 76, 82, 87, 91, 131
"Nephthys Hill", 149-150
Nepthys, 149
Nero, 226
Nestorius, 311
New Delta Project. *See* Toshka Project
New Valley Museum, 368
New Valley Project. *See* El-Wadi El-Gedid
Nikokles, 244
Nubia, 38, 152-154, 170, 184, 195, 224, 278
Nubian Salvage Campaign, 22-23, 165
Nun, 230

Octavian, 216, 228
Odysseus, 221
Ogallalla Aquifer, 357-358
oinochos, 257
Oldavai, 38
Olduvai Gorge, 35
omal, 163, 171, 240
Ondaatje, Michael, 332
oregmos, 305
Oriental Institute of Chicago, 73
Oshar, 99
Osiris, 214-215, 230, 280
ostraca, 250
 See also potsherds
Overweg, Adolf, 155
Oxbow Books, 368
Oxyrhynchus, 249, 257
Ozymandias, 18

Padi-Osiris, 27, 222-223
Paleolake Teneida, 49, 51-52, 54
Pamour, Aurelius, 253-254, 270
Parr, Dr. Ryan, 276
PCR, 275-277
Pepy I, 152
Pepy II, 152-153, 184
Pereus, 220
Petrie, Sir Flinders, 111, 130-131, 173, 198, 240
Phillipi, 216
phytoliths, 68
Piankhy, 195
Piggot, Stuart, 172
Plasmodium malaria, 273
Pleistocene. *See* Ice Age
Pleistocene period, 78
Polis, 220
Polymerase Chain Reaction Technique. *See* PCR
Pompeii, 221
Poseidon, 220, 221
Postel, Sandra, 359
potsherds, 2, 3, 144, 175
Poznan Archaeological Museum, 80, 368
Pringle, Heather, 267, 268
Processional Way, 225, 227
Psamtik I, 207
Psamtik III, 204
Ptolemies, 206
Ptolemy Lagos, 211
Punt, Land of , 152
Puss-Moth, 42

Qalamun, 162, 325
Quftis, 173
Quraysh, 318, 324-325

Ra, 146
radio-carbon dating, 40
Ramadan, 317
Ramesside period, 191
Ramses II, 18, 193
Re'-Atum, 191
recto, 247
Redford, Donald, 19
Refuf Pass, 40-41
Remelé, Phillip, 225, 226
Richardson, James, 155
Rock Drawings of Southern Egypt, 96
Rohlfs, Gerhard, 1, 2, 156, 203, 220, 225,
 328-329
Roman amphora, 2
romani, 330
Rosetta Stone, 248
Royal Ontario Museum, 24, 214, 323, 368

Sadat, Anwar, 346, 349
Sahara Desert, 1, 6
 Arabic meaning, 6
 history, 7, 10-15, 115
 weather, 7, 115
Sahel, 81, 105, 308, 362-364
Salvadora, 81
San peoples of the Kalahari Desert, 88
saqia, 309-310, 338, 344, 353, 355, 370
Saqqara, 146, 167
sarcophagus, 199-200, 207
Schwarcz, Henry, 40, 44-45
Seh Gabi, 73, 83
Selim the Grim, 325
Selima Oasis, 153
Sennusi, 329
Septimus Severus, 303
Seth, 195, 207, 229
Seven Days' War, 148
shaduf; shadufs, 181, 338, 344
Shain Esdhuti, 195
Sharpe, John, 245
Sheikh Mabruk, 67-68, 78
Sheikh Muftah, 120-125, 127-130, 132, 134-
 136, 151-152, 177-178, 187-189, 363
Sheikh Zayad Canal, 349
Sheldrick, Peter, 196-200, 202, 215, 259, 260-
 262, 266, 268, 290
Shorbag/Shorfa/Ashrif, 324-325
shosh, shoshes, 79, 162
Shoshenk, 195
Sio'h, Plain of, 2-3, 223, 232, 303, 311, 355,
 361, 369, 371, 372
Siwa oasis, 2, 8, 19, 153, 203-204, 210, 241
Smekalova, Tatyana, 161, 174-176, 242
sol invictus, 299
sondage, 141
Soranus, 272
Sothis, 230
Soukiassian, George, 143, 144-145
Southern Methodist University, 62
stagma, 305
stela, stelae; 147, 194-195, 281
"stone places of the Sahara", 73
Stonios, 286-287

Strabo, 307
Streptomyces, 272
Study of Egyptian Antiquities, Society for the, 18
suq, 321

tabula rasa, 91
tang, 57
Tebtunis, 249
tectones, 255
Tell el-Amarna, 193
temenos, 2, 224, 236
Temple of Hibis, 205
Temple of Osiris Heqa Djet, 19
Teneida, 51, 53, 148
Tethys Sea, 310
tetracycline, 272
tetradrachms, 299
Thanheiser, Ursula, 79, 81, 82, 87, 105, 122, 166, 167, 306, 309
Thebes, 189, 204, 268
The English Patient, 332
"The Grander Canyon", 9, 10
The Histories, 204
"the Ionian dog". *See* Alexander the Great
The Lost Oases, 94
The Mummy Congress, 267
Theodosius, 299
The Oxyrhynchus Papers, 250
"The Painted Rock". *See el-Muzzawaka*
The Prehistory of the Eastern Sahara, 64
The Seven Odes, 322
The Sheik, 94
"The Stone Convent". *See* Deir el-Hagar
The Times, 244
Thompson, Jennifer, 125-128, 193
Thoth, 215
"Throne of the Moon". *See* Sio'h, Plain of, 167-168
Tibesti Mountains, 72, 347
tilapia, 355
Timbuktu, 155
Timotheos, 298
tiphagion, 306
Titus, 226
Tjemehu, 187
Toshka , 350, 353
Toshka Canal, 362
Toshka Depression, 349
Toshka Project, 349-351, 356-357
touriyeh, 180, 256, 339
Travels and Discoveries in North and Central Africa in the Years 1849-1855, 155
Trimithis, 219
Tuck, Dan, 246
tufas, 41, 53
Tutankhamun, 159, 193, 260
Tutu, 281-283, 285

University College, London, 131
University of Amsterdam, 250, 334
University of Arizona, 302
University of Central Florida, 291
University of Chicago, 19
University of London's School of Oriental and African Studies, 350
University of Michigan, 250
University of Natal, 46
University of Nevada, 125
University of Pennsylvania, 51
University of Rome, 118

University of Toronto, 18, 196
University of Utah, 276
University of Toronto, 19, 65
Uweinat Mountains, 95, 113
Uwenait, 157

Valentino, Rudolf, 94
"Valley of the Golden Mummies", 211, 215
verso, 247
Vespasian, 226
Vienna Institute of Archaeological Science, 79

wadi, 7, 14, 37, 42, 52, 78, 86, 89, 332, 341
Wadi el-Battikh, 89, 78, 150
Wadi el-Refuf, 43
Walter, Johannes, 99
Wayheset, Prince, 195
Well of Souls, 256
Wendorf, Fred, 62, 88, 93, 118
    "Aterian Ponds", 62-63
    "empty desert theory", 63-64
Wermai, 191-192
Wilkinson, John Gardner, 328
Wilson, Edward O., 107
Wilson, John A., 19
Winkler, Hans, 94, 96-103, 148-149
Winlock, Herbert, 7, 24, 226, 228
Wiseman, Marcia, 40, 43, 43-44, 48-49, 65
    Dakhleh inhabitation, 65-66
    early tools, 66-67
Woidich, Manfred, 334-338
Worp, Klaas, 250-253, 278, 289

Yam, Land of, 153, 187
yardang, 9, 47-48, 51-52, 89, 98, 119, 149
York University, 84

Zagros Mountains, 74
Zeffet el Arusa, 330
Zemzemi, Zemzemi Shahab, 40
Zerzura, 332
Zielinski, Adam, 224
Zizyuphus, 306
Zoroaster, 287